THE SPECIAL OPERATIONS EXECUTIVE IN MALAYA

Our understanding of what SOE did in the Second World War against Japan, and how this influenced the turbulent post-war reordering of Asia, for a long time lagged badly behind the more concentrated study of SOE's role in the war in Europe. But the passage of time and the release of official records now makes it possible to close that gap and correct some long-held but not well-founded conclusions. What Richard Duckett did for the campaign in Burma, Rebecca Kenneison has now done for the campaign in Malaya. Her closely and carefully argued but also well-written study, the first to draw on the full SOE archive for this campaign, spells out not just how, but more important why, understanding what SOE did during the war in Malaya, and how it evaluated the situation there after the war, is necessary in order to understand how the Malayan Communist Party used wartime cooperation to develop its violent challenge to post-war decolonization. This is essential reading for those interested in clear and myth-busting explanations for wartime special operations, intelligence and the onset of the Cold War in Southeast Asia.

– Professor Brian P. Farrell, National University of Singapore

The Special Operations Executive in Malaya gives us a meticulous study of SOE's work with the Malay resistance, with the Guomindang Chinese 'guerrilla state' and with the 80 per cent of Malayan guerrillas under communist control. It also enriches our understanding of the MPAJA's attempt to squeeze others out of wartime resistance work and to preserve its post-war potential for revolution.

– Professor Karl Hack, The Open University

THE SPECIAL OPERATIONS EXECUTIVE IN MALAYA

World War II and the Path to Independence

Rebecca Kenneison

BLOOMSBURY ACADEMIC
LONDON • NEW YORK • OXFORD • NEW DELHI • SYDNEY

BLOOMSBURY ACADEMIC
Bloomsbury Publishing Plc
50 Bedford Square, London, WC1B 3DP, UK
1385 Broadway, New York, NY 10018, USA

BLOOMSBURY, BLOOMSBURY ACADEMIC and the Diana logo are trademarks of
Bloomsbury Publishing Plc

First published in Great Britain 2019

Cover design: Terry Woodley
Cover image © Hassan Muthalib

A catalogue record for this book is available from the British Library.

A catalog record for this book is available from the Library of Congress

ISBN: 978-1-78831-389-6
ePDF: 978-1-35011-857-7
eBook: 978-1-35011-858-4

Series: International Library of War Studies

Typeset by Newgen KnowledgeWorks Pvt. Ltd., Chennai, India
Printed and bound in Great Britain

To find out more about our authors and books visit www.bloomsbury.com
and sign up for our newsletters.

To the memory of
George Hess'e and Geoffrey Frank
boyhood friends
who both saw service with Force 136.

CONTENTS

ILLUSTRATIONS

Plates

Tables

Maps

ACKNOWLEDGEMENTS

This book began as a doctoral thesis, but my first investigation of the activities of the Special Operations Executive (SOE) in Malaya began when I tried to unravel my family history. As part of this, I wanted to fill in the details of the short life of my father's cousin Geoffrey Frank who died in Singapore in January 1946, following an accident in the car park of Raffles Hotel. Geoffrey, I discovered, had belonged to Force 136. But what was Force 136? What did it do in Malaya? The books that were easy to get hold of told me very little. The scarce books were not only hard to find but had a habit of disagreeing with one another. The only way to find the answers was to go back to the archives. The more I read my way through pages of yellowing foolscap, the more I realized that they held the promise of a remarkable story.

The story I have ended up telling wasn't, of course, the story I thought I'd tell. It was more complicated, more – as historians love to say – nuanced. I wasn't even a historian at the beginning: my supervisor, Mark Frost, was unfortunate enough to find himself working hard at the difficult task of trying to turn me into one, hammering the art of historical analysis into my head. How well he succeeded (or not) you can judge for yourself.

I was extremely fortunate to speak to or correspond with many people who lived through the period of which I write, who shared their memories with me: the late George Hesse, Hyacinth Hesse, Pam Mayo, the late C.E. 'Bill' Foss, the late Barry Neubronner, Tun Mohammed Hanif Omar, Dato Syed Ahmad Idid, the late Tan Sri Yuen Yuet Leng and Jack Burgess. I am also indebted to the late Reg Lawther, who agreed to be interviewed by an intermediary and provided me with a copy of his memoirs, and to his daughter Fiona who acted as an email conduit. I would also like to thank the relatives and contacts of individuals involved in World War II for providing me with information as well as copies of photographs, documents and tapes, including Terence Clifford, Ann and John Evans, Angela Frank, John Hembry, Tim Hannah, John Hay, Samuel Hui, Rozainah Kendrew, Don Levy, Stephen Brereton Martin and Hassan Muthalib. I am very grateful to Dato Dr. Wan Hashim for providing me with copies of several scarce volumes. Particular thanks are due to Puan Sri Elizabeth and Tan Sri Leo Moggie for their amazing hospitality, help and advice. I am especially grateful to Liz herself for tracking down and interviewing a number of people on my behalf, and to all her contacts and informants on her trip to Kelantan in March 2017, especially Tan Sri Lau Yin Pin and Mr. Wee Pock Soon. I am also indebted to Jonathan Moffatt who is a most generous researcher and a mine of information, to Mary Harris for sharing both her own research and encouraging words at the right moment, to Andrew Hwang for useful pieces of information and to my old friend Nicky

Ansell, who not only provided a spare room and a meal on many trips to the National Archives, but also put up with me binding on for hours about the day's discoveries. The membership of Steve Kippax's SOE list, including Rich Duckett, cannot be forgotten.

My greatest thanks, of course, have to go to my husband and my immediate family, for their help, encouragement and support.

ABBREVIATIONS

101STS	101 Special Training School (SOE school, Singapore)
AJUF	Anti-Japanese Union and Forces (used in contemporary British documents of MPAJA and MPAJU)
AMS	Askar Melayu Setia (Malay guerrilla group)
BMA	British Military Administration
FMSVF	Federated Malay States Volunteer Force
GLO	Group Liaison Officer (leader of a Force 136 operation)
INA	Indian National Army
ISLD	Inter-services Liaison Department (designation used by SIS/MI6 in Asia during World War II)
LDC	Local Defence Corps (in action 1941–1942)
MCP	Malayan Communist Party
MCS	Malayan Country Section (of Force 136)
MNLA	Malayan National Liberation Army
MPAJA	Malayan People's Anti-Japanese Army
MPAJU	Malayan People's Anti-Japanese Union
OCAJA	Overseas Chinese Anti-Japanese Army
OSS	Office of Strategic Services
PLO	Patrol Liaison Officer (leader of a Force 136 team)
SEAC	South East Asia Command
SIS	Secret Intelligence Service (MI6)
SOE	Special Operations Executive
SSVF	Straits Settlements Volunteer Force
UMNO	United Malays National Organisation

NOTE ON SPELLING

Names and places have been spelt as they were at the time, in the sources used. The one exception to this is Guomindang (then rendered Kuomintang), since this is now the widely used spelling in academic publications.

KEY CHARACTERS

Name	Role
Broadhurst, Lt. Col. Douglas	GLO, *Galvanic*
Broome, Major Richard	Second-in-command, *Gustavus*
Campbell-Miles, Lt. Col. Alan	GLO, *Tideway*
Chin Peng (Ong Boon Hua)	MPAJA (Senior liaison with Force 136)
Chrystal, Captain Robert	SOE stay-behind, attached Force 136
Colonel Itu	military commander, Perak MPAJA
Creer, John	Cut-off, attached, Force 136
Davis, Col. John	Leader, *Gustavus*
Dobrée, Lt. Col. Peter	Leader, *Hebrides*
Fenner, Lt. Col. Claude	GLO, *Humour*
Goodfellow, Col. Basil	Head, Malayan Country Section until Sept. 1943
Hannah, Lt. Col. James	GLO, *Funnel*
Hasler, Major Geoffrey	Leader, *Fighter*
Headly, Lt. Col. Derek	Leader, *Multiple*
Hislop, Major James	GLO, *Sergeant*
Ho Thean Fook	Ranker in MPAJA
Hunter, Major J. 'Jock'	PLO, *Galvanic Blue*
Ibrahim Ismail, Captain	Leader, *Oatmeal*
Killery, Valentine	Head of SOE's Oriental Mission
Lai Teck	Secretary General, MCP
Lau Mah	Perak Deputy State Secretary, MCP
Lawther, Reg	Major in MPAJA
Leonard, Major George	GLO, *Pontoon*
Lim Bo Seng, Major	*Gustavus*
McDonald, Major Ian	PLO, *Galvanic Brown*
Mackenzie, Colin	Head of SOE's India Mission
Mahmood Mahyideen, Major	Force 136 Staff
Martin, Major W. 'Paddy'	GLO, *Carpenter* (until January 1945)
Owen, Major S. 'Taff'	PLO, *Funnel Green*
Pagden, Fl/Lt. Hugh	Force 136 staff
Richardson, Lt. Col. Douglas	Leader, *Beacon*
Spencer Chapman, Lt. Col. Freddy	SOE stay-behind, attached Force 136
Tremlett, Lt. Col. Innes	Head, Malayan Country Section from Sept. 1943
Yeop Mahidin	Founder, Wataniah
Yong Kong	Key leader, OCAJA

Introduction

THE SPECIAL OPERATIONS EXECUTIVE, MALAYA AND THE HISTORICAL DEBATE

During World War II, the Special Operations Executive (SOE) ran operations from France to China and from Norway to Timor. When it folded in 1946, it was in profit to the tune of £23 million, entirely due to one of its Asian operations, *Remorse*.[1] Yet the Asian wing – known by the last years of the war as Force 136 – accounted for only 10 per cent of SOE's expenditure. Much the same seems to apply to what has been written since, with SOE's Asian operations attracting minimal attention compared to its work in Europe. Now, as then, they are the poor relations, despite the extent of the primary sources that have become available. These sources tell us about far more than merely what SOE did, and where, and when. They provide clues to colonial planning, insights into imperial intelligence gathering and, in the case of Malaya, they tell us things about the Malayan Communist Party (MCP) that we would never otherwise discover. It is almost a truism that SOE unintentionally influenced post-war politics in Europe. As I hope to show, it influenced them in Asia, too.

In the summer of 1940, following the Dunkirk evacuation, SOE was formed in London from elements of military intelligence (the unit MI(R)) and Section D of the Secret Intelligence Service (SIS or MI6).[2] Its role was to sponsor and conduct sabotage and subversion behind enemy lines. Its activities overlapped with those of MI6, whose leadership was in any case resentful at the loss of Section D to SOE. The Chiefs of Staff, similarly, were displeased to have the control of sabotage and subversion taken out of their hands.[3] Despite this ill-starred beginning, SOE eventually became active in much of occupied Europe and Asia; its activities in France, the Balkans and Greece are particularly well known.

At the time SOE was formed, Britain was vulnerable to invasion: much military equipment had been abandoned in France and the Local Defence Volunteers (later known as the Home Guard) were armed with shotguns and farm tools.[4] Short of both arms and troops, Britain was unable to reinforce the defences of its Asian empire, already exposed to external threats by the collapse of France and the Netherlands to the Germans, and then yet more exposed when Japan joined the Axis in September 1940 by signing the Tripartite Pact.[5] The British government responded to intelligence intercepts detailing the threat posed by

Japan to Malaya and Singapore by developing the defence plan Operation *Matador* during 1941.[6] However, the troops and equipment available fell short of those required, to the deep anxiety not only of the Foreign Office, but also of senior military commanders.[7] In the opinion of General Sir Alan Brooke, who became Chief of the Imperial General Staff on 1 December 1941, while it was correct not to spread Britain's forces too widely and thus too thinly, 'it left us in a lamentably dangerous position on the entry of Japan into the war'.[8] Britain, suffering from overstretch and anxious not to draw Japan into a conflict, was prepared to act only with extreme caution.[9]

In this context, SOE sent a scouting mission to Asia early in 1941, and in May 1941 the first staff of SOE's Oriental Mission arrived in Singapore, disguised as an outstation of the Ministry of Economic Warfare.[10] The aim of this body was to enable local governments to resist Axis expansion, and their plans included the formation of an intelligence network, the development of a propaganda unit and the establishment of groups capable of behind the lines activity should Japan declare war on Britain. Prior to the outbreak of the Pacific War in December 1941, Oriental Mission was obstructed by a complex web of factors (as will be discussed in Chapter 1), but after the Japanese attacked Malaya, it was summoned into action by Malaya Command. Japan's rapid conquest of Malaya stymied many of Oriental Mission's efforts, though critical groundwork was laid for later SOE activity. After Singapore fell to the Japanese, some of Oriental Mission's staff were absorbed by India Mission, another SOE body. By 1943, India Mission (later renamed Force 136) was active in Burma and, that May, launched its first operation into Japanese-occupied Malaya.

The Force 136 presence in Malaya was never large – around 360 men were infiltrated – and the Malayan guerrillas were not tested against the Japanese as were those in Burma. Nonetheless, these operations repay academic study. For one thing, by the end of the war, Force 136's Malayan operations were in contact with all the local guerrilla groups, and so these sources provide insights into events within Malaya not currently found in the historical literature. A study of the role of Force 136 in Malaya during the Japanese occupation and immediately afterwards allows a dissection of its relationships with these distinct and often complex guerrilla organizations, and gives us a penetrating new understanding of their attitudes towards each other, and towards the British. Such a study allows us to explore and re-examine, from a new perspective, the three main foci which form the basis of this book: (1) the long-term and, for the British, self-defeating impact of SOE in increasing the capabilities and expectations of the MCP; (2) the developing and conflicting political ambitions of both the British government and the communists of the MCP in Malaya through the Japanese occupation and into the uneasy peace that followed; and (3) the nature of imperial intelligence gathering during and immediately after the war. It will be argued that a study of Force 136 adds a further dimension to our understanding of all of these foci, and so broadens our view of the events that led up to the crisis point of the declaration of the Malayan Emergency in 1948.

SOE's Malayan operations

This examination is necessarily underlain by a discussion of the development of Force 136 in Malaya, which allows us to integrate its Malayan operations into the wider history of SOE. Historical studies of SOE have long been dominated by its activities in Europe, with ample coverage of, for example, France and the Balkans, a Eurocentric tendency that persists to the present.[11] M.R.D. Foot, responsible for several of SOE's official histories, in his *SOE: The Special Operations Executive 1940–1946* briskly refers any reader enquiring about Asia to the official history, Charles Cruickshank's *SOE in the Far East*.[12] However, Cruickshank's history, while a useful point of reference, fails to connect SOE in Asia to the wider story of SOE – other than to discuss the extent to which the European charter he claims that it was given was inappropriate for work in Asia.[13] Cruickshank offers only limited discussion of Force 136's relative effectiveness (e.g. in the field of wireless communications), and there is no mention that the Force's activities might have had post-war repercussions. Moreover, Cruickshank does not link its activities to techniques pioneered in Britain by SOE's forerunners, Section D and MI(R), although one of them – the idea of the stay-behind party – would prove fundamental to the establishment of guerrilla forces in Malaya.[14]

This geographically limited view of clandestine activity has been challenged in the last ten to fifteen years with the publication of a number of studies of the activity of the American Office of Strategic Services (OSS) in Vietnam and China and, more recently, of SOE in Burma.[15] Such studies give a more global perspective and perhaps allow us to move beyond the specific to draw some wider conclusions. A close investigation of Force 136 in Malaya might give us insights into British policy for Malaya, just as studies of OSS in China clarify the extent of competition there between Britain and the United States.[16]

Another feature of the existing historical literature is that SOE's Oriental Mission appears largely in isolation, as a brief blaze of rather pointless SOE activity snuffed out at the Fall of Singapore. The mission's enduring influence upon Force 136, and in turn upon later political developments, is not explored. Cruickshank speaks at length of Oriental Mission's struggles against military and civilian officialdom in Singapore, and concludes that, faced with implacable opposition there and elsewhere, it accomplished little; certainly, he does not connect its action in 1941–1942 to later events.[17] S. Woodburn Kirby, the official historian of World War II in Asia, relegates the mission to a footnote on Burma in Volume V of his work.[18] Richard Aldrich lets stand a judgement that it achieved nothing; the military historian Brian Farrell is of the view that its suggestions were woefully underused, but goes little further.[19] Richard Gough's *SOE Singapore 1941–42* details Oriental Mission's projects, but his conclusions focus on how it might have been better used for the defence of Singapore.[20] None of these authors looks forward to any lasting implications of Oriental Mission's activities, other than Farrell who mentions that young Chinese communists trained by the mission formed the nucleus of the Malayan People's Anti-Japanese Army (MPAJA).[21] Richard Duckett, in his

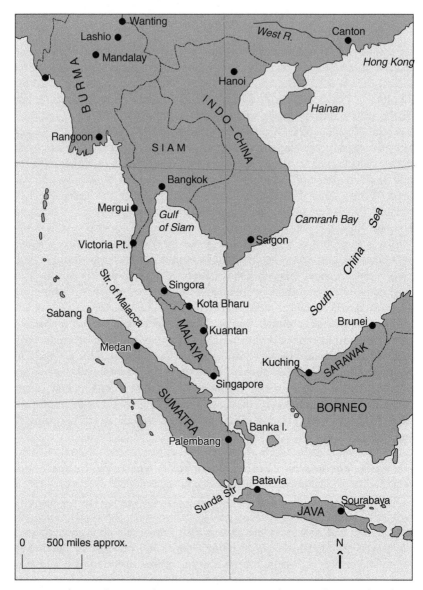

MAP I.1 Malaya and Surroundings. From Major General S. Woodburn Kirby, *The War Against Japan, Vol. V, the Surrender of Japan*, H.M.S.O., London, 1969).

doctoral thesis of 2015, was perhaps the first scholar to have suggested that SOE's Oriental Mission laid the foundations of later SOE activity in Asia – a suggestion which informs my approach here with regard to Malaya (see Chapter 1). Duckett also seeks to relate the outcome of SOE's work in Burma with that of SOE more generally.[22]

Furthermore, much of the existing literature is confusing, since it fails to distinguish between different clandestine bodies. Aldrich, examining the activities of these bodies against Japan during World War II, takes a top-down view, considering events at the level of high policy. In this respect, his book is informative, but it is evident that he is hampered by the shortage of comprehensive studies. There is, for example, confusion about the details of Force 136's activities in Malaya, with Aldrich under-estimating both the number of 'guerrilla groups' and Force 136's involvement with them.[23] An operation (*Cairngorm*) launched by OSS is described as British.[24] Similarly, Christopher Bayly and Tim Harper, in *Forgotten Armies*, mistakenly credit the successful Allied raid on Singapore harbour in October 1943 to Force 136 rather than to Special Operations Australia.[25] A recent popular history, Alan Ogden's *Tigers Burning Bright: SOE Heroes in the Far East*, discusses the activities of individuals and includes much useful background material, some not previously published.[26] There is, however, a degree of confusion in it with respect to the operations and membership of Oriental Mission and the Inter-Services Liaison Department (ISLD – a cover name widely used by MI6 during World War II).[27] While individually trivial, these repeated cases of mistaken identity confound attempts accurately to assess the scope of SOE's operations in Asia, and to fit SOE into the overall pattern of Allied clandestine action. At a basic level, it is this misleading and incomplete picture that this book seeks to rectify.

The Japanese occupation and the origins of the Malayan Emergency

The first major focus of this book, the often unintended long-term political impact of SOE's wartime alliances, has been examined in studies covering a number of different countries, particularly in the Balkans, where SOE is seen as having played a significant role in the rise to power of Tito in Yugoslavia and Hoxha in Albania.[28] In both of these countries, communist groups came to power at the end of the war, supported by the best armed and most competent of the competing guerrilla groups that had contested the field during it. Debate over the impact of SOE in the Balkans has gone well beyond SOE itself and into the activities of MI5 and possible Soviet moles.[29] Similar work has begun on the role of Force 136 in Burma, where the consequences of its actions are seen as having deepened ethnic tensions and contributed to civil war, and also on the political impact of OSS in French Indo-China.[30] However, the exact role of Force 136 in Malaya, and the precise nature of its relationship with the MCP and the MPAJA, has not yet been drawn out with full reference to the surviving records, and thus the question of the impact of the Force's actions on later political developments in Malaya, particularly the declaration of the State of Emergency, has not been addressed.

In the case of Burma, some scholars have stated that the revolt of the Karen after Burmese independence was due to Force 136 having made, it is claimed, unauthorized promises with regard to the formation of an independent Karen state. Mary Callahan states that Force 136 had 'almost no SEAC [South East Asia Command] oversight', which allowed it to make its own deals. Here, Callahan appears to overlook the role of 'P' Division, which coordinated the clandestines in SEAC from 1943, and the effective relationship between Force 136's head, Colin Mackenzie, and Louis Mountbatten (Supreme Allied Commander South East Asia).[31] Duckett's more recent research, by contrast, concludes that Force 136 had been empowered during the war to promise the Karen a distinct status within Burma after the war (which some officers appear to have interpreted as independence) in return for their support, and that the failure of the British government to stand by this promise was one of the reasons the Karen rebelled after Burmese independence.[32] Duckett's analysis places the responsibility for this chain of events on the British government, not SOE.[33] These conclusions are particularly interesting in respect of the debate over whether Force 136 made political promises to the MPAJA or not, and suggest that the terms of the agreement with these guerrillas, and the atmosphere in which it was struck, bear detailed investigation.

Where historians have noted the long-term political impact of Force 136's activities in Malaya, their approach has tended to be cursory and lacking in detail. This is true not only for works of primarily military history, where the long-term political consequences of military activity are not a major focus of the study, but also for those concerned with the ethics of warfare.[34] Michael Burleigh's *Moral Combat* devotes an entire chapter to SOE, but his only mention of the Malayan resistance is of the communist guerrillas, previously 'orchestrated' by 'the British', preparing for insurrection: he is clearly speaking of the MPAJA and Force 136, but he does not elaborate.[35]

As the literature currently stands, the events of the Japanese occupation are insufficiently considered as explanatory factors in the crisis that led to the declaration of the Malayan Emergency and how the British reacted to it. Some scholars fail even to mention the existence of the alliance between the British and the MCP, let alone delve into its longer-term repercussions.[36] Ban Kah Choon and Yap Hong Kuan are the exceptions in attempting to address the outbreak of the Malayan Emergency almost entirely in the light of the MCP's wartime activities.[37] This book will develop this line of study further, examining the MPAJA's (and thus the MCP's) attitude to competing guerrilla organizations to evaluate the degree to which the communists attempted to attain political and military dominance of the Malayan resistance during the Japanese occupation. It will also examine the extent to which the MPAJA sought to acquire stocks of arms for later jungle warfare. This will enable us to deepen our understanding of the MCP and its long-term ambitions, and to trace a path from the actions of the party during and just after the Japanese occupation to the decision by its leadership to turn to armed struggle in early 1948.

Alliances and agreements

The second major focus of this study is the context in which SOE and the MPAJA operated during the Pacific War, which requires elucidation of the nature and range of armed Malayan resistance to the Japanese. The historical literature covering the guerrillas of the Malayan interior is limited and initial misunderstandings continue to persist. The consensus has long been that the only armed resistance body of any significance was the MPAJA, which was composed almost entirely of ethnic Chinese, and supported by the MCP. As a result, the efforts of the guerrillas allied to the Guomindang and of the Malay groups have been largely overlooked. Harry Miller, a journalist who wrote in 1954, virtually ignored both the Malay guerrillas and the Guomindang forces.[38] Much the same can be said of works by Edgar O'Ballance and Cruickshank, which appeared in the mid-1960s and mid-1980s respectively.[39] By 1990, this tendency had gone a step further and the MPAJA was described as 'the only indigenous resistance' in Malaya.[40]

In 2003, an academically influential memoir appeared: that of Chin Peng, a leading cadre during the Japanese occupation and, from 1947, Secretary General of the MCP. When, in this work, Chin Peng entirely ignored the Malay guerrillas, dismissed the Guomindang-linked Overseas Chinese Anti-Japanese Army (OCAJA) as 'bandit groups' and declared that the MPAJA had been 'the only functioning resistance movement on the peninsula', he chimed with the generally accepted scholarly view.[41] He went on to argue that the MCP's failure to obtain the concessions that it felt were its due (as, supposedly, the 'only' resistance) soured its relationship with the colonial power and fed directly into the unrest that resulted in the declaration of the State of Emergency in 1948.[42] This view has strongly influenced more recent work. Bayly and Harper, for example, paint the OCAJA as 'hill gangs' rather than as the guerrillas that (as we shall see) they considered themselves to be – and as some Force 136 officers agreed that they were.[43]

This book will argue that such a scholarly perspective, which provides credence to Chin Peng's claims and gives them further leverage, has been highly misleading. The negation in the historical literature of the efforts of other groups who fought the Japanese is significant in the case of the armed Malay resistance, which served as a proving ground for young elite Malays who subsequently assumed positions of considerable authority in the independent nation. The current misrepresentation in the historical literature also disguises the extent to which the communists made wartime bids for territorial control of the Malayan interior, even if this meant overthrowing other anti-Japanese guerrillas. This is a revelation which has the potential to significantly recast how we understand the outbreak of the Malayan Emergency. Both these topics will be addressed later in this book. Finally, the privileging of communist resistance during the Japanese occupation of Malaya results in a scholarly tendency to overlook the fact that Force 136 in Malaya – like SOE in Europe – backed all sides. As a consequence, only a partial view of British wartime policy with respect to Malaya's multiple political factions has so far emerged.

Britain was seeking local allies and, like the United States in French Indo-China, was prepared to back armed communists.[44] However, unlike the United States, Britain was a colonial power hoping to return to a former possession, for whom the backing of an avowedly anti-imperialist party might have seemed ultimately self-defeating. However, this willingness to support the MCP looks less surprising when one realizes that its leader had been a British agent before the Pacific War. In an astonishing coup, in the 1930s the Malayan Special Branch acquired an agent named Lai Teck from the Sûreté Fédérale in French Indo-China, and infiltrated him to the very top of the MCP, significantly blunting the power of the MCP to act against the colonial state.[45]

The reasons that Britain was willing to back the Guomindang guerrillas of the OCAJA and support the Malay resistance remain largely unexamined. Although British policy aims for post-war Malaya, such as the creation of a Malayan Union with wider citizenship rights, are well understood, little work has yet been done which attempts to tie these to Force 136's association with the Malayan guerrillas. Tim Harper, in his detailed study *The End of Empire and the Making of Malaya*, comments that the existence of Malay resistance movements was, for the British, 'politically reassuring', but he does not explore the Malay resistance in any depth.[46] Beyond this, there is very little English-language work on Malay guerrilla movements. The only exception seems to be Wan Hashim's *Role of the Malay Guerillas: Force 136*.[47] His purpose was to recover this hidden history and recount the activities of the Malay resistance, and consequently he does not discuss the motivations that drove Force 136 to sponsor Malay operations, or whether the Malays who joined hoped to extract concessions from Britain in return for their support. The motivations underpinning Malay guerrilla movements, and British backing for them, remain unexplored.

As well as this confused and limited depiction of Force 136, and of the guerrilla forces it worked with in Malaya, there continues to be much scholarly dispute over the exact nature of the agreements made between Force 136 and the MPAJA and the motivations that lay behind them. While it is widely recognized that the cooperation between Force 136 and the MPAJA was based on an agreement signed at Blantan in Perak at the end of 1943, the terms of this agreement remain open to debate, as will be seen in Chapter 3. The Singaporeans Ban Kah Choon and Yap Hong Kuan argue that the MPAJA treated the Japanese occupation as 'but a prelude to the struggle to throw out the British and establish a communist republic'.[48] Their book is problematic, however, because Ban, who revised the book for publication, is not an historian but a professor of English. Further, possibly with the expectation that he would support the policy of the Singaporean government of the time, Yap was given unprecedented access to Special Branch files. As consequence, the work is not footnoted and so claims cannot always be tested against contemporary documents. Nonetheless, their claims regarding the MCP are worthy of investigation. One purpose of this book is to test the validity of their allegation that the MPAJA was, all along, planning a revolution, and it is a topic that will recur in chapters examining the MPAJA's relationships with the British and with other guerrilla bodies.

As for the outcome of the Blantan Agreement, some scholars argue that SOE did not fulfil its side of the deal due, perhaps due to British wariness of the communists, whereas others assert that Force 136 did arm and train the MPAJA, bringing them to the same stage of readiness as the levies of the Burmese operation, *Character*, who played a key role in the recapture of Rangoon.[49] There are also doubts about the political commitments that Force 136 did – or did not – make to the MPAJA, with some scholars arguing that political promises were made while others contend the opposite.[50] As we shall see, the issue of political promises made (or not made) by Force 136 offers important insights into British policy-making at the time. Even more significantly, an evaluation of the terms of the Blantan Agreement allows us to assess the extent to which the breaking of promises on the part of the British was a contributory factor in the decision of the leadership of the MCP to turn towards armed revolution.

To summarize, the role of SOE in Malaya remains shrouded in confusion, which serves to obscure not only SOE's role in the development of Malayan politics, but also the impact of British policy upon the Malayan resistance. There is a failure to distinguish between the different clandestine bodies, disagreement over the status of the MPAJA, and conflicting conclusions regarding the agreements between SOE and the guerrilla organizations – over what these agreements promised, why they were struck and the degree to which they were fulfilled. This book will seek to remedy some of this confusion, thus permitting the integration of the Malayan operations within the story of SOE as a whole. It will also contribute to our understanding of the Malayan Emergency, allowing us to locate its beginnings within the Japanese occupation and the struggles between the different Malayan guerrilla bodies for territorial control. This struggle can be read as another episode in the story of Malayan decolonization, as new leaders began to emerge from among the colonized, taking their political futures into their own hands.

Imperial intelligence

The third and final focus of this study is upon the activities of Force 136 as an imperial intelligence gathering service. This aspect of its role has not previously been subjected to scholarly enquiry. Scholars have begun to unpick the supposed rationality of diplomatic correspondence and intelligence, showing how bias becomes entrenched and remains invisible to those who use the data that is produced.[51] Intelligence from Malaya, it will be shown, was far from neutral: those who gathered it were, inevitably, influenced by their own prior experiences and future hopes, as well as by their informants and the level of trust that they placed in them.

At the end of 1945, as the operational reports were written, liaison officers in Force 136 produced a trove of information on the MCP. This book will explore the nature and variety of that intelligence, and the fate of the reports produced. Parallels will be drawn between the nature of the intelligence gathering process as practised by Force 136, and as carried out in Malaya in the six months or so prior to the declaration of the Emergency. This book, then, will investigate what lay in the mass of reports about MCP members produced by Force 136, and explore the reasons why this information was handled in the manner it was, and how this relates to the post-war policy of the British government for Malaya.

Sources and methodology

The relative shortage of literature on SOE in Malaya is not due to a lack of primary sources, for there are plenty of these, both official and unofficial, written from a range of viewpoints and providing a wealth of information. Indeed, the extent of sources available for Force 136's operations in Malaya provides us with what is almost an exemplar of imperialism in action, an imperialism which had lost its prestige with the Fall of Singapore, and was struggling to reassert itself in a time of social change. In the field, it faced challenges from both within (from both non-white and lower-class members of the Force) and without, in the form of the communist-backed MPAJA. The old hierarchies of class and caste were being shaken: by the war's end, a Labour government had come to power in Britain and, on the international stage, the anti-colonial United States was in a powerful position. The main shortcoming of Force 136 as an example of imperialism in action, of course, is that the majority of sources it provides have a distinct colonial bias and, even within that, are written from the privileged position of the primarily Caucasian officer class. Most subaltern voices are also those of Europeans, though there are a few exceptions.[52] This section will discuss the official and then the unofficial sources, which can be divided into those contemporary with the events they describe, and those written with the benefit of hindsight.

The available British official sources are mostly located at the UK National Archives at Kew; however, a few are held at the Malaysian national archives. A small number of official papers also survived in private hands with a collection of particular interest surviving among the private papers of Freddy Spencer Chapman, held at the Imperial War Museum. A small (and very interesting) group was discovered in the papers of C.E. ('Bill') Foss, who had retained the operational documents left to him by his major in Operation *Funnel*.

Within the official papers, the key source for a study of Force 136 in Malaya is the HS (SOE) series held at the UK National Archives. This series was gradually released to the public from 1993 and covers SOE planning, operations and personnel. However, valuable as these papers are, they have their shortcomings. Firstly, the HS series is a shadow of its original self. After SOE's own post-war bonfires, the surviving archive was passed to SOE's rival, the Secret Intelligence Service (SIS: MI6), which aggressively weeded it over the years. Consequently, by the 1970s, 87 per cent of the original documents had been destroyed.[53] It is possible, on the basis of papers surviving in private hands, to hazard an educated guess at what has been lost. Absent papers must include the accounting records of Force 136 patrols working with the guerrillas and the nominal rolls of the guerrilla units that Force 136 officers in the field produced. It is also likely that papers which were particularly or potentially embarrassing were consigned to the flames. It is here that the survival of papers in out-of-the-way places comes into its own: the Foss papers include the only known surviving nominal roll for an MPAJA patrol. Spencer Chapman's Private Papers contain an assortment of intelligence summaries, reports, letters and telegrams, including the potentially awkward information that Force 136's forerunner, India Mission, made the deliberate decision to keep some key information out of the view of the higher command.[54]

In addition, a proportion of what has survived has not yet been released. Some files have redactions that, given the context, often seem to relate to the activities of MI6. Some personnel files are not yet in the public domain, for if no proof is available of the death of the subject, the file is retained until the subject would be – or can be assumed to be – one hundred years old. It is also relevant here that SIS retained the personnel files relating to individuals who went on to work for the clandestine services.[55] It is probably for this reason that the file of Capt. Hugh Fraser of Operation *Galvanic* is not held by the National Archives, nor even listed by them: Fraser joined MI5 in 1965.[56] In addition, SIS appears to have kept back the files of those who progressed to senior military or police careers.[57]

It is worth noting that in the operational reports, which recorded work in the field, it is not always clear whether the information provided is first-hand or hearsay – first-hand information being, obviously, more authoritative, even if it provides only a partial view of events. The final point is, of course, that the HS series presents, almost exclusively, SOE's view of itself though, in the case of the operational reports at least, no official line was being toed. Men seem to have been at liberty to state their views, and some wrote very freely, showing definite signs of being 'demob happy'.[58]

To obtain the view of external bodies, trace the pattern of events and obtain information not retained on the HS files, it has been necessary to explore the holdings from other government agencies, including the Cabinet (CAB), Colonial Office (CO), Air Ministry (AIR) and War Office (WO) series. The AIR series gives an insight into the problems that confronted the Special Duties Squadrons in provisioning parties in the field. Cabinet, War Office and Colonial Office papers trace the movements of policy and war planning and give the other side of the argument in SOE's tussles with central government. Helpfully for the researcher, a vast range of papers (from the CAB, CO, Treasury and WO series) has been sifted to extract those most significant to the story of Malayan independence, and published as part of the *British Documents of the End of Empire* series, which simplified the tracking of the development of the idea of the Malayan Union, and served to explain some of the strictures placed upon SOE during the war. It was not possible to examine the records of the OSS, but the evidence suggests that these might in future provide yet another perspective on SOE, for the OSS was at times a keen competitor. Aldrich's *Intelligence and the War against Japan* relies heavily on these papers and, as will be seen, they can provide a very different take on events from that given in SOE's own files.[59] In addition, occasional use was made of the *London Gazette*, particularly for military detail.[60]

Unofficial primary sources – letters, diaries, news articles, interviews, memoirs and photographs – can be split into those produced at the time and those created afterwards. Clearly, the closer to the event a source is produced, the more authoritative it is likely to be. These unofficial sources round out the picture given in the official files, contributing personal anecdotes and details of actions not considered important enough at the time to be recorded in the official reports. They can give valuable information about key personal relationships that influenced events, such as that between the head of Force 136, Colin Mackenzie, and Louis Mountbatten (Supreme Allied Commander, South East Asia), which allowed an assessment to be made of the influence enjoyed by Force 136 in the highest levels of the British military machine.[61]

Standard historical practice is, of course, that more reliance is placed on contemporary sources such as letters, diaries and perhaps (depending upon the rigour of the journalists and the reliability of their informants) news articles, than upon information recorded at a later date. All, however, are subject to the old rule, *testis unus, testis nullus* (one witness is no witness), and it is important to test aspects of an account against other records; this also allows the sifting of the narrators into those who are more and less reliable. Further, the wider the range of sources consulted, the more possible it becomes to contextualize the information they provide, and to test its veracity.

Both memoirists and interviewees can be guilty of the wisdom of hindsight, the desire to burnish or preserve an established reputation and simple forgetfulness. The scholar Gwyn Prins, writing about historical methodology, claims that oral histories are often held 'in contempt', but adds that research indicates that, when individuals reach the stage of what is known as 'life review', their accounts 'can be remarkably precise'.[62] Even so, the words of those likely to espouse particular viewpoints repay critical study. In particular, this book will seek to interrogate what has been possibly the most influential personal memoir to shape academic opinion as to the role of the MCP during the Japanese occupation and its actions before and during the Malayan Emergency, that of Chin Peng – a key cadre during the Pacific War and the eventual Secretary General of the MCP. As noted previously, Chin Peng's memoir *My Side of History* appears to give an insider's view of the MCP, but before this view is accepted, a number of points should be considered. Firstly, he wrote it with two co-authors, calling into question the extent to which it is his authentic voice.[63] However, parts of it reprise discussions recorded, verbatim, in *Dialogues with Chin Peng*, the result of several days of round-table discussions some years earlier between Chin Peng and a group of academics.[64] The conversations of *Dialogues* formed a dry run for the memoir, and demonstrate Chin Peng's fluent and competent English. In addition, he is not on record as objecting to how his views were presented in either book. Thus, they can be taken as fair expositions of his opinions.

Beyond this, given his position, Chin Peng is to be expected to wish to present the MCP in a favourable light and his own course of action as sensible and defensible. Consequently, *My Side of History* has to be read as critically as any other memoir, and compared with information recorded at the time. While Chin Peng was highly intelligent with an excellent recall of detail, this book seeks to interrogate what he has to say. When his version of events is read against other sources – such as Force 136 reports and the claims of Malays involved in non-communist resistance groups – there are, as noted above, lacunae and perhaps some one-sided interpretations of the facts.[65] In this respect, it is difficult not to concur with Karl Hack's view of Chin Peng's memory being either 'self-consciously selective' or prone to 'convenient amnesia'.[66]

There is a tendency to privilege words, especially written words, above other sources, but, as this book also hopes to show, photographs and maps can provide insights not otherwise available. For example, photographs of the MPAJA entering the small town of Slim River at the end of the war give a clear idea of how well armed they were; an image of a group of OCAJA taken at around the same time shows that, though only possessing an approximation of a uniform (shorts and a shirt topped off with a trilby) they were all armed and reasonably well-drilled. Food supply problems are made vivid when, as is very occasionally possible, one can compare a photograph of a well-nourished officer in India before his parachute drop, and a gaunt man at the end of operations.[67] A map can show more clearly than words the distribution of Force 136 operations within Malaya, showing at a glance their concentration on the western littoral of the peninsula, ready for the landings of the planned reconquest, Operation *Zipper*.

Thus the range of available sources for a detailed study of SOE's Malaya operations and their aftermath is considerable, and forms a strong base from which to tackle the questions addressed in this book. Sources will be approached with the intention, where possible, of comparing them with other available accounts, and making connections between people, and between people and their experiences. This in turn allows a clear thread to be drawn from, for example, SOE experience in the Balkans to attitudes held by Force 136 men working in Malaya, and experience in the Malayan jungles before the war to work within them during it: 'knowing the resistance' and 'knowing the country', it will be shown, had a strong influence upon how men perceived events and consequently upon the interpretation they placed upon them in the reports they wrote.

This book will begin with an overview of SOE's Oriental Mission and its activities in Malaya: 1941–1942, underlining the key role it played in laying the groundwork for later SOE activity in the country. The following chapter looks at the development of SOE's India Mission (later known as Force 136) and its Malayan Country Section, and tackles such issues as the limited availability of suitable recruits, the motives of men for volunteering and the racial attitudes that permeated the British Empire. The following three chapters discuss in turn Force 136's relationships with the MPAJA (particularly focussing upon clarifying the deal struck between the two bodies, and the motivations that propelled them to make it), with local Malay resistance bodies, and with the guerrillas raised under the banner of the Guomindang, as well as the relationships of these local organizations with each other.

The following chapter seeks to clarify events during the difficult and deeply unsettled period between the surrender of Japan in August 1945 and the return of civilian government in April 1946. A central issue animating the analysis here is the extent to which the MPAJA still viewed itself as a revolutionary body and was prepared to use the opportunity provided by a lack of centralized control within Malaya to expand its arsenals and experiment with power. Finally Chapter 7 ('The

Tangled Mass of Unspun Fibres': Information and Intelligence in the Lead-up to the Malayan Emergency) assesses the nature and quality of British intelligence in Malaya in both the period of the British Military Administration (September 1945–March 1946) and the months leading up to the declaration of the State of Emergency in June 1948.

This book, then, will cover the arc of SOE's involvement in the Malayan scene, beginning with the arrival of Oriental Mission in May 1941 and then examining the role of India Mission/Force 136 during the Japanese occupation, before exploring the repercussions of SOE upon Malayan politics as the Emergency approached.

Chapter 1

ORIENTAL MISSION AND MALAYA, 1941–1942

For a full understanding of Force 136 – its contacts and its recruits, and its benefits and limitations as a producer of revealing and detailed primary source material for the historian – our story has to begin with an examination of Oriental Mission, the first foray into Asia of the Special Operations Executive (SOE). Historians who have discussed Oriental Mission generally concur that it achieved very little with respect to Malaya.[1] Some recognize that it trained young recruits provided by the Malayan Communist Party (MCP), who it then inserted in small parties into the jungle ahead of the Japanese advance of 1941–1942, with the intention that each group should form the nucleus of a guerrilla unit.[2] The majority also note that, in addition, Oriental Mission recruited, trained and inserted stay-behind parties, mostly consisting of resident Europeans, to harass the Japanese behind their lines.[3] However, with the exception of Paul Kratoska and Richard Gough, most appear unaware that Oriental Mission also established an escape route from Singapore, through the Rhio Archipelago to the south of Singapore and then to Padang on the west coast of Sumatra, from where evacuees were collected by vessels of the Royal Navy. At the Fall of Singapore, this route was key to the escape of several thousand soldiers and civilians. As we will see, it proved to be of enormous significance, for the escapees later provided a pool of candidates from which SOE drew many recruits, both Asian and European, for its Malayan operations. Without them, this work in Malaya would not have been viable.

This omission is symptomatic of a general scholarly confusion surrounding Oriental Mission's work in Malaya, which it is the main purpose of this chapter to resolve. At the same time, this chapter will also posit that Oriental Mission was critical in laying the foundations for SOE's later work in Malaya. The Padang escape route provided many recruits, the survivors of the European stay-behind parties became useful points of contact for infiltrating SOE operatives, and the MCP parties helped to ensure that there was an active guerrilla resistance upon which SOE was able to build.

Finally, this chapter will challenge another false assumption evident in the historiography, that much of Oriental Mission's work was political rather than military in nature.[4] In fact, this chapter will show that the mission's aims, in Malaya at least and from the beginnings of its work there, were, though sometimes politically sensitive, essentially military in both scope and form.

The activities of the mission are detailed in the reports, letters and memoranda that it generated, and which are now filed alongside the Force 136 papers. The mission's documents are of course subject to the criticism that their authors will have wanted to make the best of what they had done. However, their words can sometimes be tested by comparison with external sources, such as the diary kept by the leading Guomindang member, Lim Bo Seng. Supporting the contemporary papers are various memoirs written by those involved, some published soon after the end of the war, which contribute additional detail and can be read against contemporary accounts.[5] It is upon this mix of sources that this chapter will be based. Before proceeding, however, it is necessary to discuss Malaya itself, for it was a complex country, and its complexity had a deep influence on the nature of the special operations that SOE conducted there.

Colonial Malaya, 1941

Malaya, though a small colony in terms of land area – about the size of England – was important to the British war effort as a producer of rubber and tin. The British administration exerted comparatively close control over the country, by means both official and unofficial: it was from these various systems of control that many later members of Force 136's Malayan Country Section were eventually drawn.

Malaya was ethnically complex, and the system of government favoured the Malays – indeed, there was a tendency within the administration to view Malaya as 'a Malay country'. Malays, of all Malaya's 'nationalities' or 'races', were the only non-Europeans allowed to enter the elite Malayan Civil Service.[6] The Malay sultans also retained some of their panoply and power, especially within the Unfederated Malay States (Johore to the far south of the peninsula, and Trengganu, Kelantan, Kedah and Perlis to the north); within the Federated Malay States (Perak, Selangor, Pahang and Negri Sembilan), which lay in a broad belt across the middle of the country, they were responsible only for matters of religion and custom. However, the Straits Settlements (Singapore, Malacca, and Penang and Province Wellesley) were governed directly, as colonies of the British Crown.

Malaya's two other big ethnic groups, the Chinese and the Indians, were most numerous in the Federated Malay States and the Straits Settlements. Although there was a centuries-long history of Chinese settlement in Malaya, the majority of the Chinese population, like the Indian one, had come to the country over the previous half century to work on the tin mines and rubber estates.[7] Both groups had traditionally been seen as 'birds of passage', with the expectation that individuals would ultimately return to their countries of origin, but it was more and more obvious that they were becoming increasingly settled, with a growing proportion being native-born. Faced with this, and with the huge contribution that Chinese and Indians had made to the development of the Malayan economy,

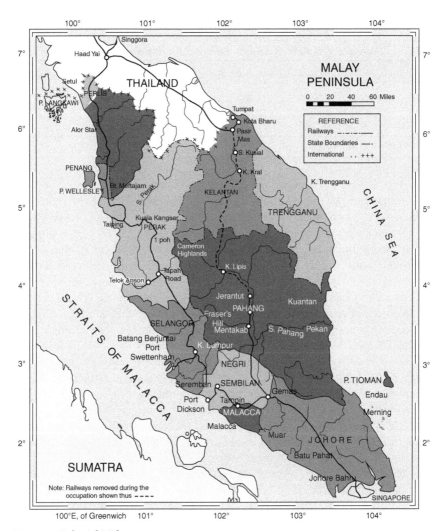

Map 1.1 Colonial Malaya.

it was becoming more difficult to defend Malay privileges. At the same time, ethnic tension, though still largely latent, was beginning to raise its head: Malay resentment at being outnumbered in what they saw as their own country was becoming more vocal.[8]

Colonial control of these groups was mostly exerted through mine and rubber estate managers, who interacted with their workforces both directly and through the patterns of authority within the labour system. European managers knew particular Chinese labour contractors, or relied upon their *kepalas* and *mandores* (overseers), and their office clerks. Through these men and also via Asians they might know socially, in the less racially exclusive clubs, at the Rotary or on sports

Table 1.1 The Malayan Population, 1941

	Malays	Chinese	Indians	Europeans	Eurasians	Others	Total
SS	309,051	922,463	148,623	18,017	13,484	12,712	1,424,350
FMS	722,626	989,635	466,056	11,149	5,286	17,300	2,212,052
UMS	1,245,675	465,892	129,523	2,200	560	28,479	1,872,329
Total	2,277,352	2,377,990	744,202	31,366	19,330	58,491	5,508,731
% of total	41.34	43.17	13.51	0.57	0.35	1.06	100

Note: Percentage calculations are my own.
Source: Condensed from Kratoska, *The Japanese Occupation of Malaya*, p. 19.

teams, they were able to tap into affective knowledge, especially if they had attained proficiency in one of Malaya's numerous languages. Their contacts, however, were mostly members of the intermediary class, who often saw the Empire as a benefit rather than a blight: these were the Asians who donated to the War Fund, not those who joined the MCP. Much the same can be said for the connections of the European members of the Malayan Civil Service, whose work brought them into contact with village headmen and an array of Asian dignitaries.[9] In this respect, the knowledge that fed into the colonial system was inevitably skewed.

Beyond the mines and rubber estates, situated mostly on the western littoral, lay the rain forests that covered 80 per cent of the country. Even these were locked into the colonial system: they were explored and mapped by surveyors, divided up for various uses ('Malay Reserves', for Malay agricultural settlement; 'Forest Reserves', for controlled felling and so on), and managed by forest officers and game wardens. Through these systems of control, the colonial state had contact with Malaya's aborigines, the *Orang Asli*, and was aware of illegal tin mining or timber felling and – an increasing issue during the Depression – illegal settlement by Chinese 'squatters', thrown out of work and onto their own resources.[10] These squatters, whose numbers increased hugely during the Japanese occupation, would become the major recruiting ground for the Malayan People's Anti-Japanese Army (MPAJA), and their main providers of food: as the guerrillas found, the jungle could not feed them (even the *Orang Asli* had difficulty in this regard).[11]

Food supply, which proved a problem for the Japanese during their time in power, had also been a concern for the pre-war British administration. Despite the production of rice in the country (mostly in the hands of the Malay peasantry), Malaya was a rice deficit country.[12] Thus, the road and rail network that was used for the export of Malaya's raw materials was also used for the import of foodstuffs. This network was at its most dense on the heavily settled western littoral (though there was a railway line, branching at Gemas, which ran up the eastern side of the country) and in itself enabled increased colonial control. During serious rubber estate strikes in mid-1941, it allowed the army and, of course, the police, to reach the estates, quell the protests and allow production to restart.[13] The police, of course, were the first line of colonial defence and an obvious source of colonial control. It is significant that, of the eight operations Force 136 dispatched to the MPAJA during the war, four were led by policemen.[14] Force 136 also looked for other men with a close knowledge of Malaya, such as civil servants, planters and businessmen: men whose daily lives had brought them into contact with Asians, and compelled them to speak Malay or a Chinese dialect. At the end of the war, the returning administration would find that these structures of information and control were seriously weakened, if not destroyed.

In a sense, it was at the lowest level of colonial control – at that of policemen who worked with Asian constables, and planters who talked daily to *kepalas*, contractors and Asian clerks – that colonial familiarity with Asians was at its greatest. The higher up the tree one moved, the more remote the Asian country became. It is perhaps significant that, of the three main army commanders in Malaya in late 1941, only General Lewis Heath, who commanded III Indian Corps, was active in the training of Asians for jungle work, whereas the General Officer Commanding, General Arthur Percival, was – as Oriental Mission would discover – entirely opposed to any such scheme.[15] It was thought that even hinting that a Japanese assault might be successful would be more than the fragile psyches of Asians would be able to bear; this was one reason why so few defences had been prepared.[16] As I shall shortly discuss, this was one of the reasons why Oriental Mission, when it arrived in Malaya, was initially unsuccessful in carrying out its plans. Even so, SOE eventually had a lasting impact in the country.

Oriental Mission: SOE starts work in Asia

As already noted, SOE was formed in London in the wake of the Dunkirk evacuation, by combining the military intelligence unit MI(R) with Section D of the Secret Intelligence Service (SIS or MI6).[17] The new organization's role was to sponsor and conduct sabotage and subversion behind enemy lines, and it eventually became active in much of occupied Europe, with SOE's work in France, the Balkans and Greece being particularly well known. Its Asian operations came under a number of designations including Special Operations Australia (SOA, also known as Z Force and the Special Reconnaissance Department – SRD) and India Mission – which became known as Force 136 in March 1944. Yet SOE was not always a popular body within British security circles. The Chiefs of Staff were displeased to have the control of sabotage and subversion taken out of their hands, and the leadership of MI6 resented both the loss of Section D to SOE, and SOE's intrusion upon spheres of activity that had previously been MI6's preserve.[18]

In May 1941, SOE set up Oriental Mission in Singapore with the cover story that it was an outstation of the Ministry of Economic Warfare (MEW).[19] Oriental Mission's head, Valentine Killery, and his deputy Basil Goodfellow had both been senior managers with Imperial Chemical Industries in China.[20] These two seemed unlikely candidates for clandestine work, but the scholar Antony Best suggests good reasons for the use of businessmen in such a sensitive endeavour. British intelligence had for decades used businessmen, journalists and missionaries in Asia as useful informants, for they could access people and places beyond the easy reach of the formal intelligence services. Businessmen were also assumed

Table 1.2 Allied Clandestine Organizations Active in South East Asia, 1940–1945

Parent Organization or Government	Branch Organization	Comments
Active in Malaya		
British		
MI6	ISLD (Inter-Services Liaison Department)	Joint operations with Force 136 in Malaya
MI9	'E' Group (concerned with evaders, POWs and Internees)	Operatives dropped to Force 136 reception committees
SOE (7/1940–1/1946)	Oriental Mission, Singapore (5/1941–2/1942)	Arranged operations in Malaya (Stay-Behind Parties)
		Set up escape route from Singapore
	India Mission: formed May 1941 with cover name GS I(k); later became Force 136 (3/1944–1/1946)	Officially Force 136 from March 1944, but not called that until the move to Kandy in December 1944. The Force's Malayan Country Section is not to be confused with the Malayan Civil Service (also MCS)
	SOA (Special Operations Australia); aka 'Z' Force and the Services Reconnaissance Department (SRD)	SOA was under F136's operational control.
SEAC (South East Asia Command) SEAC's 'P' Div. coordinated the clandestines from Dec 43	PWD (Psychological Warfare Division): propaganda	Joint UK/US project, with staff from OWI, OSS and the United Kingdom's Political Warfare Executive (PWE)
	'D' Division (deception)	Worked with Force 136
American	OSS (Office of Strategic Services)	Worked with Force 136 in Malaya
Not Active in Malaya		
British	BAAG (British Army Aid Group)	British Army Aid Group: active in China and under control of MI9
American	Naval Group China	Worked with Guomindang in China
	OWI (Office of War Information)	Propaganda: only active in Malaya as part of PWD (see above)
	BEW (Board of Economic Warfare)	Later known as Office of Economic Warfare
	MIS-X	Escape organization
French	DGER (Direction générale des étude et recherché)	Active in the former French colonial territories
Dutch	Korps Insulinde	Concerned with NEI; worked with India Mission

Note: This table shows the number and range of clandestine organizations active in Asia during World War II. The possibilities for cooperation (and competition) can be seen. 'P' Division played a critical role as referee, helping to overcome the fragmented nature of a system that had developed on a very *ad hoc* basis.

Source: The information in this table is drawn from Cruickshank, *SOE in the Far East*, pp. 61, 83 and 88; Terence O'Brien, *The Moonlit War: The Story of Clandestine Operations in South-East Asia, 1944–5* (London: Collins, 1987), pp. 28 and 223; TNA, HS 1/112; TNA, HS 1/165, pp. 31–37; IWM, 15555, Private Papers of Fraser Crawford; Richard Gough, *The Jungle Was Red: SOE's Force 136 Sumatra and Malaya* (Singapore: SNP Panpac, 2003), p. 12; <http://discovery.nationalarchives.gov.uk/SearchUI/details?Uri=C9268> [accessed 18 July 2013]; <http://discovery.nationalarchives.gov.uk/SearchUI/browse/C21394> [accessed 12 November 2013]; Supplement to the London Gazette, 19 April 1951, Air Chief Marshal Sir Keith Park, Despatch, <http://www.ibiblio.org/hyperwar/UN/UK/LondonGazette/39202.pdf> [accessed 19 November 2013].

to be reliable by intelligence staff because they shared their upper-middle class background.[21] Although there is no definite evidence that Killery had any pre-existing connections with British intelligence, Best considers that the pattern of recruitment into SOE in Asia gives 'a clear indication' that many of those recruited were already part of a colonial intelligence network.[22]

As head of Oriental Mission, Killery was made responsible for SOE activity in a vast geographical area, which included Malaya, China, Hong Kong, Shanghai, Thailand and Burma.[23] He was also aware of what he termed the 'delicate' nature of the political situation in the region at the time – that is to say, the risk of drawing Japan into open conflict with Britain.[24] When he came to write his charter, which would govern what he was to do and how he would go about it, his three main objectives were political: to prepare 'an organisation ... ready to take action to counter Japanese activities', to collect intelligence and to 'undertake covert propaganda' against the Axis.[25] It was Killery's superiors who added to his draft charter two more, openly military, aims: the formation of stay-behind parties to become active in the event of a Japanese invasion and the establishment of a paramilitary training school.[26] Even as the civilian staff of Oriental Mission worked up their contacts and developed their plans, the military trainers employed by the mission founded a military training school at Tanjong Balai, about ten miles west of the city of Singapore. Nominally a Royal Engineer's school of demolitions, it was known to SOE as No. 101 Special Training School (101STS). Its second-in-command, Major Freddy Spencer Chapman was, by virtue of the books he had written about his adventures in Greenland and Tibet, a minor celebrity. He would spend much of the war in the jungle and prove a useful contact for later infiltrations by SOE.[27]

Oriental Mission encountered critical difficulties during the course of its work in Malaya. The most significant of these was that Killery's charter committed him to obtaining permission from the British civil and military authorities in any country in which he wished to work. This was not forthcoming in Malaya and as a result Oriental Mission found itself unable to prepare for possible invasion.[28] The authorities – in the form of General Arthur Percival (the General Officer Commanding, Malaya) and Sir Shenton Thomas (the Governor of the Straits Settlements) – crushed Killery's plans for ethnically mixed stay-behind parties, and forbade the training of 'Orientals' at 101STS.[29]

These ethnically mixed stay-behind parties had been a key part of Oriental Mission's plan for Malaya, put forward in August 1941. These parties were to be selected from men familiar with the districts in which they would operate, who would then be trained in guerrilla tactics at 101STS, the mission's school. The parties would then select suitable campsites, stash dumps of stores, and return to their normal lives until they were needed. Their task would to be to cause as much disruption to the Japanese as possible (cutting their lines of communication, harassing their rear and so forth) and to gather intelligence.[30]

The idea of these stay-behind parties was neither radical nor new, for they echoed the Auxiliary Units in Britain. Developed by Colin Gubbins of MI(R), who brought his knowledge (and many of his instructors) to SOE when he joined it in the latter part of 1940, the Auxiliary Units were raised from the Home Guard in coastal districts of Britain. They contained men intimately familiar with the landscape in which they were to operate, with farmers, gamekeepers and poachers being prime recruits. Trained in sabotage and assassination, they were to lie low in the event of a German invasion and would then harry the invaders from behind.[31] Furthermore, the effectiveness of behind the lines activity in modern warfare had been proven by the Long Range Desert Group (LRDG), which was formed in July 1940. As with the Auxiliary Units and the planned stay-behind parties in Malaya, the LRDG relied upon men very familiar with the territory in which they worked, although its modus operandi was different. It operated by truck out of Egypt, attacking Axis garrisons in the Libyan desert and gathering intelligence. In September 1940, the War Office had supported a doubling in size of the LRDG, a testament to its success in the few months since its inception.[32] The British Army is considered by some academics to be 'a learning institution', and there is evidence on file that knowledge made its way from one part of the army to another via the War Office.[33] There is thus every likelihood that senior officers within Oriental Mission were well aware if not of actual clandestine activity which had been, or was being, conducted under the aegis of other units, then of the lessons derived from these endeavours.

However, despite the established nature of behind the lines activity, Percival and Shenton Thomas refused to countenance it for Malaya, though their reasons for this decision are open to debate. They expressed two particular objections, one being that any plans suggesting that the Japanese might invade would have a negative psychological impact on local Asians, and the other that the plans would be a drain on 'European manpower'.[34] Given the ban on training 'Orientals' at 101STS that was imposed by Shenton Thomas, it also appears that there was a reluctance to arm Asians. Killery himself suggested that Percival was motivated by pique, for he had not been consulted during the formulation of the mission's plans.[35] There are also two further possibilities, not put forward at the time: the British policy objective of avoiding war with Japan, and Percival's personal antipathy to defensive works.

It is difficult to assess which of these factors amounted to a genuine reason for the opposition faced by Oriental Mission's plans. It seems highly unlikely that the local population was unaware of the possibility of war, for the active Asian press ensured that many Asians were aware of the world situation. Oriental Mission, in fact, thought that Malaya's Asians would have considered the possibility of invasion.[36] The 'European manpower' argument also seems very weak, for the mission's plans called for, at most, a few dozen Europeans who, after a few weeks' specialist training, would have been released back to their normal duties.[37] This was not a drain on manpower that would have made a noticeable difference to the Malayan economy.

Shenton Thomas's ban on the training of Asians also makes little sense, for many local Asians were already under arms. The Malay Regiment was being increased from one battalion (of just over 800 men) to two; the Sultan of Johore maintained his own military force of 1,300 men; recruitment had recently started of Eurasians into the Royal Artillery; and there were over 8,000 local Asians in the various units of the Malayan Volunteers (a multi-ethnic body which functioned much like the Territorial Army in Britain). In total, at least 10,000 Malayan Asians were under arms and trained as combat troops.[38] Added to this, the Malayan Police – which Oriental Mission had been keen to use – were routinely issued with firearms.[39] Indeed, Oriental Mission's attitude towards Asians was in general more positive than that evinced by Percival and Shenton Thomas, even though colonial assumptions about the innate capacities of different ethnic groups were embedded within the planned structure of the stay-behind parties. Asian members of these proposed parties would enjoy a freedom of movement denied to the Europeans, but the idea that Europeans would lead the stay-behind parties was so deeply rooted within colonial society that it was never even discussed.[40] However, it appears from Killery's initial plans for stay-behind parties – that they be ethnically mixed, with Asian policemen as seconds-in-command – that, unlike Shenton Thomas, he placed a degree of trust in the local population.

It may be that the ban on training Asians at 101 STS was rooted not in an objection to the arming of Asians, but to their being trained in guerrilla warfare. Although it was Shenton Thomas who expressed this objection, it is conceivable that it may have originated with Percival. He had pioneered techniques of counter-insurgency in Ireland and was aware that men trained to operate as guerrillas could ultimately pose a serious threat to the colonial state.[41] Yet even as Percival and Shenton Thomas argued with Killery, some of Malaya's Asians were receiving specialized training, similar to that which would have been given to guerrillas. In the north of the country, under the aegis of the Indian Army's General Heath (a man who did not see eye to eye with Percival), a forests officer in the Malayan Volunteers raised a platoon of fifty men within the Federated Malay States Volunteer Force (FMSVF) for jungle combat.[42] The FMSVF also raised a border patrol.[43] It is not known if Percival and Shenton Thomas were aware of the existence of these sub-units.

The suggestion that Percival was motivated by pique is reflected in the Oriental Mission history, which ascribes the mission's problems to 'reactions of personalities'.[44] There may have been an element of truth in this, for Percival appeared affronted that he had not been consulted earlier about the stay-behind project, during the planning stage. In his estimation, this had led to a 'loss of valuable time' and the production of a 'faulty scheme'.[45] In fact, the alternative scheme that he outlined overlapped to a degree with what Oriental Mission had suggested, though it confined the mission to using Europeans only, for intelligence alone, and in restricted 'frontier' areas of the country.[46]

Beyond the possibilities suggested by Percival, Shenton Thomas and Killery lie two others: the pressing need for a hard-pressed Britain to avoid war with the Japan, and Percival's attitude towards fixed defences. Certainly, Percival and the Governor were labouring under contradictory priorities: to prepare for war without – and this was the more important priority – rousing Japan.[47] In 1937 Japan had invaded China, and the United States had reacted by instituting a trade embargo. Japan, now short of oil and other raw materials, was believed to be eyeing the rest of Asia and was thus seen, by the British and others, as a threat to their colonial possessions.[48] In September 1940, acting promptly after the fall of France, the Japanese moved troops into French Indo-China, thus giving them control of the airfields.[49] Britain, meanwhile, stretched to her limits in Europe, remained anxious to avoid a showdown with the Japanese.[50] Both Aldrich and Farrell see the reluctance of Percival and Shenton Thomas to work with Oriental Mission as a problem of centre and region: the official priority was to avoid 'provoking' Japan, and Malaya Command was being asked to assist with special operations which might do exactly that.[51] Certainly, these competing priorities left Percival and Shenton Thomas in a difficult position.

There is also a strong argument that Percival had an aversion to defensive works and preparations for war, and that his approach to command was 'without imagination and conviction'.[52] Malaya Command, under Percival, refused to accept offers of assistance in defence preparations from other sources. For example, in mid-1940, the Malayan Geological Survey offered its staff – surveyors and mapmakers familiar with all parts of Malaya – to the army for intelligence work, but was turned down.[53] Furthermore, according to Brigadier Simson (Malaya Command's chief engineer), when he discussed defences with Percival in mid-October 1941, the possibilities that Percival rejected included the organizing of 'Chinese and Malays into guerrilla bands to operate behind enemy spearheads'.[54] This was a suggestion very close to Oriental Mission's proposals, though there is no indication that Simson was aware of this. Simson complained that Percival refused to take *any* action in October 1941 even when offered well-considered and achievable plans.[55] Moreover, the military historian Keith Simpson argues that Percival had a negative attitude towards defensive works that is hard to explain.[56] It seems, then, that for either strategic or personal reasons Percival was reluctant to prepare for war, and SOE was not the only body whose ideas he rejected. As a consequence, as one researcher has noted, the northern shore of Singapore Island, 'the back' of Singapore, provided no more 'resistance to a would-be invader than the back of Bournemouth'.[57]

Oriental Mission's three key Malayan schemes

Once Japan invaded Malaya, on 8 December 1941, war was a reality, the conflict between centre and region vanished and Percival's objections to Oriental Mission's proposals disappeared.[58] By this time, it was too late to establish the ethnically mixed stay-behind parties that the mission had originally suggested. Instead, attention was turned to last minute scorched earth and to three schemes that would have a lasting bearing on the later operations of SOE in Malaya: a collaboration with the MCP which trained core guerrilla cadres, the raising of European stay-behind parties and the laying down of the Rhio-Padang escape route.[59]

There is every possibility that the British authorities agreed to work with the MCP because its leader, Lai Teck, was a Special Branch plant. Lai Teck was passed to Special Branch by their equivalent organization, the Sûreté Fédérale in French Indo-China, and was in position in Singapore by the mid-1930s. His information allowed Special Branch to arrest and deport many senior members of the Chinese-dominated MCP, a clearing of the ranks that allowed Lai Teck a rapid rise, such that he became the Secretary General of the MCP in April 1939.[60] The party's offer to assist in the British war effort was first made in July 1941, when the MCP volunteered its resources in the event of war with Japan but (as with similar offers from other bodies noted above) Malaya Command turned it down.[61] The MCP repeated this offer soon after the Japanese invaded Malaya, and on 19 December 1941 a meeting was held at an MCP safe house in Singapore. On one side was Lai Teck, and on the other were his Special Branch handler Innes Tremlett (later to be a key figure in Force 136), Inspector Wong Chin Yok (also of Special Branch) and Spencer Chapman, then of 101STS.[62] They quickly came to an agreement: SOE would train, arm and insert young communist cadres ahead of the Japanese advance.[63]

SOE was rushed into this agreement by the possibility of short-term gains, yet (as with special operations elsewhere) there were to be long-term consequences. The veto on the mixed parties originally proposed, and the formation by Oriental Mission of MCP parties, resulted in a Chinese-dominated guerrilla movement. This was a factor that would deepen and expose latent ethnic divisions between Malays and Chinese, particularly during 1945. A similar process operated in Burma, where Oriental Mission's recruitment of guerrillas from the 'hill tribes' accentuated the split between them and the Burmans, again with bitter long-term results.[64]

Following the agreement between Spencer Chapman and Lai Teck, SOE trained communist cadres at 101STS who provided the nucleus of the MCP's guerrilla army, the MPAJA.[65] Keen, young, and committed to opposing the Japanese, they 'included the finest men whom the school had to handle'.[66] Altogether 165 young communists were trained at 101STS, and a small number of others at a high school in Kuala Lumpur.[67] In groups of fifteen to thirty they were inserted into the jungle ahead of Japanese lines, with limited food stocks, a few weapons and generous quantities of plastic explosive.[68] The intention was that the trainees would in turn train other men, thus forming the nucleus of a guerrilla force. This, indeed, was what they did, forming the first groups of the MPAJA.

Though SOE did not create the MPAJA, the evidence suggests that its trainers gave it a good start. Men were trained at 101STS in the use of explosives and weapons such as tommy guns and, urged to pass that knowledge on to others, quickly developed an organized structure when inserted into the jungle.[69] An exception to this was the MPAJA's Perak Regiment, which had no or little input from SOE. It began as guerrilla bands as young cadres obtained weapons from battlefields such as Slim River and seems to have taken longer than MPAJA regiments further south to become a unified body.[70] This can be seen in the numbering of the MPAJA regiments: although the Japanese reached Perak before Selangor, the Selangor Regiment – where the first group of MCP trainees was infiltrated – was the 1st Regiment; the Perak guerrillas, although the first to take to the jungle, organized later and became the 5th Regiment.[71] In helping to create the MPAJA, Oriental Mission had, by default, set up a future point of contact. Later in the war, two men who had trained these young Chinese communists, the policeman John Davis and the civil servant Richard Broome, would be SOE's first emissaries into Japanese-occupied Malaya.

While the MCP parties were being trained, 101STS was looking for volunteers for its second key scheme, the insertion of European stay-behind parties. Oriental Mission searched for the recruits for these parties through an obvious colonial network, that formed by the Malayan Volunteers. At least some of the Volunteers, a month into the fighting, had come to the conclusion that their local knowledge would be largely ignored. One of these Volunteers, a planter named Ian McDonald, recorded in an account of August 1942 that they felt sidelined, performing repetitive manual labour with their language skills and local contacts not put to proper use.[72] He was not alone. M.C. Hay, a bombardier with the FMSVF Light Battery, stated in his diary that the Volunteers warned that the Japanese were likely to attempt a landing at Sabak Bernam: 'No notice was taken of this, and that is exactly what they did. That landing was unopposed.'[73] Clearly, this was not a problem in Malaya alone. A Colonial Office report on the loss of Hong Kong and Malaya noted that 'most Europeans and some responsible Asiatics' had been in the Volunteers, where they had been 'too often employed on unimportant jobs as ordinary rank and file'. Some, the report contended, would have been of more use in their regular work, whereas others could have been 'guides, interpreters and advisers' for the army. This all amounted to 'a serious waste of manpower'.[74] Percival himself admitted as much in his Despatch, submitted to the Secretary of State for War in 1946, when he commented that military units had suffered from their lack of local knowledge and that, in any future conflict, each unit should have attached to it an intelligence platoon formed of those who lived in the country.[75]

Oriental Mission readily found recruits among the Volunteers, once word reached them that they were required.[76] Training was brief, owing to the pressure of time and the lack of capacity at 101STS, and nine of these stay-behind parties were placed in the jungle, each designated by a number. Though most members were Europeans from the Malayan Volunteers, some parties included one or two Asians.[77] For various reasons, largely connected to the lack of time in which to establish themselves, not all of these parties were effective, but those that became active caused the Japanese considerable trouble. Spencer Chapman, who led No. 1 Party, based his figures on information he later gathered from local informants. He estimated that his party caused around 1,000 Japanese casualties, tied up around 2,000 Japanese troops (of the 70,000 General Yamashita had at his disposal), derailed seven or eight trains and destroyed or damaged up to forty vehicles, showing the effectiveness of guerrilla activity.[78] However, the mortality rate in these parties was shockingly high, at over 40 per cent, with only a handful of men surviving at liberty in the jungle.[79]

Some of these survivors, including Spencer Chapman and a planter named Robert Chrystal, later provided Force 136 with points of contact with the guerrilla groups of the Malayan interior. They also knew a great deal about these guerrillas and Spencer Chapman's knowledge was considered so useful that he was exfiltrated from Malaya at considerable risk at the end of May 1945. He soon produced a long and detailed report on the MPAJA, many of whose camps he had visited or lived in during the previous three years. This report gave Force 136 a vitally useful insight into the workings and structure of the MPAJA when planning its own operations into Malaya during the build up to the expected Allied seaborne invasion, Operation *Zipper*.[80]

The communist groups trained at 101STS also went into action during the Japanese advance. That they caused difficulties for the advancing Japanese may be inferred from the claim made the Japanese administrator Mamoru Shinozaki. After the war, he stated that Japanese frustration at the action of these guerrillas sparked the massacre of Singaporean Chinese known as the *Sook Ching*.[81]

The Padang escape route was the third of Oriental Mission's projects that had a lasting influence on SOE's work in Malaya. This route was established during late January and early February 1942, as it became ever more probable that Singapore would fall and the escape of useful or endangered individuals became a pressing issue. Members of Oriental Mission worked out a feasible route. They established dumps of food and water through the Rhio Archipelago to the southwest of Singapore and struck agreements with local people to help those trying to escape. To enable those fleeing to reach Padang on the west coast, arrangements were made with the Dutch on Sumatra for rest camps and transport. A basic guide to the route was prepared for circulation when the time came.[82] Men who escaped via Padang were critical to the later development of Force 136's Malayan Country Section. They included Asians, such as the young Guomindang member Lim Bo Seng who went on to be a key recruiter of Chinese agents for Force 136, and Tengku Mahmood Mahyideen who was later important to the Force's Malay operations, as well as numerous Europeans.[83] SOE estimated that about 2,500 people – soldiers, civilians and many members of Oriental Mission – were picked up from Padang, mostly by Royal Naval vessels. When the Japanese entered Padang, there were only 800 British troops remaining.[84]

Some of the escapes from Singapore were officially organized, while others depended upon the determination of the individuals involved. Lim Bo Seng had been a leading member of the Chinese Mobilisation Council, which provided labour for urgent projects during the siege of Singapore. The British administration considered that he would be at risk from the Japanese, so he was given assistance to escape. At 6 a.m. on the morning of 12 February 1942, Lim and fifteen other Chinese left by sampan, waved off by a policeman, Innes Tremlett. Once they arrived on Sumatra, Oriental Mission's Basil Goodfellow assisted them.[85] In 1943, in India Mission's Malayan Country Section, Lim would work with both these men. Relationships were being developed and networks established that would later be summoned into action.

Most British Malayans who escaped along the Padang route left later than did Lim, for they were in the Volunteers and under military discipline.[86] They included a sizeable contingent of Chinese-speakers who had worked with the hastily raised unit, Dalforce.[87] Dalforce, a group separate from the MCP parties trained as guerrillas at 101STS, was formed mostly of communist Chinese but was officered – inevitably – by Europeans.[88] Of the Dalforce officers who left Malaya by junk on the evening of 15 February, five later infiltrated into Malaya with Force

136.[89] Paddy Martin, a planter, led another escape. Told by his commanding officer at the Pengerang Battery in southern Johore that he might escape alone, he decided that this instruction was nonsensical: to leave men to become prisoners of war seemed to him 'too stupid to be considered'. He gathered a group of about a dozen (many of them British Malayans) and his Chinese contacts found the party a small vessel and a crew. Leaving on the evening of 16 February, Martin's group made their way to Tandjong Pinang in the Rhios and eventually picked up the Padang route. Martin himself returned to Malaya with Force 136, as did three others in his party, plus another with the Inter-Services Liaison Department (ISLD).[90] That the Padang route allowed many to escape is illustrated by the adventures of a group of sailors: escaping from Singapore through the Rhios, they did not pick up the official route. It took them five weeks to reach Padang; they were too late to be evacuated, and they became POWs.[91]

Conclusion

Though Oriental Mission folded following the Fall of Singapore on 15 February and that of the Netherlands East Indies the following month, some of its staff was absorbed into India Mission: they would form the core of Force 136's Malayan Country Section.[92] The obstruction Oriental Mission had initially encountered prevented it from fulfilling its short-term objectives. However, by providing points of contact within Malaya and facilitating the escape of key men, the mission eventually laid the foundations of later SOE operations in Malaya, and – it can be argued – also contributed, unwittingly, to post-war events.

The foundations laid by Oriental Mission were threefold: the European stay-behind parties, the groups of trained MCP cadres and the Padang escape route. The impacts of these intermeshed. The European stay-behind parties eased the path of later SOE infiltrations when dealing with the guerrillas.[93] Beyond this, the training, arming and insertion of the MCP parties gave the MPAJA a head start. The MCP was already well structured and used to operating below the radar and, with the addition of young cadres with some guerrilla training, the MCP was well placed to form the most dominant guerrilla grouping, especially in the Chinese-majority areas of the country. Many of the SOE men who were eventually sent to work with the guerrillas had escaped around the Fall of Singapore via the Padang route. As the next chapter will show, without the Padang escapees, and the 'knowledge of the country' that they embodied, Force 136's Malayan Country Section might not have been viable. Two of these escapees, John Davis and Richard Broome, were well known to the guerrillas they had trained and helped to insert into the jungle: again, personal points of contact would prove important, letting the SOE agents prove their bona fides to the communists.[94]

Several other conclusions may also be drawn. The first is that, contrary to Aldrich's assertion, many of Oriental Mission's activities were military in nature. It is true that the Mission's ambitions had clear political ramifications before the outbreak of the Pacific War. However, within Malaya – as in Burma – Oriental

Mission aimed to use armed men to accomplish an essentially military objective: to slow any Japanese advance and to harry them behind their lines. In the short term, because of the delays imposed by Percival and other members of the command structure, Oriental Mission did not accomplish in Malaya what it set out to do. In Burma, on the other hand, where it had more time to establish its units, the mission enjoyed considerably more success.[95]

The treatment of Oriental Mission by the higher command feeds into debates about the Fall of Singapore. Was it inevitable due to inadequacies of supply and organization consequent upon the war in Europe, or speeded by the nature of those in command in Malaya? Had Percival not been so averse to defensive strategies, it is conceivable that the ethnically mixed parties proposed by the mission would have been as successful as Spencer Chapman's group in harrying and slowing the invaders. By the time the Japanese were in Johore, just north of Singapore, their supply lines were creaking under the strain, and the blowing of bridges and derailing of trains further north might have had a critical impact upon their supplies of ammunition and food.[96] This in turn might have made worthwhile the landing of the reinforcements that were en route from the Middle East.[97]

As it was, Singapore fell to the Japanese, surrendering on 15 February 1942.[98] The main armed resistance that survived the Japanese onslaught was that of the communist guerrillas in the jungles, trained and armed by SOE. They became Force 136's obvious local allies once SOE was again able to turn its attentions to Malaya. The result was an armed communist force with strong ambitions and a sense of conviction that it was owed a position at the post-war political table. When Oriental Mission trained and inserted communist cadres to form the guerrilla core, the first steps were taken along the road to the Malayan Emergency.

Chapter 2

MALAYAN COUNTRY SECTION, FORCE 136:
RECRUITMENT, COMPOSITION AND TRAINING

On the 14 April 1942 off the coast of Ceylon, a Welsh freighter, the *Anglo-Canadian*, turned her guns on a 60-foot coastal trading *prahu*, the *Siderhana Johannis*, and destroyed her as a danger to shipping. Watching from the deck of the *Anglo-Canadian* were eighteen men who had just been rescued from the *prahu* after over a month on board. She had been one of the last vessels out of Padang on Sumatra before the Japanese took the town, and unsuitable though she was for the open sea, they had sailed her across the Bay of Bengal with the last of northeast monsoon. Five of them were members of Oriental Mission, including the policeman John Davis and the civil servant Richard Broome.[1] Davis and Broome soon persuaded Colin Mackenzie, the head of SOE's India Mission, to take them on.[2] Davis, Broome and a handful of others were to become the core of India Mission's Malayan Country Section (MCS).

This chapter outlines the nature of MCS and discusses both the insights it provides into British colonialism and into clandestine work in Asia during World War II. The multi-ethnic nature of MCS is revealing about the day-to-day workings of British colonialism, illuminating the attitudes of some Asians towards the Empire and of Europeans towards Asians, as well as the complexities of multi-ethnic ventures. An examination of MCS also allows us to explore the motivations that drew Europeans to fight in Malaya, and led Asians to appear to support the Empire. Investigating the work of MCS provides insights into the interactions of Allied clandestine bodies, and the limitations and challenges that circumstances forced upon SOE.

Historical studies that cover the Japanese occupation of Malaya and the interregnum that followed tend to overlook or at least obscure the role of Force 136 (as India Mission later became known), or to concentrate upon only one aspect of the Force's activity in the country. The scholars Ban Kah Choon and Yap Hong Kuan focus on the activity of the Malayan People's Anti-Japanese Army (MPAJA) and the ultimate political ambitions of the Malayan Communist Party (MCP). Despite Force 136's close involvement with the MPAJA, Ban and Yap do not make clear that the Force was part of SOE, but appear to view it and SOE as different but parallel organizations.[3] Where a detailed analysis of Force 136 is provided in the scholarly literature, the emphasis is overwhelmingly on the first

India Mission operation into Malaya, *Gustavus*, which linked up with the MCP.[4] However, *Gustavus* was far from being the only important Force 136 operation launched into Malaya, and the focus upon it presents a skewed picture that fails to show the extent to which the Force aided the MPAJA and worked with other guerrillas. Though the Force is discussed in passing in a number of other works, it has never been comprehensively examined.[5] As a result, the overall pattern of its activity has been difficult to discern and the repercussions of this activity have not yet been adequately discussed.

Force 136's MCS was complex in its composition, and the sources that relate to it cannot be fully comprehended unless that is kept in mind. These sources include the files of the HS (SOE) series, which can be broadly split into two: those covering planning and liaison (with government departments, other clandestine agencies and South East Asia Command) and those concerned with operations, detailing work in the field with the guerrillas. The men who wrote these letters, memoranda and reports came from a wide range of backgrounds, and their personal attitudes and previous experiences influenced the conclusions they reached during their service in Force 136. These differences in background sometimes resulted in conflicting conclusions being reached about the same events. For example, Force 136 officers who infiltrated into Malaya came to very different conclusions about the MPAJA, depending upon whether they were British Malayans or men who had previous SOE experience in the Balkans. As will be shown later in this book, understanding such differences refines our analysis of the information Force 136 produced and thus revises our understanding of wartime Malayan resistance, the events of the interregnum and the origins of the Malayan Emergency.[6]

This chapter will begin by situating SOE within wider Allied strategy in Asia after the Fall of Singapore. It will then move on to discuss Force 136 recruitment, how the men were trained and the motivations that impelled them to volunteer. The Force's position and role with regard to other clandestine bodies will then be discussed, and finally its performance in the field will be assessed.

India Mission/Force 136: Malayan Country Section

From an Allied perspective, World War II reached its nadir after the Fall of Singapore. In March 1942, the Japanese won the Battle of the Java Sea and took control of the Netherlands East Indies. Burma fell and by the end of May the Philippines had surrendered. In Europe, the Germans were far into Russia, poised to push either towards Moscow or towards the Caucasus (in the end, they opted for the latter strategy). Allied policy was 'Europe first', and insofar as Britain had a priority within Asia, it was Burma, not Malaya.[7] Burma was strategically more important, for the Japanese occupied much of the country and were convincingly menacing the Indian border.[8] Though India was internally unsettled, with the Quit India movement actively challenging the Raj, the retention of India was vital to British strategy. Britain's Asian operations were based there, and the country was a key reservoir of troops, with Indians fighting in North Africa and two Indian divisions stationed in Iran and Iraq lest the Nazis break through at Stalingrad.[9] Beyond its strategic importance, Burma was also much more accessible than Malaya, for it could be reached by air, whereas Malaya was accessible only by submarine. Even though there had been suspicions in 1941–1942 that the Burmese population was apathetic towards the British, perhaps even hostile, the importance of defending the Indian border saw SOE restart operations in Burma in early 1943.[10]

Despite the low priority of Malayan operations at this time, infiltration into Malaya was in the minds of members of Oriental Mission even before they had outrun the Japanese advance. When the *Siderhana Johannis* party of eighteen men, including the five from Oriental Mission, was selected to leave Padang on Sumatra for Ceylon in March 1942, they were chosen on the basis of their specialized knowledge and their contacts in Malaya.[11] Their ethnicity also seems to have played a role: the party included a Japanese Eurasian, as well as Davis's Malay police driver, Jamal bin Daim, and Broome's Chinese servant, Lo Ngai Soon. Over a dozen former members of Oriental Mission, including John Davis and Richard Broome, who had trained and infiltrated the MCP parties, soon moved to 'SOE India' – India Mission, the body that later became known as Force 136 – to form the core of MCS.[12] This meant that once the high command began to consider the reinvasion of Malaya, MCS already existed.

India Mission was under the overall control of Colin Mackenzie, a World War I veteran who had been a director of the international haberdashery company J & P Coats in Asia between the wars. He came to India to begin SOE's operations there in October 1941, having been requested by the viceroy, Lord Linlithgow.[13] In a contemporary report by SOE, his tact was credited with being the dominant factor in the lack of infighting between the different sections of Force 136, and he was the only head of an SOE overseas mission to survive in a post from appointment to the end of the war. As a result, Force 136 enjoyed a continuity of command from which other SOE missions did not benefit.[14] Within India Mission, MCS was headed first by Basil Goodfellow (previously of Oriental Mission) then, from September 1943, by the policeman Innes Tremlett. It appears that Tremlett was Lai Teck's handler, so his appointment may indicate a desire within Force 136 to make the most of prior knowledge and keep watch, as far as possible, on the MCP.[15] The challenge for heads such as Mackenzie and Tremlett was to find men with specific skills, and of particular ethnicities, by mobilizing colonial and military networks. But while India Mission's Burma Country Section could tap into the thousands of Burmese troops who had retreated from the country, its MCS had only a small pool available to trawl.[16] The potential risks that recruits faced were well understood: all the recruits were volunteers, and it appears that the Europeans at least were expected to make their wills before infiltrating.[17]

As one might expect in a society governed by racialized assumptions (and as had been the case with Oriental Mission's initial plans), it was assumed that Europeans would lead Force 136 operations. Racialized attitudes towards Asians, and European assumptions about the capabilities of Asians, became recurring features during the course of SOE's activities in Malaya. For John Davis, European leadership was vital on the basis of prestige. When he was told that he might not be able to remain ashore after the first *Gustavus* sortie (the first India Mission foray to Malaya), he argued that if a European did not remain behind, the 'loyalty' of the Asian agents would be lost. He also claimed that a European leader was important to give the party 'leadership and drive'.[18] In making these arguments, he was saying two things: that British prestige could not afford to allow Asians to detect any failure of courage, and that the Asians themselves were not capable of running the operation, though he does not specify whether this was due to their personalities, to their levels of education or to flaws inherent in their 'race'.

David Cannadine discusses issues of race and class in the British Empire, particularly from the mid-nineteenth century until its demise in the mid-twentieth. He argues that although the British used race as a key classifier of their imperial subjects, these subjects were also ranked by class. This ranking system was also tied to 'notions of superiority and inferiority', though it predated any 'scientific' notions of racism.[19] As a consequence, Cannadine claims, there were two subtly intertwined visions of empire: one based on race and the other upon social position, with neither vision totally dominant, but both influencing beliefs and behaviour.[20] Although Cannadine has been strongly challenged for over-simplifying the complexities of British imperialism, seriously under-estimating the importance of race and focusing too much on elites, his analysis is still relevant to understanding Force 136.[21] Lim Bo Seng – a wealthy, upper-middle class Chinese – and Tengku Mahmood Mahyideen – a Malay noble – both held commissioned ranks within the Force, in contrast to the non-commissioned officers (NCOs), many of whom were white and from lower middle- and working-class backgrounds.[22] Here, attitudes towards class and race intersected. MCS assumed that Europeans would lead and the Asians would follow, while a lower-class background generally led to a lower rank. However, these attitudes came under severe pressure as the war progressed, with both Europeans from less elite backgrounds and some Asians elevated to positions of authority within Force 136, and relied upon as never before. Men who would have been unlikely to have served as officers in the country before the conflict, including a carpet salesman and a Eurasian, descended by parachute, with considerable authority vested in them.[23]

It was obvious during initial recruitment that anyone infiltrated would be going in 'blind' and so would need extensive local knowledge. It was also evident that Europeans would not be able to act alone: Asian agents would be essential, especially those with local knowledge and local contacts they could tap for advice, help and information. Consequently, almost all Force 136's early recruits had lived in Malaya, with a handful from the Netherlands East Indies and Borneo. The importance placed on local knowledge is illustrated by a request made to the Colonial Office for the transfer of an officer to SOE for work in Malaya. When it became clear that the man in question had never actually reached Malaya, although he was 'of a very suitable type' and 'keen', the decision was made not to press for his transfer.[24] As more operations became established, the initial importance of recruits having local knowledge diminished as they were going to existing teams which included people who knew the local landscape and spoke local languages. As a result, towards the end of the war, an increasing proportion of men were infiltrated, both British and Chinese, who had never been to Malaya before. Some, however, had the advantage of previous operational experience with SOE, mostly in the Balkans and France.

MCS tapped into imperial networks of knowledge and control to find the people it wanted. Though much disrupted by the war, these networks were still very effective. Europeans were tracked down in a variety of ways, including through the escape lists kept by Malayan organizations.[25] There is no direct evidence of Force 136 using word of mouth contacts, but it is hard to believe that these were ignored, and they were certainly favoured by the Inter-Services Liaison Department (ISLD). According to Boris Hembry, who led ISLD's Malayan operations, finding Europeans was 'easy' via what he called 'the old boy net'.[26] It seems that men who had fought and escaped together, some of whom had been friends already, continued to keep in contact.[27] The military passion for paperwork also helped, for it enabled men to be traced via documents such as movement orders.[28]

If finding potential European candidates was 'easy', turning them into agents was more complicated. The indications are that of the men approached, around a quarter were either not fit enough for the hard physical conditions they would experience behind enemy lines, or did not want to undertake special operations work. Another quarter could not be released from their current employment. Of those taken on, several proved unsuitable for work in the field and either pulled out or were never sent on operations.[29] Obtaining the release of men from other duties was a lengthy process, requiring persuasive letters to the authorities in question. If, for example, a man had found employment in another colony, SOE had to approach the Secretary of State for the Colonies, who would in turn write to the colony's governor. Sometimes the tone of these letters was pleading ('officers with Malayan experience are so few and so essential'), at other times it was slightly more robust. In one case, the Secretary of State informed a colonial governor, 'I should wish to agree to his release for this duty unless you see strong objection.'[30] Replies to such requests often stipulated that a man would not be released from his current employment for several months.[31] Sometimes men who had been approached 'pulled every possible string' to ensure their own release to SOE.[32]

Before being sent to Ceylon or India, men were often brought back to Britain for initial training, and some also took a course with the Malayan Planning Unit (MPU) as they were expected to transfer to Civil Affairs work as soon as any fighting was over.[33] The MPU had been formed to redesign and simplify Malayan governance and forge a unified Malayan nation, with a long-term commitment to Malayan self-determination.[34] This redesigned polity was to be called the Malayan Union, and proposals included the removal of Malay privileges and extended citizenship rights for non-Malays. Plans such as this would help the British government convince the Unites States that, having agreed in September 1942 to return to the colonies according to the principles of the Atlantic Charter, it meant what it said.[35] However, in the short term, the MPU's intention was to regain the former colonial hold and exploit Malaya's natural resources.[36] Comprised of colonial officials, and reliant upon the Colonial Office for guidance, the unit was nonetheless attached to the War Office in London. Between the end of Japanese rule and the establishment of the Malayan Union there would of necessity be a period of military governance, and it was for this that the MPU sought to prepare the SOE trainees.

With all of these factors in the mix, recruitment and training were very time-consuming. A new candidate had to agree to join SOE, be released from his current work and then be trained. In a typical case, it took a year from the first bid to recruit a future member of Force 136 until he was infiltrated into Malaya.[37]

If anything, though, the recruitment of Malays and Chinese proved even more difficult. In 1942, there were 5,000 Chinese in Calcutta who were being formed into a Service Corps by the businessman Lim Bo Seng, but when the former policeman John Davis investigated, he found that very few were suitable for special operations. When Basil Goodfellow – then head of the nascent MCS – realized that there were around 400 Malayan Chinese in Chungking (the war capital of Nationalist China), he asked Lim Bo Seng if he would use his personal connections with General Tai Li (of the Chinese secret service) to intercede for SOE and see if any of these men could be transferred.[38] Lim obtained Tai Li's agreement, and it is likely that his role in this respect was critical. Tai Li was no friend of SOE and had been a moving force behind the expulsion from China of Oriental Mission's China Commando Group in 1942.[39] Lim recruited, among several dozen others, Tan Chong Tee, who later wrote a detailed memoir of his experiences with Force 136.

By the end of 1942, the SOE had also decided to recruit Malays, for reasons that will be discussed in detail in Chapter 4. Major Tengku Mahmood Mahyideen, who worked with MCS as both recruiter and propagandist, played a key role in such recruitment and went to considerable lengths in his endeavours. He visited Britain to try to recruit Malays living in England and paid a visit to Sir Edward Gent, the head of the MPU to discuss post-war British policy for Malaya.[40] In planning his propaganda, he identified closely with the Allies: 'it is we who will gain the final victory'.[41] He broadcast propaganda for the Allies into Malaya under the pseudonym 'Raja Mopeng' ('the masked Raja'), assisted by another Malay, Tun Suffian.[42] Yet even with the Tengku's assistance, the recruitment of Malays proved as difficult as the recruitment of Chinese. In the end, several Malays were found by a former Malayan Volunteer gunner, Peter Dobrée, who had escaped in a leaking dinghy from Singapore, and scouted through both Malay naval personnel and Malay – or Malay-speaking – Hajis stranded in Mecca by the war.

Mention must also be made of one final source of what were termed 'native agents' for SOE: the practice of mounting what was, in essence, state-sponsored piracy. SOE's conducting officers (who saw agents into the field) were given an additional duty on their submarine sorties: to capture the crews of coastal vessels they encountered and bring them back to Ceylon. At the Mahara Examination Centre, which was founded as a result of collaboration between ISLD, SOE and the American Office of Strategic Services (OSS), these crews were presented with the bald alternative of either becoming Allied agents, or spending the war in internment. Those held at Mahara were not always well treated, but even so many were prepared to become agents, some because it provided them with a route home, others because the Japanese had treated them so badly.[43]

The final large group recruited to Force 136 operations consisted of the eighty or so Gurkhas who were parachuted into Malaya towards the end of the war. The involvement of the Gurkha groups resulted from what can be read as an act of expiation on the part of a Gurkha officer. This officer survived the battle at Slim River, in which the Gurkhas suffered very heavy casualties, and escaped from Malaya. His original suggestion was that Gurkha NCOs be dropped into Malaya to contact the large number of Gurkha POWs (prisoners of war) believed to be there, to release them and then form them into guerrilla units. Force 136 adopted this idea and the recruitment and training of Gurkhas began.[44] In the end, these trainees were not used to contact Gurkha POWs but to strengthen the MPAJA.[45] Five platoons were dropped into Malaya before the Japanese surrender, and at least one other afterwards.[46] Finally, two Eurasians, both Malayan refugees, were recruited once they were old enough for army service.[47] The ethnic mix of teams in the field was thus very diverse.

Though MCS was responsible for its own recruitment, the training of Force 136 operatives was organized by India Mission, which by the end of 1943 had established training facilities in India and Ceylon. However, some new recruits used SOE training facilities in Britain, if these proved to be more convenient.[48] Men were trained in infiltration methods (usually via a parachute course), jungle warfare, demolitions and intelligence.[49] Though India Mission remained chronically short of all supplies, from Sten guns to compasses, by September 1943, it had an effective training system and a rationalized supply branch.[50]

Force 136 volunteers were from diverse backgrounds, and they also varied in the impulses that drove them to risk a return to occupied Malaya. The British Malayans seem to have been motivated not only by a need to contribute to the overall war effort, but also by a sense of duty to Malaya and a desire to recover their lost honour.[51] These motivations are expressed most forcefully by one of the Padang escapees who, perhaps tellingly, wrote of himself in the third person. Colin Symington stated 'that something within him has been dead' since his escape: partly trauma, as his narrative seems to acknowledge, but also an awareness 'that he had fled', even if under orders.[52] Bobby Ross, of the Federated Malay States Volunteer Force artillery battery, wrote soon after his escape that the surrender of Singapore left his unit 'terribly distressed'; he later joined Special Operations Australia.[53] Though it cannot be directly proven that the British Malayans who returned with Force 136 shared these sentiments, it is a reasonable extrapolation that they did.[54] Peter Dobrée, at one time a dairy farmer in Malaya and, like Ross, a gunner in the Volunteer artillery battery, recalled looking back at Singapore from the leaking dinghy in which he had left: 'I felt very bitter. I swore an oath that I would return.'[55] He parachuted into northern Perak in December 1944.[56]

Asian motivations included the desire to push back the Japanese – one shared by many of the Europeans – and also the hope of future political rights. In the case of Lim Bo Seng, the Chinese businessman who joined Force 136, the former motivation loomed large and was inspired by a specific regional context: that of the Japanese invasion of China, the country of his birth.[57] Lim had a record of anti-Japanese activity dating back to the late 1930s and had assisted with the war effort as a member of the Chinese Mobilisation Council in Singapore, which provided labourers to the administration.[58] In the final days before the city's fall, and aware that he and his comrades would be marked men when the Japanese arrived, the British helped them escape.[59] Another Chinese fired by an urge to 'fight the enemy' by participation in a patriotic war in the Chinese homeland was Tan Chong Tee, who recounted in his memoir how he had travelled to China in 1940 to do exactly that, but had been diverted into college studies.[60] When the opportunity arose for military service in the 'Nanyang' – broadly speaking, South East Asia – he claims that he jumped at it, eager to drive the Japanese from Malaya.[61] Tan became one of Lim Bo Seng's recruits, the 'Dragons'. Another member of this group was Yee Tian Song, who argued later in his life that he had been inspired by earlier Chinese heroes, and that the Chinese recruits were mostly motivated by 'a sense of righteousness'.[62] Although in the Dragons' case there is no mention of any desire for political rights, it is hard believe that this was not a consideration. Chinese identity might have been in flux in Malaya during the 1930s and 1940s, with much of the community still more concerned with events in China than with events in Malaya, but by the late 1930s there was a growing feeling among middle-class Chinese that they were being unfairly excluded from the politics of the colony.[63]

The acquisition of political rights, however, was clearly at the forefront of the motivations of the Chinese Force 136 recruits from the west coast of Canada, where there had been a significant Chinese presence since Chinese labourers had built the Canadian-Pacific Railway.[64] Canadian Chinese had, in the pre-war era, been excluded from public office and the professions. When the war broke out, as there was no conscription in Canada, young Chinese in Vancouver made the decision themselves that they should try to enlist, in the hope that their campaign for civil rights would be boosted. Several young Chinese did so, but were all turned down.[65] However, as the tempo of the Asian war increased during 1944 and the reinvasion of Malaya drew closer, Force 136 cast its net in search of potential Chinese recruits, and the young Chinese Canadians were given a second opportunity. As South Africa and Australia had banned Chinese immigration, the only accessible pool of Chinese in the British Empire was the community in Canada. It took Force 136's representative four months to secure permission from the Canadian authorities for SOE to recruit and train Chinese Canadians, but eventually 143 were sent to India and Australia for work all over Asia.[66] Of these, nine went into Malaya prior to the Japanese surrender.[67]

Political ambitions and their attendant expectations were also crucial to some of the Malays who joined Force 136. The Padang escapee Tengku Mahmood Mahyideen was the younger son of the last Sultan of Patani (a Malay-majority state in southern Thailand) and had been Director of Education in the northern Malayan state of Kelantan before the war.[68] An officer in the Kelantan Volunteer Force, he remained with British forces during the retreat, and it was deemed important to evacuate him due to his 'sympathy for the British'.[69] He joined Force 136 – India Mission as it was then – in 1942, recruited by Dennis Ambler, a civil servant who had also escaped via Padang.[70] However, his motivations for assisting the British extended well beyond any sense of 'sympathy', and looked to the future of the

Malay population. From a long memorandum he wrote for the Colonial Office it becomes clear he was driven by an urge to represent the Malay population.[71] Moreover, later information suggests that he understood that if he supported the British he would obtain a bargaining chip should they return to power.[72] One scholar has claimed that the Tengku wished to bring Patani into British Malaya, and then work for Malayan independence.[73] In addition, Mahmood Mahyideen had another good reason to oppose the Japanese. His father's cousin was, at the time, Sultan of Kelantan – and Kelantan was one of four Malay states that the Japanese, to the disgust of Malaya's Malays, ceded to Thailand in mid-1943.

Force 136 and other clandestine bodies

To understand the context in which Force 136 operated, it is also necessary to recognize the sometimes overlapping and occasionally conflicting aims of the clandestine organizations operating in Malaya, and the tensions that could result from this. At the start of its operations, Force 136 jostled for scarce resources with ISLD (the manifestation in Asia of MI6), 'E' Group (handling escapers and evaders), the Psychological Warfare Division (PWD: propaganda), 'D' Division (deception) and the OSS – a situation that was not resolved until the creation of 'P' (Priorities) Division. This body was agreed between Mountbatten and General William Donovan of the OSS and was imposed upon the clandestine organizations from above at the end of 1943.[74] 'P' Division coordinated and prioritized clandestine work and ensured that it meshed with the regular forces. It also encouraged the clandestines to share resources, and Force 136 appears to have had a reputation for helpfulness to other clandestine bodies.[75] Force 136 teams in the field took 'E' Group drops (though they sometimes complained about having to do so), and when the men of a Force 136 operation in Malaya, *Oatmeal*, were captured by the Japanese, wireless contact with them was passed to 'D' Division as soon as Force 136 became aware that the party had been compromised.[76] This cooperation extended to the teams in the field, where men from different organizations often – perhaps usually – worked cooperatively. The tensions that existed at this level tended to be no greater than those that could flare between different Force 136 operations when one operation discovered another was working in its territory, or there was pressure on dropping zones.[77]

There were, notoriously, at the commencement of SOE's operations in Malaya, as across Asia, major tensions at the highest level between it and ISLD, whose parent body (MI6) had been displeased to lose Section D to SOE in mid-1940.[78] However, these tensions largely dissipated in relation to Malaya from late 1943, when Innes Tremlett, the former policeman, took over MCS. He and Boris Hembry, who was responsible for the Malayan side of ISLD's work, became friends and the two departments developed an effective modus vivendi, though there were still points of stress.[79] Force 136 operations in Malaya, for example, would take drops of both stores and 'bodies' (as parachuting agents were unnervingly known) for ISLD, and on one occasion, an ISLD agent and a Force 136 officer set out together into northern Malaya on a planned joint operation.[80] The evidence is, therefore, that the British clandestine bodies in the field in Malaya established a reasonable, if not perfect, modus vivendi.

The situation with OSS was rather different, for it involved international rather than merely intra-national rivalries. OSS's founding father and wartime director was the anti-isolationist and Anglophile William Donovan.[81] British policy-makers were suspicious of him (perhaps partly due to his anti-colonial leanings) and assumed his organization to be plotting the foundations of post-war American trade – involving, inevitably, expansion into markets the British wished to dominate.[82] The British were right to be concerned, for the OSS saw itself 'as providing long-term strategic intelligence of benefit to American commercial and political interests, well beyond the war's end'.[83] In effect, the OSS in India was seeking information about future British mercantile and political aims; SOE in China, naturally enough, was attempting to gather the same information about the United States.[84]

From the beginning, as Aldrich observes, the intelligence relationship between the United States and Britain was ambiguous: even as the OSS was being formed with British advice late in 1941, the British were concealing from the Americans the existence of Oriental Mission in Singapore.[85] Suspicions endured from then until the end of the war. In March 1942, an internal SOE review of American plans expressed the concern that US propaganda would 'increase considerably American influence in British possessions'.[86] The OSS was firmly – and correctly – convinced that the British in India were keeping a very close eye on OSS staff and operations there, and doing their best to exclude OSS operations from a number of countries.[87] The British were similarly convinced that the OSS was working against them. Col. Lindsay Ride of the British Army Aid Group was, by July 1945, completely certain that General Wedemeyer, by then the commander of US forces in China, was doing everything in his power to exclude the British from 'Kwan Tung' (Guangdong) until he could claim there was no need for Ride to operate in the area.[88]

In October 1942, an initial agreement was reached between SOE and OSS, in which OSS took the role of the 'junior partner'. Within months, however, OSS had slipped the leash with which SOE's Mackenzie had sought to constrain it, and was accused by India Mission officers of trying to turn the Kachin of Burma against the British.[89] It was clear that OSS and SOE needed a revised relationship, and it was this that spurred the creation of 'P' Division.[90]

Despite this official agreement and apparent cooperation, there is direct evidence in the Force 136 documentation that Mackenzie was under instructions from London to dissuade the Americans from operating in Malaya, a country in which the British planned to reassert imperial control.[91] What is less clear is the extent to which the British blocked American operations into Malaya solely because they were American operations, rather than because they were unrealistic or clashed with pre-existing British plans. Aldrich states that some OSS plans for Malaya displayed an over-optimistic attitude towards local conditions and political alliances, making British objections to them entirely reasonable.[92] Other American schemes, however, were so like Force 136's own that the Force suspected that the Americans had a mole inside 'P' Division. In the second half of 1944 both OSS and SOE had plans to insert Malay agents into northern Malaya, and Force 136 HQ even suspected that the OSS operation, *Jukebox*, had been cooked up 'to steal the thunder' from the Force's equivalent operation, *Oatmeal*.[93] OSS believed that its *Jukebox* operation was thwarted by the refusal of the Malay agents of SOE's *Oatmeal* to infiltrate with it, blaming SOE for turning them against OSS.[94] However, there is no mention in the *Oatmeal* report that *Jukebox* ever entered its considerations.[95] From the perspective of OSS, Force 136 had stood wilfully in their way, determined to keep Malaya as an exclusively British field of operations. On the British side, the suspicion that OSS was managing to obtain information on British plans from 'P' Division endured to the end of the war.[96] British and American competitiveness distracted the clandestines on both sides from the immediate priority of overwhelming the Japanese.

The month after the argument over *Jukebox*, in December 1944, Force 136 was firmly told by 'P' Division that OSS could not be excluded from Malaya.[97] In the wake of this, OSS sent Operation *Cairngorm* into Malaya, without fully informing Force 136 of who was in it or what they planned to do. So far as Force 136 was concerned, it appeared that yet another of their plans had been reworked by the Americans, since some of the *Cairngorm* objectives – in so far as the Force understood them – clashed with those of the proposed Force 136 operation, *Hebrides*.[98] The staff of Force 136 can only have felt vindicated when *Cairngorm* failed to come up on the air and went missing for most of the rest of the war.

There is no suggestion that Force 136 did anything to hamper or hinder *Cairngorm*, for the Force had no parties on the ground in the vicinity at the time. *Cairngorm*, in fact, was impeded by conditions within Malaya that no one could have foreseen, for its members fell into the hands of the 6th Regiment of the MPAJA, which held them as 'virtual prisoners' until almost the end of the war.[99] Nevertheless, the disappearance of *Cairngorm* gave Force 136 (and the Colonial Office) exactly the lever they had craved since 'P' Division had compelled them to work with OSS. They could now argue convincingly for their existing line, that the British and the Americans should present a united front to the MPAJA, since any other approach could have political results that would be desirable to neither the United States nor the United Kingdom.[100] It took until the following May to hammer out the final agreement, but Force 136 got exactly what OSS had suspected it had wanted in Malaya all along: virtually total control over OSS agents, with them integrated into Force 136 operations as intelligence sections.[101] While some wrangling did continue, Force 136 was thereafter prepared to accept OSS operatives into Malaya, since they were entering on Force 136's terms. Indeed, in July 1945 the Force was almost pleading with OSS to send a party to Operation *Beacon*, whose only European officer, Douglas Richardson, was in need of assistance. Force 136, overstretched by this stage, had no one suitable available to drop to him, and the Force 136 officer was delighted to receive the OSS agent.[102] Beyond this, Force 136 men on the ground were helpful to OSS: Jim Hannah, the commander of Operation *Funnel*, sent a signal warning that 'four thousand half Japs half mixed troops' had gone into the jungle and had the potential to reach *Cairngorm*'s operational area.[103]

In sum, relationships with the OSS were similar to those with ISLD: often positive and helpful on operations, but conflicted higher up the tree. The Force's interactions with both of these bodies indicate the fragmented nature of the intelligence operations, and the complex competing national and departmental interests which often resulted in friction between units. The most senior officers of Force 136, viewing matters from a more strategic perspective, were anxious to limit American influence in former British colonies, whereas more junior officers, struggling with difficult conditions on the ground, had no objections to American assistance.

Force 136 in the field

Force 136's main functions in Malaya were the collection of intelligence and the formation of guerrilla patrols. Ultimately, this activity was designed to support Operation *Zipper*, the spearhead of the planned Allied reconquest of Malaya, originally proposed for November 1945. To this end, South East Asia Command wanted to establish Force 136 parties within Malaya, particularly along the western littoral where *Zipper* would come ashore and begin two advances, north to Kuala Lumpur and south towards Singapore.[104]

Initially, it was almost impossible for Force 136 to establish operations within Malaya. Until long-range Liberator aircraft became available to the Force in late 1944, the only way into Malaya was via submarine.[105] Though submarines had a much larger payload than the adapted Liberators, the difficulties of moving stores from the submarine to the coast, and then from the coast to the operational area, meant that airdrops were far preferred: the men and containers could be landed far from the Japanese. Indeed, for both the *Gustavus* and *Carpenter* operations the difficulties of submarine infiltrations would prove almost to be their undoing: *Gustavus* had to leave its wireless equipment near the coast, which meant that contact with base was eventually lost, and *Carpenter* was unable to bring all its stores ashore.[106]

For India Mission, 1943 was essentially a year of development and experimentation with early operations that were run into enemy-occupied territory being primarily seen as exploratory. The difficulty of submarine operations, and the greater strategic importance to the high command of Burma, meant that only one operation, *Gustavus*, infiltrated into Malaya before October 1944. *Gustavus*, led by the policeman John Davis (who had helped to train and insert the keen young communists in early 1942), was launched in May 1943 to establish regular contact with Malaya, to discover the fate of Europeans believed to be at large, and to obtain intelligence.[107] Although it reached an agreement with the MCP at the end of 1943, the stranding of its wireless equipment on the coast and the collapse of the submarine rendezvous system that had been arranged meant that it was out of contact with Force 136 headquarters until early 1945.

During this period of hiatus, Force 136 continued to try to establish operations in Malaya. Yet full approval for the raising and arming of guerrillas in Malaya was not given by Mountbatten until June 1945. Despite this, a detailed scheme for supporting guerrilla groups had been developed in August 1944.[108] Indeed, 'P' Division, without official approval, soon backed operations to raise guerrillas.[109] In October 1944, Force 136 launched two operations in Malaya. *Carpenter* was infiltrated by submarine to make contact with the MPAJA in south Johore, and the ill-starred *Oatmeal* by flying boat to contact Malays in the northeast of the country. *Carpenter*'s contact with the MPAJA was successful and it established a wireless link to Colombo, which encouraged Force 136 to plan additional operations. Operation *Funnel* was planned to drop 'blind' into Perak, but as it was, contact with *Gustavus* was re-established and the advance group of *Funnel* was able to drop to a reception party.[110]

From this point on, the tempo of infiltrations picked up rapidly, and *Funnel* was soon followed by other operations sent to the MPAJA (see Table 2.1).

Table 2.1 Force 136's Malayan Operations

Date of first infiltration	Area of Malaya	Name of operation	Leader	Guerrilla group
11.5.43	Perak	Gustavus	John Davis (ex-police)	MPAJA HQ
22.9.44	South Johore	Carpenter	'Paddy' Martin (planter, SSVF)[a]	MPAJA 4th Regt
31.10.44	Kelantan	Oatmeal	Ibrahim bin Ismail (regular soldier)	Malays (unsuccessful: captured)
16.12.44	Upper Perak/ Kelantan	Hebrides	Peter Dobrée (dairy farmer, FMSVF)	Malays (AMS) and OCAJA
25.1.45	West Pahang	Beacon	Douglas Richardson (surveyor, FMSVF)	Malays (Wataniah)
24.2.45	West Pahang	Pontoon	George Leonard (game warden)	MPAJA 6th Regt
26.2.45	Kedah	Fighter	Geoffrey Hasler (rubber industry, JVE)	Malays (AMS)
26.2.45	Perak	Funnel	James Hannah (businessman)	MPAJA 5th Regt
26.2.45	Kedah	Sergeant	James Hislop (planter, FMSVF)[b]	MPAJA 8th Regt
8.4.45	Lower Pahang and Negri Sembilan	Multiple	'Bill' Headley (Malayan Civil Service, FMSVF)	Malays (unsuccessful)
30.5.45	Selangor	Galvanic	Douglas Broadhurst (ex-police)	MPAJA 1st Regt
26.6.45	North Johore	Tideway	Alan Campbell-Miles (planter, JVE)	MPAJA 3rd Regt
2.7.45	Negri Sembilan	Humour	Claude Fenner (ex-police; infiltrated 30.7.45)	MPAJA 2nd Regt

Note: This table shows the significance of the Malayan Police and Volunteers to Force 136. SSVF: Straits Settlements Volunteer Force; FMSVF: Federated Malay States Volunteer Force; JVE: Johore Volunteer Engineers; AMS: Askar Melayu Setia (Loyal Malay Soldiers); OCAJA (Overseas Chinese Anti-Japanese Army – Guomindang).

[a] This operation was temporarily commanded by Major Durward Sime (formerly a visiting manager in the rubber industry and a member of the SSVF) after Martin's death in action, and eventually, from June 1945, by Lt. Col. Ian Wylie (a former policeman).

[b] After the Japanese surrender, Hislop was replaced by Lt. Col. David Alexander (TNA, HS 1/117, Major J.A. Hislop, Operation *Sergeant* GLO's Report, p. 6).

The first successful drop into a Malay-majority district was that of Operation *Hebrides* in December 1944, and three more Malay operations followed (see Table 2.1). By the time of the Japanese surrender, thirteen Force 136 operations were active in Malaya and the Force had infiltrated about 320 men. Of these, approximately 140 were Europeans, around two thirds of whom were officers. The infiltrated agents included several Canadians, some Frenchmen and two Danes, nearly sixty ethnic Chinese, around thirty Malays, eighty-five Gurkhas and a handful of others.[111] The majority of these men, and virtually all of the equipment, were dropped by the RAF Special Duties Squadrons. The equipment included almost 4,800 assorted arms, generous quantities of ammunition and explosives, uniforms, medicines, food and money (sometimes faked Japanese notes, sometimes gold).

Operations with the MPAJA were all arranged in the same way. A Group Liaison Officer (GLO) led each operation; he commanded his own small headquarters staff – usually a second-in-command and two wireless operators, with perhaps a medical officer and orderly – and several 'patrols', each led by a Patrol Liaison Officer (PLO). Patrols were named in a colour sequence approximating the order in which they arrived in the country (Orange, Green, Blue, Brown, Slate and Pink).[112] The composition of a Patrol Liaison Team (PLT) generally followed the 'Jedburgh' format widely used by SOE in Europe: a commanding office, a second-in-command, an NCO wireless operator, and, if necessary, a translator, an instructor, or both. Operations with the Malays and the Guomindang were organized differently, with – at least in the case of Operation *Beacon* – locally recruited guerrillas, who often had prior military experience, taking the place of infiltrated liaison officers.[113]

Though Force 136's Malayan operations, unlike those in Burma, were never able to prove their strategic worth, it can be argued that they generally succeeded in what they set out to do. Of course, one might expect that in their reports infiltrated officers would claim that this was the case, but the evidence they present indicates that their assessments were correct. The guerrilla patrol with *Funnel Slate* ambushed a party of Japanese which was pursuing them, killing five for no guerrilla casualties.[114] Ten guerrillas with *Galvanic Blue* encountered a mixed party of Japanese troops and Malay police, totalling fifty men. In the ensuing fire-fight, the guerrillas wounded two of the police and shot a Japanese officer in the eye and, again, suffered no casualties themselves.[115] These encounters were by no means unique.[116]

Of the thirteen operations Force 136 launched into Malaya, three encountered serious difficulties: *Gustavus*, *Oatmeal* and *Multiple*. *Gustavus*, as discussed above, was out of contact with Force 136 headquarters for over a year. During this time, as we will shortly see, its intelligence network was rolled up by the Japanese.[117] *Oatmeal*, however, was betrayed to the Japanese soon after infiltration.[118] Its troubles and those that beset *Multiple* will be covered in Chapter 4. Yet, despite the problems these operations encountered, Force 136, at the point of the Japanese surrender in Malaya, had helped arm and train just over 5,000 guerrillas.[119] This was accomplished by Force 136 personnel operating in small groups which, plainly

Table 2.2 Armed Guerrilla Forces Trained by Force 136, Disbanded Late 1945

Guerrilla Organization	Armed guerrillas disbanded, October–December 1945
MPAJA (communist-run)	4,480
Malay Organizations	384
OCAJA (Guomindang-aligned)	358
Total	5,222

Source: The data in this table are drawn from the copies of 'Appendix G' appended to the operational reports in HS 1/107 and HS 1/117–HS 1/123. A considerable number of MPAJA were being held in reserve by the MCP as a 'secret army', the Malay movements had many unarmed men with them who were in the early stages of training, and a number of OCAJA absconded prior to disbandment (having recently been seriously depleted by fighting with the MPAJA), so these figures, though they look precise, are really only approximate. Due to some confusion in the records, there is also a possibility that the OCAJA total has been undercounted by 120 armed men.

enough, do not function in the same way as larger formations, for the personal relationships within them develop differently. As the military sociologist Jacques van Doorn argues, armies manage violence via a structured hierarchy.[120] In small teams, the role of the military hierarchy diminishes and personal initiative and improvisation become more important.[121] This can be seen in the operation of the Force 136 patrols deployed in Malaya, where initiative was highly valued, and close and trusting personal relationships were essential in allowing teams to survive and even thrive in difficult conditions.

Force 136 operatives were in danger from the point infiltration began, sharing the risks faced by submariners and aircrew. Blind landings were riskier than those to reception parties, but both were dangerous: in a night drop to *Galvanic*, one man landed in a pool on a tin tailing and drowned beneath his parachute.[122] Injuries were not uncommon: Major Ian McDonald of *Galvanic* 'treed' on landing, and ended up with a damaged back and hand.[123] Once in Malaya, operatives faced the same risks of illness, hunger, betrayal, capture and combat as did the guerrillas of the MPAJA.[124] Lim Bo Seng died in custody after being betrayed and Paddy Martin, the first leader of Operation *Carpenter*, was shot dead, along with two MPAJA members, in a Japanese assault on a camp in Johore in January 1945.[125] The environment was challenging: hot, humid, hilly, malarial, leech-ridden and bitterly cold at night at high altitudes. Radio contact was difficult, with report after report complaining about the problems of generating adequate power.[126] Poor wireless contact coupled with the proportion of failed sorties – when the planes could not find the dropping zone, or had to turn back because of bad weather or technical problems – could mean lean times for the men on the ground. Since 20 per cent of sorties failed, and food supplies from within Malaya were often limited, some patrols went very hungry, with one Air Operations Report noting that a patrol had suggested that their operation be renamed *Skeleton*.[127] Operatives had also been warned that once *Zipper* was launched, their life expectancy was a short one: the Canadian Chinese were told three weeks.[128] As a result of these risks and dangers, the pressure on the men was intense. In a small team, the failure of one man was difficult for the team as a whole, and as a consequence of this, officers were highly critical of men who did not measure up to expected standards.[129]

Force 136 rated what was called 'efficiency', a party's ability to work cooperatively and hold together under pressure, as vital to the success of teams in the field. The Force also saw 'efficiency' as more important than either early arrival in the field or maintaining good relations with other clandestine bodies. Early in 1945, Force 136 had the opportunity to coordinate its Operation *Funnel* with an ISLD operation, *Evidence*. *Evidence* had a higher priority with 'P' Division than did *Funnel*, so two joint drops (rather than an ISLD drop followed by a Force 136 drop) would have brought *Funnel* operatives into the field earlier than would otherwise have been the case. ISLD agreed to this (perhaps due to the friendship between ISLD's Hembry and Force 136's Tremlett), but when Jim Hannah of Force 136 was asked to lead the first drop, he declined, even though Force 136 operations in Malaya were at a critical stage.[130] There was 'a certain amount of dissension in the ISLD party and he [Hannah] felt that with the few days left at his disposal an unhappy party could not be made into an efficient one, and it was vitally necessary that it should be efficient because of the difficulties which would be encountered on the chosen DZ [dropping zone]'. As a consequence, the ISLD party dropped first, with no Force 136 representation.[131]

In addition, Force 136's small infiltrated units had to achieve 'efficiency' and cohesiveness under the leadership of a colonial officer class. These officers, as the language of their operational reports revealed, had a tendency to reinforce clear racial and social hierarchies, 'other' their Asian allies and accentuate difference. The game warden George Leonard (*Pontoon*) noted that he had 'Experience handling natives'; Jock Hunter (*Galvanic*) commented that with 'native guerrillas you either click or you don't'.[132] Claude Fenner, who led Operation *Humour* – and was a senior policeman during the Malayan Emergency – considered that 'normal' Chinese habits included 'prevarication and procrastination'.[133] Similarly, Major David Alexander with Operation *Funnel* complained about 'inevitable Chinese interference' in the work of the medical officer with his patrol.

At the same time, and within the framework of colonial judgements made on the basis of 'race', senior European officers trusted and relied upon their individual Asian subordinates and often commented favourably on them in their personnel reports. Hunter described his interpreter, Ted Wong, as brave and tireless; Major Owen of *Funnel Green* thought that his radio operator, Yeung Wai Chong, was 'A really first class man' who worked very hard and very well.[134] At times, colonial racial tropes were simultaneously reinforced and challenged. Derek Headly wrote of his Eurasian sergeant, Bobby Neubronner, 'I consider he is quite an exceptional Eurasian. He does not suffer in any way from an inferiority complex.'[135] Other officers gave assessments of Asians that ran counter to racialized myths. While the perceived inability of Malays to keep a secret was a recurrent theme, and seemed to be regarded, at least by Geoffrey Hasler of *Fighter*, as a racial trait, Douglas Richardson, working on the other side of the Main Range, commented upon the remarkable security demonstrated by both the Malays and the *Orang Asli* with whom he had had dealings.[136] Sometimes European officers objected to what they saw as the blatant racism of their colleagues: Claude Fenner was critical of his subordinate, Major B.G. Phillips, for referring to an MPAJA patrol leader as 'his Chief Monkey' and the patrol's HQ as 'the monkey house'.[137] Within a racialized structure, in which Europeans tended to regard Asians as inferior, there were several gradations of view.

In the case of Operation *Gustavus*, there are indications that issues of racism and colonial prestige combined in a toxic mix that, even if they did not damage the operation itself, certainly worsened some of the interpersonal relationships within it. Though the 'Dragons' – the Guomindang Chinese recruited in Nationalist China by Lim Bo Seng – recruited into Force 136 had limited military experience (at least two of them were recruited directly from their studies), they held high ranks in the Chinese army, frequently higher than those of the British officers under whom they served. Yet despite being officers in the army of the Republic of China, Force 136, for 'security reasons', sent them on operations in the uniforms of British Other ranks.[138] The security justification is credible: had the MPAJA discovered the British had planted men in their camps associated with the Guomindang army, their mistrust of the British would only have intensified. Nonetheless, the Dragons of *Gustavus* would have remained aware of their actual ranks, and perhaps suspected that British anxiety to retain racial prestige had resulted in their symbolic demotion. At the end of the war, when the security risk no longer existed, the British high command still refused to allow the Dragons to display their actual badges of rank, because 'it might have unfortunate results on the status of British Liaison Officers whose ranks would almost always be lower than those of the Chinese Officers'.[139]

To at least one Dragon, Tan Chong Tee, it appeared that relations within *Gustavus* were undermined by British racism. Tan stated in his memoir that Europeans in Force 136 'still behaved very much like the colonial master with the Chinese at their beck and call' and added that Lim Bo Seng told him that 'the British are difficult to get along with because of their arrogance'. Tan allows this generalization to stand indicating, perhaps, that his run-ins with John Davis had a stronger impact upon him than did the calm and conciliatory role taken by the senior officer Richard Broome who, Tan wrote, 'treated the trainees as friends'.[140] Poor relations between the Nationalist Chinese and the British in *Gustavus* would have hardly been helped by the fact that before leaving China, Tan had been instructed by Wu Tieh-cheng, a leading politician in the Chungking government, to spy on Force 136. He recorded in his memoir that his instructions were to 'Send us information on training skills and secret weapons used by the British'.[141]

In Tan's view – contrary to the picture presented by the Force 136 officer John Davis – *Gustavus* was riven by suspicion and ill-discipline.[142] The *Gustavus* network was rolled up in 1944, resulting in the arrest of half a dozen agents and, ultimately, the death of Lim Bo Seng.[143] Betrayal could have come from a range of sources, including the activities of the MCP traitor Lai Teck, without the operation's internal problems playing any part.[144] However, that tensions existed within *Gustavus*, with issues of race at the root of them, cannot be denied.

Gustavus was not the only operation in which there were tensions between operatives of different backgrounds. Douglas Broadhurst, the GLO of *Galvanic*, accused 'many' of the Dragons of 'pompous self-esteem' and of thinking themselves above 'the menial tasks that are the inevitable lot of all operatives of whatever rank'.[145] His sweeping judgement of the Dragons, however, was not entirely supported by the personnel reports he wrote about the agents under his command. Although he wrote scathingly about one of the Dragons who worked for him, he described the other, Tong Shu Shan, as 'a valued and much appreciated man'.[146] Broadhurst did, however, impose a clear hierarchy in his view of his Chinese allies: he viewed the Canadian Chinese Force 136 recruited as 'enlightened', by which we must assume that he meant more Westernized, more like Europeans in outlook.[147] The Canadians, it seems, complied with the 'civilizing' mission of the Empire, whereas the Dragons did not.

Conclusion

Despite these evident internal tensions, the difficulties presented by the climate and topography and the problems of communication and supply, eleven of the thirteen operations launched into Malaya by Force 136 succeeded in accomplishing their objectives, entirely in the case of most, and in part in the case of *Gustavus*. Contact with the guerrillas was made, wireless contact was established, arms were dropped and training was begun.

Exploring the detailed evidence provided by Force 136's documents allows us to draw conclusions at several levels about the operation of this military unit: at the international, the national and the personal. Internationally, it reveals the competition between Britain and the United States for post-war control in Asia, with both parties trying to gain or maintain toeholds in countries dominated by the clandestine services of the other. At a national level, our study indicates that the initial rivalry between Force 136 and ISLD (acquired from their parent bodies, SOE and SIS) was substantially eased for the Malayan operations by the close relationship between the head of ISLD's Malayan operations, Boris Hembry, and Innes Tremlett of MCS. Hembry and Tremlett mirrored the attitude of the men on the ground who, though they sometimes resented the members of other organizations, were on the whole willing to work with them in pursuit of local aims. At this level, even international rivalries died away – as in the case of Operation *Beacon*, whose leader was delighted to receive assistance from a member of OSS.

At the personal level, a mixture of motivations was in operation: expiation, an eagerness to defeat the Japanese, and the search for political rights. A man like Tengku Mahmood Mahyideen could look like a supporter of the British Empire and yet, when his motivations are scrutinized more closely, prove to have been a nationalist in deep but temporary disguise. Others, such as the Canadian Chinese, were completely frank about what inspired them to join Force 136: they were seeking equality for their community back in Canada, and would risk their lives for the Allied cause to attain this end.

Although a wide range of men came together in Force 136, to cooperate and pursue a common aim, the Force was nonetheless deeply influenced by imperial notions about race and by attitudes towards social class. The leading roles (from staff officers to senior liaison officers in the field) were dominated by upper-middle class Europeans, with a sprinkling of upper class Asians. However, as the war progressed, necessity (indicated by the difficulties in recruitment) began to wear down this tidy hierarchy. War sometimes (though not always) broke down barriers between people, and confounded expectations. For example, the Eurasian former Volunteer, George Hesse was recruited locally by the planter Ian McDonald. The two men established a friendship that endured until McDonald's death.[148] At other times, existing colonial racial attitudes caused ill-feeling in projects that were already difficult: from Tan Chong Tee's account it appears that his clashes with Davis – perceived by him to be rooted in ingrained colonial attitudes towards race – compounded the difficulties faced by Operation *Gustavus*.

While the levies raised by Force 136 in Burma had the opportunity to prove their worth in the first half of 1945, when they helped the Allies overwhelm the Japanese in the region just north of Rangoon, the guerrillas which Force 136 assisted in Malaya never had this opportunity and never engaged in more than limited skirmishes with the Japanese.[149] Nonetheless, the evidence presented in this chapter suggests that they would have been equally useful had the British tried to retake Malaya by force. The startling new insights that Force 136 sources reveal about the activities of these guerrilla armies, with respect to both the British and to each other, are the focus of the following three chapters.

Chapter 3

'A DEAL WITH THE DEVIL': FORCE 136
AND THE MPAJA[1]

At the end of December 1943, in a jungle camp at Blantan in northern Malaya, a handful of men held a conference to agree the terms of the unlikely alliance between Force 136 and the Malayan People's Anti-Japanese Army (MPAJA), a guerrilla body sponsored by the resolutely anti-colonial Malayan Communist Party (MCP). The MPAJA's membership was almost entirely Chinese, and it had a strong emphasis on education – including political education.[2] Supported by a civilian network, the Malayan People's Anti-Japanese Union (MPAJU), it took action against both the Japanese and those it termed 'traitors'.[3] Acting for the MPAJA was the former Special Branch agent Lai Teck, calling himself 'Chang Hong'. With Lai Teck was Chin Peng, an important cadre despite his youth. He would lead the Malayan National Liberation Army (MNLA) against the British during the Malayan Emergency.

Facing Lai Teck were three Special Operations Executive (SOE) officers authorized to act as military representatives of Admiral Mountbatten, the Supreme Allied Commander, South East Asia Command. These were John Davis and Richard Broome, who had worked with Oriental Mission to train and insert the first parties of communists ahead of the Japanese advance in 1942, and Lim Bo Seng, the Chinese businessman who had been key in the recruitment of the 'Dragons' to SOE.[4] Lai Teck was, it seems, recognized by Davis. Davis later recalled that he found the moment of meeting Lai Teck at Blantan 'the most "difficult and strange" of his life'.[5] What Davis didn't know was that Lai Teck was now working for the Japanese. At the end of two days of negotiations, a deal was signed by Davis, Broome, Lim and 'Chang Hong'. Chin Peng was not invited by his leader to append his signature, and as the stay-behind Freddy Spencer Chapman, who the MPAJA had brought into the camp a few days earlier, was not a 'representative' of Mountbatten, he also did not sign.[6]

The Blantan Agreement, and the subsidiary understanding of April 1945 that covered how it should be carried out, underlay all later cooperation between Force 136 and the MPAJA and would have consequences stretching beyond the end of World War II. The exact nature of these agreements is still disputed, though their terms, and how they were fulfilled, relate to an ongoing historical debate as to the size and effectiveness of the MPAJA. In addition, some historians claim that the

British reneged on their side of the deal, arguing that this was a contributory factor to the violence leading to the State of Emergency in 1948.[7] Moreover, the bargain itself – what it said, what it did not say – is revealing about the development of British policy for Malaya for the post-war period.

As much research has demonstrated, bargains, written and unwritten, explicit and implicit, are a key factor in understanding the mobilization of particular groups of people during wartime, and some of the events that follow. Nicoletta Gullace credits the Great War with hastening women's suffrage in Britain, finding that women who participated in the war effort keenly felt the injustice of being unable to vote, when conscientious objectors could: citizenship was now about patriotism, not about possessing a male body.[8] The Vietnam War was likewise perceived as a deal by civilians involved. Peasants moved to hill country in the early 1960s, lured by larger landholdings and patriotic duty, to feed the soldiers and protect the entrances to the Ho Chi Minh Trail. By the 1980s, with the war over, they felt neglected by the government when their wartime sacrifices for the future of the nation were not rewarded, while others received government assistance. War had been a time of moral clarity: the peace, as they stayed poor and others grew wealthier, proved confusing and disappointing.[9]

The same principle applied in the British Empire during and after World War II, although the bargains that developed varied from place to place. In India, the source of multitudes of Imperial troops, the attitudes of many soldiers were transformed and Indian officers could not see why Britain should remain in India, once Japan was no longer a threat.[10] As these examples show, people view their participation in warfare as more than service to their nation: they also perceive it as their half of a deal, in which they expect to receive political or economic gains in return, even if no explicit bargain has been struck.

A number of works have examined the activity of the MPAJA during and just after the Japanese occupation of Malaya and have discussed the relationship between the MPAJA and Force 136. Yet despite its later significance, the exact nature of the key agreement struck between the two bodies is currently open to dispute. Some historians, as does Chin Peng himself, trace at least some of the roots of the Emergency down into a soil of promises made, and broken, by the British. Chin Peng contends that the British committed themselves to more than they wished.[11] Christopher Bayly and Tim Harper are more explicit, stating that during the April 1945 discussions (when the second, verbal, agreement was struck), 'Force 136 officers had been allowed to go further in promising that the MCP would not be required to register as a political party after the war, as part of the new liberal imperialism of the Malayan Planning Unit'.[12] This claim is repeated in Bayly and Harper's later work, *Forgotten Wars*.[13] Caroline Elkins, in her review of this book, repeats and strengthens their argument, contending that the British 'disavowed any war-time alliance or promises, particularly to the MPAJA' and that this 'only added to the nationalists' mounting bitterness'.[14] In essence, the claim is that the British reneged on explicit undertakings that they had made, worsening an already tense situation and fuelling the growing unrest.

By contrast, some scholars claim that no political promises were made. Cheah Boon Kheng, whose work on the MPAJA mainly focuses on the interregnum – the unsettled period between the surrender of Japan and the return of the British – asserts that political matters were excluded from discussion when Force 136 and the MPAJA made their deal.[15] Similarly, Ban Kah Choon and Yap Hong Kuan are clear that neither the first nor the second deal included any political promises.[16] Ban and Yap's essential thesis is reflected in the title of their book: *Rehearsal for War*. They conclude that the MCP used the Japanese occupation to prepare for eventual rebellion against the British and agreed to cooperate with SOE as this cooperation allowed them to pursue their own aims.[17] Ban and Yap also argue that even before the arrival of Force 136 the MPAJA was an efficient fighting force.[18]

If Ban and Yap are correct in their claim that the MCP used the Japanese occupation to prepare its forces for eventual revolt (and this chapter will provide compelling evidence that it did), we are faced with an important question: if the MPAJA was, as Ban and Yap also claim, effective without British input, why was it willing to enter into an agreement with representatives of a government which it did not trust and whose rule it did not wish to see again? This issue of political concessions – part of the backdrop to arguments about the Emergency's causes – remains clouded.

As this chapter will show, homing in on the bargains struck between Force 136 and the MPAJA is historically illuminating for it allows us to test not only these but other arguments made in the scholarly literature. Some scholars imply that, aside from political promises, SOE failed to fulfil undertakings to arm and train the MPAJA made in the agreements. Richard Aldrich, who has suggested that Force 136's senior officers were more concerned with political rather than military matters, has stated that, though the British armed the MPAJA, the main purpose of this was 'retardation'.[19] Paul Kratoska has broadly concurred, observing that the Chiefs of Staff's planning committee mistrusted the communist-inspired MPAJA and relegated it almost to the role of a service corps – intended to provide labour, intelligence and guides.[20] By contrast, Charles Cruickshank – the official historian of SOE in Asia – considers that, by the war's end, the MPAJA had been welded into as competent a fighting force as the levies of Force 136's Burmese operation, *Character*, guerrilla forces that played a significant role in the reconquest of Rangoon.[21] In other words, there is little scholarly consensus not only about the promises the British made to the MPAJA, but about the degree to which they were fulfilled. A bargain seen as such a key element in some historians' explanations of the outbreak of the Malayan Emergency remains poorly understood.

The deal agreed between Force 136 and the MPAJA also raises the issue of the British government's wartime intentions. As we will see, while the Malayan Planning Unit's moves towards eventual self-government for Malaya indicate that self-rule had been accepted by Whitehall, there was still no desire among the Chiefs of Staff to promote a broadly left-wing guerrilla movement to a position of power. As Kratoska observes, the Chiefs of Staff were not enamoured of the MPAJA; they worried about internal security after Malaya's recapture from the Japanese, and foresaw political issues arising from Britain's reliance upon a predominantly Chinese force during the reconquest of a country where the Chinese did not have equal rights.[22] Mountbatten also understood these issues, though he appeared less worried than the Chiefs of Staff by the risk of later security problems. It seems he had shorter-term military aims in mind, being keen to recruit local allies to speed up Malaya's recapture.[23]

This chapter will examine the interrelated and unresolved questions concerning SOE's deal with the MPAJA by addressing the reasons behind it, and the *explicit* undertakings contained within it. Our discussion will then move onto examine – in the light of the existing literature which frames 'war as a bargain' – the *implicit* promises the MCP believed were bound up in that agreement, and the extent to which explicit promises were kept. We will then explore the impact of the MCP's implicit understanding of its bargain with the British, before concluding with a consideration of whether Force 136, by backing the MPAJA, bolstered the political hopes and aspirations of the Malayan communists.

The path to Blantan

From the outset of SOE's Malayan operations, the political implications of any deal with the MPAJA comprised one of its primary concerns. In many countries where SOE operated, it worked with local guerrillas, either raising units or forming alliances with pre-existing groups. The Americans did the same, working with local troops who had escaped the Japanese in the Philippines, and with the communists in French Indo-China. SOE was prepared to work with communists in the Balkans, despite concerns about the future, for they provided the most effective local anti-Axis forces.[24] However, the selection of allies in Europe was one thing; choosing them in a former – and, as SOE expected, future – British possession was another.[25] To further complicate the matter, SOE, in choosing to work with the communists in Malaya, was fully aware of the likely reaction of another Allied power, the Guomindang government in China. The backing of a majority-Chinese communist party in a country with a large Chinese population had the potential to cause friction with Guomindang allies.

From August 1942, and, more than a year before South East Asia Command was created with Mountbatten at its head, India Mission was permitted to operate in Malaya and so began working towards a combined intelligence and guerrilla role.[26] SOE, despite political concerns, sought out the MPAJA as its first Malayan ally, partly as a result of the contacts the British had already developed through the training they had offered to the MCP cadres of the left-behind parties in 1942. After the Fall of Singapore, John Davis and Richard Broome, then both of Oriental Mission, had briefly returned to Malaya from Sumatra and ascertained that the MCP left-behind parties that they had inserted had become operational.[27] In May 1943, Davis and five Chinese agents infiltrated into Malaya to contact a resistance they hoped would still be active.[28] Though Davis's immediate aims, as agreed with Mackenzie, were to establish both a submarine link with India and an intelligence system, it is clear from the agreement made between Davis and the MPAJA at the end of 1943 that he was authorized to cooperate militarily with the guerrillas.[29]

News that Davis had contacted the MPAJA arrived in India via submarine rendezvous, and in October 1943 a concerned memorandum was dispatched to Colin Mackenzie, India Mission's head, written by SOE's adviser on Chinese affairs. Though it optimistically concluded that the MPAJA was 'probably the rallying point of all activist elements in Malaya who are anti-Japanese', it noted that 'any undue prominence given to the label "communism" is a mistake, as it is likely not only to alarm ZP [the Foreign Office] … but even more so the Kuomintang Government of Chungking'.[30] At this stage of the war, the Chungking government was a key ally in a number of SOE operations in China. Force 136 was also recruiting Malayan Chinese who were living in China.[31]

Within a matter of days, the decision was made – apparently by Mackenzie – to 'play down the use of the word "communist" and stick to "Anti-Japanese Union" ' – which, apparently, 'sounds quite snappy' in Chinese'.[32] This guidance seems to have been taken to heart; the intelligence summary that resulted from the November submarine rendezvous explained that 'There are no difficulties between them [the MPAJA] and other resistance groups, and communist influence is not, so far as can be ascertained, paramount'.[33] Force 136 was keen to work with the MPAJA because SOE already had contacts within it, making it easier for infiltrated men to prove their bona fides.[34] Though many members of the MPAJA were not communists, to rise up in its ranks one had to be a member of the MCP, or at least claim to believe in communist doctrine.[35] To ensure that Force 136 could work with the MPAJA, SOE deliberately glossed over its links with communism.

At the same time, the British well understood that any deal they struck with the MPAJA would strengthen the MCP's hand, increasing both its credibility and its capacity. That they chose to make one was no doubt a consequence of the awareness of some members of Force 136 that the MCP was led by Lai Teck, a British agent who had helped weaken the MCP from within. What SOE could not know was whether their informer had escaped the 'screening' of the Chinese by the Japanese or, if he had, whether he would still be prepared to work for them. This issue is not discussed in the available documents, but whatever was known about Lai Teck in this period, SOE plainly decided that an alliance with the MPAJA was worth the risk.

Further up the official hierarchy, the decision also received support, though the same concerns were expressed about the communist nature of the MPAJA. Mountbatten was in favour of maximizing the use of guerrilla forces.[36] The Joint Planning Staff agreed with this overall aim, but was concerned that arming any resistance movement could lead to difficulties with 'internal security after the recapture'.[37] These senior military figures also picked up on Mountbatten's more subtle political concern that British support for the predominantly Chinese MPAJA 'might invite pressure to secure these privileges [enjoyed by the Malays] once hostilities are over'. To assuage Mountbatten's anxieties, the planners agreed to push for the promulgation of the post-war constitutional policy of equal political rights, and to encourage support for non-Chinese resistance.[38] In effect, the British high command understood that any bargain struck with the MPAJA would have implications beyond its wording, however tightly that might be drawn. This anxiety meant that the Chiefs of Staff instructed Mountbatten to offer such support to the MPAJA as would allow 'control' over them.[39] Mountbatten – a man, according to the SOE historian, M.R.D. Foot, 'who did what and went where he liked' – would appear to have interpreted this as allowing him to approve Force 136's determined build-up of the MPAJA, which it had in any case already begun to arm.[40]

The delay in informing Whitehall of the communist control of the MPAJA reveals wartime tensions, at a high official level, between Britain's imperial centre and colonial periphery. Towards the end of the war, Mountbatten finally informed the Joint Planning Staff of the MPAJA's long-term aim 'to achieve an independent Republic of Malaya', claiming that this information had 'become available' since he first reported to them.[41] It is possible that he was being disingenuous, but it is also possible that Force 136 had deliberately sat as firmly upon its knowledge of the close involvement of the MCP in the MPAJA as its earlier telegrams had implied it would. Force 136 was eager to get the job done in Malaya as quickly as possible, using the MPAJA's help (by offering the bribe of citizenship if possible) whereas the planners and military chiefs in London worried about due process and the long-term risks of armed, trained communists in an imperial possession. It is also worth noting that Force 136's Malayan Country Section used the opportunity of working with the MPAJA to gather information on its leadership. It is unlikely that it was pure coincidence that the head of the section was Innes Tremlett, who had been Lai Teck's handler before the war, and that, of the four former Malayan policemen who were infiltrated, all went to MPAJA operations.[42]

As for the question of why the MPAJA was willing to do a deal with Malaya's former colonial rulers, the answer lies in both the strengths and weaknesses of the MPAJA. The MPAJA was never short of recruits; it had considerable support from rural Chinese; it enjoyed a measure of autonomy and it was active against the Japanese. Yet its recruits were mostly drawn from among the squatters in the villages along the jungle fringe, who had left unworked estates and mines for a life of smallholding in the hills. Spencer Chapman noted that most recruits were 'coolie and jungle types', who were typically barely educated: 'only one in a hundred can read a map'.[43] The MPAJA had the manpower but if it was to turn itself into an effective fighting force, its recruits needed training, and the MPAJA had few trained soldiers in its ranks.[44] Besides this, its village supporters were liable to suffer Japanese reprisals should the MPAJA take anti-Japanese action, which not only forced the guerrillas to flee deeper into the jungle, but burdened them with refugees.[45]

The MPAJA was also profoundly weakened from within by the actions of Lai Teck. Arrested early in the Japanese occupation and interrogated by Major Onishi of the Kempeitai, he agreed to work for the Japanese, and began to ingratiate himself with his new masters.[46] In May 1942, he betrayed the Singapore Town Committee to the Japanese.[47] Then, at the very end of August 1942, a meeting of forty communist representatives was organized to begin at a camp near

Batu Caves, with Lai Teck due to join them on 1 September. On the night of 31 August, the Japanese attacked. Half the delegates – all of them senior members of the party – were killed, along with their bodyguards and cooks. At a stroke, the Japanese wiped out many able and experienced MCP leaders, including graduates of No. 101 Special Training School (101STS).[48] During the lead-up to another major meeting in Perak a few months later, more key members were arrested – and yet no one in the party totted up the clues.[49] Chin Peng later reflected that it was 'quite extraordinary' that the cadres didn't spot Lai Teck for what he was until the war was over.[50]

This gutting of the MCP and MPAJA ensured Lai Teck's survival, and also weakened the whole communist organization, leaving it in greater need of external assistance than might otherwise have been the case. The underground nature of the pre-war MCP and the risks of a guerrilla life had already sent a chill breeze of paranoia through the psyche of the MPAJA, and the continuing betrayals made it more paranoid still. Any communist suspected of going over to the other side was disposed of as a 'traitor'.[51] The evidence suggests that over the course of the occupation between a third and a half of those killed by the MPAJA were 'traitors', real or suspected, though many of these were from outside the organization.[52] Ban and Yap argue that the Batu Caves massacre effectively cleared Selangor of capable communist leaders, which resulted in Perak becoming a more important base for the MPAJA.[53] This can of course be read the other way: the Perak MPAJA was probably no stronger than it would otherwise have been, but the Selangor MPAJA was considerably weaker.

The MPAJA, already short of experienced leaders, was further hampered in its activities by the lack of autonomy given to local commanders. Spencer Chapman, who spent over three years with the guerrillas, complained that junior leaders had 'never been fostered', which may explain why they were reluctant to act beyond strictly defined spheres of control.[54] This was coupled with painfully slow communications, leading to long delays between a suggestion being put forward, and action being taken.[55] All the power was at the top, and since local groups of MPAJA were often out of contact with their own hierarchy they were unable to act decisively.

Aside from this sclerotic control, the MPAJA was beset by shortages that limited its operational effectiveness. In many places it was short of food, and everywhere it lacked adequate arms and ammunition. The Japanese occupation was a time of increasing shortages, for the economy collapsed and insufficient rice was imported to feed the population. The Japanese currency, derisively known as 'banana money' for the illustrations that adorned it, devalued rapidly.[56] In an attempt to deal with supply problems, the Japanese administration set up a rationing system, but the shortages were so severe that ration quantities were often merely theoretical.[57] The death rate rose markedly, with diseases such as malaria and influenza felling increasing numbers. By the war's end, Javanese labourers were dying in the streets of Singapore and children had been stunted by several years of poor nutrition.[58]

The MPAJA's troops could not merely hole up in the jungle, because the jungle could not feed them.[59] To overcome this problem, food supplies were brought in from outside. Those who Spencer Chapman called 'the outside workers' – the propagandists – were often 'charming and delightful people' and thus good ambassadors for the MPAJA. These 'outside workers' were very active in the villages, building up the MPAJU so that food lines could be established.[60] The civilian network of the MPAJU provided the link between the guerrillas and the local people, raising subscriptions, organizing the porterage of food to the camps and rooting out informers.[61] It was the forerunner of the Min Yuen, the MNLA's civilian network during the Emergency, and it was one method by which the MPAJA increased its influence. The best propaganda was the reality of happy, well-ordered camps and the 'charming' propagandists themselves.[62] Throughout the Japanese occupation, supplies of food came into the jungle from the squatter settlements, despite the terrible reprisals that the Japanese sometimes inflicted on peasants they suspected of assisting the guerrillas.[63]

Nonetheless, despite the efficiency of the MPAJU, food supplies from beyond the jungle were often inadequate, and also vulnerable to the Japanese, who might discover and close the routes used by the porters who brought food from the villages to the camps. The MPAJA used two tactics to assist it in such circumstances. In the north of Malaya, the leadership carefully fostered an alliance with the jungle aboriginals, the *Orang Asli*. Aid from this quarter, Spencer Chapman noted, was especially valuable when 'we are on the run or our food lines are closed'.[64] In addition, the MPAJA's soldiers often grew some of their own food. The 7th Regiment in East Pahang, which had with it large numbers of civilian refuges from Japanese 'drives', had, by 1944, established seven large plantations.[65] Food was also grown in Johore.[66] However, these efforts were always vulnerable to Japanese attack: the 7th Regiment was driven from its extensive plantations by Japanese forces during 1944.[67] Though there were times of comparative plenty, food was almost always in short supply.[68]

Consequently, despite the work of the MPAJU, the assistance of the *Orang Asli* and the food crops raised in the jungle, the guerrillas were often malnourished. The senior Force 136 men Davis and Broome reported from Perak in September 1943 that 'the camps are very badly off for food', with almost no vegetables or meat being provided.[69] When the Force 136 doctors arrived – in response to a request made by the MPAJA at the Blantan meeting – one calculated that the guerrillas' own rations, exclusive of food provided by Force 136, provided between 1,000 and 1,200 calories per person a day – around half of what was needed.[70] A liaison officer with the same regiment noted that the guerrillas had been hungry for so long that, while the Force 136 men could miss a meal or two and not suffer too badly, 'the Chinese had been living on such meagre rations for so long that that each meal was a major event and they could not offord [sic] to miss one and carry on'.[71] The food supply organization was there, but the food was not.

All this left the members of the MPAJA prey to illness and weakened by deficiency diseases. Reg Lawther, a major in the MPAJA in east Pahang, saw a direct connection between the low diet and the ill health endured by the guerrillas, with beriberi 'a common disorder in the camps'.[72] Ho Thean Fook, the MPAJA foot-soldier in Perak, suffered from scurvy.[73] Already weakened by malnutrition, the guerrillas were less able to cope with attacks of malaria. Some camps were more malarial than others, but a doctor arriving in Perak in April 1945 considered that the infection rate for malaria, which worsened the anaemia caused by the poor diet, was a hundred per cent in the camps with which he had contact.[74] One of the doctors' first actions was to issue to multi-vitamins to everyone in the camps, as well as the anti-malarial, mepacrine.[75] Malnutrition also left the guerrillas very vulnerable to jungle ulcers: a leech bite or small scratch could swiftly turn into an ulcer, ranging in size from a sixpence to a saucer.[76] In addition, the guerrillas had almost no access to medicines until the arrival of Force 136. The guerrilla Ho Thean Fook, who had spent time with a medical family in the small town of Papan, acted as a 'roving doctor', but his supplies were limited.[77] At one point he had sulphonamide pills, permanganate of potash, stale tea, and quinine; later on, he entered a camp with quinine, rice bran and red palm oil as his entire medical armoury.[78]

The guerrillas were organized and enthusiastic, but they were not fit and healthy troops, and nor were they well armed. The early guerrillas had gathered together what they could, collecting arms abandoned after the fighting at Slim River, and being given or buying other weapons.[79] They were directed to collect arms by their leadership, which also prescribed the hierarchy of the patrols that they formed.[80] Oriental Mission likewise urged the communists to arm themselves just before Singapore capitulated.[81] Once the battlefields had been cleared, however, it was difficult for the MPAJA to obtain additional weapons, other than by raiding police stations and Japanese stores.[82] The MPAJA ended up with a variety of armaments – 'a hell of a collection', according to George Hess'e, who acted as the armourer in a camp in Selangor – but it did not have very many of them, and a large proportion was in poor repair. Those that the guerrillas did have they sometimes found difficult to use.[83]

According to Ho Thean Fook, a patrol of sixty guerrillas might only have fifty weapons, including a few side arms such as pistols.[84] Reg Lawther states that there were not enough weapons to go round and that a guerrilla going on sentry duty had to go to the armoury to collect a gun.[85] This information is broadly supported by that given by Spencer Chapman and other Force 136 officers, who noted that most patrols – which were still rarely more than about a hundred strong – were not fully armed.[86] The Force 136 reports make it clear that arming the patrols was a key issue. Major Sime, with Operation *Carpenter* in late 1944, stated that 'one of the factors governing our relationship with the AJF [Anti-Japanese Force: MPAJA] was the number of weapons we could give them'.[87] The MPAJA's shortage of guns was compounded by a shortage of ammunition, which degrades rapidly in tropical climates unless carefully kept.[88] This was impossibly difficult for guerrillas living in hastily erected accommodation and sometimes on the run. The early infiltrations of Operation *Gustavus* reported that ammunition sent in had to be waterproofed and their reports noted that the MPAJA was 'very poorly equipped and has very few guns and very little ammunition'.[89]

As a result, the MPAJA was unable to carry out concerted attacks on the Japanese. The MPAJA's own account of its activities states that it launched 340 individual anti-Japanese operations, claiming to have killed 5,500 Japanese troops, though it is not clear if this figure includes Malayan recruits to Japanese forces.[90] Japanese records are at odds with this, stating that there were 600 Japanese casualties (of whom over 250 were killed) and 2,000 from among their locally raised forces.[91] There is very little evidence to establish which set of figures is the more accurate. Cheah places more reliance on Japanese records, and his conclusion is in line with the comments made by Force 136 officers who were active with the MPAJA.[92]

To an extent, the number of casualties that the MPAJA inflicted on the Japanese is an irrelevance. The significant factor is that the MPAJA deprived the Japanese of free access to territory that the Japanese considered they had conquered. Despite the difficulties it faced, the MPAJA – and, by extension, the MCP – was experimenting with territorial control, moving itself and many of its supporters beyond the reach of Japanese. There were areas of the Malayan hinterland where the writ of the Japanese did not run, or only ran if Japanese troops were actually present. Ho Thean Fook, though he offers no dates, records MPAJA attacks on police stations in Perak. One such attack had the aim of keeping the Japanese away from what Ho termed the guerrillas' 'frontier', a choice of word indicating that, to the minds of the guerrillas at least, they inhabited an area that they held against the Japanese.[93] Japanese researchers arriving in Singapore late in 1942 to study the rubber industry were told that it wasn't safe for them to visit the estates.[94] In some places, the cadres were able to print propaganda, news-sheets, maps and, in one case, even money. They also sheltered a number of evading Allied troops.[95]

All of this indicates that the MPAJA enjoyed a reasonably high degree of autonomy within the jungle, though the guerrillas were under continual threat from informers and direct attack. However, the MPAJA was never able to press home a consistent offensive against the Japanese because, as Cheah states, they 'were too badly armed to carry out any major operations' until the early part of 1945.[96] This lack of major offensive activity indicates the great logistical problems faced by the MPAJA and here lie the practical problems that propelled the MPAJA into an agreement with the British.

The explicit bargain: the Blantan Agreement

The deal signed at Blantan gave both sides what they wanted and was, on the face of it, straightforward. It bound the MPAJA to receive Force 136 liaison officers and to accept their tactical command, in exchange for food, money, medicines, arms and training (see full text in Appendix A). Lai Teck also agreed that the MPAJA would continue to assist the British until peace was restored. Force 136 had potential troops in sight, just where it wanted them, and the MPAJA had won the promise of the supplies that were desperately needed if they were to take the fight to the Japanese and – if Ban and Yap are correct – prepare for later rebellion against the British.

When Lai Teck finally told his senior cadres of this alliance, in October 1944, he justified it by claiming it would further the MCP's long-term plans. He advertised the agreement to the MCP's senior men as an opportunity for the MPAJA to be split into two parts, one (the open army) for ostensible cooperation with the British, the other (the 'secret army' or Mi Mi Tui) to arm and train in secret. Once the British landed in force, the 'secret army' was to challenge them for control of Malaya by seizing public buildings and police stations in the towns and controlling as much territory as possible.[97] This was consistent with the MCP's pre-war manifestos and Chin Peng saw it as 'a rousing call to revolution'.[98] It was also consistent, as will be seen in the two following chapters, with the MPAJA's behaviour towards other resistance forces. As Chin Peng later admitted, 'Central' – that is, Lai Teck – had told them to conserve their strength (such as it was), develop the guerrillas and organize the masses: the aims of the MCP went beyond the ejection of the Japanese to the ejection of the British.[99]

The link between the signing of the Blantan Agreement and Lai Teck's 'rousing call to revolution' indicates that the MPAJA entered the agreement in a spirit that cadres like Chin Peng considered entirely in line with the MCP's stated aim of overthrowing the imperial power and instituting a republic. The British, however, would have viewed this as bad faith, for it seems that the MPAJA's leadership never intended to abide by the Blantan deal's final clause. The clause stated, 'That cooperation shall continue during the period in which the [British] army is responsible for the maintenance of Peace and Order in Malaya.' This was the period in which Lai Teck promised his cadres that the MPAJA would rise up against the British, and transform Malaya into a socialist republic. Both sides acted in tune with their ulterior motives: SOE for ruling out political concessions at the very beginning, and Lai Teck for signing up to assist in the post-war period when he had – or, at least, told his cadres he had – exactly the opposite intention. Lai Teck, it seems, was playing a long game: maintaining his popularity with the cadres and the Japanese, while keeping open a path back to the Special Branch fold.

Due to communication problems, it proved impossible to put the written agreement into operation for over a year and, for the agents of Operation *Gustavus*, 1944 became a year of dashed hopes and disasters. The submarine rendezvous system by which they had kept in touch with Force 136 HQ collapsed, as it became too dangerous for the submarines to come close enough inshore for contact to be made. With some of the heavy wireless equipment Davis's party had brought in still stranded near the coast, and the rest of it captured by the Japanese, they could not get news of the deal out of the country.[100] Then, in March 1944, the Japanese rolled up the intelligence network formed by Lim Bo Seng and his agents; Lim would die in Batu Gajah Prison following torture.[101] Although it seems that Lai Teck did not betray the whereabouts of the British officers to the Japanese, Ban and Yap believe that he did betray Lim Bo Seng to the Kempeitai. It would, they state, have been typical of him to rid himself of a troublesome opponent while appearing to be acting entirely for the benefit of the Japanese.[102]

Not until February 1945 was wireless contact resumed.[103] By this stage, the tide of the war was running strongly in favour of the Allies, after the profound 'strategic, operational and tactical turnaround' that had taken place from early 1943 to the middle of 1944.[104] The guerrilla forces raised and armed by the Force

136 operation, *Character*, were about to prove their worth in Burma, speeding the British reconquest of Rangoon.[105] This gave SOE – and, one assumes, Mountbatten – a lever to use when arguing with Whitehall for concessions for the MPAJA.[106] Military planners were given a striking demonstration of what could be accomplished by a well-directed guerrilla force; Malaya was next on the list, and thus the guerrilla build-up there needed to begin.[107]

By this time, however, Malayan Country Section was a step ahead. Even before the *Gustavus* operation had achieved wireless contact, Force 136 had operatives with the MPAJA in Malaya who were in contact with its HQ, in the form of Operation *Carpenter* in south Johore, whose agents had infiltrated 'blind' by submarine.[108] Local Chinese recognized its leader, Paddy Martin, who had been a planter in the district before the war, and put the party into contact with the MPAJA; furthermore, the operation had already received at least one drop of arms.[109] Operation *Funnel* in Perak was also underway, with arms and personnel having been dropped in February, in the immediate wake of wireless contact from northern Malaya being, at last, established.[110]

In the middle of April 1945, Davis and Broome, unaware of Lai Teck's alternative plans but in contact with Force 136 headquarters, met again with 'Chang Hong' to lay down the form of the liaison between Force 136 and the guerrillas. This time the agreement (see Appendix B) was only verbal, though it was relayed by radio to Colombo for confirmation. It bound the British to specific sums of money, the provision of a doctor to each MPAJA regiment, and a 'Group Liaison Officer' (GLO) to each regiment and a 'Patrol Liaison Officer' (PLO) to each patrol, who would all be accepted by the MPAJA.[111] Chin Peng adds that, 'Each liaison officer was to be accompanied by a platoon of Gurkhas.' During a break, Lai Teck assured his men that they should not worry about the Gurkhas, for there would only be a platoon (twenty to thirty) of them against a company of guerrillas (approximately 120 men).[112] Force 136 records are less clear about the planned number of Gurkhas, though it seems that fewer platoons were planned for than Chin Peng claims. The Gurkhas are sometimes described as 'guards' for the liaison officers, but it is clear that their prime function was to support – 'stiffen', in the parlance of the operational reports – the guerrillas.[113]

Around 200 Force 136 operatives were infiltrated to the MPAJA between the establishment of wireless contact and the end of the war, along with thousands of weapons.[114] Medical personnel were infiltrated, and all teams also had medical supplies and offered basic care to the guerrillas. Jungle ulcers were so widespread that junior officers took to treating them.[115] The officers felt that 'doctoring' improved and strengthened the bonds between them and the guerrillas.[116] Major S.F. Owen with the patrol *Funnel Green* also noted the difference the medical supplies provided had on the patrol: 'from the time medical kit came in sickness went right down'.[117] He – like other officers – also commented on the value of food drops.[118]

Undoubtedly, Force 136 had a noticeable impact on the operational efficiency of the MPAJA. An active programme of training was undertaken, with one MPAJA patrol beating the local Gurkha group's time for stripping a Bren gun.[119] These patrols were also outfitted. Major Owen was unusual in recording the detail of his drops, which included 380 sets of battledress and 100 pairs of jungle boots for a patrol of about 190 men, but it is fair to assume that most patrols were similarly supplied.[120] All of these examples are drawn from the reports of just one operation – *Funnel* – but similar ones can be found in those of other operations.

Initially it was planned that the MPAJA would be ready to go into action in support of the Allied reinvasion force of Operation *Zipper* in early September 1945. Due to the precipitate surrender of the Japanese, the war ended on 15 August 1945, and the *Zipper* landings were unopposed. However, the indications are that the MPAJA would have been ready for action; indeed, its effectiveness has already been noted in Chapter 2. Jim Hannah, GLO of *Funnel*, was 'convinced that the M.P.A.J.A. would have put up a very good show' and his view was broadly shared by other officers.[121] The official assessment was much the same, stating that although the Japanese had tried to wipe out the MPAJA associated with Operations *Carpenter* and *Funnel*, they had not succeeded. This assessment considered that the 'main problems' would not have been the readiness of the guerrillas, but (given the pressure on Special Duties Squadrons at this time) keeping them supplied with 'food and ammunition'.[122] This requirement for additional food and ammunition again makes it clear that the MPAJA needed Force 136's external assistance to become militarily effective.

Those who took part in Force 136's operations in Malaya will have wanted to cast them in the best possible light, yet the detailed information from the field – like the performance of Owen's Bren gunners – indicates that their positive assessment was a fair one. The precise size of the MPAJA is difficult to assess, for other guerrillas and reserves from the villages came into the camps overseen by Force 136 in the run-up to disbandment in December 1945. Nevertheless, it appears that Force 136 had brought around 4,000 troops to a point where they were battle ready before the war's end.[123] The MPAJA had become a far stronger force than it had been before: fitter, healthier, better armed, better trained, and of more potential help to the Allies, and in the event of an invasion they were capable of effectively harrying the Japanese behind their lines and cutting their lines of communication. In one striking instance, the MPAJA assisted civilians in the rescue of downed American aircrew, who were later evacuated by submarine.[124] The increased strength of the MPAJA is revealed by the evident unwillingness, towards the end of the war, of increasingly depleted Japanese forces to launch open confrontations. In Selangor, for example, the Japanese Army knew where the guerrilla camps were but did not attack them.[125] Indeed, as will be shown in Chapter 5, the MPAJA was strong enough by this stage to take control of territory from other guerrilla groups.

The implicit political bargain

Neither of the agreements between Force 136 and the MPAJA included any political promises about the post-war polity. However, SOE was aware that any guerrillas it

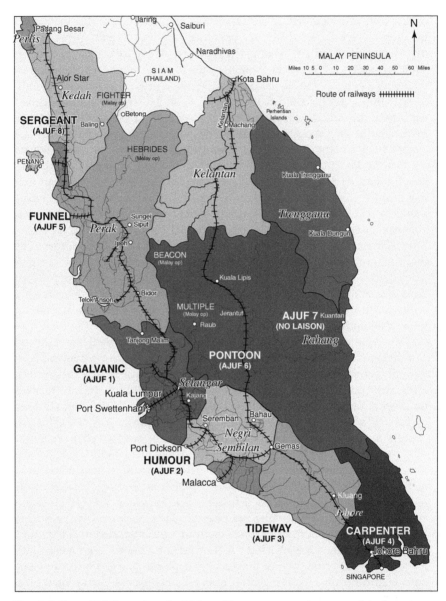

Map 3.1 Force 136 Operations in Malaya. The seven operations named in large type (Sergeant, Funnel, Galvanic, Pontoon, Tideway, Carpenter and Humour) were all with the MPAJA. The others (Fighter, Hebrides, Beacon and Multiple) were infiltrated to work with Malay guerrillas. Beacon is placed further north than its final area of operations, as is Multiple. The MPAJA's 7th Regiment ('AJUF 7') was sent a liaison team in the form of Operation Siphon after the Japanese surrender.

Source: Based on a map in HS 7/165.

worked with might have bigger ambitions than a short-term military alliance, and that there might be attempts to extract political concessions. Certainly, SOE officers in the field were aware that the MPAJA had its own agenda. Force 136 officers commented drily that, somehow, it was always the airdropped containers with cash and arms that the guerrillas could not (allegedly) locate, and they were frequently irritated by the activity of the MPAJA's political organizers, who they perceived as 'agitators' who indoctrinated the foot soldiers and disrupted training.[126] All this caused tensions between the two sides, but there was a tacit acceptance by Force 136 that they could do little to prevent these things from happening. In effect, an unwritten, implicit deal underlay what was openly agreed: SOE accepted that it would have to tolerate behaviour from the MPAJA that it considered undesirable, and the MCP worked quietly away to consolidate its power.

In November 1943, even before the Blantan Agreement had been signed, SOE already understood the value of political promises and concessions to the MPAJA and had begun to move to an official consensus on what form these might take. One result of an SOE meeting with the Colonial Office was the official decision that no one who worked against the Japanese would be penalized for their pre-war political activities. At the same time, SOE was told that awkward issues such as the post-war status of the MCP should be sidestepped, and the most that SOE officers were permitted to convey about political citizenship to the guerrillas was that 'a greater degree of civic equality' was being considered.[127] A few days after this meeting, Alec Peterson, a Force 136 staff officer, wrote to the Colonial Office outlining the political questions to which Force 136 felt answers would be useful 'in the coming months'. These included future political rights for Malayan Chinese and British policy towards 'Chinese Party Organisations'.[128]

However, despite such efforts to extract specific answers from the Colonial Office, the nearest that SOE ever came during the war to obtaining permission to offer the MCP any formal recognition was in August 1944, when Edward Gent, of the Malayan Planning Unit (MPU), wrote a brief memo to Col. Taylor, SOE's Director of Overseas Missions. It stated that officers in the field could tell the guerrillas that it was 'hoped' that a Malayan citizenship would be created after the war, and offered to people who had lived there 'for very many years' and that the British 'intention' was to alter legislation such that 'a society or organisation will not be considered illegal unless declared to be so'.[129] This was extraordinarily vague: what was meant by 'hoped' and 'very many years'? Moreover, it gave the MCP no assurance that the British would not declare any communist organization instantly illegal the minute the war was over. There is no evidence whatsoever on the file that this anodyne official intimation of future hopes was taken any further, nor even of any reply from Taylor to Gent. In any case, if Gent's statement was passed on to the guerrillas, it promised them nothing concrete whatsoever.

Various sources indicate that Force 136 officers going into the field were given clear instructions about the answers they could give when pressed about political issues by the MPAJA. Major Tom Wight, with Operation *Sergeant* in Kedah, stated in his report that he had been told that he 'must not get mixed up in politics', and had strictly obeyed this order.[130] His commanding officer commented that Wight 'did not like the type of Chinese we were working with' (i.e. communists) and was exasperated by his obstinacy, for Wight interpreted his orders to mean that he should not work with men involved in political activity.[131] At the other end of the country, Lloyd Chin Fen, a wireless operator with *Carpenter*, explained in a later interview that Paddy Martin (*Carpenter*'s original leader) had told him that 'he felt a bit sorry for them [the MPAJA] because they did not get what they wanted' in discussions that Martin had had with them. Chin Fen understood Martin, in this respect, to have meant discussions about political concessions.[132]

In the case of Wight, his reluctance to talk politics with the MPAJA came despite the fact that by the middle of 1945, when he was dropped into Malaya, British policy for post-war Malaya had become more definite. Whitehall had clarified the citizenship rights Britain would offer under its Malayan Union plan and had also proposed to rescind the pre-war Societies' Ordinance, which deemed all unregistered organizations illegal. However, Cabinet had not yet approved any of this.[133] What is more, according to an early draft of the British citizenship policy in Malaya, it was stated that it would not 'be possible to make an Order in Council until the Rulers have ceded jurisdiction in their states to His Majesty': in other words, until the Malay sultans agreed to a rewriting of their treaties with the British Crown.[134] Consequently, no concrete promises could be made to any resistance fighters in occupied Malaya until its Malay rulers had agreed to cede such of their remaining powers as would enable a Malayan Union to be formed.

Despite this difficulty, some British officials pushed hard to allow political promises to be made to the MCP, among them Mountbatten and Colin Mackenzie, who wanted Force 136 officers in the field to be able to make future British policy known to the MPAJA. Mountbatten was driven by more than expediency, for he was a man of liberal instincts, and this was no secret from those around him.[135] The Force 136 staff officer Alec Peterson, who had by this stage been seconded to Mountbatten's staff, recorded in his private memoir, 'One thing I was quite certain of was that the European 'empires' ... should not survive after the war and since this was also Mountbatten's conviction we spoke quite freely.'[136] One might argue that Peterson was recalling both his own opinions and Mountbatten's in the light of later events, but Mountbatten's attitude towards the Burma National Army does not conflict with Peterson's view.[137] In Malaya, Mountbatten was also keen to see increased racial equality, with a general push towards a Malayan citizenship.[138]

Whitehall, constrained by various factors, did not share Mountbatten's enthusiasm. On 11 May 1945, he approached the Foreign Secretary directly, asking for Force 136 to be allowed to tell the MPAJA of Britain's plans for the post-war constitution, particularly regarding the future equality of the Chinese.[139] On 7 June the Chiefs of Staff informed him that 'Post-war policy for Malaya has only received provisional approval of Cabinet for planning purposes...no publicity of policy can be made and you should ensure that your clandestine organisations impress upon the resistance movements that any association with them is purely military.'[140] Before anything could be said to the MPAJA, the new policy had to be approved by Cabinet which, in mid-1945, was insulated by distance and preparing for the elections of 5 July. In any case, the new policy still depended upon the assent of the Malay Rulers.

This official position was passed on to Force 136 liaison officers in the field, who were instructed to tell the MPAJA 'that we are not prepared to discuss political issue [sic]. Active cooperation against the Japanese in conformity with Allied Military Authorities will be to their advantage. Further than that liaison officers should not go.'[141] A vague hint of future possible benefit, its type (political or monetary) unspecified, was all that could be offered. This continued to be the situation into August 1945, when Mountbatten, writing again to the Chiefs of Staff, complained that the current interpretation of the directive under which Force 136 was operating in Malaya 'interdicts any discussion of future constitutional policy'. He explained in this memorandum how important it was that the new policy should be revealed.[142] His comments were promptly passed up the line to the Colonial Office.[143] However, Cabinet had still not settled the matter when Japan surrendered on 15 August. On that very day, Tremlett, head of Force 136's Malayan Country Section, wrote tetchily that his agents in the field had 'never been able to assure the AJA [Anti-Japanese Army a.k.a. the MPAJA] or its leaders that they will not be treated as outlaws' due to 'the general policy of the Colonial Office to make no statements'.[144]

Ever politically astute, Mountbatten appears to have realized that those who had helped the British eject the Japanese felt that they had earned some measure of payback.[145] The Chiefs of Staff and the Cabinet did not share his sense of urgency. The MCP, however, most definitely did. Within a week, Lai Teck had released the 'Eight Point Programme', outlining the MCP's plans for Malaya: a democratic government 'with electorate drawn from all races', freedom of speech and so on.[146] In late August, Claude Fenner, the leader of Operation *Humour*, signalled Colombo with details of this manifesto. He seems to have felt that the MCP had stolen a march on the British, in advertising its intentions before the British had broadcast theirs. This resulted in a cipher telegram from Mackenzie to London on 29 August, pushing for permission to announce future intentions as to 'a) status of domiciled Chinese b) attitude to organisations and associations previously considered? [sic] illegal'.[147] A reply came by return, assuring Mackenzie that the wheels were in motion, but adding that the matter was not coming before Cabinet until 4 September: as ever, SOE in Asia was not a high priority in Whitehall.[148] So far as Chin Peng was concerned, following the Japanese surrender the MCP enjoyed only 'tacit recognition' from the British.[149] The history of Force 136 in Malaya (written in March 1946) falls very closely into line with this belief, stating that on 24 September Force 136 officers were, at last, permitted to inform the MPAJA that 'a Society was legal until its members by their behaviour over-stepped the Law'.[150] Finally, the communists knew they would not be 'outlaws' after all. Yet it seems that they were still in ignorance of British plans for citizenship.

Clearly, absence of evidence is not the same as evidence of absence, and it remains impossible to prove that no British officer ever promised the MCP that it would be recognized and that the Chinese would be equal citizens with the Malays. However, if any did so, then they acted contrary to the orders of the Colonial Office, as relayed via the Chiefs of Staff to Mountbatten. Everyone in the chain – Mountbatten, Mackenzie, all the way to men in the field – knew exactly what could not be said, though what might have been implied by actions in the field is another matter. The new citizenship policy was finally announced in the press in the middle of October 1945.[151] The lapsing of the requirement to register an organization does not seem to have been similarly advertised, though it was the policy of the British Military Administration (BMA).

According to Harper, during 1946, Edward Gent, now Governor of Malaya, felt sure that the MCP must have been promised during the occupation that they would not need to register as a political party. Finding no relevant paperwork in Kuala Lumpur, he wrote to London to ask if any existed. The reply he received informed him that Force 136 had been instructed that its officers could give such an assurance, but that it was not known whether they had done so or not.[152] Considering that, at the close of the war, Mackenzie believed his officers were *not* allowed to give such an assurance, Gent's correspondent would appear to have misinterpreted the information on file, and so contributed to the later mistaken assumptions of several historians. Gent must have been incredulous that a policy developed so long before the end of the war had still not been granted official sanction by its end.

For their part, what the leadership of the MCP and MPAJA seem to have believed was what British women believed earlier, and Vietnamese peasants believed later: that if help and assistance were given to the war effort, some form of payback was both deserved and expected.[153] It was this sense of expectation, rather than Britain's betrayal of the explicit wartime promises it had made, that appears to have underlain the breakdown in MCP's post-war relations with the British, as the recollections of Chin Peng appear to confirm. Chin Peng does not accuse the British, as historians including Bayly and Harper have done, of committing themselves to written concessions that they then denied. Rather, he regards the MCP as having received a raw post-war deal, in that that the MCP was seriously unrepresented in the advisory councils of the BMA. The implication in his memoir is that he felt the agreement at Blantan went beyond what was written: 'embedded' in it, he recalls, were 'the seeds of our eventual armed struggle'.[154] But the 'turning point' came with 'brutal crowd control measures' applied during strikes in October 1945, along with the arrest and conviction of the MCP man Soon Kwong. From Chin Peng's viewpoint, any willingness that the MCP had to cooperate with the British was destroyed by these acts of bad faith on the part of the BMA.[155] In other words, an assumed rather than explicit bargain had been broken. That the MPAJA had already deceived the British by developing their 'secret army' during the war does not seem to have influenced his conclusions.

Conclusion

This chapter has examined the factors that brought SOE and the MPAJA to make a forced marriage of convenience in Malaya during the Japanese occupation, and has discussed the terms and nature of that agreement. SOE was searching for local allies, and while it avoided making any explicit political promises, it was nonetheless aware that an implicit undertaking was likely to be assumed by the MCP. The MCP needed arms and food to let it attack the Japanese – and to lay the foundations for the future revolution it expected to have to fight if it was ever to come to power in Malaya – and so its leadership entered into an agreement with Force 136 that included no political concessions. Nonetheless, its senior cadres considered that an implicit bargain had been struck. Neither side was completely open with the other; had they been, it is unlikely that the agreement would ever have been made.

Thus, although the British build-up with the MPAJA began on a purely military footing, it had profound political implications. The evidence indicates that the explicit military promises made by SOE were kept. Though Force 136 was working, as Aldrich states, to control the MPAJA, it did, as he also acknowledges, deliver to it considerable stores of arms.[156] Indeed, additional men were being trained, and they were being armed with newly developed equipment.[157] Mountbatten, spurred by his experiences in Burma, wanted to make as much use as possible of these guerrillas 'to facilitate and accelerate the advance of my forces in Malaya', and the planning committee of the Chiefs of Staff broadly agreed with him.[158] There were tensions within the chain of command, with Mountbatten working to bring his superiors round to his own point of view.

If no explicit promises were broken, it appeared to the MCP that the British denied that any implicit bargain had been struck or assumed. The guerrillas had hoped for concrete indications of British gratitude in the form of a clear share in forming the post-war polity, but this was not forthcoming. There had, in fact, been bad faith on both sides: the British had done everything they could to dodge the need to make political concessions, and the MCP had used the British to help them build up their own guerrilla army.

The British, keen to obtain intelligence and armed assistance in the fight against the Japanese, had armed guerrillas with an avowed anti-imperialist platform. They were, however, themselves not united: men like Mackenzie were willing to downplay the degree of communist control of the MPAJA to persuade those up the line to support his plans; Mountbatten was willing to take allies where he could find them if it would reduce military casualties in the short term; and the Chiefs of Staff wanted to see the MPAJA 'controlled' if it was to be used at all. In the end, Mackenzie and Mountbatten got their way and the MPAJA was, by mid-August 1945, well armed and prepared for battle. As Ban and Yap argue, the period of its alliance with Force 136 can be seen as a 'rehearsal', not for a war against the Japanese but against the British.[159] The cadres who took to the jungles in 1948 were able to make use of training they had received from the British, and arms they had received from the British, to take their war to the British.

Though Force 136 concealed the politics of the MPAJA from those further up the military hierarchy, it scrupulously fulfilled its written promises to the guerrillas. As for parts of the implicit bargain – citizenship rights for the Chinese, the MCP being permitted to operate in the open – they were both offered by the colonial administration in the last few months of 1945.[160] However, with the collapse of the Malayan Union and the shift to the Federation of Malaya, the citizenship rules were tightened considerably.[161] The MCP felt excluded from the political process, though it continued to operate openly (it was not banned until after the declaration of the State of Emergency).[162] The MPAJA's wartime struggle earned it the sympathy of the rural Chinese, and the much greater strength that came from its deal with Force 136 almost certainly increased its stock among them. The Force's involvement also gave credibility to the MCP's argument that it deserved a political voice. The MCP was stronger for the material input of Force 136, for its cadres had received military training, and it had banked a share of the disbandment bonus awarded to its fighters.[163] It had also, as will be shown, obtained a considerable arsenal of up-to-date weaponry.

This chapter has discussed the relationship between Force 136 and the MPAJA. What has not been examined, however, are the dealings of these two bodies with the other guerrilla organizations that operated in Malaya during the Japanese occupation. Yet these interactions – with both Malay guerrillas and those allied to the Guomindang – are deeply revealing, particularly as regards British concerns about Malaya's ethnic mix and the desire of the MCP to exert its hegemony over the Malayan interior. These will be the focus of the following two chapters.

Chapter 4

'EXPECT TO MEET YOU SHORTLY': FORCE 136 AND THE MALAY RESISTANCE[1]

In mid-July 1945, Yeop Mahidin, an assistant district officer in the eastern state of Pahang, hastily signed off a letter he was writing with the disconcerting words, 'Have to close now owing to presence of hostile persons.'[2] The letter was taken by courier into the jungle to its recipient, a Force 136 officer who understood the risks Yeop was running and who assured him in a later communication, 'If you and your family ever think it advisable to take a holiday in the country we are ready at any time to welcome you!'[3] The two men barely met until after the Japanese surrender, yet they placed absolute trust in each other and worked energetically towards a shared aim. Their work together, conducted through letters passed by couriers, recruited hundreds of young Malay men into an anti-Japanese guerrilla force.

This chapter will examine the activities of the Malay resistance, which existed independently of the communist guerrillas, and test the contention made by M.R.D. Foot that 'There is some sound evidence to suggest that, had they ever been given the chance, there were plenty of Malays who would gladly have joined in the struggle against their Japanese oppressors.'[4] Foot's comment implies that the Malays were never 'given the chance' to resist. Yet, as Yeop's and other stories will show, there were indeed Malays who willingly joined the anti-Japanese resistance, although their motives for working with the British were perhaps more subtle than they might initially appear. Recovering this hidden history allows us to contest and revise what Foot describes as 'the usual current doctrine' of a communist-dominated resistance, a doctrine that has remained largely unchallenged, certainly in the English-language literature, for seventy years.[5] Some historical accounts imply that there was never a Malay resistance by not mentioning the fact that one existed. Other accounts directly deny its existence. Yet this resistance story acts as a counterweight to narratives which stress the mobilization of the Malays by the Japanese, illustrating that, in some localities at least and from comparatively early in the occupation, there were Malays ready to act against their new rulers. The Malay anti-Japanese resistance had important legacies, both in the late colonial period and the political life of independent Malaysia, for it brought to the fore young elite Malays who would emerge as leaders of their community. It was also revealing of the relationship between politically active Malays and the communists.

The story in which they figure has the power to influence our perceptions of the occupation, of the Emergency and of Malaysia itself.

Currently, the story of Malayan armed resistance is dominated by the Malayan People's Anti-Japanese Army (MPAJA), and overshadowed by Chin Peng's influential memoir. It is perhaps inevitable that this should be the case: the MPAJA was, without any doubt, far larger than the Malay guerrilla forces. The MPAJA was also later reborn as the Malayan National Liberation Army, the communist insurgent army of the Malayan Emergency. With this dramatic second act to consider, it is little wonder that the wartime activities of Malay groups such as Wataniah fell into the shadows, outshone by the dominant narrative. The Malay elite was to some degree complicit in this disappearing act: Abu Talib Ahmed argues for what he terms 'bio-data blackout syndrome', whereby individuals contributing to the Malaysian Who's Who in the decade after independence downplayed their involvement with the Japanese and, to a lesser extent, the British during the occupation. In effect, both imperial 'brands' – the Japanese one more so than the British – had come to be seen as toxic. Abu Talib contends that this was because 'both courses of action only served the interests of either Britain or Japan', with those supporting the British 'merely fighting for the colonial state'.[6] To an extent Anthony Stockwell concurs with this, noting that in the few years immediately after the war, when Malay confidence in the British hit a nadir, association with the British, whatever the motives that underlay it, 'could be more than an embarrassment – it could be a political liability'.[7]

Chin Peng also had a hand in the shelving of this resistance story. He must have known of the existence of independent Malay guerrilla groups, but does not mention them in his ghost-written memoir, nor did their existence crop up in the round table with academics that resulted in *Dialogues with Chin Peng*.[8] He either decided that they had been irrelevant, or that it was in his interests to make it appear so. In this, he was merely following the lead set by numerous authors, both academic and popular, writing since the 1950s, who either ignore the Malay resistance entirely or discuss it only fleetingly. Harry Miller's book of 1954 entirely omits the Malay resistance, despite including a chapter about the Japanese occupation; much the same can be said of Gene Z. Hanrahan's account of 1971.[9] In an article in 2007, Hew Strachan describes the Malayan Communist Party (MCP), which sponsored the MPAJA, as '*the* agent of anti-Japanese resistance' [my italics] as if it had been the only one.[10] Thomas Mockaitis goes so far as to describe the MPAJA 'the *only* indigenous resistance' [my italics].[11]

Here and there the Malay resistance exists as a shadowy backdrop to the events that dominate the stage, such as the formation of the United Malays National Organisation (UMNO).[12] Some of the more recent works do outline the existence of armed Malay forces, but almost nowhere do they feature for more than, at most, a few pages.[13] However, even here there is confusion. *Forgotten Armies* describes the group named Wataniah as 'a cell of Malay fighters', which understates both its scope and its intent, and Cheah Boon Kheng argues that British mistrust of the Malays was such that it was not until 'the closing stages of the war' that the British became involved with the Malay resistance – when, as we shall see, the British had been at least considering creating a Malay resistance from late 1942 or early 1943, and launched their first Malay operation in the same month as they launched their second to the MPAJA.[14] The literature covering this period gives the impression that a significant majority of the Malay community was not interested in opposing the Japanese in any forceful way.[15]

The main exception to the near-oblivion into which the Malay resistance has faded is the work of the Malaysian academic Wan Hashim, who in 1994 was responsible for the publication of the diary of Lt. Col. Douglas Richardson, who led the Force 136 operation *Beacon*, which linked up with Wataniah in Pahang.[16] Furthermore, in 1993 he had produced a narrative account of the Malay resistance based on oral sources, drawing upon the experiences of both the Malay guerrillas and members of Force 136.[17] His work indicates that the Malay resistance was broadly based and that guerrilla recruits came from all strata of Malay society, from the elite via the middle classes to rural paddy-planters. However, only a few copies of this work were produced in English and their circulation was extremely limited. Malay-speaking academics, however, sometimes reference this book.[18]

As with any post-hoc account, one must handle the words of Wan Hashim's interviewees with care, and the same caveat obviously applies to other interviews and the available body of memoirs. However, the availability of Richardson's diary and the gradual opening of the HS series in the British National Archives enable us to read later material against contemporary records. In addition, there is a mass of material in the papers of Mubin Sheppard, the administrator and scholar, at the Malaysian National Archives.[19] Some of this material was gathered for, and includes drafts of, a detailed (but unpublished) book about the Malay operations written by Derek Headly who lead Force 136's Operation *Multiple*. These papers also contain some items dating to just after the war, or which clearly reference immediately post-war sources.

Understandably perhaps, the small size of the Malay armed groups which eventually came under the wing of Force 136 – a total of around 400 armed men (as opposed to around 4,500 raised by the MPAJA) – has made them easy to discount as irrelevant in the English-language scholarship on Malaya during World War II. However, it is important to recognize that they nevertheless formed the main – and practically the only – conduit of contact between the British and the Malay population during the occupation.[20] A proper study of the interactions of Force 136 with Malay resistance fighters thus allows us better to understand the attitudes of these groups towards each other and to further illuminate the post-war relationships between the British authorities and Malay leaders.

This chapter will therefore examine the context in which Malays opted to associate with British-sponsored armed resistance, reviewing the manner in which the Malay community's relationship with the Japanese shifted over the first half of the occupation. It will then examine the motivations behind the formation of the Malay resistance – as expressed by those involved – before discussing the activities of the resistance and its relationship with Force 136 and the MPAJA. Finally, the long-term legacies of Malay resistance will be assessed, with some discussion focusing on what clues these wartime relationships between Malay guerrillas, Force 136 and the MPAJA give us as to the pattern of future events after the war.

The context of the Malay resistance

As will be shown, at the beginning of the Japanese occupation the majority of the Malay population was, broadly speaking, willing to cooperate with the new rulers. However, as the occupation progressed, a change in attitude towards the Japanese penetrated large sectors of Malay society, particularly following the cession of four Malay-majority states to Thailand in 1943. Force 136 exploited this, particularly via contacts with former allies, and developed a small Malay resistance which it used both as an anti-Japanese force in Malay-majority areas of the country, and as a counterweight to the power of the MCP.

What Foot terms 'the usual current narrative' has tended to stress not Malay resistance to the Japanese, but the existence of a Malay 'fifth column', consisting largely of the members of the radical Malay nationalist organization, the Kesatuan Melayu Muda (KMM), whose leader, Ibrahim Yaacob, had contact with Japanese intelligence prior to the invasion.[21] This narrative, reflected clearly in the memoir of the KMM's vice-president, Mustapha Hussain, is essentially teleological: the KMM was anti-colonial, Malaya attained independence within two decades, the KMM helped to blaze the trail, and so it deserves investigation.[22] This 'current narrative', then, largely neglects those Malays who resisted the Japanese invasion, and from whose surviving ranks many Malay guerrillas would later be drawn.

Indeed, almost the only Malays who are mentioned as resisting the advancing Japanese are the men of the Malay Regiment. The story of one of their number, Lt. Adnan Saidi, killed by the Japanese after the fighting for Pasir Panjang Ridge in Singapore, has become a Malaysian legend. The Malay Regiment was formed in 1935 after the success of a trial unit had proven wrong those Europeans who were convinced – in line with the martial races theory – that Malays would make poor soldiers. Recruited from all over the country, and always heavily oversubscribed, the regiment was from 1940 increased from one to two battalions (totalling 1,255 men by 1 December 1941).[23] The British laid down that the regiment would only be deployed for the defence of Malaya.[24] It took huge casualties during the final defence of Singapore: by the surrender, between 5 and 10 per cent of the regiment's fighting men had been killed.[25] The only other full-time Malay troops were the 1,300 men of the Johore Military Forces (JMF), the Sultan of Johore's personal army.[26]

For many Malays, especially those from rural areas, the JMF and the Malay Regiment offered social mobility, prestige, steady employment and regular meals. Contemporary records show that new recruits to the Malay Regiment gained weight and height within a year of joining.[27] The motives of those Malays who joined the various volunteer forces raised by the colonizing power are harder to dissect. Bayly and Harper contend that 'at least some' joined for the sake of the diversions offered at the clubhouse, feeling that there was a Boy Scout air about the whole enterprise, at least in peacetime.[28] However, recruits cannot have failed to notice the reality of volunteer service, for they were trained for war with rifles, howitzers and heavy machineguns.[29] Whatever their motives, around 6,000 Malays belonged to the various Volunteer units by the outbreak of the Pacific War; an unknown number served with the Local Defence Corps (LDC).[30] Altogether, when the Japanese landed, there were over 8,500 Malays under arms (6,000 Volunteers, 1,225 in the Malay Regiment and 1,300 in the JMF) – more men than would be disbanded from the MPAJA at the end of 1945. Given the size of the Malay population, this was not a huge number, but it provided the bedrock of later guerrilla recruitment.

The desertion or willing disbandment of considerable numbers of Malays during the retreat is sometimes seen as being due to a lack of willingness to continue to back the British.[31] This was no doubt a factor for some, but for others it was rooted in a reluctance to continue fighting a rear-guard action when their families had been left behind Japanese lines. For example, the wives and children of the Malay Regiment's troops were brought to Singapore in January 1942, and the regiment remained cohesive and determined until it was overwhelmed.[32] The failure to evacuate families and the consequent impact on the soldiers was noted at the time. Of the Malay jungle unit trained in the north, it was said that they 'were really good in action', and would have done better yet had their families been evacuated.[33]

Disbandment came as a bitter blow to some of the Malays involved in the fighting. Yeop Mahidin, then an assistant district officer in Kuala Lipis, was an officer in the LDC. Like most other Malays who were under arms, when offered the opportunity to demobilize, he opted to return home – though he was given some weapons to bury to make use of if he could.[34] These men, who had fought on the same side as the colonial state would later, as might have been expected, prove willing to resist the Japanese.

However, at the outbreak of the Japanese war, most Malays were not involved in any military activity. The Malay population was also much less politically mobilized than the people of, say, India, with little articulation of anti-colonial sentiment or Malay nationalist impulse – the exception being the relatively recently formed KMM.[35] While Anthony Milner has argued that what he terms the '*ancien régime* of the Malay world' was threatened by liberal European ideals and critiqued from within by Malay thinkers who applied these ideals from the first half of the nineteenth century, even into the 1930s the bulk of the Malay masses, the *rakyat*, gave their first loyalty to their state and their sultan.[36] The Malay rulers encouraged this loyalty to bolster their own power, and it was so significant and strong that it had a word of its own: *kenegarian*.[37] The emergence of the idea of a Malay nation was slowed by a combination of Malayan history (the Malay states of the peninsula had never formed a single polity) and the nature of British governance (which varied from state to state, and relied upon indirect rule).[38] The idea of the *bangsa*, the Malay nation, had been born only in the 1920s, in the writings of the journalist Eunos Abdullah, and the concept of 'Malayan' was only in embryonic form.[39] As is shown by the writing of Mustapha Hussain of the KMM, before the Japanese invasion Malay nationalism was by no means a mass movement.[40]

Abu Talib Ahmad argues that though some rural Malays, influenced by Japanese propaganda and hoping for cheap consumer goods, were quite positive about the Japanese takeover, most were simply stunned.[41] Yet despite widespread indifference and the manner in which the majority of Malays in the civil service (Yeop Mahidin included) returned to their posts under the Japanese, and despite the efforts of the KMM and the Japanese to advertise the idea of what they termed the Greater East Asia Co-Prosperity Sphere, within a few years it appears that much, perhaps most, of the Malay population was disenchanted with the new order – some of the KMM included. This evidence is admittedly localized, but where it exists – for Upper Perak, for Pahang, for Kelantan – it is, as will be shown, entirely convincing.

This disenchantment and alienation resulted from several factors, of which the collapse of the economy, Japanese brutality and cession of four of the Malay states to Thailand by the Japanese were the most critical. The economic decline was dramatic, and led to hunger and deprivation.[42] The collapse of the rice import trade did not benefit local Malay rice-producers, for the Japanese requisitioned their surplus without adequate compensation. Consequently, Malay farmers grew less rice rather than more, since, as they reported to one Force 136 officer, 'the Japs take it anyway'.[43] This, coupled with the poor maintenance of irrigation systems and recruitment of men for forced labour, saw the Malayan rice harvest drop by almost a third during the occupation.[44] The collapse of the harvest, coupled with the reduction in imports – especially acute from 1944 onwards – forced reliance on other crops. Some nicknamed this period of deprivation the 'Tapioca Age' after the deeply unpopular root crop that was eaten instead of rice.[45] Malaria control also declined and malnutrition became widespread, leading to a significant increase in the death rate during the occupation. Deaths in the Malay states rose from 92,000 in 1940 to 146,000 in 1944, the last full year of the occupation.[46] Hunger was coupled with alienation, for Japanese policy allowed non-Malays to occupy land in Malay Reservations, blocks set aside for occupation by future generations of Malay farmers. Malay officials rose up almost as one to object to this change and Malay agriculturalists felt that their security was threatened.[47]

While the hunger brought by the Japanese took time to become established, the brutality they introduced arrived immediately and ran the full gamut from slapping and looting to rape and murder. The argument has long been put forward that the methods used within the Japanese Army caused troops to consider brutality as acceptable not only towards the enemy but also towards civilians.[48] Yuki Tanaka concurs with this, arguing that brutal behaviour flowed down the pyramidal structure of the army, meaning that many of the troops had no compunction in visiting it further down the hierarchy, upon non-Japanese civilians.[49] At its most extreme, this resulted in massacres. Although Malaya's Chinese bore the brunt, there were nonetheless massacres of Malays, perhaps the best known being that of around ninety men of the Malay Regiment at Bedok in Singapore.[50] During the invasion itself, fear of rape was both widespread and justified, and village women concealed themselves under houses.[51]

Table 4.1 Population Distribution in Malaya, 1941

State	Malay	Chinese	Indians and Others	Malays as % of Population	Total Population
Kedah	341,294	108,445	75,719	65	525,458
Kelantan	369,256	23,363	15,362	90	407,981
Trengganu	186,580	16,956	2,207	91	205,743
Perlis	46,441	8,227	3,182	80	57,850
Sub-total	943,571	156,991	96,470	79	1,197,032
All States of British Malaya	2,277,352	2,377,990	853,389	41	5,508,731
Malaya less states ceded to Thailand	1,333,781	2,220,999	756,919	31	4,311,699

Source: The raw data for this table are drawn from Kratoska, *The Japanese Occupation of Malaya*, p. 19, using figures from the estimated census of 1941; any errors of calculation are my own. Slightly different figures, based on Japanese sources, are used by Cheah (*Red Star over Malaya*, p. 28), but the result is much the same.

The Japanese further alienated their new subjects by insisting upon behaviour that conflicted with Malay beliefs. They insisted that people bow towards the Japanese imperial palace, a practice offensive to many Muslims.[52] A refusal to bow often resulted in a slap to the face, inimical to Malay manners and deeply resented. Some Malays were turned to resistance by violence inflicted upon them as the result of the refusal to comply with orders they considered unethical. Yeop Mahidin, the assistant district officer, felt he had no alternative but to stay at his post. To begin with, the Japanese seemed reasonable, but when he refused orders to procure a woman for a Japanese colonel, he found himself arrested, beaten and tied to a flagpole for three days, and his attitude to the Japanese was transformed to opposition.[53] Refusal to join various Japanese forces such as the Butai (in this context, border police) led to reprisals against men's families and kampongs. Press-ganging into a security unit was a form of forced labour and reduced the pool of young men available for both rice production and guerrilla recruitment. Throughout the occupation, personal rights were violated and violence was normalized. The response of many in the population was defiance. Even Butai members defied the Japanese: when sent ahead to engage guerrillas they would fire into the air, 'and then return to their officers reporting a victory'.[54]

The researcher Wan Hashim's sources in Upper Perak stated that their alienation from the Japanese was rooted in resentment of the 'Tapioca Age', unhappiness about Japanese brutality and the lack of consumer goods.[55] It seems that to these Malays, the cession of four Malay states (Perlis, Kedah, Kelantan and Trengganu) to Thailand was a lesser concern. For politically conscious Malays, however, this gift from the Japanese to Thailand for that country's cooperation in 1941 was a crucial act. From 1899, Thailand incorporated those of its tributary states not dominated by the British into the Thai administrative system, including the Malay-majority kingdom of Patani.[56] Under the nationalist government of the late 1930s, Thailand adopted a policy of forced assimilation of minorities. As a consequence, thousands of Malays left the area for Malaya and Saudi Arabia, spreading the word of events in Thailand through all levels of Malay society.[57]

All of the four states ceded to Thailand were Malay-majority states, and without them, the Malays in the rump of former British Malaya were even more outnumbered than they had been before. The Japanese cannot have reasonably expected that the Malays would meekly accept this abrupt sundering of their country. Mustapha Hussain of the KMM, who had once tentatively supported them and who had begun to lose faith in early 1942, deeply resented this move.[58] Although the Thai administrators were themselves reasonable, and the sultans retained nominal authority, the Kempeitai remained active in the four states, and some of the Thai laws promulgated there disadvantaged local Malays.[59] To the Malays, this must have looked like two sets of colonizers, rather than just one as before.

These three factors – economic decline, brutality and the cession to Thailand – were not the only ones leading to disillusionment in the Malay population. Civil servants found the Japanese more authoritarian than the British had been.[60] At least some of them discovered that formerly routine tasks that had been their responsibility and which involved an element of authority – such as controlling land offices and writing reports – ceased to be asked of them. One Malay district officer observed that the burden of his job now involved persuading the population to grow more food and generally obey the Japanese.[61] Towards the end of the war, Yeop Mahidin caustically noted that the main function of Japanese civil officers was 'spying on … Government Servants' and 'Bossing the District Officers'.[62] Malays of all social classes thus had reason to regard the Japanese with disfavour as the war moved into its final year.

Moreover, resistance began to appear to be a more realistic option. All-India Radio was beamed into Malaya and, as described in Chapter 2, the Special Operations Executive (SOE) member Tengku Mahmood Mahyideen, broadcast propaganda as 'Raja Mopeng'.[63] There were a few middle-class Malays who retained 'unsealed' radios and, from news broadcasts out of India, they had a clear idea of how the war was going and understood that the Japanese were losing.[64] However, Malay support for Force 136 should not be seen as outright support for Britain as a colonial power. Abdul Razak Hussein, one of Yeop Mahidin's lieutenants, later claimed that when the Pahang Malays saw the British leave in 1942, 'we did not want them back'.[65] He was explicit that it was Japanese brutality and the cession of the four states to Thailand that turned him against the Japanese.[66] The British were to be preferred as rulers, though Abdul Razak, at least, did not want them back as a permanent fixture.

Independent Malay resistance to the Japanese

When current scholarship addresses Malay resistance to the Japanese, the focus is entirely on the Malay guerrillas.[67] Yet Malay resistance included not only guerrilla activity but also sabotage and infiltration of the civil service. Many of those involved in these latter activities were from the colonial intermediary class which had prospered under the British. There were those, such as Mahmood Mahyideen, who wished to bring the Malay-majority states of Thailand back into British Malaya. Others appear to have been moved by a desire for Malayan independence.[68] These last two groups both considered their a work as means of gathering bargaining chips for use in post-war political negotiations.

The Malay population was, in general, not well equipped for armed resistance. When the Japanese invaded, local Chinese – some embittered by the Second Sino-Japanese War, others seeking profit – gleaned the battlefields for weapons and equipment, and when unemployment hit the estates and mines where they worked, they moved to farm on the jungle fringe.[69] In contrast, rural Malays mostly stayed rooted in their villages, making them an easier population for the Japanese to control. Many Malays lost the arms they possessed before war, such as shotguns used to scare elephants and wild pig from their fields, because the colonial licence stubs for their weapons remained in the local police stations, making it easy for the Japanese to disarm them.[70] Even so, a few Malays sought from the beginning to oppose the Japanese. In *The Malay Regiment*, a short work written for the Department of Public Relations immediately after the war, the civil servant Mervyn (later Mubin) Sheppard described the resistance activities of some of the regiment's survivors early in the Japanese occupation. For example, Lt. Khalid bin Hashim, who had fought at in the Malay Regiment's last stand at Pasir Panjang on Singapore Island, initially worked as a fisherman, hoping to contact an Allied submarine.[71] Thwarted by Japanese rules obliging him to stay inshore, he instead arranged access to guns and ammunition for organized anti-Japanese activity should the British invade, and allocated these to members of a Malay group he had recruited. He and his group also committed acts of arson, which resulted in Japanese reprisals. It was these that convinced Khalid to stop.[72]

Even as Khalid was finding a safer course, Yeop Mahidin in Pahang was exploring the means of resistance available to a man in his position. His experience tied to the flagpole had convinced him to use the 'mean trick' of appearing to collaborate while working towards his own ends. He began by contacting the MPAJA, who told him that Malays were prominent in fighting units.[73] After a few months of active assistance, he overheard a conversation that convinced him that the MPAJA had plans to take over the country and so he 'more or less withdrew'. He then decided to focus on his own organization – the one that became Wataniah ('Homeland').[74]

The available sources for the early part of Wataniah's existence consist entirely of oral testimony. However, it is important to note that the claims made expand upon, and do not contradict, what was recorded immediately after the end of the war by Force 136's Douglas Richardson. According to Yeop, he sought the Sultan of Pahang's permission for the formation of a resistance body as early as 1942.[75] During 1943, Yeop gathered a nucleus of officers while working in Bentong and then, when transferred to Raub, he recruited around 250 Malays and established a jungle training camp. Wataniah was also responsible – the information for the timing is unclear – for raids against the Japanese and the Indian National Army using not only the arms Yeop had buried earlier, but also salvaged and raided arms and grenades.[76] Prior to the arrival of Force 136, Yeop was hampered by arms shortages and could to do little more than harass the Japanese and was certainly in no position to launch a full-scale guerrilla war. Wataniah was so closely kept a secret that right up until the end of the occupation, the Japanese blamed Yeop's raids on the MPAJA.[77] This was also a line of thinking that Yeop, as an employee of the Japanese, would have been able to encourage.

Yeop Mahidin could not have known it, but his organization bore direct parallels to the Noyautage de l'Administration Publique, an arm of the French Resistance. This arm aimed to win sympathizers throughout the public services, so that permits and papers could be obtained, policemen persuaded to look the other way and civil servants selected who would lead their departments after liberation.[78] Yeop had agents in the Posts and Telegraphs Department in Raub, ready to act should the British invade.[79] A number of Yeop Mahidin's lieutenants were also civil servants (such as Abdul Razak). In addition, in 1944 the Japanese sponsored the formation of a Malay Association in Pahang, with Yeop Mahidin as the president of the Raub section.[80] He used this 'to call members of the association to RAUB and at a series of meetings appointed [Wataniah] agents in various towns'.[81] By the time Richardson of Operation *Beacon* arrived in the area, Wataniah had sufficient penetration and support among civil servants and administrators for Yeop to be the first port of call for anyone seeking Malays sympathetic to the anti-Japanese cause. Richardson dispatched his agent Roslan bin Johar, a local man, to approach a number of leading Malays in the outlying villages, seeking a high-level contact, and a school inspector visited Yeop on Roslan's behalf.[82]

In sum, the evidence suggests that in some areas of Malaya at least, there was considerable sympathy among the Malay community for anti-Japanese activity. These resistance networks were often unarmed, but alert to the possibility of an expansion in their activities.

Force 136 and the Malays: motivations

Force 136 chose to encourage Malay resistance for a combination of short-term military gains and long-term political management. In the short-term, the British were eager to lay their hands on good intelligence, for the purposes of both reinvasion and post-invasion planning.[83] At the time of the infiltration of *Oatmeal* (the first Malay operation), John Davis's party in Perak (*Gustavus*) was still out of contact, and Operation *Carpenter*, in Johore to the south, had barely come up on the air.[84] The British were also alert to the long-term consequences of backing only the MPAJA. Though it was never openly stated, it is highly likely that there was a desire within Force 136 to have a counterweight to the communists – both as guerrillas, and in whatever negotiations might take place in the post-war period. As we saw in Chapter 3, Force 136's senior staff was well aware of communist involvement in the MPAJA, but chose to downplay this.[85] What was clearly articulated, however, was a feeling – recorded by Colin Mackenzie, Force 136's head – that the Malays should be given 'the greatest possible share' in the victory over the Japanese, so that they would not be on the back foot in relation to the Chinese when the post-war settlement was negotiated.[86]

Mirroring him were Malays who saw their involvement in an armed, British-backed force as a way of advancing their own claims for self-government and eventual independence.[87] Once again, war provided a chance to strike political bargains. Wartime Malay 'loyalty' to the British became a Malay asset in the independence struggle: having proved themselves amenable to wholeheartedly assisting the British, sections of the Malay elite could make constitutional demands when their community was later relied upon to provide many of the police and troops used against the communists during the Emergency.[88] In the post-war era, members of the British administration in Malaya sometimes found themselves working with men who had cut their political teeth in the anti-Japanese resistance. For example, Yeop Mahidin became the head of the Home Guard, an armed force used to relieve the police of static guard duties during the Emergency.[89]

Force 136's dealings with Malays were always going to be more difficult than with the MPAJA, for the Force had no obvious points of contact. Nevertheless, the proposed operations were considered justified in both military and political terms. Initially, Malay resistance was imagined in terms of the formation of 'a useful intelligence organisation'.[90] Reports about the fight put up by the Malay Regiment at Pasir Panjang had not yet become generally known and most British soldiers and officials still did not see Malays as capable of being transformed into competent fighters. However, by the time Force 136 produced its operational plans, Malay operations had been designed along the same lines as those to the MPAJA, and there were to be guerrillas as well as intelligence agents.[91] The main objective of this guerrilla force would be to harass the Japanese and cut their lines of communication, once the British reoccupation force came ashore.[92]

Within Force 136, a number of senior officers gave strong support to Malay operations, including Dennis Ambler, an escaped Volunteer.[93] He and Mackenzie were supported in their efforts by the broadcaster Tengku Mahmood Mahyideen. The Tengku had been a captain in the Kelantan Volunteers, and escaped via Oriental Mission's Padang route. He was the second son of the last Sultan of Patani and, as outlined in Chapter 2, he was seeking to increase his post-war leverage over the future of the Malays in Thailand.[94] During the war he wrote a long minute outlining some of his aims, which recommended that, to increase the sympathy of the Malays for the idea of 'Malaya', the power of the Malay states should be reduced, with the sultans relegated from local rulers to representatives in an upper house. To further this forging of a nation, he wished to see a Malayan citizenship granted to those – Indians and Chinese included – who could speak fluent Malay and were already British subjects.[95] The Tengku was clearly motivated by long-term political ambitions, wishing to see the Malay states of southern Thailand incorporated into a unified Malaya.

Force 136 and the Malays: joint operations

Force 136's planning for Malay operations began in late 1942 or early 1943. The first attempt to launch a Malay operation was in August 1944, and the first infiltration

(Operation *Oatmeal*) was accomplished at the very end of the October of that year – shortly after Operation *Carpenter* went in blind with the aim of contacting the MPAJA in Johore.[96] Operation *Oatmeal* infiltrated successfully by flying boat, amongst the Perhentian Islands off Malaya's northeast coast, but it was betrayed within days to the Japanese. The quick thinking and courage of the all-Malay party, coupled with information from a clandestine party in Thailand, informed Force 136 that *Oatmeal* was communicating under duress.[97]

The betrayal of Operation *Oatmeal* led Force 136 to cancel further infiltrations, for there was now no way into Malaya from the west or northeast, for the routes used by the *Gustavus* and *Oatmeal* operations were now compromised. Nevertheless, the Force remained keen to proceed with Malay operations. Two months later, however, in December 1944, the Royal Air Force (RAF) made long-range Liberators available to the Force.[98] The rest of the Malay operations – *Hebrides* (the first, landing blind in Perak on 16 December 1944), *Beacon*, *Fighter* and *Multiple* – were all infiltrated in this way.[99] Though Force 136 could not have known it at the end of 1944, the betrayal of *Oatmeal* was the exception. All the other operations Force 136 mounted were well supported by the Malay populations to whom they were dispatched: they were kept secret and provided with food and recruits. With the exception of *Multiple*, they all armed and trained Malay guerrilla units: Wataniah with *Beacon* and the Askar Melayu Setia (Loyal Malay Soldiers: AMS) and Anak AMS (Child of the AMS) with *Hebrides* and *Fighter* respectively.

Although the Japanese became aware of the presence of Allied agents working with Malays, this was not necessarily because of the work of local spies or informers. Excited rumour was a major factor.[100] Other factors also played a role: Geoffrey Hasler, in Kedah, noted that planes supplying several operations – three with Force 136 and another with the Inter-Services Liaison Department (ISLD: MI6) – all approached their dropping zones along the same route, which was observed by the Japanese. The Japanese then increased their patrols in the vicinity of these drops and made endless enquiries of the local people, who, thoroughly frightened, took to the jungle.[101] Almost anything could offer clues: in the straitened circumstances of Japanese-occupied Malaya, even a new sarong was enough to raise the eyebrows of the curious.[102] The suspicions of Japanese troops in the *Hebrides* area were alerted when they noticed the disappearances of young men from the local kampongs, and confirmed when they discovered that a length of parachute cord had been tied to a hoe belonging to a man in a road working gang.[103]

However, Japanese efforts to glean additional information from local Malay communities were rarely successful. Lt. Col. Dobrée, who led *Hebrides*, later claimed that the Japanese tried to infiltrate informers into his camp. These men would, on arrival, report all the downriver news to Dobrée and leave with whatever propaganda 'we thought best calculated to spread alarm and despondency amongst them [the Japanese]'.[104] Major Hasler of *Fighter* was similarly untroubled by informers. He found himself able to move freely through much of Kedah, and commented that he 'could have been "sold" to the Japs time and time again'. Yet only twice, and then indirectly, did information reach the Japanese about him.[105] The Japanese could not even rely on the Malay police. In fact, Richardson, leader of Operation *Beacon*, saw the police as a source of recruits to his cause rather than a source of danger.[106] Yeop Mahidin nonetheless felt it unwise to drop basic security precautions, and chastised Richardson for giving arms to a man whose bona fides he had not adequately checked.[107]

Aside from protecting the operations from the attentions of the Japanese, rural Malays in Perak, Kedah and Pahang provided much active assistance to Force 136. The first and most obvious requirement was food. Local people planted extra food to support the men of Operation *Hebrides*, and they also received assistance from a most extraordinary quarter.[108] A Chinese convert to Islam known as Mandor Salleh had been contracted by the Japanese to cut a road trace from Ulu Perak to Batu Melintang in Kelantan, with a Japanese engineer to check the work and three elephants to do the heavy lifting. The engineer only rarely checked on Salleh, and never on a Friday. Consequently, on Fridays Salleh used the elephants to bring in food supplies to the guerrilla camp. This convenient system endured until the engineer paid an unexpected visit and found the elephants missing.[109] Whenever the Japanese were alerted to the presence of clandestine forces, the supply of food inevitably became more complicated. When villagers in Kedah fled from the Japanese, Hasler's party found that their food supplies were temporarily cut off.[110]

Once food supplies were established, the next requirement was for recruits. Hasler complained not about the lack of recruits but about the shortage of the right 'type'. He would have preferred to recruit men with experience in the police, the Malay Regiment or the Volunteers but was unable to find any until after the Japanese surrender.[111] Both Dobrée and Richardson, however, were able to find guerrilla recruits with exactly those backgrounds, who provided military experience and assistance with training.[112] Dobrée also recruited a team of agents who operated as far away as Penang, Kuala Lumpur and even Singapore, as well as in Kelantan and Thailand.[113] Some of this recruitment was carried out via local civil servants who – like those in Wataniah in Pahang – were disenchanted with the Japanese. Finally, the helpfulness and cooperation of local headmen was relied upon by all these operations. Two of the operations – *Hebrides* and *Beacon* – drew on a local support network drawn from all strata of Malay society, from paddy-planters to sultans. The Sultan of Pahang was the titular head of Wataniah, and Dobrée's agents included both an adopted son of the Sultan of Perak, and a future sultan of the state. Disillusionment with Japanese rule appeared widespread, though due to Japanese requirements for labour young men were not in plentiful supply.[114]

The risks that Force 136's local helpers were willing to run indicate the degree of Malay disillusionment with Japanese rule.[115] In early 1945, the Japanese conducted a large 'drive' against *Hebrides*, and many villagers fled their homes with the guerrillas. Two key supporters, Mandor Salleh and the local district officer at Grik, were both arrested.[116] Yeop Mahidin, right under the noses of the Japanese administration in Raub, was perhaps the most exposed, and this is reflected in the surviving documents, which include typescripts of the letters he and Richardson secretly exchanged. Yeop's couriers took similar risks, even though information was often carried in 'On Government Service' envelopes, which were not usually opened at checkpoints.[117]

As was the case with the guerrillas Force 136 raised with the MPAJA, the Malay units armed by Force 136 were never put to the test. The indications are that they would have proved their worth as a fighting force had this been necessary. They provided an able intelligence network, with *Hebrides* in particular sending much valuable intelligence back to Ceylon, including key information such as Japanese troop dispositions and the results of bombing raids.[118] When they did fight the Japanese, the Malay guerrillas proved effective in action. For example, when the Japanese came after Operation *Hebrides*, the guerrillas killed six Japanese and left another wounded, as against two guerrillas captured.[119] Although the number of Malay guerrillas remained small, at the time of the Japanese surrender these Malay units were expanding rapidly. Wataniah had reached a total of 1,000 men, if recruits awaiting training are included, though its armed strength was far smaller.[120] Plans were also underway to suborn the police. By the end of the war, 120 border police and twenty civil police in Pahang were waiting to be supplied with hand grenades and arms to allow them to rise against the Japanese when necessary, and a Giyu Tai (Volunteer Corps) platoon at Raub was poised to change sides. Similar preparations were afoot with Operation *Fighter* in Kedah.[121]

Only one Force 136 operation directed at securing Malay collaboration was a total failure. Operation *Multiple* never reached its designated area of action (lower Pahang and Negri Sembilan) and never recruited any guerrillas. Derek Headly, who led *Multiple*, was able to recruit two Malay policemen – formerly members of the Malay Regiment – as assistants, and some local Malays were helpful. Nonetheless, he was never able to establish a resistance base.[122] Headly noted that the headmen of the Malay kampongs were worried about 'Chinese political aims'.[123] To discover why *Multiple* so completely failed, it is now necessary to examine what these aims were, which of the 'Chinese' held them, and how they were expressed.

Table 4.2 Malay Guerrilla Forces Raised (Excludes Unarmed Agents; Includes Troops in Training but Not Untrained Recruits)

Operation	Armed	Unarmed	Total
Hebrides	112	40	152
Beacon	173	71	244
Fighter	99	7	106
Total	384	118	502

Source: TNA, HS 1/121, Lt. Col. P.G.J. Dobrée, *Hebrides* Operational Report, Apps. F and G; TNA, HS 1/123, Lt. Col. J.D. Richardson, *Beacon* Operational Report App. F; and TNA, HS 1/121, Major G.A. Hasler, *Fighter* Operational Report, App. G. The *Hebrides* figure may include a degree of overlap, as the armed force of the AMS was disbanded on 24 October 1945, whereas forty unarmed AMS were disbanded on 1 December; equally, unarmed recruits may have left the camp at this time too.

Malay resistance and the MPAJA

Close reading of some of the Force 136 operational reports makes it clear that the MPAJA did everything in their power to scuttle Force 136's Malay operations before they even began. Operation *Beacon* was delayed in its travels to its operational area by an encounter with an MPAJA party, whose initial welcome turned frosty when *Beacon's* leader Richardson explained his mission to them. Richardson felt there was a lack of 'really free contact' with the MPAJA, though he charitably ascribed this to his own 'lack of understanding of their outlook and ways of thinking'.[124] In fact, the MPAJA's opposition went right to the top ranks of the party. The man Richardson dealt with was a cadre of the MPAJA's 5th Regiment known as Lau Mah, which was based in Perak. Richardson did not know it, but Lau Mah was Deputy State Secretary of Perak, second in the state only to Chin Peng.[125] Richardson found that Lau Mah's unit promised assistance, but continually baulked and delayed him. After about a month's delay, he and the *Multiple* party who had been dropped to him made 'a complete breakaway', leaving with all their goods, arms and porters.[126] From then on, Richardson avoided the MPAJA entirely, and when he arrived in his operational area, near the small town of Raub, he impressed upon the local Malays and *Orang Asli* that total secrecy was essential.[127]

In the operational reports of Operation *Multiple* (which parted from Richardson's group), its leader, Derek Headly, complained repeatedly about obstruction from 'the Chinese' – which, given the type of obstruction and the context, meant 'the MPAJA'. They would, he said, provide him with food, but sought to halt all his other endeavours. Ultimately, he was unable to establish his operation or recruit more than a handful of Malay guerrillas, a failure he ascribed firstly to the obstacles thrown in his path by the communists, and only then to other issues, such as difficulties in obtaining enough porters and being forbidden by Richardson to contact Malays in an area he wished to keep entirely secure.[128]

The other two operations, *Fighter* and *Hebrides*, had less to do with the MPAJA, yet when they did they also found them uncooperative. Geoffrey Hasler, who led *Fighter* from Perak through both jungle and populated country to central Kedah, recorded that the MPAJA leader he first met received him 'cordially' but that 'the cordiality was much toned down when I said I intended to recruit, train and arm Malays'. Hasler tried to make contact with Jim Hislop of Operation *Sergeant*, who was working with the MPAJA, but discovered that the MPAJA delayed sending his message until they knew Hislop was moving out of the area.[129] Dobrée had no direct contact with the MPAJA during the occupation, but by the time of the Japanese surrender his indirect experiences had not caused him to look upon them with favour. He noted that one of his Force 136 agents, a young Malay named Sarpin bin Shahabudin who had parachuted in, had been 'kidnapped by the Three Stars [MPAJA]. He is presumed to have been killed.'[130]

Overall, then, the relationship between Force 136's Malay resistance operations and the MPAJA was not a good one – not in Pahang, not in Perak, and not in Kedah. The resistance to cooperation came not from Force 136 but from the MPAJA, who were obstructive and dishonest. This was not – as will be shown in the next chapter – because the Malay and Chinese communities could not work together, but rather a consequence of the MPAJA's political ambitions. As several of their leaders told members of Force 136, their ultimate plan was to drive out the British and rule the country themselves.[131] Since, as the leadership of the MPAJA must have realized, the majority of politically aware elite Malays did not desire a communist government, it was in the long-term interests of the MCP to keep the Malays as politically and militarily weak as possible and to deny them centres of armed power around which they would later be able to coalesce. Many Malays saw the MPAJA's attitude towards them as a form of domination and bitterly resented it. The resultant tension came to an explosive and deadly head during the interregnum.

The difficult relationship between the mass of the Malay community and the MPAJA was a Gordian knot, tangled with suspicions on both sides. Pre-war, relations between Malays and Chinese were already potentially fraught. Malaya's Chinese dominated trade and commerce, from which many Malays were effectively barred due to the Islamic prohibition on charging interest. Most small village shopkeepers were Chinese, and it was to them that Malays had to turn for credit during lean times of year, which led to difficult village relations.[132] When the war reached Malaya, Malays opposed the overwhelmingly Chinese MPAJA because it sought to achieve political dominance in a country they regarded as their own. The avowedly communist ideology the MPAJA embraced was seen as godless and at odds with Islam. To Yeop Mahidin, the communists and the Japanese were 'two sets of heathens'.[133] It should be noted that this was not an inevitable cause of division, as is shown by the alliance of Muslims and communists in launching anti-colonial resistance in modern Indonesia during the 1920s, and the career of the Indonesian freedom fighter Tan Malaka. Yet the reality was that in Malaya before the war membership of the Communist Party remained 90 per cent Chinese, a fact C.F. Yong attributes to the actions of the British Special Branch and to Malay opposition to the MCP's stated aim of abolishing the sultanate.[134]

The MPAJA, in turn, did not trust the Malay community, viewing Malays as Quislings because of their initial willingness to work with the Japanese, and as anti-Chinese because of the way Malay police, under Japanese direction, mistreated local Chinese.[135] In addition, the Japanese stoked this cycle of mistrust: their differential treatment of Malaya's communities might not have been deliberately calculated to increase racial unrest, but that was its result. For obvious reasons, the Japanese raised troops from the local Malay and Indian communities, but rarely from the Chinese. Malays joined organizations such as the Giyu Tai (Volunteer Corps) and the Giyu Gun (Volunteer Army) – both of which were likely to be used against the MPAJA – while Indians were recruited into the Indian National Army.[136] Although Chinese could not join the Giyu Gun, they could join the Giyu Tai, and some of them did so. Nonetheless, the security forces overseen by the Japanese, including the police, continued to have a Malay majority. In the occupiers' eyes, the Chinese were in competition only with the Eurasians for the status of least favoured community. They were watched, more often searched at roadblocks and lived under a permanent cloud of suspicion.[137]

The upshot of this differential treatment was that the MPAJA, according to Spencer Chapman, viewed Malays 'as rather treacherous and dangerous savages who will help anybody that will feed and protect them'. As a consequence, MPAJA officers did not let Malays who contributed to the Anti-Japanese Union know of their main camp locations. They were also reluctant to arm Malays. Spencer Chapman did note that a handful had 'been trained to fight in small camps built in the edge of the jungle', though it is unclear if he observed this directly or was relying upon the reports of others.[138] Derek Headly concurred with Spencer Chapman's reporting of the MPAJA's suspicion of Malays when he wrote that the former saw the latter as merely 'hewers of wood and drawers of water'. Nona Baker, an Englishwoman who survived the war with the MPAJA in eastern Pahang, noted that Malay police who defected to the MPAJA with their weapons were disarmed and used as field hands.[139] Moreover, although at the beginning of the occupation Malay was the *lingua franca* in the MPAJA camps, the MPAJA's official language ultimately became Mandarin.[140] To any thoughtful Malay observing the scene, what was being threatened was not only an ethnic dominance, but a cultural one as well.

For their part, Wataniah and other Malay resistance fighters avoided alliances with the MPAJA. For example, Yeop Mahidin was deeply suspicious of the Pahang MPAJA, and elected to keep news of Wataniah's existence strictly away from them.[141] This development allows us to locate the earlier roots of the ethnic tension that flared between the Malays and the Chinese towards the end of the Japanese occupation, and to add further to studies that have examined this. Cheah has concluded that actions by the MPAJA during 1945 sparked these tensions, in particular its cadres' pursuit of Malay 'collaborators'.[142] It now seems possible to take this argument further, to argue that the MPAJA began to rouse Malay anger earlier, by generally (though not entirely) excluding Malays from armed roles within the MPAJA, and by doing their utmost to stymie Malay guerrilla operations supported by Force 136.

Conclusion

The British supported the idea of a Malay guerrilla resistance for the sake of ethnic balance, lest Malaya's Chinese community be able to claim special treatment after the war. This would have been politically difficult to manage in a country where the Chinese did not enjoy equal rights with the Malays. It is also possible that, aware of the risks of post-war disorder, Force 136 was attempting to provide a force to act as a counterweight to the communist MPAJA.

To date, the Malayan resistance story has almost entirely focused on the MPAJA, to the point where the MPAJA is sometimes viewed as the only armed guerrilla force active in Japanese-occupied Malaya and the extent of this Malay resistance, underlain by increasingly disillusionment with the Japanese, has previously been largely hidden. The Force 136 archive, however, indicates that by the later part of 1943 and early 1944, many Malays, at least in the states of Perak, Kedah and

Pahang, were willing, even eager, to assist Force 136 against the Japanese. Indeed, when Force 136 arrived, Wataniah in Pahang was already in operation, recruiting its own agents among employees of the Japanese-run administration, and ready to work with Force 136.

In contrast to the cooperation that Force 136 enjoyed from many sectors of the Malay community in forming a Malay resistance, in this endeavour it met only obstruction and opposition from the communist MPAJA. By the time Force 136 agents arrived in the state of Pahang, Wataniah's leader was so suspicious of the ultimate aims of the MPAJA that he kept his organization a secret from the communist guerrillas. That his suspicions were well-founded is indicated by the difficulties encountered by the leaders of the operations *Beacon* and *Fighter*, who met delay, hostility and obfuscation from the MPAJA. Indeed, the Force 136 operation *Multiple* was so blocked and hindered by the MPAJA that it failed to establish an operational base and was unable to raise a Malay guerrilla unit. It seems from this that the MCP was determined to draw all armed resistance into its own hands, and to prevent the Malay community from pursuing its own political ambitions. In this determination to dominate the resistance, the MCP was echoing the behaviour of communist partisans in Europe, particularly in the Balkans and Greece.

Small though it was, the Malay resistance is important to a better understanding of Malaysian history, for it uncovers the legacy of some of its leading figures as important Malay nationalists or key members of the Malaysian armed forces. Two of Yeop Mahidin's lieutenants in Wataniah, Abdul Razak Hussein and Ghazalie bin Shafie, went on to have eminent political careers in the independent nation. The leader of Force 136's only all-Malay operation, Ibrahim bin Ismail, became head of the armed forces in 1971.

It is in the actions of some of these men that we can find one of the reasons for the fading of the Malay resistance from the historical record. The indications are that what Abdul Talib Ahmed dubbed 'bio-data blackout syndrome' afflicted some prominent Malaysians when they discussed their wartime history, for they did not wish to appear to have assisted the Japanese or the British, but instead to be seen as nationalists to their backbones. Beyond this, of course, the MPAJA was not only much bigger than the Malay resistance, but was also the forerunner of the Malayan National Liberation Army of the Malayan Emergency, and these factors have caused it to dominate the stage. In its efforts to suppress an independent Malay resistance one can see the MCP planning for its future dominance of Malayan politics. As the next chapter will show, MCP cadres did not only work against elements of the Malay community in this way, but also attempted to undermine and extinguish the armed resistance offered by their political rivals, the Guomindang.

Chapter 5

'THE KUOMINTANG STATE': FORCE 136 AND THE OCAJA[1]

In April 1945, a Malay headman, Toh Misai, and a Guomindang guerrilla leader, Yong Kong, died in an ambush as they travelled by boat along the Galas River to the aid of a British stay-behind, Robert Chrystal. This single incident weaves together many of the threads of the story of the wartime *ulu* – the upstream areas – of Kelantan. Unravelling these threads vividly expands our understanding not only of wartime Malaya, but of its post-war history as well. Toh Misai, Yong Kong and their escort were gunned down not, as one might have expected, by the Japanese, but by members of the Malayan People's Anti-Japanese Army (MPAJA).[2] They were victims of a war within a war, as they moved through a remote district which was effectively decolonized and self-governing. More than three years earlier, the writ of the British had ceased to run there, while that of the Japanese had never been established.

The focus of this chapter is the Guomindang-allied Overseas Chinese Anti-Japanese Army (OCAJA), and its relationships with other guerrilla movements and with SOE. The story of the OCAJA leads us deep into the Malayan interior, particularly in the north of the country, and appears to show that during the Japanese occupation there developed here not only a rival resistance army to the MPAJA but a proto-state with an active economy and even a currency. The existence and, tellingly, the demise of this proto-state indicates the extent to which the Malayan Communist Party (MCP) became nearly as concerned with crushing its Malayan competitors as it was with opposing the Japanese, at least in a part of Malaya where the Guomindang provided an active alternative to a communist-controlled guerrilla movement. The quarrels and bloodletting between the MPAJA and the OCAJA were a striking echo of the conflicts that had raged from 1939 between communist forces and the Guomindang army in China for the control of guerrilla bases behind Japanese lines.[3] This chapter also reveals how early the MCP began to position the MPAJA as the only legitimate resistance force worthy of the term 'guerrillas'. Even during the occupation, MPAJA representatives delegitimized Guomindang units by describing them as nothing but groups of robbers and bandits.[4]

This discourse of banditry has, since the late 1940s, deeply influenced scholarly and popular accounts of the OCAJA.[5] Typically, the OCAJA has been presented as a loose agglomeration of unreliable, ramshackle and thieving bandits, who ran up the Guomindang flag to give themselves some legitimacy despite being almost bereft of genuine political convictions. Historians have dismissed the OCAJA as a more-or-less criminal sideshow, small, insignificant, hardly better than the Triads, comprised of a collection of 'hill gangs' and 'robber bands' of 'small-town racketeers' who were 'poorly led, ill-trained and badly disciplined' and who, when they emerged from their 'jungle lairs', were 'distrustful of the Malays'.[6] C.F. Yong and R.B. McKenna, in their dissection of the Malayan Guomindang between 1912 and 1949, imply that the OCAJA made no significant contribution to wartime resistance in Malaya at all: 'With the exception of some KMT [Kuomintang: Guomindang] participation in the anti-Japanese resistance movement, including the British-controlled Force 136 and the KMT-directed Overseas Chinese Anti-Japanese Army (OCAJA) active in Perak and Kelantan, the Malayan KMT movement was practically dormant and virtually defunct.'[7]

Other scholars also tend to minimize the OCAJA's impact. Charles Cruickshank comments that the Guomindang 'occasionally clashed with AJUF [MPAJA]'[8]. C.C. Chin and Karl Hack state that around the small town of Gua Musang the MPAJA fended off 'other insurgent groups from the north, who they labelled "bandits", and which may have included KMT elements'. Though Chin and Hack raise a note of suspicion about the terminology chosen by the MPAJA, they also infer that the possible 'KMT elements' came 'from the north', thus implying that the MPAJA was on the defensive rather than on the attack.[9] Anthony Short adds complexity to the picture, for he comments of Upper Perak that 'it is almost certain, although hard to substantiate, that the greater part of whatever fighting the MPAJA did was with the KMT resistance rather than with the Japanese'.[10]

This chapter will try to take this story further, using a detailed exploration of the OCAJA's political rise and demise in northern Malaya, to uncover a story that ultimately leads us to rethink the beginnings of Malayan decolonization and the origins of the Malayan Emergency. For the MPAJA's determination to overwhelm the OCAJA, which became increasingly apparent as the Japanese occupation drew towards its close, shows the communists seeking to achieve hegemony over the Malayan interior well before the British administration returned.

The main primary sources that underpin these claims are colonial accounts. Nonetheless, they lie outside the 'prose of counterinsurgency' critiqued by the subaltern historian Ranajit Guha in his discussion of the British representations of insurgents in colonial India, for they were produced by Europeans who identified closely with the OCAJA and saw its resistance struggle from within.[11] The most significant of these reports were written by three men: the district officer John Creer, who was cut off during the Allied retreat; the rubber planter Robert Chrystal, who entered the jungle with an Oriental Mission stay-behind party; and a young officer named John Clifford, who was dropped to Operation *Hebrides* to work with the OCAJA early in 1945.[12] Their relations with the OCAJA were not always easy. Creer and Chrystal both disliked certain OCAJA leaders and objected to some of their actions.[13] Nonetheless, they were broadly supportive of the group and held a high opinion of several of the military commanders. At the war's end, Creer went so far as to identify as 'my best friend', without qualification, one of the senior men, Yong Kong, whom he described as an opium smoker, former merchant and contractor at the small settlement of Manek Urai, and founder of the Kelantan OCAJA.[14] John Clifford also identified closely with the OCAJA, writing of 'the men' like any young officer writing about his troops and defending them stoutly against accusations of banditry.[15]

Thus, even though all these authors operated within the colonial system and wrote about the OCAJA from that perspective, sometimes resorting to generalizations about 'the Chinese', they were not complete outsiders, but incomers embedded within the group.[16] Their accounts, simultaneously 'colonial' and 'insurgent', appear reliable, for they often support each other. Their main limitation is their geographical scope, for Creer, Chrystal and Clifford spent their time mainly in the states of Kelantan, Trengganu and Perak. Kelantan and Trengganu were Malay-majority states, and were among the four states handed by the Japanese to Thailand in 1943.[17] For the districts they cover, however, these accounts provide considerable detail. Robert Chrystal's ghost-written account, though composed more than fifteen years after the events it relates, adds detail to the picture.[18] Much of the information it contains coincides with the versions given in the two reports written at the war's end by Chrystal and Creer.[19] Moreover, certain characters and events are still remembered in the local area.[20]

The overall aim of this chapter is to test the claim made by the senior OCAJA man, Yong Kong, that what existed in Upper Perak and Ulu Kelantan by late 1944 was a 'Kuomintang State'.[21] We begin with the question of whether the OCAJA can be described as a guerrilla army, before assessing the degree to which it developed a functional state. After this, we discuss the 'state's' relationships with the MPAJA and Force 136, and then finally examine the 'bandit' trope that has had such an impact upon how the OCAJA has been viewed, by scholars and others, for the last seventy years.

War-making and state-making: the Guomindang 'army'

Charles Tilly, writing of early modern Europe, argues that war-making and state-making were 'interdependent', and that banditry, policing and war-making were merely different points along a continuum of control of populations by means of violence or the threat of violence. He argues further that governments organize and monopolize violence in order to enjoy the benefits of power and to allow them to suppress dissent or overrun competitor states, while claiming to 'protect' the population.[22] The OCAJA, as will be shown, suppressed other violent groups in the areas it controlled and launched regular attacks on the Japanese and the police, making it clear that it was both 'monopolising violence' and 'making war'. Was it, at the same time, making a state?[23] In the light of current scholarship, Yong Kong's claim for the existence of the 'Kuomintang State' is a radical one. His own unit, after all, has been tarred with the bandit brush.[24] What was he: a bandit, oppressing the people and in flight from the law, or a guerrilla, protecting the people and making the law?

While the arrival of the MPAJA upon the Malayan scene is reasonably well understood, the advent of the OCAJA is not. It appears from Force 136's reports that it had its genesis in early to mid-1942, in the bonding together of groups of jelutong tappers united by their politics and their opposition to the Japanese.[25] This anti-Japanese sentiment was clear among Malaya's Chinese pre-war and had been sparked by the Japanese invasion and conquest of large parts of China. These potential guerrillas may also have been inspired by some form of central directive issued by the Guomindang, as well as by the brutal treatment meted out by the Japanese to Guomindang members in Kelantan.[26] Very early in the occupation, five men were executed at Pasir Puteh, some for refusing to reveal the whereabouts of the account books of the local branch of the China Relief Fund.[27] The story was similar in Kota Bharu, where several Guomindang members, including the head of the Chinese Chamber of Commerce, were arrested and killed.[28] This pursuit of the Kelantan Guomindang can only have served to persuade its members to remove themselves as far from the Japanese as possible, and inspire them to resist. There is no evidence that the twenty-five Guomindang members who were trained by Oriental Mission's school, 101STS (No. 101 Special Training School), in January 1942 ever participated in the OCAJA. This force appears to have arisen spontaneously.[29]

Members of the OCAJA were drawn from across the social strata. Some were lower middle class – timber and labour contractors, small-time merchants – whereas others were woodcutters and jelutong tappers.[30] The bandit trope, however, was not entirely without foundation, for others who later came under the OCAJA's banner were responsible early in the occupation for raiding and robbery.[31] In February 1942, Creer was in a camp that was attacked and was later convinced that among the attackers were men who belonged to the OCAJA. He also blamed one OCAJA man for most of the robberies around Gua Musang during 1942.[32] Even so, this does not negate the reality of the guerrilla resistance that these men offered. After all, the MPAJA also recruited bandits, though it expected these new recruits to submit to the rigid discipline it enforced.[33] Phil Billingsley argues that, in China, 'bandit activities were frequently the precursors of rebel movements'. This would appear to have been the case in wartime Malaya.[34]

From early 1942, the OCAJA began to assert its own authority and to organize as an army. According to Creer, one OCAJA leader in Kelantan used his power to 'put down the banditry then prevalent, executing some of the culprits'.[35] This suppression of banditry and the concomitant restoration of civil order seem to have marked the consolidation of scattered groups into a more coherent whole, and the attainment of some legitimacy in the eyes of the local population. By the end of 1942, the OCAJA around Pulai was sufficiently well organized that when the local people said they could not feed all 200 guerrillas, they split into three groups and dispersed. One group went to the Thai border, one to the nearby village of Kundor and one remained in Pulai.[36] The shift from 'bandit' to 'guerrilla' was well underway. Rather than operating as independent roving bands, Guomindang-linked resistance fighters were beginning to act like a cohesive army.

The OCAJA, however, did not possess the rigid internal discipline for which the MPAJA was noted. MPAJA camps adhered to a strict timetable which, according to Freddy Spencer Chapman (who spent three years with them), consisted of daily chores, drill and education, and ended with 'lights out' and cries of 'Good night, Comrade!' at 9 p.m.[37] Creer and Chrystal, with the OCAJA, describe an entirely different way of life. Neither mentions a daily timetable, *samsu* (rice wine) was regularly consumed and they were even free to acquire hangovers at a wedding.[38] It is no wonder that the MPAJA ranker, Ho Thean Fook, who encountered the OCAJA in Perak considered their discipline 'lax' compared to what he was used to.[39]

Though poorly trained and inadequately armed, the OCAJA endeavoured to behave like an officially sanctioned force. Its members took on the trappings of a legitimate army, wearing, when they could, a uniform of a cap with a single star, civilian shirts, blue trousers and grey puttees. Like the MPAJA, they divided themselves into 'regiments' and 'companies': the Kundor detachment, for example, identified itself as 'the No. 3 Coy [Company] of the Kelantan Regiment'.[40] They had recognized headquarters, such as the one at Kuala Betis that oversaw operations in the Nenggiri valley.[41] The replacement of leaders seems to have been via consensus rather than violence, so that although Creer described one leader as 'a petty warlord type', this leader survived his replacement by another.[42] In addition, certain military procedures were in force: sentries were posted, bugles were used for signalling and the men were regularly drilled.[43] The OCAJA's overall lack of training, and their reluctance to accept any, exasperated Creer, but he had great respect for their toughness and determination, and was aware that the OCAJA rated combat experience above 'soldierly bearing'.[44]

The OCAJA, however, was similar to the MPAJA in that it was chronically short of arms, and it went about obtaining them in much the same way. Like the MPAJA, its soldiers carried out raids on police stations, and at least one leader purchased weapons gathered from the battlefield at Slim River.[45] There was an allegation in the *Straits Times* a few years after the war that, during the evacuation of Malaya ahead of the Japanese, a train was damaged and those who later formed the OCAJA looted arms from the wreckage.[46] In a similar way, the MPAJA looted the contents of an arms truck during the British retreat.[47]

Ultimately, however, the OCAJA can claim to be a guerrilla movement rather than a self-appointed police force, because it willingly took up arms against the Japanese. The OCAJA's first major action was in January 1943, when they attacked the town of Gua Musang. The Japanese forces were either killed or driven from the town and, according to Creer, 'about fifty' Malay civilians were killed, including women and children. Creer adds that the guerrillas destroyed the town 'to deny it to the Japs'. In return, the Japanese, when they returned in force to the area a week or so later, burnt down all the houses between Gua Musang and the village of Pulai.[48] A few months later, the Japanese attacked the Kundor guerrillas but, according to Robert Chrystal, who was there at the time, this attack was 'abortive'.[49] Chronically short of both ammunition and weapons, the OCAJA also attacked police stations, such as those at Tomo in Thailand and Lenggong in Perak, in an effort to seize arms. The Lenggong attack resulted in a reasonable haul of arms but expended hundreds of rounds of irreplaceable ammunition.[50] Later in the occupation, one OCAJA leader, Wong Shin, on the run, short of food, and trying to find Chrystal who he had heard was in difficulties, 'led his men into Kuala Gris and drove out a rabble of Malay police and press-ganged Chinese under three Japanese'.[51] In addition to these armed excursions against the Japanese, the OCAJA punished Chinese collaborators.[52]

Though Creer regarded some of the OCAJA's attacks as foolhardy – he pleaded with the Kundor guerrillas not to launch the 1943 assault on Gua Musang, for fear of the inevitable reprisals against civilians – he considered them to be 'tough', adding that 'toughness was a very desirable quality in a guerrilla'.[53] None of this fighting is mentioned by Creer or Chrystal as anything out of the ordinary, and so it is fair to conclude that the OCAJA was consistently active against the Japanese. The Guomindang guerrillas, however, were always constrained by their low supply of arms and ammunition, with Creer commenting that ammunition was not only in short supply but also often dud.[54]

When undertaking operations, the OCAJA also had to assess how many of their own men they could afford to risk, and also the impact of likely reprisals on the local people, for if they grew disenchanted with the OCAJA, the supply of new recruits would be likely to dry up. The recruits, however, appear to have kept on coming, and there is no suggestion in any of the sources that recruitment was forced, suggesting at worst that service with the OCAJA was preferable to waiting in vulnerable villages for the next Japanese labour drive, and at best that the OCAJA enjoyed active local support. The OCAJA took recruitment seriously and treated it as any army might. At least by the last months of the war, it is clear that it had instituted an elaborate, almost bureaucratic system, for processing volunteers. John Clifford described this system vividly:

> We had a recruiting office in BETONG [Thailand] … run by our own 'herb' doctor. System of admission was by obtaining a chitty from one of the big Towkays [merchants] in town, all of whom were our supporters. Having produced this chitty as to loyalty and trustworthiness, recruits were physically passed by the doctor and then allowed to enter our recruits [sic] camp on the outskirts of town… they were then formed into convoys and bringing that particular weeks [sic] supply of rice and food were allowed to enter the Base camp for military training and the issue of a weapon.[55]

This was not the behaviour of a gang of robbers. Rather, the OCAJA was behaving like the army it claimed to be. There was no doubt, however, that it was a very small force. Following the losses it suffered during 1945, only 358 armed men were demobilized in December 1945, with another 123 unarmed.[56] It seems unlikely that the OCAJA had ever been able to muster more than a thousand. Yet despite its small size, it had controlled a population of around 100,000 people.[57] It seems, then, that the typification of the OCAJA as 'bandits' and 'robbers' is unjustified.

'The Kuomintang State'

Like the Guomindang 'army', Yong Kong's 'Kuomintang State' had an unimpressive start before it developed into an impressive wartime reality. Its birth was chaotic, for though the OCAJA operated in a Malay-majority area, it initially behaved poorly towards the local Malays. The Gua Musang raid of early 1943 killed Malay civilians and most, if not all, of the members of the Japanese garrison killed then were Malay policemen. Furthermore, Creer reports that the guerrillas defiled the bodies of the dead, eating pieces of human heart and liver in the victory feast.[58] In Perak, on the other side of the Main Range, there was mutual mistrust between the OCAJA and local Malays. According to Creer, some of the 'Malay peasantry' near Kuala Temengor had admitted to him that they 'had instigated the Japs to murder innocent Chinese', following which the OCAJA took violent reprisals against these Malays.[59]

However, later in the war, relations between the OCAJA and the local Malays thawed considerably, at least in the *ulu* of Kelantan. In this area, the relationship between the Malay community and the OCAJA seems to have followed a reasonably clear trajectory, with decreasing violence and increasing cooperation. As we have seen with the Gua Musang raid of January 1943, the OCAJA killed Malays, including women and children. It appears that possibly during the rest of 1943, and certainly during 1944, the OCAJA 'taxed' the local population.[60] Despite this, when the OCAJA sought cooperative contact with the Malay community during 1944, some Malay leaders reciprocated, including a *penghulu* [headman] and a senior policeman.[61] Both sides, encouraged by Creer and Chrystal, recognized the benefits of cooperation.[62] By September 1944, local Malays were 'importing' goods into the 'state' to supply the OCAJA.[63]

However, the relationship remained fraught, with spasmodic acts of violence perpetrated by both sides.[64] Probably because of this continuing unease, the OCAJA leadership encouraged Creer and Chrystal to undertake propaganda work among the Malays, an activity further revealing of their state-making ambitions.[65] Creer was aware of the benefits of cooperation, commenting that it was always his aim 'to maintain the best possible relations between Chinese and Malays'.[66] He and Chrystal emphasized that, in their view, though the OCAJA were difficult as overlords, control of the area by the communists would be worse for the local Malays.[67] Ultimately, the relationship between the OCAJA and the Malays of this remote part of Kelantan developed to the point where Malays were recruited into the OCAJA. This was in direct contrast to the MPAJA's approach to Malay recruitment and an indication that the OCAJA had a more valid claim to be a representative national resistance, even if it did have its roots in a foreign political party.[68] Some of the OCAJA's Malay recruits were under the command of a Chinese named Lee Fung Sam, who had formerly operated in Pahang where local Malays, according to Creer, 'spoke well' of him.[69] Since Lee Fung Sam, who was a fighting man, led a detachment of Malays, the likelihood is that at least some of the OCAJA's Malays were armed. Towards the war's end, some Kelantanese Malays were even giving the OCAJA ammunition.[70]

Despite the propaganda work and the general rapprochement that took place, Creer noted some continuing dissent between these two groups, and that relations between the predominantly Chinese OCAJA and the Malay population of the 'Kuomintang State' were not always harmonious.[71] The stay-behind Chrystal objected to 'Chinese arrogance' towards Malays, and noted that those Malays in the OCAJA camps were generally (though not always) employed on the lowlier chores.[72] Creer accused some of the OCAJA of reprisals and heavy-handedness towards the Malay population.[73] For their part, local Malays, when the opportunity presented itself, were not averse to making life uncomfortable for the Chinese.[74] Even so, the 'Kuomintang State' was spared the cataclysmic ethnic violence that bedevilled the western coastal littoral from the final months of the Japanese occupation into the early part of 1946 (this is discussed in Chapter 6), and in general there seems to have been a degree of trust between the OCAJA and the Malay population, which developed from a shaky start to a reasonable working relationship.

Two factors may explain the change in the relationship between the OCAJA and the local Malay community. First, as discussed in the previous chapter, many Malays, at least in northern Malaya, became increasingly willing to resist the Japanese. By mid-1943, the Japanese had recruitment targets for labour for military projects, and the Kelantanese Malays, like Malays and Chinese all over the country, found themselves conscripted, and even press-ganged by the Japanese. Many of these labourers were taken to work on the Burma-Siam Railway and word filtered back into Malaya about the appalling conditions suffered by conscripted labourers: by the end of the war, about 40 per cent of the labourers had died.[75] The year 1943 was also when the Japanese ceded four of Malaya's northern (and predominantly Malay) states to Thailand, further alienating many Malays. Although these states were nominally under Thai rule, Japanese liaison officers and troops were still present.[76]

Second, as increasing numbers of Malays turned from the Japanese, they found the OCAJA wooing them. The evidence indicates that the OCAJA leadership was politically competent enough to understand that it had to be able to rely on the local majority population – the Malays. By mid-1944, the elderly leader Yong Kong had developed a good working relationship with a senior Malay headman, Toh Misai ('Grandfather Moustache').[77] Wong Shin, another OCAJA leader, was astute enough to make use of whatever prestige Creer and Chrystal retained and, early in 1945, sent them on a public relations tour around the Malay kampongs.[78] In short, as many Malays began to find the Japanese less acceptable, the OCAJA's behaviour towards them became more conciliatory.

Like Malay civilians, some Malay policemen turned against the Japanese and became increasingly willing to cooperate with the OCAJA. These police may have been influenced by an additional factor. In Kelantan at least, there is evidence the police were in conflict with another Japanese-sponsored organization, the *Jikeidan*, a blend of an auxiliary police force and a spy network reminiscent of the East German Stasi, by which neighbour kept watch on neighbour and reported any irregular goings-on. In 1943, the police and the *Jikeidan* in Pasir Puteh, Kelantan,

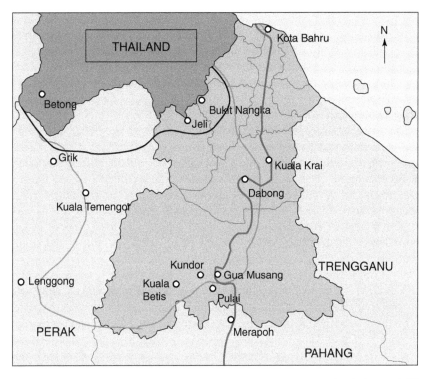

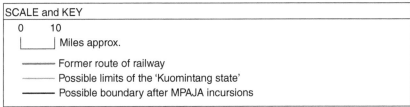

Map 5.1 Kelantan and the 'Kuomintang State', showing the possible extent of the 'state' after MPAJA incursions.

disagreed about working practices to the extent that it affected cooperation between them. Then, early in 1945, reports were received that *Jikeidan* members in the state had been involved in criminal activity.[79] By this stage, the police were sufficiently disillusioned with the Japanese for Creer, Chrystal and the OCAJA to regard them as allies rather than as agents of the Japanese and to be working with them. By April 1944, Creer was in contact with Che Shaari, the chief of police in a district bordering the 'Kuomintang State'; by the September of that year, Che Shaari was providing the OCAJA with salt 'and other supplies'.[80]

Malay policemen also supplied up-to-date intelligence to the guerrillas, who, for example, learned within days of the capture of the *Oatmeal* party.[81] By this time, Creer noted, 'the Malays of Kelantan, including the police force south of K[uala].

Krai were wholeheartedly with the KMT and ourselves'.[82] By July 1945, Creer's party included seven Malay policemen and another Malay, previously a detective in Malacca, regularly visited Kota Bharu, returning with both intelligence and rice.[83] All of this gives us a different perspective on the relationships between Malays and Chinese during the occupation. While in many places it became adversarial and even violent, in the *ulu* of Kelantan it grew increasingly cooperative as the occupation progressed.

The 'Kuomintang State' went far beyond dealing with the police for rice and salt, for it also sustained and drew revenue from a surprisingly successful wartime economy.[84] The timber trade in the *ulu* of Kelantan remained active throughout the occupation. In 1944, an agreement was struck between the Thai and Japanese governments for the felling of 96,000 cubic metres of timber a year in the northern jungles.[85] This may in turn have been due to the encouragement the Japanese were giving to the coastal junk trade, which fed through into a boom in junk construction, apparently linked to the import of rice.[86] The *ulu* was, of course, controlled by the OCAJA, and the only way to get the timber out of the 'state' was to raft it down the Galas. Enough cargoes of timber, rice, bananas and bamboo were brought down this river by raft or *prahu* to make it worth the OCAJA's while to establish a 'customs post' at Dabong, at the eastern limit of the OCAJA's 'state'.[87]

By the second half of 1944, the OCAJA had extracted all it could by means of 'tax' and blackmail. Yong Kong then revealed a facet of his abilities not previously seen. Faced with a fall in 'tax' revenues, he did what chancellors of the exchequer continue to do, and started printing money. As Chrystal recounted:

> Pages from school exercise books were cut roughly to the size of pre-war Malayan notes, stamped with the white Kuomintang star on its blue ground and signed by the 'Finance Minister', Yong Kong. These notes were given to traders in payment for foodstuffs purchased, and later redeemed by exchange for Japanese notes.[88]

Bemused, Chrystal enquired of Yong Kong how this system was supported:

> Going into his hut, the Chinese came out with a small set of delicate scales. Holding them up, he said there was nothing wrong with their currency as it was based on a gold standard. It was true enough, Chrystal discovered. There was gold in the Galas river and its many tributaries … and many Chinese were panning the precious dust from the sand of the river beds. They were forced to sell it at a low figure to the guerrillas, who then shipped it to Kota Bharu where it fetched a very high price in the Japanese currency.[89]

This currency was brought back into the *ulu* and Yong Kong's notes were redeemed against it. This system probably alienated the goldwashers, but they had always existed at the limits of the law and can have experienced little change of status.[90] Yet, in a broader sense, it stimulated the local economy. The goldwashers were paid a controlled price for their gold by what was effectively a state monopoly, which used its substantial profits to pay the population to support the guerrillas, which in turn stimulated local commerce. The sale in Kota Bharu of the exported gold enabled the import of goods, such as salt, which were not otherwise available.

The OCAJA's economy and the protection it offered were such that new settlements sprang up within the state, just as they did in areas where the MPAJA was the dominant force. A pre-war population of about 2,000 Malays around Klian Intan and Kroh, in Upper Perak, was joined by Chinese smallholders. By 1948, 15,000 had settled in the vicinity; given the history of population movements within Malaya, the likelihood is that the majority came during the war years, pushed to resettle by unemployment and their desire to avoid the Japanese, and drawn in by the vitality of the local economy. Similarly, 13,000 Chinese settled near Grik, also in Upper Perak.[91] This influx of new settlers would have been lower to the east of the 'Kuomintang State', since Kelantan and Trengganu did not have as many estate and mine labourers as did Perak. However, two new villages developed just north of Gua Musang, and their Chinese occupants, formerly shopkeepers or rubber tappers and now rice farmers, came into the bounds of the 'Kuomintang State' when the Japanese pulled out of the area in August 1944.[92] Although there is no firm evidence, it is highly likely that some of the produce of these villages was either bought by or 'donated to' the OCAJA. By the end of the war the OCAJA had extended its reach, buying rice in Siam (partly with Force 136 funds) and importing it into the 'state'.[93]

Aside from overseeing an active economy, 'taxing' the local population and printing money, it is clear that the 'Kuomintang State' controlled and policed large swathes of territory. Creer and Chrystal enjoyed considerable freedom in Upper Perak and the *ulu* of Kelantan. They both relate lengthy journeys, during which they were untroubled by the presence of the Japanese or their agents – in fact, in these accounts, the absence of the Japanese is not even worthy of comment.[94] Creer recounted a stay in a 'border' village, in which he sounded unconcerned about the risks of betrayal, kidnap or capture.[95] The OCAJA, in fact, had posted sentries along the border of their realm to determine who could enter. About forty miles of the route of the east coast railway came within the 'Kuomintang State', and the OCAJA maintained guards across it where it entered the 'state'. The OCAJA's control of this section of the railway at least partially explains why the Japanese had to give up the operation of this length of track, and their decision to send its rails to Burma, where they were more strategically useful.[96] The telephone lines could easily have been destroyed by the OCAJA, yet they chose to retain them, since OCAJA members used these lines themselves. To ensure that telephone communications were maintained, the OCAJA even issued safe-conduct passes – virtually visas – stamped with the twelve-pointed Guomindang sun, to linesmen entering OCAJA territory at Dabong. The Japanese at Merapoh (forty-five miles south) told the linesmen to keep these passes, as they could use them again on their return trips.[97] In effect, the Japanese had tacitly acknowledged that an area of territory – that held by the OCAJA – was beyond their control.

By the end of the war, the OCAJA was also showing a notable degree of diplomatic competence. High-level contact with the Thai armed forces was assured when some of its leaders established contact with Col. Patom Chulananda (Officer Commanding, South Siam).[98] In the broad swathe of territory that they controlled, in their political relations with the local populace, in their deft management of taxation and the economy and in their capacity to print money, Guomindang forces in Malaya revealed themselves in possession of, if not a fully formed state, then at least a proto-state.

'Two warring factions': the OCAJA and the MPAJA[99]

The MPAJA's negative attitude towards an independent Malay resistance was matched by their approach to one sponsored by the Guomindang. The pre-war relationship between the MCP and the Malayan Guomindang had not been a good one, for it was strongly influenced by events in China. The first communist party in Malaya, the Nanyang Communist Party, formed from left-wing elements within the Malayan Guomindang in 1928.[100] This followed the violent purge of communists from the Guomindang in China, ordered by Chiang Kai Shek in 1927. Thereafter, as in China, the two Malayan parties never saw eye to eye. They found it hard to combine into an anti-Japanese front following the outbreak of the Sino-Japanese War in 1937, with the Guomindang objecting to the 'belligerently anti-British' attitude of the MCP.[101]

As John Creer tells it in his contemporary account, the MCP sought to exert its own authority and lost no time in trying to subvert and undermine the OCAJA. During 1942, communist emissaries arrived in Pulai, and tried to draw OCAJA members around to their own political viewpoint. They were not successful. One tried to teach the OCAJA guerrillas *The Red Flag* but, according to Chrystal, his 'only reward for his pains was the sight of his *samsu*-swilling audience rolling with laughter on the floor'.[102] The MPAJA members then returned to Pahang but, early in 1943, came back with teachers who set about educating the OCAJA in 'singing, politics and drill'.[103] More communists joined these emissaries, visiting additional camps and working with the local population, and for a time the OCAJA and the MPAJA cooperated. But their relationship became increasingly tense, and splits also emerged in the attitudes of the local people, some of whom came to support the MPAJA while others increasingly resented its growing influence.[104] It is worth noting at this juncture that the population of Pulai was predominantly Hakka-speaking. The OCAJA drew its Chinese membership largely from just a couple of dialect groups, particularly Cantonese and Kwangsai, whereas the MPAJA seems to have been dominated by speakers of Hakka, Hokkien and Hylam.[105] The communist emissaries may thus have played upon by dialect-group sympathies.

The difficult and worsening relationship between the OCAJA and the communists was not improved when OCAJA guerrillas, on their way to make a peaceful visit to a visiting MCP official in February 1943, were fired upon by MPAJA guerrillas, with four of them being killed. In this instance, the MPAJA leader brokered a peace.[106]

Eventually, however, the OCAJA leadership took firm action against the MPAJA. In late 1943, Yong Kong ejected communist propagandists from the Kundor camp, claiming that his group of the OCAJA was not receiving its fair share of funds raised in Kuala Lipis. Early in 1944, the Kundor OCAJA arrested an emissary carrying a letter from the Pulai MPAJA to another OCAJA camp further north, which attempted to suborn this group by urging them to join the communists. The emissary – who had formerly been with the KMT and was thus probably viewed as a traitor – was killed, as was an MPAJA guerrilla in the search party sent to look for him. A month later, the MPAJA exacted its revenge, attacking Yong Kong and his men when they visited Guomindang sympathizers in a nearby village, killing several of them. This situation – of mistrust and sporadic killing, including of civilians – continued through the year.[107] At one point, the OCAJA took a communist prisoner, killed him and ate his heart and liver.[108] Yet the OCAJA were not alone in indulging in this practice. Spencer Chapman noted of the MPAJA that 'the liver and heart of traitors and Japanese prisoners was eaten in some camps' when other foods were short.[109] Both guerrilla groups thus stand accused of committing atrocities and defiling the bodies of the dead.

The level of conflict between the MPAJA and the OCAJA increased during 1944, and, in Crystal's view this benefitted the Japanese. Since the MPAJA and the OCAJA were now so busy killing each other, the Japanese, during August 1944, were able to withdraw their troops from Gua Musang to Merapoh, leaving the field clear for the two groups to fight it out.[110] In the scholarly literature, this withdrawal is sometimes presented as an MPAJA victory over the Japanese, rather than as what it was: a tactical withdrawal. The effect of this war within a war was to neuter the OCAJA as an anti-Japanese resistance force, for at this time Yong Kong became concerned that if his own men attacked the Japanese their undefended camp would be seized by the MPAJA. In October 1944, the OCAJA guerrillas raided the MPAJA camp at Pulai, but this was to be one of their last offensive actions. In February 1945, the situation spiralled into outright war when the MPAJA opened an assault on the OCAJA that, over the course of the next few months, almost entirely overwhelmed the 'Kuomintang State'.[111] This was a war between two armies, not – as it is sometimes presented – the putting down of banditry.[112]

By mid-1945, the 'Kuomintang State' had been overrun. Chrystal estimated the attacking MPAJA force at 2,000 men but this seems unreasonably high, given the difficulties of the terrain, the ever-present problems of food supply for large guerrilla formations, and the overall size of the MPAJA.[113] First, the OCAJA were driven out of the Pulai-Kundor area. By the end of May, the MPAJA, using arms and ammunition airdropped by Force 136 for use against the Japanese, had taken Dabong and killed a number of important OCAJA leaders, including Yong Kong, whose death was reported to Chrystal by a young Malay teacher who survived the ambush on the Galas.[114] As the OCAJA forces fled, they were accompanied by large numbers of refugees, whom they found almost impossible to feed.[115] The OCAJA signed a truce agreement sponsored by *Hebrides*, but the MPAJA did not respond to requests that they should sign it too.[116] The fighting between the OCAJA and the MPAJA gave the Japanese an opportunity to exert their authority: they moved in behind the MPAJA and began rounding up the population around Dabong and taking charge of the *ulu*.[117] By July, the Japanese were deep within the 'Kuomintang State', threatening OCAJA positions at Jeli and Bukit Nangka.[118] Meanwhile, the MPAJA had attacked OCAJA camps near Grik and Lenggong in Perak.[119] The 'state' had been reduced to a small area close to the Thai border.

It appears that all that stopped the MPAJA driving the OCAJA ever further north was the protection given to the OCAJA by Force 136, whose men and supplies began to reach them in the middle of 1945. Supplied with arms, ammunition and wireless communications, the OCAJA was able to resist its complete destruction. The MPAJA was also deterred from attacking the OCAJA when it became clear that any attack by them on the OCAJA would quickly be reported to Force 136 officers assigned to it. The Japanese also eased off the pressure they had placed on the OCAJA, for they had other concerns, having been driven from Merapoh by a combined force of armed Malays and MPAJA, under the orders of Lt. Col. Leonard of *Pontoon*. This combined force held the town, despite several Japanese assaults, until the end of the war.[120]

Beyond the sentried borders of the 'Kuomintang State', the MPAJA in its dealing with Guomindang-allied guerrillas adopted the same tactic of persuasion followed by force. Creer recounts that the OCAJA leader Lee Fung Sam had operated near Raub in Pahang. Lee Fung Sam's group had resisted efforts by the MPAJA to win them over, but eventually some members of the MPAJA entered the camp 'as self-invited guests', only to open fire on those waiting to greet them. Lee Fung Sam claimed to have been in contact with other OCAJA groups in Perak and Selangor, and said that they too had been taken over by the MPAJA.[121] He may well have been telling the truth, for Lee's account is partially corroborated by that of a Chinese, Ong Sin Bin, who survived when the Royal Navy sank a junk off the Malayan coast. Ong claimed that independent groups of Guomindang, including some armed men, existed in Perak, Selangor, Negri Sembilan and Johore; Force 136, however, did not consider his information entirely reliable.[122] However, a bandit with Guomindang sympathies certainly operated near Pusing in Perak. He was drawn into an alliance with the MPAJA, but when he and his band tried to break away he was ambushed and killed.[123] Chin Peng confirms the existence of Guomindang-allied groups in Johore, though he delegitimizes them by describing them not as guerrillas but as 'bandit groups claiming to represent Kuomintang interests'.[124] If this is the same group described by Spencer Chapman and others, then they were eventually rounded up by the MPAJA, with eighteen of those captured being killed and the others used as porters.[125]

The subversion and domination of groups who were either allied to the Guomindang or politically neutral suggests that the MPAJA sought to expand its zone of influence right across the Malayan interior and establish itself as the only legitimate resistance against the Japanese from early in the occupation. In his influential autobiography, Chin Peng is very blunt about the attitude of the communists towards the OCAJA: he says that the group in south Kelantan 'directly threatened our control of the central Highlands and we had to drive them out'.[126] The MPAJA was effectively at war with two enemies during the Japanese occupation.

The manner in which the MPAJA behaved towards other anti-Axis fighters directly echoes the actions of some communist guerrillas in Europe. In Poland, SOE-trained parachutists assisted armed bands during 1943. These groups realized that there were partisans in the same area, officered by and in contact with the Soviets, well supplied, and under orders to eliminate nationally conscious or aggressive Poles. At the end of the year, the partisans captured the SOE-linked group and the officers were dispatched to Lubyanka prison.[127] SOE operatives in Albania observed how communist partisans would attack nationalist partisans with supplies provided by the British, or force SOE agents with the nationalists to leave them, even when those nationalists were providing active resistance to the Nazis.[128] An SOE leader on Crete concluded that the communists' aim was to control the entire resistance movement, so that they could dominate the post-war settlement.[129] These SOE officers would have agreed with a later assessment that 'the [Malayan] Communists were obviously not prepared to tolerate any resistance forces which they themselves could not control'.[130]

The OCAJA and Force 136

While at least one scholar claims that the OCAJA was not 'under the wing' of Force 136, and another that Force 136 did not supply them with arms, the reports on file show that, in fact, the OCAJA received considerable support from the Force.[131] Although Force 136 and South East Asia Command were reluctant to supply the OCAJA with arms, for it was politically awkward to support both the OCAJA and the MPAJA, some weapons were still dropped to them, including seventy-eight Sten guns, nineteen carbines, four Bren guns, and ammunition.[132] These drops included money (for food), and demolition stores; medical assistance and training were also given by Force 136 to the OCAJA.[133] Drops to Clifford's party included a sewing machine, which was used to convert parachutes into shirts.[134] All OCAJA parties were also provided with wireless equipment and trained wireless operators by Force 136.

Although Force 136 had agreed to work with the OCAJA, there remained a degree of distrust between the OCAJA and some of the Force 136 officers. Dobrée, the commander of Operation *Hebrides* and the senior Force 136 liaison officer in contact with the OCAJA, was certainly not a fan of it. He later wrote, 'I was not happy about arming the KMT guerrillas. I did not trust them' and accused them of operating via 'terrorism and oppression'.[135] Yet even he had to admit that the OCAJA guerrillas were, at times, effective allies, and eventually he urged Force 136 to arm them.[136] After all, it had been the OCAJA leader, Yong Kong, who ensured that Creer and Chrystal were put into contact with *Hebrides*.[137] When Dobrée is read closely, all his face-to-face dealings with the OCAJA appear to have been successful. It was the stories and rumours about them that seem to have influenced what he thought of them.

In return for the assistance it received, the OCAJA cooperated with Force 136 right through the interregnum. On 22 August 1945, a week after the Japanese surrendered, John Clifford took his detachment from their jungle camp into Betong in Thailand, to meet Japanese and Thai officials, though this detachment soon moved to Kroh in Upper Perak to keep the peace until Indian troops arrived in late September.[138] Chrystal and Dobrée took a mixed force of OCAJA and Malays to occupy Grik, also in Upper Perak; Creer, by now accompanied by the Force 136 officer Major Bromley-Davenport, controlled Kota Bharu with a mixed force similar to Chrystal's.[139] Creer was relieved to find that the administration of Kelantan '… was a going concern. No disturbances had followed the Japanese surrender and, thanks largely to [the Malay civil servant] Dato Stia, the machinery of Government had never ceased for a moment.'[140]

In early December, when all guerrilla forces were disbanded, most of the 350–500 OCAJA members surrendered their arms without complications. However, some of the men whom Creer had left with Bromley-Davenport in late September declined to do so. They wrote to Force 136 to explain saying 'the arms we are having were obtained by our bloodsheds with the Japanese', adding that they had suffered 'tremendous hardships…in our struggle for peace and democracy'.[141] This behaviour and other unruliness fed into the impression of them as bandits. Several factors underlay the difficulties Force 136 encountered with OCAJA units as disbandment approached. When Chrystal, after three and a half years of strain, hunger and illness, was dispatched to Kuala Lumpur, the OCAJA of Upper Perak lost a familiar officer.[142] To compound this problem, Dobrée (though he considered one local leader, Hong Chee, to be 'moderately evil' and another, Tai Man, to be 'evil indeed') was nonetheless confident that these OCAJA would give no trouble, and was absorbed by administrative affairs.[143] Instead of dealing with Force 136 officers known to them, Hong Chee, Tai Man and their men found themselves faced by a replacement for Chrystal, one Captain Gabb, who had no sympathy towards the OCAJA. According to Gabb, Tai Man and Hong Chee were 'cold, almost threatening' towards him, and he promptly deemed them 'outlaw types', describing them in racialized terms as 'Kwangsai Chinese coolies of the most ignorant sort… bullies who would think nothing of taking to gang robbery'.[144] A proportion of this unit fulfilled his expectations and, behaving like the bandits he considered them to be, absconded with their weapons. A later assessment of events concluded that these OCAJA had been 'tactlessly handled'.[145] In Perak, Dobrée had attempted to maximize his control of men he considered 'pirates' by bringing them into the OCAJA after the Japanese surrender.[146] However, this 'rabble of hooligans and bandits' – who had never been part of the wartime OCAJA – soon absconded, lending further credence to the bandit trope.[147] In contrast to these two groups, those men who had worked with John Clifford since March 1945 disbanded peacefully and without difficulty. Clifford was quite clearly in sympathy with the OCAJA, considering that the desertions in Perak had been the consequence of unfair handling by the British.[148]

The OCAJA, then, was generally cooperative, but British control of them was tenuous and depended upon the relationship that had been forged between a unit and its British liaison officer. Creer also lamented that 'the death of YONG KONG at the hands of Communists in April 1945 has made the KMT ten times more difficult to control'; he added that the death of Yong Kong's 'No. 2' the following month was 'also most unfortunate'.[149] Creer thus connected the loss of these two men with the diminished discipline of the OCAJA, but whatever the causes of the disbandment difficulties, they fed into the perception that the OCAJA was a rabble of bandits, not a guerrilla army.

The trope of banditry

The presentation of the OCAJA as nothing more than a gang of bandits can be dated back to the Japanese occupation, and the efforts of the MPAJA to exert its hegemony across the Malayan interior. Richard Broome of *Gustavus*, the second European to infiltrate into Malaya, noted in his report that the MPAJA denied the existence of any Guomindang resistance movement, though he appears to have been a little suspicious, noting that it was 'quite probable that AJUF [MPAJA] labels as bandits genuine K.M.T. guerrillas'. A further reason for Broome's belief that there were probably no Guomindang guerrillas is that even Force 136's own Guomindang Chinese agents working in Malaya had heard nothing about a Guomindang organization.[150] This was almost certainly because these agents were active along the coast and the OCAJA was based far inland, but as a consequence Broome was left in ignorance of the OCAJA's existence: as far he knew, there were bandits, but there were no Guomindang guerrillas.

In addition, it appears that the description of the OCAJA as thieves and bandits was used by the senior MCP cadre Lau Mah. When Douglas Richardson of Operation *Beacon* was delayed by a party of MPAJA on his way to Pahang in March 1945, he was informed that this detachment had been driving a 'robber gang' out of the district. His source for this information is not clear, but he had discussions with Lau Mah, who told Richardson a great deal about what the local MPAJA had been doing, so the term 'bandit' may have originated with him.[151] Richardson was also told that these 'bandits' abducted women, an allegation repeated by Chin Peng in his memoir, but nowhere mentioned by Chrystal, Creer or Dobrée.[152] According to George Leonard of *Pontoon*, in late May 1945 he encountered 'LAO MAH' who told him that he was an officer with the 5th Regiment of the MPAJA and had been fighting 'bandits' on a front north of Gua Musang.[153] This was, of course, the place and time of the MPAJA assault on the OCAJA. Lau Mah's account, as related to Leonard, broadly correlates with the version of events given in Chin Peng's memoir.[154] The use of the term 'bandits' for the OCAJA extended to the top of the MPAJA hierarchy.

While Force 136 reports were sometimes more nuanced than the accounts of men like Chin Peng, overall they still reinforced the perception of the OCAJA as bandits. Many Force 136 officers were influenced by the MPAJA, and so descriptions of the OCAJA as 'bandits' permeated the higher levels of the Force's contemporary intelligence. The diverging views of the OCAJA held by Force 136 are drawn together in a report from late in the war. The report's author notes that 'an ex-Malay civil servant' – who can only be Creer – 'has confidence in the K.M.T. and states that he could soon build up considerable armed levies', but at the same time observes that the MPAJA described the OCAJA as 'untrustworthy Chinese bandits'.[155] However, despite the element of balance in reports such as this, within a few years popular discourse would come to paint the OCAJA as thieves and robbers.

The failure of some OCAJA elements to disband contributed to the development of the 'bandit' trope post-war, but the MCP also played a key role. Initially, the MPAJA was prepared to term former OCAJA men as 'guerrillas'. In June 1946, a group of 150 former OCAJA came into Lenggong to surrender, as clearly shown by a contemporary press photograph that shows the leader of this group with a Guomindang banner.[156] When a *Straits Times* article claimed that they had been members of the MPAJA, a representative of the MPAJA wrote to object to this, referring to them as 'Kuomintang guerrillas'. However, within two years the terminology had changed. When press articles appeared covering a new campaign to stamp out banditry in northern Malaya, Chen Tien – who had had led the 4th Regiment in Johore – promptly wrote to the *Straits Times*. He emphasized that the MPAJA had disbanded peacefully, but that the 'bandits' of the OCAJA had not, adding that the MPAJA had carried out 'an intensive campaign' against 'these gangs of bandits'.[157] The MPAJA now denied that the OCAJA had been guerrillas, instead reinforcing the 'bandit' trope.

That some Guomindang fighters did turn to banditry post-war only strengthened the 'bandit' stereotype. A large anti-bandit drive in early 1948 came across 'a big military jungle training school', and not until April 1949, after the beginning of the Malayan Emergency, did the final group surrender. At this point their bandit careers came to an end, though their battle against the MCP did not. The press report commented that many of the men wished to assist the government against 'the Communists'.[158] This they went on to do: some of them went on to become members of the Kinta Valley Home Guard – essentially armed sentries – during the Emergency.[159] Yuen Yuet Leng, a former senior policeman, has also confirmed that a number of these men joined the police in Grik.[160]

These were probably the same men who Chin Peng describes as being controlled by Special Branch during the Emergency but who had been 'Kuomintang bandits… pillaging outlaws' in the occupation'.[161] Denying the legitimacy of the OCAJA suited Chin Peng very well. By reducing an effective anti-Japanese resistance to 'pillaging outlaws' he decreased the legitimacy of the OCAJA, while increasing that of the Malayan communists, bolstering their claims to have been 'the only functioning resistance movement on the peninsula'.[162] Indeed, Philip Deery argues that, when discussing the communist insurgents during the Emergency, the motive in using the term 'bandit' is 'to deny the legitimacy of the opponent'.[163] In his memoirs Ching Peng elects to use a term once used of him and his insurgents to describe the OCAJA.[164]

Though the Guomindang took a share of the 'honours' in the immediate post-war period, parading with a huge Guomindang banner as well as marching with the MCP through the streets of Singapore, and joining them in demobilization parades in the peninsula, its role in the resistance struggle quickly slipped from popular memory. This overshadowing of the OCAJA's alternative, legitimate, resistance was symbolically completed when, in 1962, Chrystal's experiences were serialized in the *Straits Times*. Although one article was clear about the difference between the Guomindang and the communists, its headline trumpeted, 'It's Civil War now between the Reds – Rival Groups of Communist Guerrillas Battle Each Other.'[165]

Conclusion

Although the OCAJA fought the Japanese and developed a proto-state in northern Malaya during World War II, they have come to be remembered as bandits and this trope dominates the scholarship. Though it is true that, before the war, some of the men who later joined the OCAJA made their living outside the law, and while it is also true that the remnants of the movement turned to banditry for some years afterwards, in the intervening years they not only challenged the Japanese, but also posed a distinct threat to the hegemony of the MPAJA. They did not merely dominate a sizeable area of mountainous and jungled country by brute force, but controlled it with able political and economic management. They kept watch on who went in and out, suborned the local police, issued 'visas' and extracted 'excise duties' from reluctant traders. They also, after a rocky start, cooperated with Malay headmen, pointing to the possibility of constructive relations between Malay and Chinese communities in this period, in contrast to the murderous ethnic violence that convulsed parts of the coastal littoral during 1945–1946. The OCAJA's grasp of governance and their effective grip upon the local gold trade enabled them to issue their own currency. While a proportion of its income was used for *samsu* – and probably opium if it was available – it also fed and maintained an armed force of several hundred men. If, as Chin Peng, claimed, there were 300 such guerrillas active in south Kelantan, the total probably approached 800 at the peak: there were sentries and camps near Dabong, a substantial group across the watershed near Lenggong, and others near the Thai border. What we may never know is how many guerrillas were allied to the Guomindang across Malaya, nor how many could have been raised under their flag had they received the support enjoyed by the MPAJA.

It clearly suited Chin Peng to present the OCAJA as bandits, for it allowed the MCP to present itself as having offered 'the only resistance' to the Japanese.[166] As 'the only resistance', the party hoped to increase its political influence in the post-war period. Chin Peng strongly implies that the communists felt themselves entitled to representation after their wartime struggles.[167] It also perhaps suited the British to overlook the existence of the OCAJA. If the MPAJA had been the only ready-made armed resistance available to back, the British could believe that they had had no choice but to arm them to oppose the Japanese, and that therefore the boost this gave to the MCP could not have been avoided. This, however, is only speculation.

As well as giving us a whole new vantage point from which to view the extent and the limits of the Japanese occupation, the story of the OCAJA demonstrates the early birth of the MCP's ambition to exert its hegemony across the country, and its willingness to use force to achieve this. It also shows us that the British, via the intelligence reports submitted by officers in the field, were in possession of some detailed information about not only the aims of the MCP, but also about their methods.[168] Moreover, it demonstrates that not all anti-Japanese resistance was in the hands of the MPAJA, and that Malays and Chinese could work with each other, as well as with the British, to oppose the Japanese.

The story of the OCAJA indicates that the MCP was seeking to dominate the Malayan interior from the first year of the Japanese occupation – and that this domination of other Malayan communities, both political and racial, by persuasion or by force, might have mattered to it as much as resisting the Japanese. This wartime behaviour indicates that the MCP never fell back from its ultimate aim of taking political control of Malaya. This was an aim that, as we shall see in the following chapter, caused considerable friction between the MPAJA and Force 136, and also within the party, during the interregnum that followed the Japanese surrender.

Chapter 6

'REVOLUTIONARY SPIRIT': THE POST-WAR PERIOD, AUGUST 1945–APRIL 1946[1]

At just after midnight on 15 August 1945, under a clear and starry sky, Ghazalie bin Shafie, a senior member of Wataniah, answered a knock on his door. It was a friend, who whispered in his ear. The Japanese, he said, had surrendered. Ghazalie looked heavenward and the stars, he said, 'were twinkling as if winking at us to confirm the news'.[2] The war was over but – as Ghazalie would quickly notice – the form that peace would take was by no means settled. Malaya was on the threshold of a period of political struggle, strikes and ethnic violence, during which the Malayan Communist Party (MCP) would seek to influence the future political form of Malaya.

As the previous two chapters have shown, the MCP had consistently aimed to dominate the resistance movement and concentrate the maximum power and credibility into its own hands, in exactly the same manner as had communist parties in the Balkans and Greece. The means varied: if 'evangelism' and persuasion failed to work, violence was used. As the fighting with the Overseas Chinese Anti-Japanese Army (OCAJA) demonstrated, violence was resorted to even if it gave the Japanese access to areas from which they had previously been excluded.

Throughout the war, the MCP's guerrilla wing, the Malayan People's Anti-Japanese Army (MPAJA), had remained an almost entirely Chinese organization, with Mandarin as its official language and few Malays given combat roles.[3] This was a factor that would be significant during the interregnum, the period between the Japanese surrender on 15 August 1945 and the return of British troops during September 1945. The interregnum lasted from around three to four weeks in towns such as Penang, Kuala Lumpur and Singapore, to over to six weeks in the more remote areas of the country.[4] Gradually, however, civil affairs teams from the British Military Administration (BMA) arrived in all parts of Malaya and were cast into a situation for which they were not prepared. They had expected to follow behind a conquering army (as had administrative teams in Burma), not to have to take control of the whole country after a sudden surrender.

Several historians provide detailed studies of both the interregnum and the period of the BMA, and have reached a broad consensus. The Japanese surrender created a power vacuum, and the interregnum was marked by considerable ethnic violence, which drew out latent ethnic tensions that had existed before the war.

The unsettled conditions continued even after the interregnum came to an end, with the strikes of the later months of 1945 and the first quarter of 1946 met by increasing British repression.[5] At the same time as the British tried to quell these strikes, they were faced by an upsurge of Malay nationalism, roused in objection to the proposals of the Malayan Union, which aimed to curtail Malay privileges and widen citizenship rights for members of other ethnic groups. This upsurge of nationalist sentiment culminated in the formation of the United Malays National Organisation (UMNO).[6]

Moreover, throughout this period, the British struggled to recover lost prestige in the teeth of challenges from all sectors of Malayan society. To begin with, many Malayans welcomed the returning British with open arms. In Singapore, a Force 136 staff officer named Hugh Pagden commented that when he went to the Chinese Protectorate building, the crowd in the street 'cheered itself hoarse'.[7] In the town of Kuala Lipis in Pahang, George Leonard of Operation *Pontoon* was followed around 'by hordes of cheering people' and greeted by a towkay who 'wept openly on my shoulder... and dug into his back yard and supplied us with Allsop's Ale, with ice'.[8] Yet as the more astute observers noted – Hugh Pagden among them – this delighted welcome was based, as much as anything, upon relief, and there were, moreover, Malayans who were less than thrilled to see a British administration returning, with the mood varying from disinterest to hostility. In Negri Sembilan, a BMA administrator noted that some members of the community were 'apathetic' about the return of the British, and others only 'mildly relieved'.[9] Further north, a young officer with the British Army saw 'overt animosity' in the behaviour of Indian shopkeepers.[10] Furthermore, the body through which the British initially attempted to recover their shattered prestige, the BMA, was flawed by corruption and unable to rule effectively or provide adequate rice to feed the country, due to a combination of its own failings and international shortages; the euphoria thus quickly soured.[11] On all of this, the broad sweep of scholarship concurs.

Nevertheless, some points of disagreement remain in the historical literature. One of these is the extent to which the interregnum is seen as the opening act to a period which, though violent and unsettled, was also one of great political hope and expectation. Many Malayans, and not just the MCP alone, campaigned for increased democratic rights and sought to influence the shape of the future state. Christopher Bayly and Tim Harper, as well as John Springhall, present the BMA period as a brief 'Malayan Spring' during which political doors were opened, newspapers sprang up and artistic life throve.[12] Ultimately, this sense of hope was crushed by what Springhall terms 'clumsy and heavy-handed British military rule' which turned again to 'repressive but convenient pre-war measures' such as banishment.[13] '[T]he popular democratic will', as seen by Bayly and Harper, had proved too strong a challenge for a weakened empire, even though the MCP leader Lai Teck had revised his orders to the MPAJA and was explicitly urging a united front rather than armed revolution.[14] By contrast, Cheah Boon Kheng, as well as Ban Kah Choon and Yap Hong Kuan, see this period as primarily one of conflict, with Cheah describing the murderous strife between the Malay and Chinese communities as 'a tragedy in which the two major races were driven headlong into a deadly conflict', with the MCP also seeking to 'discredit the BMA'.[15] For Ban and Yap, 'the signs of impending trouble [between the British and the MCP] were everywhere...The war was over but another was clearly in the making'.[16] In addition, while Springhall as well as Bayly and Harper view the challenge to the colonial state as coming from the grassroots during this period, Cheah, Ban and Yap see it in narrower terms as emerging primarily from within the MCP – and also, in Cheah's case, from the upswing in Malay nationalism indicated by the formation of UMNO.

Another important aspect of the interregnum that historians have yet to agree upon is the MPAJA's stockpiling of arms during the interregnum and the early part of the BMA period. Cheah states that after the disbandment of the MPAJA, 'it was reported that only old-type weapons had been turned in'.[17] As we shall show, the MPAJA in fact surrendered virtually all the modern weapons that Force 136 had issued to individual guerrillas. Nonetheless, there remained valid (as it turned out) suspicions among British officers serving in Malaya as to the fate of weapons that the Special Operations Executive (SOE) had dropped to the MPAJA that had allegedly gone astray.[18] As for the degree to which the MPAJA looted for arms and other goods after the Japanese surrender, this too, in the current literature, remains an open question. Cheah mentions only in passing that, early in the interregnum, the MPAJA guerrillas made 'repeated attacks' on Japanese troops and local police to obtain their arms.[19] Bayly and Harper, by contrast, contend that the MPAJA negotiated for arms with the Japanese, again early in the interregnum, prior to the wide promulgation and acceptance of Lai Teck's revised directive to the MCP concerning their planned anti-colonial rising against the returning British.[20]

Using additional documents from the Force 136 archive, which have become available since these earlier studies were published, this chapter will revisit the question of how, why and to what extent the MPAJA obtained additional arms following the Japanese surrender.[21] It will also re-examine the familiar story of the BMA's rule over Malaya, adding, from the ground level, new understandings of what has been termed the British 'reconquest' of Malaya.

The documents this chapter draws upon were the product of the direct reconnaissance work of the Force 136 teams and of the information that emerged from their networks of diverse Malayan contacts, who were often well placed to know of local events. To take one example, Ian McDonald, a liaison officer with *Galvanic* in Selangor, included among his close contacts the Mother Superior of the Klang convent, a senior Ceylonese clerk in the local administration, the leader of the Chinese community in the town where he was based, a Japanese who had been resident in Malaya for twenty years, half a dozen ex-Volunteers (a group of Eurasians, three Chinese), the district officer (who must be assumed to have been Malay) and a Tamil doctor.[22] Nor was McDonald unique in the broad spread of his contacts: other Force 136 officers were in touch with locally resident Danes and members of the Indian National Army.[23] When Jock Hunter (the leader of *Galvanic Blue*) returned to Kuala Lumpur in August 1945, he soon visited the family of Gorbex Singh, a cricketing comrade from before the war.[24] Force 136 officers also had contacts deep in the Malayan jungles, with many officers noting the assistance given to them by the *Orang Asli*.[25]

In this chapter, a consistent effort has been made to establish the reliability of Force 136 reports during the interregnum by reading them against sources available from within the MPAJA. These other sources often corroborate the claims made by Force 136 officers. For instance, the Force 136 claims of widespread looting by the MPAJA during the interregnum are backed up by Chin Peng. As we shall also see, Force 136's assertion that the MCP's 'outside organization' was taking the law into its own hands during this period is supported by the testimony of the MPAJA foot-soldier Ho Thean Fook who tells us that, at least within the area of Perak where he was based, this was clearly the case. This is not to say that Force 136 was aware of everything that happened during the interregnum. In numerous cases it is clear that while many Force 136 officers had suspicions about the activities of the MCP, the information that some of them received was partly controlled by the MCP and the resulting shallowness of their intelligence left them if not entirely ignorant, then poorly informed. This lack of concrete knowledge is especially revealed by the case of Lau Mah, who was presented to Force 136 as a Chinese translator. A number of officers who mentioned Lau Mah in their reports picked up on the considerable (and to their minds negative) influence he wielded over the rankers of the MPAJA. However, it appears that none of them realized, or at least reported, the fact that this same Lau Mah was the Deputy State Secretary of the Perak MCP.[26]

Indeed, while Force 136's view at ground level was impressive during the interregnum and after, when it came to decisions made at the very top of the communist hierarchy in Malaya it remained completely in the dark. In mid-August 1945, according to Chin Peng, Lai Teck pulled the MPAJA back from launching a coup d'état. He announced instead that both the 'secret army' and the MPAJA were to disband, but that the 'secret army' would leave its weapons stashed and waiting.[27] The reports of Force 136 officers make no mention of Lai Teck's directive: it clearly remained secret from the British. They do, however, refer to the release of the Eight Point Programme – a document so anodyne that Admiral Mountbatten's adviser Esler Dening thought it 'irreproachable'.[28]

Despite these limitations, the remainder of this chapter will show that the Force 136 archive – principally but not exclusively the reports written by its officers – provides numerous insights pertaining to the local political situation in Malaya in the four to six months following the war. In particular, these sources shed new light on the activities and attitudes of the MCP in this period, and on the internal tensions to which it was prey. These tensions included those that arose as a result of the duplicity of the party's leader, the past and future double agent Lai Teck, and those that emerged between moderate cadres prepared to accept his revised directive and their more radical comrades, who, according to Chin Peng, were filled with 'revolutionary spirit' in the immediate aftermath of the war.[29] The chapter will then move on to a discussion of the varied manner in which the MPAJA was represented by Force 136 officers, and how this mixed picture was edited, unified and presented to those further up the hierarchy. Finally, an assessment will be made as to how far the Force's reports offered a warning to the British about the potential of the MCP to lead a future armed insurgency.

'Revolutionary spirit'? Looting for arms and other goods

The terms of the Blantan Agreement bound the MPAPJA to continue to cooperate with the British for as long as 'the [British] army is responsible for the maintenance of Peace and Order in Malaya'.[30] Subsequently, South East Asia Command issued orders in mid-August 1945 that instructed the MPAJA guerrillas to stay out of the towns and avoid all contact with the Japanese, an order that John Davis understood to be untenable: why, he wondered, should these fighters have to remain 'half-starved in the hills'?[31] On around 22 August, the MPAJA headquarters gave the order for its guerrillas to enter the towns and take control of the administration.[32] Guerrillas then began to slip away from their Force 136 liaison officers, joining members of the Malayan People's Anti-Japanese Union (MPAJU) already in the towns and other settlements of Malaya. Many of Force 136's former allies were now out of its sight and beyond its control.

As we noted in Chapter 3, Lai Teck had all along had other plans that involved the MCP using the 'secret army' as well as the MPAJA to seize control of Malaya, and it was these plans that the MCP's cadres initially sought to fulfil as they moved into the towns. Before Lai Teck's revised directive was circulated, his cadres had a week of preparing, as Chin Peng put it, 'to target the returning colonial power'.[33] Careful reading of Chin Peng's memoirs indicates that he was in no hurry to pass on Lai Teck's new orders to the MPAJA. Though Chin Peng received these orders on 19 August, he then visited John Davis (on Lai Teck's orders), but not until 25 August did he begin to spread the word through northern Malaya of the order for the 'open army' to surrender its arms, and the 'secret army' to stash its weapons.[34] When this revised order went out, some cadres seem to have interpreted the order to stash the weapons of the 'secret army' as preparation for the coming revolution, and thus as tacitly permitting the acquisition of further arms. Chin Peng states that some cadres approached Japanese troops to ask them to come over to the MPAJA, bringing their weapons with them.[35] Of the Japanese arms obtained by the MPAJA, he says that some were abandoned, but that 'many were acquired after negotiations with senior officers in Japanese garrisons'.[36] In this way, he implies that a substantial part of the eventual armoury of the Malayan National Liberation Army (MNLA) came from these sources, rather than from Force 136 airdrops.[37]

The MPAJA's negotiations with the Japanese and their allies for arms are likewise a recurrent theme in the Force 136 reports. In Ringlet, in the area of operations of the 5th Regiment, a free Dane named Rasmussen reported to a Force 136 liaison officer that MPAJA guerrillas were dealing with the Japanese for arms, and that they had contacted local units of the Indian National Army, also requesting arms.[38] That Force 136 officers were well aware of the risk of Japanese weapons coming into the hands of the MPAJA is revealed by the fact that the subject was raised three times in the correspondence of the Malay Operation *Beacon* in Pahang.[39] Force 136's Field Intelligence reports twice reported that, as late as mid-September, and long after Lai Teck's new orders should have been known to all MPAJA regiments, the Japanese were either selling or giving guns to the MPAJA near Kulim in Kedah.[40] There are also claims in Force 136's operational reports that the communist guerrillas, especially in areas out of contact with the MPAJA HQ, were seizing police arms.[41] John Creer, who was in Kelantan until late September, reported that communists had obtained police weapons from a Japanese in Kuala Krai.[42] There is, therefore, overwhelming corroborating evidence from Force 136 officers and their informants that the MPAJA was obtaining arms from the Japanese and the police, and that this activity continued well into September, weeks after it would have been reasonable to expect the MPAJA units in question to have received Lai Teck's new orders.

Aside from Japanese arms, the Force 136 archive also provides strong evidence that the MPAJA retained considerable quantities of arms dropped into Malaya by SOE. Chin Peng claimed in his memoir that the MPAJA stashed 5,000 weapons at the end of the war, of which only 10 per cent (500) had come via Force 136, thus implying that 90 per cent of the weapons later held by the MNLA consisted of battlefield pick-ups, shotguns, seized police arms and weapons obtained from the Japanese.[43] However, Chin Peng's assertion needs to be read against Force 136's consolidated arms return for Malaya.[44] This return includes totals for each type of weapon introduced into the field, as well as for any category not issued by Force 136 but nonetheless handed in by the various guerrilla groups. Its data appears to have been arrived at by collating the figures for weapons dropped into the field and the numbers handed in to the Force 136 operations during disbandment. Each operation submitted its own arms return, which showed how many arms, of which type, it had issued, and how many had been handed in (including those of types that had not been issued).[45] When the figures in all of the operational arms returns are added together, the total of weapons issued to guerrilla patrols or lost to the Japanese (around 3,200 arms altogether) is lower than the total shown as issued in the consolidated return (4,765).[46] This implies that the consolidated return gives the totals for all weapons infiltrated into Malaya by SOE, including those in containers not recovered by Force 136.

It appears that much of this deficiency was due to the MPAJA informing Force 136 officers that containers of arms, dropped by SOE, had gone astray and were lost, when in fact the arms concerned had been spirited away by the guerrillas. The operational arms returns indicate that although the Malay operations returned all weapons issued (there is no suggestion, anywhere in the Force 136 archive, that arms dropped to Malay guerrillas went missing), consistent hints and claims are made by liaison officers that arms containers dropped to the MPAJA had a tendency to disappear. The liaison officers would be told that a container, or containers, could not be found.[47] According to Chin Peng himself, the guerrillas were under instructions to secrete all the weapons that they could if airdropped containers landed away from Force 136 operatives.[48]

The consolidated return also indicates that more weapons were handed in (5,497) than were dropped by Force 136 during the war (4,765). Of the weapons

Table 6.1 Weapons Infiltrated but not Recovered by Force 136

Main weapons missing, by type	Issued	Recovered	With absconded guerrillas[a]	Number deficient	% deficient
Pistols, all varieties[b]	848	395	7	446	53
Sten guns	1647	1253	21	373	23
.30 carbines	1909	1590	2	317	16
Total	4404	3238	30	1136	26

Notes

[a] These were the OCAJA guerrillas who refused to disband. See Chapter 5.

[b] This excludes on the Verey light pistols; of the eight dropped, seven did not reappear. They were useful for jungle signalling and were used by the MNLA early in the Emergency. See *Straits Times*, 20 June 1948, p. 1.

Source: TNA, HS 7/165, Calculated from 'Weapons issued to and recovered from the field in Malaya'.

handed in, the ones most in surplus were those that were either less desirable for jungle warfare or of an unknown age and condition: shotguns (1,104, of unknown age, type and state of repair), .303 Lee Enfield rifles (690, which were standard British Army issue and therefore almost certainly gleaned from the battlefields in 1941 and 1942) and assorted pistols (250, again, of unknown age, type and state of repair). In other words, as the MPAJA officer Reg Lawther recalled, the MPAJA kept the best weapons.[49] It was worth the MPAJA's while to hand in arms with little fighting value, for each disarmed and disbanded guerrilla was paid a bonus of $350, $200 of which was claimed by the MCP.[50]

During the war, SOE dropped arms into Malaya packed into containers, usually with several types packed together. If the containers had gone randomly astray, one would expect approximately the same proportion of each type of weapon to be missing.[51] However, the percentages of weapons not recovered from the guerrillas vary from zero (for a variety of silenced pistol, Bren guns, and 3" mortars), through to 16 per cent of carbines, 23 per cent of Sten guns, 35 per cent of the lightweight EY rifles and 69 per cent of .45 automatic pistols.[52] Indeed, altogether, more than 50 per cent of all pistols dropped into Malaya by Force 136 disappeared from the view of the British.

What is particularly interesting about Force 136's consolidated return is not the number of weapons handed in, but what it reveals about those that went missing: they were the arms most suited to jungle warfare and assassination. Of the weapons in notable surplus, the excess pistols were of unknown type and condition, and it is not clear either what ammunition they took. For the MPAJA it would have made sense to retain guns that were in good repair and used ammunition that was available from British or Japanese stocks, and therefore to retain, preferentially, new pistols which used British ammunition. As for the shotguns and Lee Enfield rifles, both were heavy and long, and therefore unsuitable for jungle warfare. The Lee Enfields were not popular with the guerrillas, despite possessing considerably more firepower than shotguns.[53] Reg Lawther, of the MPAJA in east Pahang, described the Lee Enfield as 'an unwieldy weapon for use in the jungle because of its length and weight ... It often got entangled in the creepers and foliage'.[54] Shotguns, with their short effective range, were useful only for close-range ambushes.[55]

On the other hand, the weapons recommended for jungle fighting by military training manuals were the short, comparatively light machine carbines (such as the Sten, of which 373 vanished into the Malayan jungles), pistols and knives, and perhaps also light rifles.[56] The Sten was a popular weapon with SOE units, and had the advantage of being a simple weapon, easy to use, maintain, dismantle and conceal, and with a minimal kick when fired.[57] Its rapid rate of fire also meant that its user did not require elaborate target-shooting training and practise. Pistols were also useful for assassination, the incidence of which, as will be discussed in Chapter 7, increased sharply in the approach to the Malayan Emergency. Bren guns, which had considerable firepower, appear to have been returned as they were hard to use: Chin Peng said of them that they 'were just too big for us to control without proper instruction'.[58] They were also heavy, weighing over 20lb.

Press reports from mid-1948 onwards indicate that communist insurgents in Malaya made frequent use of, in particular, Thompson submachine guns (Tommy guns), Stens and pistols.[59] The fondness for pistols coincides with the substantial proportion that disappeared. The insurgents' Tommy guns would have come from the battlefields in 1941–1942, for all of those – and more – supplied by Force 136 were handed in at disbandment. (Although, again, the Tommy guns that were handed in were in unknown condition, and the $350 disbandment bonus may well have been a lure). Stens, however, were not produced until early in 1941, were not in bulk production until late 1942 and did not arrive in Asia in any quantity until 1944.[60] Thus the Stens used by the insurgents can only have come from Force 136 drops.

In sum, Chin Peng's claim that, of the 5,000 weapons stashed by the MPAJA at the end of the war, only 500 came from Force 136 sources does not seem to be entirely accurate.[61] Certainly, some of the weapons dropped by SOE were genuinely lost – perhaps 10 per cent (the percentage is unlikely to have been higher, given that all of some categories of weapon dropped were recovered). If a 10 per cent rate of loss is a fair estimate, this would mean that the MPAJA retained around 600 Stens and carbines, and about 400 pistols – a thousand guns in total. Force 136, then, appears to have provided about 20 per cent of the MNLA's arsenal. This figure of around 20 per cent seems credible, for it is reflected in the press reports of seizures from arms dumps before the Emergency. Of arms whose original source can be judged, 36 were Stens or American carbines, and almost certainly came from Force 136 drops, whereas about 125 were likely to have been either battlefield pick-ups or obtained from the Japanese.[62] In other words, a little over 22 per cent of the guns recovered from these dumps came from SOE sources. A figure of 20 per cent is not particularly high in itself, but the key thing to bear in mind is that this 20 per cent was almost entirely comprised of those types of gun ideal for future insurgent activity. As a result of its association with Force 136, the MCP had a bigger, and much better, arsenal for jungle warfare and assassination. SOE's unintended contribution to the MCP's arsenal was therefore considerable, greater than Chin Peng suggests, and also of superior types of weapon for the purposes intended. It is not beyond the bounds of possibility that the former members of

Force 136 shot dead during the Emergency fell victim to SOE weapons, loaded with SOE ammunition.[63]

As well as arms, the MPAJA and other communist bodies looted various goods during the interregnum, either for distribution to increase their own prestige, to use later or to sell to raise money, as both Chin Peng and the Force 136 reports confirm. Chin Peng states that, though some people bought rubber from the Japanese during this period, 'we [the MCP] just seized [it]' and stored it in warehouses for 'we had the weapons to protect our interests'. The party made $2 million (Straits) when the rubber market restarted.[64] In addition to rubber, Force 136 officers in Johore, Pahang, Negri Sembilan and Perak reported that the communists spirited away supplies of rice and other items.[65] It is unclear if the MPAJA planned to sell the rice (virtually a currency at a time when the Japanese scrip had been demonetized on orders from Whitehall) or distribute it as a means of increasing its own prestige and authority, or both. In any case, the reality was that food was still in short supply and the BMA was struggling to feed the population.[66] The MCP also engaged in some deft fundraising, for example by insisting that vehicle owners purchase 'licences' from the local 'People's Committee' – which seem to have been the reincarnation of the MPAJU.[67]

Read alongside what Chin Peng himself tells us in his memoirs, Force 136 reports indicate that the MPAJA was preparing itself for a future conflict. The cadres appear to have made a broad interpretation of Lai Teck's revised orders instructing them to surrender the arms held by the 'open' MPAJA and to stash those held by the 'secret army'. They took the opportunities presented by the chaos of the interregnum and the early BMA period to obtain additional weapons for the future armed struggle that Chin Peng, perhaps with the wisdom of hindsight, has told us he felt the MPAJA 'would, undoubtedly, be [waging] five to ten years hence'.[68] The cadres also acted promptly to ensure a flow of cash for the MCP's coffers through the looting of rubber. The stocks of rice they acquired, on the other hand, might have been held for later distribution to the population, as a way of increasing the popularity and legitimacy of the party, or feeding their army in the field. This begs the question: should it have been clear to the British from the intelligence recorded by Force 136 officers that the MPAJA was likely to pose a direct armed threat to the power of the colonial state?

The MPAJA: influencing the population

Some of the Force 136 reports surveyed for this chapter also provide considerable evidence that the MPAJA and the People's Committees, through their control of a considerable proportion of Malaya's small towns, used the power vacuum as a time to strengthen their organization, both materially and in terms of the political legitimacy they enjoyed among the wider population.[69] These reports substantiate the claim made by Bayly and Harper (drawing upon Cheah) that 70 per cent of the urban areas of the peninsula were under communist control.[70] So far as Spencer Chapman could see, Kuantan and much of Malay-majority east Pahang were being run by the 7th Regiment of the MPAJA, which had formed local unions and dominated local society via control of the administration.[71] There is also clear evidence in the Force 136 documentation that, if the MPAJA did not control Kuala Lumpur, it certainly exerted considerable authority there.[72]

The Force 136 reports also tell us that the MCP was trying to prepare the population for rebellion. Near Ringlet, the free Dane Rasmussen told Force 136 that a local MPAJA leader had told him 'that if the M.P.A.J.A. did not get their demands from the British Govt. they would use their arms to obtain them'.[73] According to the local Force 136 liaison officer, this same MPAJA leader made speeches of a 'nationalist kind' to the population in Ringlet and Kampar that were so strong in tone that the Force 136 officer felt constrained to put across 'the British point of view'.[74] Ho Thean Fook (who also served as translator to Force 136 officers) recounts that a woman in his hometown of Papan told him that the MPAJU 'have told us not to be too happy. They warned us that the war wasn't over yet'.[75]

The MPAJU and some units of the MPAJA sought to reinforce their status as the scourge not only of the Japanese, but also of those who had supported them. The same direction from Lai Teck that instructed the MPAJA to go into the towns also told local parties to set up People's Committees.[76] Force 136 reports give us an insight into how these committees took over the running of the towns, doing everything from imposing price controls and organizing rationing to the production and distribution of propaganda.[77] These committees also made arrests and held public trials of alleged collaborators. A patrol leader of the MPAJA's 5th Regiment held trials in Ringlet, just over the state boundary in Pahang.[78] In Johore, a Force 136 officer accused the local MPAJA of 'murder and intimidation'; another in the same area reported that the communists had beheaded three men.[79] In eastern Pahang, the area under the sway of the 7th Regiment, trials were held with no defence being offered to the accused.[80] Policemen were killed in districts as far apart as Karak (Pahang) and Seremban in Negri Sembilan.[81] The MCP, backed by the MPAJA, was assuming the mantle of the state, meting out brutal justice via its own courts.

The Force 136 documents also show that, besides storing arms and supplies in readiness for the next conflict and preparing the people for revolution, communists also killed or intimidated people they thought were too close to the British. Major G.A. Hasler, leading Operation *Fighter* in Kedah, reported that a *ketua kampong* (village headman) he knew had been killed, adding 'I can only imagine that he was murdered because he had been working for me.'[82] An MPAJA guerrilla, Cheng Kian Koon, who had been sent to India for training by John Davis and later infiltrated into Malaya, was killed after the Japanese surrender by the communists, who believed him to be a traitor.[83] Similarly, Creer relates that a Chinese who had assisted him during his time in the jungle had been 'beaten up and driven from his home' at Ringlet by communists.[84] The MPAJA man Ho Thean Fook recorded in his memoir that Kai Loh Weng, a Chinese who had formerly belonged to the Royal Army Service Corps, and who had been instrumental in providing arms for the communists at the beginning of the Japanese occupation, was nonetheless killed by the 'outside organization' at the end of the war.[85] In Negri

Sembilan, MPAJA cadres entered the 'agricultural settlement' of Fuji-Go, some miles east of the town of Bahau. Many of its residents were Eurasians, some of whom had moved there to escape the threat of arrest and torture that had hung over them in Singapore, or who had already suffered at the hands of the Kempeitai. A detachment of MPAJA guerrillas entered the site the day after the occupants had enjoyed a victory party and reprimanded them for singing 'God Save the King'. They also arrested three members of the settlement, threatened to execute them and put them on trial.[86] These trials, beatings and killings continued even as the British began to exert control over Malaya. In mid-September 1945, Force 136's Field Intelligence summaries reported that the district officer of Kluang in Johore had vanished.[87]

Historians have noted the fact that such activity created tensions between the communists and other groups, particularly Malays, though some Chinese were also alienated.[88] Cheah has argued both these points, noting that some aspects of the communists' behaviour during this period served to convince many people that communist rule would be terrifying.[89] As Cheah observes, the behaviour of the communists towards the Malay-majority police force and local officials (also often Malays), antagonized Malay sentiment and roused Malay communities who then attacked Chinese villagers.[90] In Malay memory, he says, the interregnum was remembered as a time of terror – as, indeed, it still is by those who were children at the time.[91] As Cheah further argues, the manner in which the MPAJA acted towards Malay police and officials, and reacted during the ethnic strife, was short-sighted, but also a consequence of a cycle of events that was out of their control.[92] The administrator John Gullick observed that, to Malays who shortly assumed positions of leadership within their community, these incidents were 'a demonstration of what the Chinese, if they ever obtained political control, might do'.[93]

The Force 136 reports support Cheah's claims, and extend them beyond the western littoral of Malaya that is the focus of his study. They also reveal a further startling dimension: Japanese involvement in fanning post-war racial tension.[94] In Pahang during the interregnum, news reached Wataniah that the Sultan of Pahang, who had recently passed through Kuala Lipis en route to his *istana* at Pekan, had not arrived home. In fact, the sultan, who had been travelling with some valuable goods, had been waylaid by a small party of Europeans and Nationalist Chinese under the command of an officer of the American Office of Strategic Services, who belonged to the Force 136 Operation *Pontoon*.[95] The sultan and his party were quite safe, if somewhat bored, being accommodated in a shed on a pineapple plantation.[96] However, the Japanese propaganda officer in Raub produced a script that was to be translated into Malay and distributed through the town, which gave a quite different impression: 'can there be any means of saving H.H. [His Highness] from the hdnas [sic] of these brigands? Do not we, the Malays, feel sorry and ashamed of the bully made by these rogues on His Highness ...?' The task of distributing this leaflet was given to Ghazalie bin Shafie – he who had admired the twinkling stars the night he heard of the Japanese surrender – who was employed by the Japanese as an administrator but was also one of Wataniah's lieutenants.[97] To his mind, this script had only one purpose: 'to stir the feelings' of the Malays 'to go against the Chinese.'[98] Ghazalie did not know what had become of the sultan but, wise to the danger of ethnic strife, he ensured that the posters were never displayed. The Japanese attempt to envenom local race relations did not succeed.

One final point that emerges from a study of the Force 136 information relating to the interregnum is that the contest between the communists and other guerrilla organizations for territorial control – which we discussed at length in Chapter 5 – did not end with the surrender of Japan. Despite their best efforts, the communists were not able to control all the towns that they attempted to enter, for some were already in the hands of other guerrilla groups. Parties of OCAJA and Askar Melayu Setia (AMS) guerrillas entered a number of towns ahead of the MPAJA, thus denying the communists the control they sought. Robert Chrystal relates a confrontation that occurred when the MPAJA tried to enter a town garrisoned by the OCAJA. He and Peter Dobrée had heard of the surrender, but due to the illness of their radio operator they had not received the standstill order that instructed them to remain in the jungle. Consequently, they took a mixed group of AMS and Guomindang guerrillas into the small town of Grik in upper Perak to maintain order. Then, at the request of the Sultan of Perak, who was fearful of a communist takeover, Dobrée took the AMS to Kuala Kangsar.[99] Soon after, the MPAJA attempted to enter Grik, but were prevented from doing so by Chrystal and the Guomindang. During the resulting confrontation, Chrystal negotiated with the MPAJA with 'sten-guns cocked and aimed at our stomachs' and later recalled, 'I've never been more scared in all my life.'[100] On 8 September, another mixed party, again of AMS and OCAJA, entered Kota Bharu to take control of the town, on the urging of an officer of the American Office of Strategic Services who was worried about the communists.[101] At the end of August, Wataniah occupied Raub with Operation *Beacon*. Douglas Richardson, who led *Beacon*, made no mention of encountering any MPAJA in the town.[102] Thus, though the MPAJA was clearly the strongest armed guerrilla force in Malaya at the end of the war, it is clear that in some areas non-communist guerrillas were able, and indeed encouraged, to deny it control over towns and settlements.

Force 136: the interpretation of information

In spite of everything the officers of Force 136 had recorded as having taken place – the revolutionary speeches to prepare the population for a future conflict against the British, the disappearance and stashing of British and Japanese arms, the looting of supplies, the killing of British allies and the political domination of many small towns – no warning emerged from the Force 136 reports as to the immediate and likely threat that the MCP posed to the returning colonial power. Two main factors explain this failure. The first is the variability in the behaviour of the MPAJA across Malaya. The second is the different ways in which the Force 136 officers interpreted the activities of the MCP and the MPAJA. As a consequence, as we shall now discuss, no clear intelligence picture emerged of the revolutionary potential and intentions of the MPAJA, and at the same time the MCP's push to dominate Malayan political life was obscured.

Read as a whole, Force 136 reports show that at the end of the war the MPAJA hardly behaved as a unified force; rather, there existed a wide spatial variability in the reactions of its various regiments and patrols to the defeat of the Japanese and the return of the British. One or two regiments were consistently willing to cooperate with Force 136 during the interregnum. The 1st Regiment, in Selangor, was universally noted for its cooperation. In Selangor's capital, Kuala Lumpur, the former rubber planter, Jock Hunter, described in his report the manner in which Cheng Nam, the MPAJA patrol leader with whom he worked, assisted in halting the looting that was going on in the town.[103] Another former planter, Ian McDonald, recorded the considerable assistance he was given by the patrol he was with, including their reliable guardianship of a stock of sheet rubber worth around $375,000 and their assistance in routing a party of bandits who had taken over a police station.[104] But in other regiments, in the weeks and months after the war, there was considerable variation from patrol to patrol in their attitude towards the British. At least two regiments were not well controlled by the MCP and required serious pressure from the MCP hierarchy to bring them into line with Lai Teck's new directive not to push for an immediate post-war revolution.

Most probably, the considerable variation in the attitude of the MPAJA towards the British from one patrol to another was a result of the varying levels of radicalism among its senior cadres. While Major Grant of *Funnel Orange* found the MPAJA in the Ringlet area defiant and out of his control, Majors Owen (leading *Funnel Green*) and Ross (of *Funnel Blue*) had few complaints to make, at least until the run-up to disbandment. Where Force 136 officers did have problems, they tended to pin these precisely on particular men, such as the 5th Regiment's military commander Col. Itu, and Lau Mah, who as we have noted, was a high-ranking figure within the Perak MCP, though the Force 136 officers knew him only as an interpreter.[105]

Moreover, though Lai Teck and other senior party leaders tried to impose tight control during the Japanese occupation, slow communications within the Malayan interior meant that some units had acted with considerable independence. Regiments at the limits of contact from the MPAJA's headquarters (such as the 6th and 8th Regiments) or out of contact altogether (as was the case with the 7th in eastern Pahang) were those that most consistently defied Force 136's instructions. During the war, they had either been reluctant to accept Force 136 liaison officers or, as in the case of the 7th again, not wanted any, and by the time of the Japanese surrender, the Force 136 officers who had contact with them mistrusted them. The 6th Regiment, in western Pahang, was described by its liaison officer, Major George Leonard, as being 'uncontrolled, anti-British, not organised, and non-cooperative' and 'a bunch of bandits'.[106] Major Jim Hislop, with the 8th Regiment in Kedah, was not allowed into the MPAJA's camps, and his mistrust of them permeates his report.[107] It took a visit by Chin Peng, and a change of leadership within both the local MPAJA and the Force 136 team to bring this regiment into line with Lai Teck's August directive.[108] The 7th Regiment had never wanted to work with the British and, in any case, did not receive a liaison team from Force 136 until Operation *Siphon* was dropped to them after the surrender.[109] Ultimately, it required the intervention of both Freddy Spencer Chapman (known to the regiment from the Japanese occupation) and the MPAJA high command before the regiment agreed to cooperate with the returning colonial power.[110] Even then their cooperation was, in Spencer Chapman's view, 'anything but gracious'.[111]

This, then, was the first blurred lens that clouded the picture presented by Force 136 of the MCP during the interregnum. On top of this was laid another: the varied interpretations that Force 136 officers placed upon what they observed. In general, officers who found their MPAJA patrols or regiments cooperative wrote much the same things: that the MPAJA had been helpful, well disciplined and so on. However, when Force 136 officers encountered difficulties with the guerrillas, their reactions varied greatly depending on their backgrounds. The main contrast was between those officers who were British Malayans or had some other prior experience in Asia (who accounted for all of the Group Liaison Officers – GLOs – and about half the Patrol Liaison Officers), and men with prior SOE experience in the Balkans (a minority of about half a dozen).[112] As will be shown, the British Malayan officers tended to make precise distinctions between the MPAJA and other communist bodies, whereas officers who had spent time with Balkan partisans saw all communist organizations as different arms of the same body and made broader generalizations. Those with Balkan experience appear to have become deeply cynical about the Malayan communists.[113]

Another reason why the MPAJA's revolutionary potential did not come through clearly in the Force 136 reports was the proximity of many British Malayan Force 136 officers to their patrols. This tendency of liaison officers to draw close to resistance bodies was noted in a memo to Edward Gent: 'in the course of time the LO [Liaison Officer] becomes rather embued [sic] with the views of the resistance movement to which they [sic] are attached'.[114] This judgement probably applied most of all to the British Malayan Force 136 officers, because they all spoke at least some Malay and were able to converse directly with the guerrillas. Indeed, the quote above referred specifically to the former Malayan policeman John Davis, a fluent Cantonese speaker. It certainly appears that when members of this group of officers saw or heard of communist extortion, abduction and murder, they tended to blame it on other communist bodies – such as the MPAJU and the People's Committees – rather than the MPAJA.

The result was that the MCP's armed wing, the MPAJA, frequently appeared in Force 136 reports as quiescent and easily controllable. Even Ian McDonald in Selangor, who, according to his personnel report, 'had little or NO sympathy for Chinese guerrillas and their aims', was careful to differentiate between the behaviour of his patrol, and that of the 'three-star impersonators' who were 'looting and extorting' in outlying districts.[115] Similarly, the policeman Claude Fenner, GLO of Operation *Humour* in Negri Sembilan, drew a clear distinction between the guerrillas under his nominal command and 'certain irresponsible and lawless elements of communist sympathies, probably members of the Anti-Japanese

Plate 1 Major W.P.S 'Paddy' Brereton Martin.
Courtesy of Steven Brereton Martin.

Plate 2 Canadian Chinese, a Nationalist Chinese, and Capt. M.G. Levy.
Courtesy of Don Levy.

Plate 3 Yeung Wai Chong, 'A really first class man'.
Courtesy of the late Bill Foss.

Plate 4 Major Reg Lawther of the MPAJA.
Courtesy of the late Reg Lawther.

Plate 5 Effective MPAJA action: Japanese lorries after an MPAJA ambush, Perak, August 1945.
Courtesy of the late Bill Foss.

Plate 6 Zain Hussein (*Hebrides*) and Ibrahim Ismail (leader of *Oatmeal*).
Courtesy of Hassan Muthalib.

Plate 7 OCAJA, Force 136 and Malay guerrillas working together, Upper Perak.
Courtesy of Hassan Muthalib.

Plate 8 Guomindang flag on display during celebratory march, September 1945. Australian War Memorial.

Plate 9 Colonel Itu and Lt. Col. J.P. Hannah. The two men were in contact after the war. Photo courtesy of Tim Hannah.

Plate 10 MPAJA guerrillas beneath a victory arch, Slim River, August/September 1945. Some members of *Funnel* can be seen in the front row.

Courtesy of the late Bill Foss.

Plate 11 'Bandit camp', early in the Emergency, found by a team of 'Ferrets'.
Courtesy of the late Bill Foss.

Union', who he blamed for 'systemised extortion' which inflamed the Malay population.[116] Certain Force 136 officers were very trusting of the communists in general, and optimistic about the future. John Davis, the most senior Force 136 man on the ground in Malaya, had been hopeful at the end of July 1945 that the 'give and take' policy adopted with regard to AJUF (Anti-Japanese Union and Forces: the MPAJA and the MPAJU combined) would 'reduce the chance of anti-British policy being adopted by them at a later date'.[117]

In fact, only a small minority of the British Malayans who worked with the communists became deeply suspicious of the MPAJA, and these were the men who worked – or tried to work – with the three regiments who were independent of its central command: the 6th, 7th and 8th Regiments. George Leonard, GLO of the Force 136 team with the 6th Regiment, reported with approval Spencer Chapman's description of the regiment's leader as a 'two faced double-crossing bastard', and was adamant in his report that the local MPAJU was 'run and organised by the regiment'.[118] Yet even Leonard ultimately came to the view that, in the weeks leading up to disbandment, the regiment became 'friendly and cooperative', thanks to a mixture of judicious management and the persuasion applied by John Davis, who had paid a helpful visit. Leonard gave the impression that the difficulties he had encountered were due to a group of 'troublemakers' rather than to sentiments held by the bulk of the MPAJA rank and file.[119]

Much the same attitude can be found in the Force 136 reports from Kedah, the area overseen by Operation *Sergeant* where, as noted above, it took a reshuffle at the top to improve relationships between Force 136 and the MPAJA. Here, the new GLO, though he admitted that the local MPAJA 'had been guilty of abduction, murder, looting and anti-British propaganda', complained that the Force 136 liaison officers previously in post 'made no distinction between AJUF, communists and bandits', thus appearing to concur with the widespread view that the armed wing of the MCP was somehow divorced from the rest of the organization.[120] In general, the official view seemed to be that the MPAJA was overall a reasonable body. The first page of the operational report written by a former Malayan policeman Lt. Col. Douglas Broadhurst, with the 1st Regiment in Selangor, expresses his gratitude to the guerrillas for their assistance, especially during the interregnum.[121] If negative views about the MPAJA were expressed, among a generally favourable body of reports, they were usually limited to a particular individual (such as the 'interpreter' Lau Mah) who caused 'trouble' or 'was not a pleasant type'.[122] This attitude towards the MPAJA persisted, even though a number of officers, including John Davis, were well aware of the existence of guerrilla patrols with whom they had had no contact – in other words, they were alert to the possible existence of a communist 'secret army'.[123]

In contrast, Force 136 men who had served in the Balkans described in their operational reports what they considered to be disconcerting parallels between the activity of communist organizations in Malaya and those they had left behind in Europe. Hugh Munro, with Operation *Sergeant* in Kedah, commented that the 'methods and political propaganda' of the MPAJA in Kedah were 'identical to that of their Balan [sic: Balkan] friends'; he was sure that they had contemplated an uprising, 'in keeping with the "General Plan, all countries for the use of"' adopted elsewhere'.[124] Bertie Wright with *Carpenter* in Johore, at the opposite end of the country, noted that the 'political set-up of A.J.F. [Anti-Japanese Force: MPAJA] was exactly the same' as that of the partisans with whom he had worked in Albania: 'the real leader was the political chap', not the military commander.'[125] Both men accused the patrols they were with of variations on the themes of deceit and extortion.[126] Another ex-Balkans officer with *Carpenter*, Dare Newell, discovered, when he went on reconnaissance, that the MPAJA patrol he worked with had misled him about the conditions prevailing in the nearby town of Rengam after the surrender. Once he was in Rengam, he found the Japanese far more helpful than the local communists.[127]

In contrast, the British Malayans of *Carpenter* did not see this MPAJA regiment as either radical or particularly difficult. While their reports were not entirely positive, and though they noticed activities that should have worried a returning administration, they did not express the type of deep concerns recorded by Newell and Wright. For example, although David Trevaldwyn, a British Malayan planter who led *Carpenter Blue*, reported that the leader of the MPAJA patrol was extremely anxious to obtain as many weapons as possible, he failed to connect this to any wider strategy. This was the case even though, by the time he wrote his report in December 1945, he would almost certainly have heard about the activity of some of the more radical regiments.[128] The planter Neville Reddish, who led *Carpenter Orange*, likewise reported positively about the MPAJA men he worked with, and recorded no difficulties with them.[129] It appears that it was only the ex-Balkans officers with *Carpenter* who expressed long-term concerns about the MPAJA.

From the relevant Force 136 personnel reports, it also becomes clear that British Malayan officers in *Carpenter* did not take the concerns expressed about the 4th Regiment by Newell, Wright and another Balkan veteran, Capt. G.E.A. Whyte, entirely seriously. The personnel report of the ex-Albanian officer Capt. McCloy (Wright's second-in-command) described him, like Newell, as having been biased against the communists.[130] Only two men who had Balkans experience wrote generally positive reports on the MPAJA: Major Philip Thomson-Walker with *Galvanic*, who found that the MPAJA to have been extremely cooperative, and Major T.A. Wilson with *Funnel*.[131] The patrols with *Funnel*, as already noted, seem to have varied from the radically anti-British to the obliging, and *Galvanic* was attached to the ever-helpful 1st Regiment in Selangor, who had assisted Jock Hunter in quelling the looting in Kuala Lumpur.

On the whole, the reports by men who had served in the Balkans indicate that they saw the communists as organized and ruthless, echoing the comments made by Nigel Clive, an MI6 officer who worked in Greece. He reported at the time that the misdeeds of the communist forces made the rather questionable Republicans 'look innocent', and was convinced that the communists would practice the 'brutal elimination' of their opponents if they entered the towns, given their attitude towards justice in the mountain areas they controlled.[132] Similarly, W. Stanley Moss, with SOE on Crete, regarded the communists as merciless and self-serving.[133]

Significantly, those British Malayan member of Force 136 who were not with the MPAJA – those with the Malay guerrillas and the OCAJA – expressed views of the MPAJA that were almost universally negative. John Creer and Robert Chrystal expressed the strongest opinions, probably a result of their unhappy experiences with the communists during their three and a half years in the jungle.[134] In addition, Creer's 'best friend', the OCAJA leader Yong Kong, had been killed by them. As we have already seen, the MPAJA in Kedah, in northern Malaya, proved to be difficult for even the MPAJA's leadership to control, and in Perak Chrystal had further negative experience of the communists, when they attempted to enter Grik during the interregnum. In his eventual report, Chrystal warned, 'There may be trouble later from the Communist sponsored unions in Malaya.' The MPAJA, he concluded, were 'semi-educated gangsters'.[135] Chrystal had long since lost the sympathy he had once had with the communists' ambitions, and, like some of the ex-Balkans men, made a wider comparison, referring to the MPAJA conducting 'terrorism on Russian lines'.[136] Creer was likewise highly critical of the communists, stating in his report that they 'exterminated all who opposed them, of whatever race, sex or age, with the cruelty of fanaticism' and that they would go on breaking their promises for 'as long as we let them'.[137]

In summary, the potential for Force 136 to provide useful intelligence on the MPAJA after the Japanese surrender was undermined by the bifurcated manner in which it reported on them. There was a cleavage between the broadly positive language used of the communists by the British Malayans and others with Asian experience who were with the MPAJA, and the suspicious and oppositional terminology employed by disillusioned men who had either worked with guerrillas opposed to communist forces, or who drew parallels between the Balkans and Malaya. Though some of the British Malayans who had worked with the MPAJA did express concern at the widespread nature of communist activity, perceiving it as a challenge and as a threat, they tended – like Claude Fenner and Ian McDonald – to make a distinction between the MPAJA and the MCP. The officers who expressed forebodings were men who had worked with guerrillas opposed to them within Malaya, or had already seen communist bodies move from guerrilla warfare to running the government in Albania. In their minds, the parallels were too stark to be missed.

Conclusion

Through detailed exploration of the Force 136 archive, this chapter has suggested that although the MCP pulled back from immediate rebellion in August 1945, during the interregnum many of its cadres still considered the MPAJA to be a fundamentally revolutionary body. Consequently, they were sufficiently receptive to the idea of a future armed struggle that, even as they generally obeyed their leader's orders to fall back upon a political approach and worked to build up the party's base among the masses, they also salted away all the arms and ammunition that they might need in future. These arms were gathered from whatever sources were available: the MPAJA's own arsenals, the police and the Japanese. But the shotguns and rifles obtained in this way were not ideal weapons for jungle warfare, and so the MPAJA turned to supplies dropped by Force 136, arming itself with jungle weapons: machine carbines, pistols and lightweight rifles.

At the same time as the jungle caches were being laid down in boarded pits and cave systems, the MCP seized goods later saleable for cash. It also extended its meting out of post-war justice beyond Japanese collaborators to include those it felt to be close to the British. However, the pursuit of 'collaborators' embroiled the MCP in the ethnic unrest of Malaya's western littoral on the side of the Chinese, and compounded the alienation that already existed between the party and many Malays. In the long term, this would prove to be part of the MCP's undoing, for without broad-based support from the Malay community, it would have no hope of controlling the countryside during the Emergency.

The behaviour of MPAJA units immediately after the Japanese surrender also indicates a cleavage within the MPAJA, between cadres who were either well disciplined or genuinely moderate in their outlook, and those who were more radical in their approach, for not all MPAJA units reacted to instructions from their own leadership in the same way. Some were – outwardly at least – entirely cooperative with Force 136. Others defied the Force 136 officers until brought into line by their own high command. Yet others – for example, one of the patrols with *Funnel* – continued to jib at the constraints placed upon them almost up until disbandment.[138]

In terms of how the colonial authorities viewed the political situation after the war, the mixed picture provided by Force 136 was made yet more confusing by the manner in which its officers interpreted the MPAJA's actions. The range of these interpretations appeared to depend upon three things: where an officer had lived before the war, which guerrilla body he was associated with in Malaya and whether or not he had served in the Balkans. Men who were with non-communist guerrillas or who had been with SOE in the Balkans were especially critical of the communist guerrillas, and drew parallels between Malayan communist bodies and communist activity in other places. Two members of this group, Chrystal and Hugh Munro (with Operation *Sergeant*), were seriously concerned that the communists would press for their ends by violent means in the future; Munro rightly predicted 'that arming communists in Malaya would act as a boomerang on ourselves'.[139]

Yet, although the information in the Force 136 reports is confused, conflicting and contradictory, it is in hindsight nonetheless possible for the historian to analyse it, to break it apart and then put it back together into a coherent overall picture. Carefully read, the operational reports combine to give a picture broadly borne out by later events. The MPAJA men were praised for their steadfastness as allies during the occupation and for their assistance (in some places, at some times) during the interregnum, and criticized for what was seen as their obstinacy and defiance (in other places, at other times) during that same interregnum. They suggest too that the MPAJA had policies and plans of its own, to which the British were not party: 'uncontrolled' men came in for disbandment. That the communists retained an arsenal was 'public knowledge'.[140] The psychological and practical potential of Malayan communism to revolt against the British were both suggested: there were 'fanatics' among the leaders, networks of activists in every state, weapons hidden in the jungle.

Yet this overall picture was precisely what the intended readers of these reports failed to recognize. As a result, the extent of the MCP's potential threat to the colonial administration was overlooked. As the Colonial Office itself confessed, it was caught off-guard when violence and assassination reached such a pitch in Malaya in mid-1948 that the Malayan Emergency was declared.[141] The question of how the information in the mass of the Force 136 reports came to be missed by the Colonial Office will be tackled in the following chapter.

For all their limitations, the overall picture provided by the Force 136 reports cannot help but affect our view of the period between the surrender of Japan and the outbreak of the Emergency – those few years termed the 'Malayan Spring' by the novelist Han Suyin.[142] Bayly and Harper, focusing on the early part of 1946, see this period in lyrical terms, in contrast to the violence of the latter part of 1945. They argue that the MCP, with Lai Teck re-elected as Secretary General on a surge of support, at this time moved away from violence towards a united front espousing racial harmony. The MCP was entering the political field opened up by what they describe elsewhere as 'liberal imperialism' – a field soon closed down by the British administration which responded to strikes and rallies with old-style colonial repression.[143]

Yet the evidence presented in Force 136 reports, written by those close to and even – in the case of Creer and Chrystal – arguably within guerrilla movements, tells a rather different story. Lai Teck might have been re-elected on a moderate platform, but the MCP contained cadres who had worked hard and consistently to prepare both party and people for armed revolution. These cadres declared that they would turn to revolution if they did not succeed by other means. They knew that boarded pits contained weapons carefully greased for long-term storage. They remembered that the rural masses had supported them against the Japanese, and expected that they would be likely to support them again. According to Ho Thean Fook, some cadres were already deeply suspicious of Lai Teck before his unmasking, including a group of 'secret army' guerrillas at Gunong Hijau in Perak, who had never been in contact with Force 136.[144] For radical cadres like these, the democratic effort to obtain political concessions was merely a diversion, even an aberration. The secret army had been waiting; the true path to political change involved taking up arms once more, and returning to the jungle.

Chapter 7

'THE TANGLED MASS OF UNSPUN FIBRES': INFORMATION AND INTELLIGENCE IN THE LEAD-UP TO THE MALAYAN EMERGENCY[1]

By late May 1948, less than three years after the end of World War II, an atmosphere of tension and paranoia had permeated Malayan life. Over the previous month there had been two killings and several cases of arson reported in the press, all of them connected to either labour disputes or the labour unions.[2] The European planting community was in a state of some anxiety, and its members were not alone, for their mood was shared by Chinese businessmen. Tan Kim Puay, the owner of a remote sawmill in Selangor, was suspicious and on edge. He had been involved in a dispute with sections of his workforce, culminating in a lock-out. The Factory Workers Union had written to inform him that he was not to dismiss the four men who he blamed for his labour difficulties.

Towards the end of the month, Kim Puay's *kepala* noticed a Chinese, dressed as a Malay but lacking the traditional *songkok*, or cap, in a coffee shop close to the sawmill, talking to an *Orang Asli*. Kim Puay ensured that both the local forester and the police were alerted. On 2 June, four men arrived at the sawmill saying that they were searching for work and asking to speak to either Kim Puay or his brother. The local forester happened to be nearby, and he was sufficiently suspicious to inform the brother, who came to the sawmill with a small posse of policemen. When they arrived, a running gun battle broke out between them and the four men. Two escaped, but the other two ran into a swamp and were arrested. They had with them two pistols, a hand grenade, a dagger and a length of rope. Kim Puay was inclined to pin the blame on the labour union for what he can only have seen as an attempt on his life, and perhaps that of his brother.[3] A fortnight after the Tan brothers' close call, as a result of a spate of political murders, arson attacks and robberies sparked by a change of tactics decided upon by the Malayan Communist Party (MCP), a State of Emergency was declared. It would last for twelve years.

Lai Teck had again begun to inform on the MCP to the British, but he was unmasked as a traitor by his comrades in early 1947. More radical cadres took the helm and in March 1948 they pulled back from the political stance that he had championed and began again to prepare for revolution. They launched a campaign described by the Governor-General of Malaya as 'the rule of gun and knife'.[4] Strike action turned violent, the murder rate rose and the British administration, following five killings in a single day, declared a State of Emergency in mid-June. The MCP, though it had as yet no detailed plans, was already calling former guerrillas to arms.[5] The Malayan People's Anti-Japanese Army (MPAJA) was reincarnated as the Malayan National Liberation Army (MNLA), and former members of Force 136 found themselves again under arms, fighting their former allies.

The scholarship examining the outbreak of the Emergency in Malaya can be divided into two main strands, one exploring the failure of the Malayan administration to foresee the coming insurgency and the other focusing on the reasons behind the MCP's decision to return to the jungle. Regarding the lack of preparedness, there is a wide acceptance of the idea that the government (in both Malaya and London) was, to a degree at least, caught out. However, scholars differ as to the apportionment of responsibility. Philip Deery places the blame at the top, suggesting that Whitehall was too preoccupied with other concerns connected to the beginning of the Cold War – the formation of NATO, the containment of the USSR – to spare Malaya sufficient attention.[6] The Greek Civil War had sparked the Truman Doctrine in early 1947, and the globe was splitting into two ideologically opposed blocs, with Western governments increasingly suspicious of communism in all its guises.[7] Simultaneously, nationalist movements were gathering momentum and, in the immediate post-war period, the British Empire faced considerable tension and violence in countries such as India and Palestine.[8]

By contrast, Robert Heussler contends that British administrators in Singapore and Whitehall shared responsibility for the lack of readiness to face insurrection, with both displaying 'a continuing reluctance to face the facts'.[9] Some scholars take this further, arguing that the colonial administration in Malaya and Singapore was focusing on the wrong issues, or was out of touch with local political realities, and that there were major failings within the Malayan Security Service (MSS).[10] Anthony Stockwell argues that head of the MSS, John Dalley, issued warnings that were too 'diffuse'.[11] For both Anthony Short and John Coates, the problems of a remote administration were compounded by the failings of the MSS, and the loss of its key informant, Lai Teck, Secretary General of the MCP, who fled Singapore early in 1947, leaving the MSS desperately short of information on the MCP's intentions.[12]

The other key historiographical debate revolves around the underlying factors within Malayan society that led to the insurgency, and whether the MCP urged the population towards revolt, or responded to pressures from below, in the form of increasing rural unrest. For Tim Harper, Malaya was enduring 'the second colonial occupation', and the MCP was reacting to events, not so much planning for revolution as being carried toward it by a 'spiral of rural terror'.[13] He argues that the deepening social crisis in rural Malaya – low wages, high prices, unemployment, the decision by the government to move wartime 'squatters' out of the Malay and Forest Reserves and, finally, a serious tightening of union regulations – led to a popular rural revolt which the MCP rode rather than drove.[14] Harper further argues that John Dalley was so distracted by Malay politics that the MSS failed to pay sufficient attention to the brewing unrest.[15] The MCP, meanwhile, was disenchanted by its failure to influence the structure of the Federation of Malaya which, when inaugurated on 31 January 1948, enshrined Malay privilege.[16] Bayly and Harper, then, see the situation from the grassroots up: they accept that the MCP was feeling excluded from the political sphere, but see the motive power of the Emergency as being generated by the exasperation and desperation of the evicted peasant and the underpaid tapper.

Karl Hack, by comparison, approaches the study of the Emergency's origins from an international strategic rather than a local social context. While he agrees that the Emergency did not simply result, as has been claimed, from instructions issued by the Soviet Union at the Calcutta Youth Conference of February 1948, he still sees it as being at least partly precipitated by Soviet international policy. Although the communist-inspired revolts which broke out across Asia in 1948 were not, he notes, a direct consequence of orders from Moscow, they did result from the eagerness of local parties to adhere to the 'two camps' line expounded by Andrei Zhdanov at the founding meeting of the Cominform in September 1947. Zhdanov declared that the world was divided into two, the 'anti-imperialist and progressive camp', headed by the USSR, and the 'imperialist and anti-democratic camp', led by the United States. Hack argues that this line was advertised at the Calcutta Conferences, and went on to influence national communist parties, ultimately inspiring the spate of Asian communist risings (in India, Burma and Malaya) during 1948. Supporting his argument by reference to the chronology of events, he states that it is impossible to argue that the MCP was driven to act by a rising tide of violence and strike action, because both violence and strikes had fallen to a post-war low in the early months of 1948. It was not until the MCP met in March and decided to move towards open revolt six months later that the upsurge of violence, intimidation, and assassination began.

Hack also argues that although the British administration of Malaya was deeply suspicious of the MCP, it acted rationally within the constraints operating upon it, which were determined by its lack of concrete knowledge concerning the party and its desire not to appear excessively oppressive.[17] If it banned the MCP before it had compelling evidence of its involvement in arson, theft and murder, the state would appear oppressive and this would, counter-productively, drive the MCP underground, making it even harder to monitor.[18] The Colonial Office had used repressive tactics within days of the institution of the Malayan Union in April 1946, when ten members of the MCP who had been arrested some months earlier were banished.[19] As Hack observes, it also used tough methods to try to bring the Malayan unions to heel.[20] Yet repression was not in step with the mood of the times, and so Malcolm MacDonald, the Governor-General of Malaya, resisted banning the MCP.[21] The Malayan Union, after all, was meant to allow for a free press, free association and the building of a Malayan nation. If things panned out as expected, it would let Britain exploit the colony in the short term while satisfying the Americans (and the requirements of the Atlantic Charter) by promising self-rule in the medium-to-long term.[22] An outstanding question, however, is whether the colonial administration's knowledge of the MCP, its motivations and its future plans could have been more detailed.

In the last chapter we saw how the rich source of information contained in the Force 136 reports, which covered the MPAJA's (and MCP's) revolutionary activities during the interregnum and the period of British Military Administration (BMA), was drawn from a varied network of informants. This information revealed that communist organizations (including the MPAJA) had killed people they considered too close to the British, looted weapons and supplies and had begun preparing segments of the population for revolution. These reports, however, were very diverse in their views of the MPAJA and the post-war threat it posed. In the absence of a single overarching report, the threads of information these sources provided were not tied together and so no coherent picture of the political situation emerged.

This chapter takes further the issue of British intelligence in Malaya prior to the outbreak of the Emergency by its examination of the political information available to the Malayan administration and the Colonial Office during the first half of 1948. It then moves on to examine the parallels between the disparate nature of the information presented in the Force 136 reports, and the lack of any clear picture of communist activity in the intelligence reports upon which the colonial administration relied in the run-up to the Malayan Emergency. On the face of the matter, it appears that a straightforward intelligence failure affected the Malayan administration and the Colonial Office in the first half of 1948. Scholars have often quoted the comment made by John Dalley, head of the MSS, on 14 June 1948:, 'At the time of writing there is no immediate threat to internal security in Malaya although the position is constantly changing and is potentially dangerous.'[23] Two days later, three white planters and two Chinese were shot dead, in the spate of killings that led the Emergency to be declared.

Finally, this chapter will examine whether this apparent intelligence failure was something more complex, indicative of tensions within the colonial chain of command which meant that detailed knowledge about the country and the prevailing political mood failed to get through to senior administrators or went deliberately unheeded.

Sources of political information and pre-Emergency failure of analysis

In terms of local information flows, the post-war colonial administration of Malaya faced a much more difficult situation than that presented by the country pre-war, for the war itself had largely decimated the networks on which the state had previously relied. The reduction in this access to Malayan society and the knowledge base it represented ran from the top of the colonial hierarchy to its distant reaches, to the estates, mines and forests. Many officials and managers who took up appointments in Malaya after the war were newcomers. For Edward Gent, the Governor of the Malayan Union, it was his first overseas appointment.[24] Though some pre-war members of the Malayan Civil Service returned to work in the country in the year after the war, their numbers were much depleted and a considerable number of new men, some with no previous experience of Malaya, also joined the service. Most of these newcomers lacked – at least to begin with – networks of Asian contacts able to supply them with useful information about local conditions.[25] This distancing of Europeans from Asian society also applied to the estates and mines: war, deaths in captivity, and retirement had thinned the European staff, and their local contacts were thus also lost.[26] In some places, the number of Asian staff had decreased as well: during the Japanese occupation, the Malayan Forest Department lost forty-six members while on duty, most of them probably killed by guerrillas.[27] A vital cadre of knowledgeable colonial servants had been lost, just as the administration was about to spark a conflict with the MCP for control of the Malayan hinterland by seeking to remove squatters who had moved to the forests during the war.

British access to affective knowledge was also weakened by Asian resentment. Many, Chinese and Eurasians especially, felt that they had suffered for the Empire, and resented the post-war treatment they received. The colonial colour bar remained in certain employments, and Asians who had fought in the Malayan Volunteers, as well as Asian government servants, were indignant about inequitable treatment.[28] Asian resentment permeated the work of the administration, with one district officer noting that some of members of his staff were 'truculent' and uncooperative.[29] Hugh Pagden, who had been a Force 136 staff officer and had numerous contacts and friends in the Malayan Chinese community, wrote later that the disaffection with the British began with the corruption of the BMA and the appalling behaviour of sections of the army in the early months of the reoccupation, coupled with a failure to punish collaborators and quash 'gangsterism'.[30] That the administration made alienating mistakes in its dealings with the population can be seen from complaints that arose from the 1946 King's birthday parade in Singapore. The men of the Straits Settlements Volunteer Force, who had fought in the defence of Singapore in 1942 and some of whom at least saw themselves as loyal subjects of the Empire, were asked to marshal but not to march, and were so unhappy about this that it was difficult to find sufficient volunteers to do the job.[31]

To add to these administrative difficulties, in March or April 1947, the British lost their pre-eminent Malayan informant: the MCP's Secretary General, Lai Teck, whose complex treacheries had finally laid a snare for him that he could not escape. Lai Teck, having been a critically important Special Branch agent in the years before the Pacific War, was again run as an agent post-war, this time by the MSS. However, as rumours about him circulated among his comrades, the noose began to tighten and Lai Teck, realizing that the he was no longer trusted, left the country.[32] Nonetheless, even though (as Short memorably puts it) 'the light at the top of the stairs went out', the colonial government still possessed a torch or two, for information still came in, apparently from one or more agents placed within the MCP who continued to report upon it.[33]

In the years that led up to the Emergency, the Malayan administration (including the Colonial Office) had available to it three formal streams of political and social information: Security Intelligence Far East (SIFE), the army and the MSS. SIFE was the British government's central point for the collation and distribution of intelligence in Asia. Formed in 1946 and based in Singapore, it included agents from MI6, but it was headed by MI5. SIFE reported principally to the Joint Intelligence Committee, not to the Colonial Office, and its reports focused upon strategic long-term trends that affected Britain's interests.[34] Although there was some overlap with the work of the MSS, SIFE did not deal with political intelligence as a distinct category; its coverage appears to have been limited to economic trends and external threats.[35]

Instead, the earliest post-war intelligence reports used by the British administration came from the army's Malaya Command. They were based on the work of the military Field Security section and included elements of political intelligence. As the Colonial Office noted of these summaries, which it received from April 1946 when it took over responsibility for the colony from the BMA, Malaya presented a 'grim picture', beset by political changes, shortages (especially of rice) and economic difficulties that made it harder to govern.[36] There is a clear comprehension in these reports that food supplies, prices and strikes were all different aspects of the same problem.[37] Strikes feature early in them, with a connection being drawn between strike action and the communists.[38] In the intelligence summary of 23 February 1946, for example, a letter published in the *Malay Mail* is quoted. It appeals to Chau Yeung Pan (who had led the Selangor Regiment of the MPAJA) to put a stop to 'the strike fever' and accuses those who had called the strike of intimidation and stifling public debate.[39] However, the army, though aware of the MCP, paid more attention to Malaya's Chinese Triad gangs, as well as to the potential impact of the Indonesian revolution upon Malayan politics, which from a military perspective was not, at the time, unreasonable. Soldiers, after all, were more likely to be called out in pursuit of bandits and armed revolutionaries than political agitators. What is more the British had, in 1945–1946, become heavily embroiled in events in Indonesia.[40]

The stream of information that most focused on Malayan politics – including, of course, the MCP – was provided by the MSS's *Political Intelligence Journal.* Initially, the *Journal*, which was produced twice a month, was distributed within the upper levels of the MSS itself, to senior policemen, senior administrators, and the MI5 representative for Malaya. Copies were also sent to Calcutta Special Branch (to whom information about Malaya's Indians would have been of interest). However, not until early 1948 were issues of the *Journal* routinely sent to the Colonial Office.[41] As the *Journal* seems to have been the Colonial Office's main source of information regarding the political scene in Malaya immediately prior to the declaration of the Emergency, it is entirely possible that the failure to dispatch it to Whitehall earlier had lulled the Colonial Office into a false sense of security regarding Malayan politics.

With regard to their potential to gather useful information on the MCP, both SIFE and the MSS suffered from a lack of funding and shortages of staff.[42] Dalley complained that he only had 138 of the 172 MSS staff he should have had, meaning that he was almost 25 per cent below establishment. Documents, he wrote, 'are piling up untranslated', because he could not pay translators enough to lure them from better paid and easier jobs.[43] Information was therefore distributed late and without analysis. The effectiveness of the MSS was also impeded by its organizational structure and its relationship with the police, neither of which was in line with post-war recommendations.[44] Whereas the pre-war Special Branch had powers of arrest, the MSS did not; it could only pass on its recommendations to the police and hope they took action. Furthermore, the unified pre-war police force was now divided into two, one part operating in Singapore and the other on the peninsula – a situation that contributed to poor co-ordination.

The problems inherent in the structure of the colonial intelligence system were compounded by the enmity between Dalley and SIFE. MI5, the most powerful body in SIFE, considered Dalley an untrustworthy empire builder and they believed that he would sabotage any mole they might plant within the MCP, should he find out.[45] Some scholars see a personal animus on the part of SIFE in its actions towards Dalley, as demonstrated by their suggestion that he was a coward for having attempted to escape from Singapore just before it fell to the Japanese.[46] One recent study claims that Sir Percy Sillitoe, SIFE's head, 'subverted the MSS within the machinery of colonial administration' even before the declaration of the Emergency.[47] Beyond all of this, however, lay a fundamental failing shared by the MSS and the Colonial Office: the inability to distinguish 'information' from 'intelligence'.

'Information' versus 'intelligence'

At the end of 1945, Force 136's failure to produce a critical analysis of its operational reports foreshadowed the difficulties that would beset the Malayan administration less than three years later. Neither the leading men of Force 136 nor the mandarins of the post-war Colonial Office seem to have made a distinction between 'information' and 'intelligence'. Christopher Bayly, in *Empire and Information*, argues that knowledge is key to the endurance of imperial control, making the point that there is a clear division between 'information', which 'implies observations perceived at a relatively low level of perceptual definition' and 'knowledge', 'which implies socially organised and taxonomised information'.[48] One could take this a step further by reference to military views of 'intelligence', for example that of the US Marine Corps, which see it as pertaining to the opposition. The raw material provided by a source is analysed to discover its 'implications for decisionmaking [sic]' and the final product is 'knowledge that provides a meaningful assessment of the situation'.[49] 'Intelligence', here, is the *process* of analysis, as much as what is produced. In 1945, there was a failure to analyse fully what the various Force 136 liaison officers had to say about the communists. In 1948, nobody analysed what was known about communist activity, as the MCP turned towards armed rebellion. The issue was not, as has sometimes been assumed or suggested, that the administration had no information; rather, it had a plethora of detail, but lacked analysed intelligence.[50]

The failure of Force 136 to produce a summary report on the Malayan guerrilla movements may have been due to the death of Innes Tremlett, the head of Force 136's Malayan Country Section, in an air crash in October 1945.[51] There is a possibility that Tremlett, with the reports of all the Malayan operations available to him, might have produced a summary report which balanced the hopeful conclusions drawn by the British Malayans attached to the MPAJA against the more cynical and anxious comments made by those officers who were either with non-communist guerrillas or who had worked in the Balkans. However, the likelihood is that, as a former policeman himself, he would have set more store on the comments made by the policeman who led the operations – men like John Davis and Douglas Broadhurst who, as we have seen, had a good opinion of the MPAJA.

The failure to produce such a summary report provides a surprising insight into the weaknesses of imperial intelligence gathering, and makes the intelligence failure that followed later somewhat more explicable. As it turned out, there was very little time for any Force 136 reports to be circulated between their writing, in mid-December 1945, and the final winding-up of the unit in the first weeks of 1946.[52] The probability is that they were not circulated at all, for none has a circulation list included with it. As recorded in the Introduction, such paperwork as had survived the bonfires in Kandy, where the Force was headquartered by the end of the war, was ultimately passed to SIS.[53] It remains unknown if any of the documents thus archived were ever consulted by post-war Malayan administrations.

Another factor explaining why detailed information was not transmuted into useable intelligence was the optimism for the future within the colonial administration and the military hierarchy, in itself perhaps a product of post-war euphoria. The policemen who had served with Force 136, and who returned to work in Malaya, had been in general positive about the MPAJA in their reports, with any reservations they expressed subsumed by an implication that the part of the MCP with the greatest potential to threaten the colonial state – its armed cadres – was also the part with which understandings could be reached and with whom good relationships had already been forged. The policeman Douglas Broadhurst, the leader of *Galvanic*, described the leader of the MPAJA's 1st Regiment, Chau Yeung Pan, in glowing terms: he was 'charming' as well as 'open and frank'.[54] John Davis, Force 136's most senior man in Malaya, also a policeman, spoke of the 'sense of responsibility' of the leadership of the MPAJA. Indeed, at the end of 1945, Davis retained a conviction that 'the MCP are not planning armed disorders ... but intend to press their aims by political methods', and his optimism was to endure almost to the Emergency.[55] He was correct in that the MCP was not *planning* armed disorders in 1945; he did not, however, make the point that it had the potential (and, as some of the cadres seemed to demonstrate, the desire) to cause them if the 'political methods' did not bear the desired fruit. The policemen's views on the MCP's political advisers were less positive, but were buried more deeply in their reports.

The optimistic mood meant that warnings were dismissed. In October 1945, Robert Chrystal spoke about his report to a senior army officer in Kuala Lumpur. The officer's reaction was that, in the wake of the Yalta Conference, there was absolutely no need to worry. Chrystal responded with a saying he had learnt from Creer's friend, the old OCAJA leader Yong Kong: 'You can't treat with a snake – it only knows how to bite.'[56] To Chrystal, the MPAJA's cadres were not comrades in arms, but reptiles poised to strike. Yet Chrystal's comments were buried in a mass of unsorted data in which the most optimistic reports, if they were ever seen, were those likely to have the most influence.

In 1948, the intelligence problem was similar. As had been the case at the end of 1945, there was a failure to analyse what information existed, rather than a failure to access information. The MSS, despite its permanent staff shortage, gathered a large amount of data, but laid it out in such a way that it was difficult to understand. Despite their length, its *Journals* lacked a contents page (though indexes were eventually produced), and often came with supplements and appendices.[57] Each edition opened with a 'General Summary' of the contents, which was nothing more than that: a summary, not an analysis. No indication was given of which information was part of a troubling pattern, and which was not. Only rarely was the information graded, so that the reader usually had no ready idea of its standing in the usual intelligence ranking.[58] Split up as the *Journals* are by 'race', beginning with the Malays, moving on to the Chinese and the Indians (and, rarely, the Eurasians), before discussing 'Mixed and Miscellaneous Organisations' (including the MCP) and then tackling 'General Subjects' such as 'Political Influences on Education' and 'Political Influences on Labour', it is hard to follow a thread across the ethnic groups or to focus on one part of the country.

In particular, the organization of the MSS *Journals* obscured the full influence of the MCP, since references to the party were scattered though each edition, rather than being drawn together. The 'General Summary' of the *Journal* of 15 January 1948, for instance, mentioned the New Democratic Youth League ('the Chinese communist-controlled organisation') in three places on one closely-typed foolscap page, without any attempt to relate these parts of the puzzle to one another. Not until page nineteen was a section dedicated to the MCP: a little over half a page. The communists' efforts to control schools (in competition with the Guomindang) and their involvement in the Malayan trade union movement do not feature until page twenty-one ('Political Influences Upon Education' and 'Political Influences Upon Labour'). It must have therefore been easy to open a *Journal*, read the summary and then the next few pages and conclude – from the slavish way which the summary followed the order of the rest of the journal – that Malay nationalism (including influences from Indonesia) was the administration's biggest headache or, as some have suggested, Dalley's personal obsession.[59]

For colonial officials, it would have been equally easy to read about the All Malaya Council of Joint Action (AMCJA) but remain vague about its communist connections because, although the information was available, it was not always clearly flagged up.[60] The AMCJA was formed in late 1946 with the aim of influencing the development of the new Malayan constitution that was to replace the Malayan Union, a process that many Chinese felt was biased against them.[61] But according to Chin Peng, the MCP, working at this time via a united front, gradually came to dominate the AMCJA: eventually, he tells us, 'it was firmly under our influence'.[62] It was clear that the MSS knew of this connection, and their intelligence was sound: they reported that the AMCJA representative in London was assisted by known communists.[63] Yet when Oliver Morris, a senior Colonial Office official, wrote a long minute outlining what he viewed as the major points raised by the *Journals* of February and March 1948, he failed to infer the degree of communist influence on the AMCJA – due, almost certainly, to the scattered nature of the information, and the fact that no reference was made in those editions to information previously recorded. Ironically, he was still congratulated by David Rees-Williams, a minister in the Colonial Office, for 'drawing a connected thread from the tangled mass of unspun fibres'.[64] From this remark, it appears that his analysis was considered if not definitive, then at the very least adequate.

Chin Peng in fact argues that the failure of the AMCJA to influence the form of the Federation – which replaced the Malayan Union on 31 January 1948 – was one of the factors that pushed the MCP towards armed rebellion.[65] Objections to colonial rule in Malaya went well beyond the MCP, but the MCP provided the most active opposition – a point that is also not clear from the *Journals*. Even within a subheading such as 'Political Influences Upon Labour', the writers of the *Journals* made no attempt to separate out unions influenced by the Guomindang, those influenced by the MCP and those where control was disputed, though the information given is often very precise.[66] Furthermore, they provided virtually no analysis of the social trends driving political activity, either in Singapore or the peninsula. Strikes over pay were mentioned, but living standards were not discussed. The activities of the AMCJA were described, but the reasons for its existence ignored.

Though the *Journals* do not present a clear picture of the communist movement in Malaya, the repeated (but scattered and unconnected) mentions of the MCP and other communist bodies did have one effect on its readers: it convinced some colonial officials that Dalley had become somewhat obsessive about communism. In February 1948, Sir Franklin Gimson, the Governor of Singapore, wrote to inform Henry Bourdillon, the head of the Colonial Office's Eastern Department, that consideration was being given in Singapore to the MCP, and to investigating ways of combating it 'in Schools, Trade Unions and Youth Organisations'. Though he went on to admit that 'the situation here is dangerous' he also disclosed that 'I am not quite sure whether some of the pictures painted by Dalley ... are not too lurid. I think he tends to assume that any agitation is communist and then looks for evidence in support of this, whereas he should really proceed in the other way.'[67] This view – which must have been seen as authoritative, since it came from a senior administrator on the ground – was highly influential. Two months later, Bourdillon commented that Gimson's remarks about Dalley's attitude towards Malayan communism had led him to modify his views.[68] Two months before the Emergency was declared, and just as violence and strike action began to increase, senior men at the Colonial Office were deciding that the 'communist menace' in Malaya was not all that Dalley had cracked it up to be.

It did, however, begin to dawn on some officials in the Colonial Office that, while the *Journals* were packed with *information*, what they did not contain was *intelligence*. In February 1948, the Colonial Office civil servant Morris wrote a review of a recent *Journal*, and among his conclusions was the following observation: 'These detailed reports may have the effect of hiding the wood by the trees, and I think we must leave it to the local authorities to draw their deductions, make their appreciations and advise the Secretary of State on major trends of public opinion.'[69] The Colonial Office was aware that major trends were not drawn out and that analysis was lacking but not until 18 June 1948, the day the State of Emergency was expanded to cover all of Malaya, did it seem to understand the implications. On this day Morris finally noted that what was needed from Malaya were 'appreciations, not factual summaries'.[70] Two weeks later, the conclusion was finally drawn that 'the authorities [in Malaya] seem to have very little idea of what constitutes good intelligence'.[71] As the Malayan civil servant Brian Stewart would later note, the *Journals* contained no 'strategic threat assessment', having just the 'occasional gem inserted among the chaff' yet 'Mandarins and Generals alike were apparently content to accept the document in this patchy form'.[72]

In the weeks which followed the declaration of the Emergency, as the officials of the Colonial Office realized that what they had at their disposal was not 'intelligence' but 'information', they shifted the blame back to the Malayan authorities. Here, as Harper observes, 'recriminations dominate the record'.[73] Yet at least some of the fault for the poor quality of the intelligence belonged to the Colonial Office: blaming Malaya's administration, or the MSS, was far from fair. The weakness of the MSS, its failure to produce analysed 'intelligence', could not be laid entirely at Dalley's feet. It was a consequence of systemic failings, themselves traceable back an impoverished Empire trying to do too much with too little.

The Colonial Office does not appear, at this stage, to have received the SIFE reports on a regular basis. However, a SIFE report of May 1948 was received by the Colonial Office just after the beginning of the Emergency. This report, according to a minister in the Colonial Office, 'betrays no inkling whatever of the impending trouble in Malaya and consists ... of nothing but scraps of gossip about various communist personalities, most of which gossip any assiduous press cutter could have got together'.[74] Although one must accept, given the timing of this minute, that the Colonial Office was offloading blame, it is strikingly critical. Once again, it appears that what was available was information rather than intelligence.

No other intelligence body was able to fill in for either the MSS or SIFE. MI5 produced a review entitled 'The Chinese Factor in South East Asia', but while the Colonial Office regarded this as being of 'rather more use' than SIFE's offerings, this was hardly a ringing endorsement. Incidental information was also fed to the Colonial Office by a number of other, more minor sources. For example, the Labour Department's monthly and yearly reports were found to be useful but (unsurprisingly) 'limited in scope'. In sum, the Colonial Office considered that the MSS was obsessed by communism, SIFE by the Guomindang and the CID by the Triads.[75] Whitehall – in this case the War Office – had also chosen to close down a potential additional source of political intelligence by ending the army's role in collecting political intelligence.[76] In a letter to the War Office, Col. Neville Grazebrook of the Malayan General Staff complained that the army had then been obliged to rely upon the MSS, in whose 'voluminous' reports 'the gravity of the situation [regarding the MCP] was never sufficiently stressed'. If he was shifting the blame, he was doing so justifiably. He admitted 'that we at G.H.Q. didn't foresee and anticipate the present struggle' and is fair-minded enough to mention, not once but twice, that the MCP's decision to turn to armed struggle seemed only to have been taken in April, thus giving the MSS very little time to obtain this information, to check it and then circulate it.[77] The MCP's decision to prepare for armed struggle had in fact been taken towards the end of March.[78] According to several sources, its Central Committee had intended that no decisive action should be taken until later in the year, but as it happened, some more militant cadres slipped the leash, and the MCP was no more prepared than was the government for the State of Emergency.[79]

The army's own intelligence was far from faultless, though its reports sound authoritative. For instance, a 1947 summary included a list of men attending a political conference in Delhi, one of whom was 'H.B. Tallala [sic]' who was 'alleged to have been a collaborator with the Japanese'. Yet Benjamin Talalla, a Sinhalese converted to Christianity, was highly unlikely to have collaborated. He had sent his two oldest sons to Britain to join the RAF (Royal Air Force); in 1941, he and his brother had laid on a curry tiffin for 400 Australian soldiers; and during the occupation, he and his entire family were imprisoned by the Japanese.[80] Such confusion is indicative of the British state's loss of local knowledge in Malaya. There were people who could have provided this knowledge, contextualized it and then turned it into intelligence, but it appears that they were ignored by the administration.

Force 136 and intelligence failures prior to the Emergency

It can also be argued that Malaya's post-war colonial administration further compounded its inability to convert 'information' into 'intelligence' by failing to make use of surviving sources of local knowledge. The administration had to hand a source of inside intelligence on the MCP, in the form of those members of Force 136 who had returned to the country. Yet in the welter of pre-Emergency information in the Colonial Office files, their voices are entirely silent.

As the Malayan Emergency approached, the administration was faced by a confusing and complex set of circumstances. There was no clear, conclusive picture of the political situation on the ground in Malaya upon which to base future – or even short term – colonial policy. Just before Christmas 1947, the labour adviser to the Secretary of State for the Colonies returned from Malaya, announcing that he had seen 'no substantial and serious discontent'.[81] In contrast, six weeks later, the former Special Operations Executive (SOE) man Walter Fletcher, now an MP, informed Parliament that the Malayan population was becoming restive, since so much of what the country earned was being siphoned off by the British government.[82]

Despite the disparity of viewpoints at the highest levels, little effort seems to have been made by the Malayan administration to seek clarification by probing the knowledge of those, such as the former officers of Force 136, who had good contacts with the MCP, or of others, such as planters and mine managers, who via their dealings with labourers and labour contractors had some understanding of the motive forces at work in the rural areas.[83] Several former Force 136 officers kept in close contact with former members of the MPAJA, with Jim Hannah going to considerable lengths to find steady jobs for some former guerrillas.[84] Pagden, who had returned with the BMA, was an entomologist who sometimes took ex-MPAJA men on his collecting trips and had considerable contact with Chau Yeung Pan, the leader of the 1st Regiment in Selangor. In fact, Pagden got on so well with these contacts that when he went away on tour, they gave him a letter of introduction to other ex-MPAJA associations and urged him to visit them.[85]

Yet, so far as this study has ascertained, Colonial Office records make no mention of these ex-Force 136 members between the Force's disbandment in early December 1945 and the outbreak of the Malayan Emergency. If these men were tapped as a source of intelligence, they were tapped only at a very local level. Later, both Hannah and Pagden stated that they had passed their concerns and information to those further up the administrative hierarchy. During 1946, Hannah, convinced that some MPAJA had remained under arms, went so far as to meet up with Col. Itu and Lai Teck to persuade them to pursue their political aims by peaceful means.[86] In his memoir, Hannah, formerly commander of Operation *Funnel*, claims that he regularly passed information to the administration, and even directly to Sir Edward Gent himself, information that he received from trusted sources. As Hannah wrote later, Gent 'just didn't want to believe anything I said and eventually he turned to me angrily and said… "The trouble with you, Hannah, is that you see a Communist behind every rubber tree".'[87] Hannah makes no mention of ever passing information to the MSS.

Pagden, likewise, does not seem to have been tapped by the MSS. Shortly after the Emergency was declared, he submitted a lengthy report to the Colonial Office, in which he explained that he had quickly come to view the communists as 'a menace' and had submitted information on them to the Malayan administration early in 1946. He nonetheless wished to see the communists treated fairly, and he gives an account of one such incident in which he illustrates how, in the early days of the new administration, the local knowledge and assistance provided by Force 136 officers were only reluctantly accepted. In early September 1945, a Malay policeman was murdered in Johore and an MPAJA man, Choo Kau, was then sentenced to death for the crime. Pagden, then in Singapore, and having received 'a flood of petitions' from Chinese interested in the case, discovered that among the failings of the prosecution's case, a significant witness who knew Choo Kau and had witnessed the killing had not been called to give evidence. This was Durward Sime, who had been a senior liaison officer with Force 136's Operation *Carpenter*. When Pagden told Sime what had happened, Sime went at once to Johore to see the officer handling the case but 'was told to mind his own business and to get out'. Pagden submitted a report, complete with Sime's version of events, which exonerated the convicted man, and it was this report, it appears, which secured his release. 'If Choo Kau subsequently turned bandit', wondered Pagden, 'who could blame him?'[88]

Compounding this apparent reluctance on the part of the administration to use the former Force 136 officers as an intelligence source was the failure of these men to agree about the level of the threat offered by the MCP to the colonial state. To the former policeman John Davis – a man with many contacts, who spoke fluent Cantonese, spent much time with Asians and was working as Commissioner for Labour in Pahang – the scene appeared confused. In the latter part of 1947, he thought that 'politically things are quietening down a bit'.[89] He was, at this time, in contact with Chin Peng, and believed him to be a man who was looking to settle down.[90] To Davis, it seemed that Malaya, though uneasy, was edging towards a more stable future.

It was not only the ex-Force 136 men who were not tapped. Even former MPAJA men who took up jobs with the new administration, such as Reg Lawther who worked for the Harbour Board Auxiliary Police in Singapore, do not seem to have been questioned.[91] There is also a tantalizing possibility as to why Gent cut himself off from the information that could have been provided by former members of Force 136. Though Hannah was an accountant and Pagden a government entomologist, it appears that Gent had a deep animus against planters, a role to which many of the former Force 136 officers – McDonald, Hunter, Trevaldwyn, Owen, to name just a few – had returned. According to the author Noel Barber, at around the time the Emergency was declared, one Malayan Civil Servant recorded in his diary Gent's comment to him that 'planters make me sick'.[92] The planters, as we will see, would later accuse Gent over what they saw as his failure to act decisively as unrest and violence increased.

Force 136 and the continuity of local knowledge

As contemporary newspapers noted, the tempo of Malayan life changed from early April 1948. Up until April 1948, as Hack has shown, violent crime and strike days had been falling.[93] This fall was irregular, but it was reasonably steady. In 1946, there had been 421 murders; in 1947, 220 – an average of around eighteen a month. In January 1948, there were only seven; the same total was recorded for March.[94] However, this overlaid a country that was still profoundly unsettled. There was deep poverty, the administrative apparatus had not yet recovered from the chaos of war, and the issue of squatters, left over from the days of the Japanese occupation, had not yet been resolved.[95]

From April 1948, the strikes and the violence began to increase. There was no doubt that the MCP was using intimidation, something that was also obvious from the pages of the *Journal*.[96] Accurate information existed but – as we will see – it did not seem to penetrate the Colonial Office. As the Australian general John Coates argues, the administration was out of touch.[97]

If the Colonial Office remained unaware of the fundamental shift in the Malayan political atmosphere, former Force 136 officers soon noticed it. Jim Hannah, though he had no official position (he was an accountant with Perak Hydro), retained a network of informants. He had long been aware of the existence of the MCP's 'Secret Army'. During May, he heard rumours that former MPAJA men were 'melting back into the ulu in twos and threes' and reported these to Davis.[98] By 9 June 1948, he was writing to Davis and predicting 'a crop of hold-ups and murders before June is out'.[99] In early June, Pagden received a letter from a friend, a successful Chinese businessman, who saw the increase in strikes and murders as 'the beginning of much more trouble to come'; this businessman dated the dawn of his anxieties to a month or more previously.[100]

Simultaneously, the European planters – with good local knowledge and close to life on the estates – were becoming increasingly anxious and were eager to prompt the administration to take action. As one of their representatives related in detail that when a Malayan business delegation met with the Secretary of State for the Colonies a week after the Sungei Siput killings, they had been deeply concerned about the trend towards strikes, violence and intimidation, and had met with Gent during May. He wrote to them on 25 May following this meeting, agreeing that the disturbances on the estates were due to the activities of 'subversive political elements'. However – again according to the planters – on 15 June, the day prior to the Sungei Siput killings, Gent had called for a conference in Kuala Lumpur to discuss the labour problems. The memorandum that accompanied this invitation stated that neither the estate employers nor the workers believed that the 'disturbed labour conditions' were the result of the abuse of the trades unions by either criminals or communists. The planters, utterly baffled by this complete about-face on Gent's part, could only conclude that he had hoped to obtain broad agreement with his memorandum, allowing him to send a soothing despatch to Whitehall.[101] It appears that the observations of the planters matched those of men like Pagden and Hannah: as disturbances and intimidation increased, those with local knowledge were uttering warnings almost in concert.

By this time, Malaya had seen the re-emergence of another tactic used by the communists during the Japanese occupation, and noted in the reports of the Force 136 officers: that of targeted killing. In the course of four weeks, MCP squads killed twenty-two men.[102] These killings did not just focus, as some have suggested, upon managers and foremen.[103] Careful analysis indicates that, while managers and foremen were among the dead, the largest single category of those killed consisted of six members of the Guomindang, some of them office holders, who died in the month leading up to the 16 June: the communists, having pursued members of the Guomindang during the Japanese occupation, were pursuing them again.[104] While four of these men were foremen, and thus in a position to urge labourers to ignore union demands, two of them are noted only as shopkeepers.[105] Added to these were the killings of others who had challenged the power of the communists in various ways: four men who had crossed swords with them in court (as witnesses in intimidation cases, including two tin mine labourers); an MPAJA man who had, in the words of the *Journal*, 'broken away'; a man who had refused to go on strike; one who was noted as being 'anti-communist'; and an estate owner who resisted the MCP's demands.[106] In all, fourteen men were killed who had a record of opposing the MCP, either politically or in court.[107] (For details, see Appendix C.) Men like Hannah and Pagden had their fingers pressed precisely to the country's pulse. The MCP was re-awaking as a revolutionary force, and it was doing so in a manner entirely consistent with its behaviour during the Japanese occupation and the interregnum.

By around this stage, Hannah states in his memoir, two of his 'informers' reported to him that the MCP leadership was planning to go underground. He passed this news on to the police in Ipoh, who had already heard about it from their own sources. They in their turn passed it up the line – only to be told that 'Hannah was talking through his hat as usual'.[108] Yet the MSS had received this information too.[109] It was rated, however, as B2 and B3 – that is to say, as information from a reasonably reliable source that was only probably or possibly true, not confirmed.[110] Dato Seri Yuen Yuet Leng, a retired senior policeman, supported the unconfirmed nature of this information. He stated that the police had many suspicions, but nothing upon which they were able to act.[111] The colonial state found itself stranded in a sea of suspicions, unable to act decisively without appearing unduly repressive. The administration did what it could with the information that it had: on 14 June, it was announced that emergency legislation was on being prepared.[112] Two days later, the insurgents shot five men in one day: three European planters at Sungei Siput, and two Chinese, one elsewhere in Perak, one (a Guomindang member) in Johore. Yet even at that stage, no threat assessment had been produced.

Once the State of Emergency had been declared, the colonial administration moved quickly to locate former members of Force 136 in order, finally, to tap them for information about the MCP.[113] John Davis found himself returned to the Malayan Police within a matter of hours: he was in Kuantan working as a Commissioner of Labour when news of the Sungei Siput killings came in. Summoned by telephone, he took charge, immediately, of the police in West Pahang.[114] Pagden too was soon asked by the administration about what he knew. Drawing on his many contacts within the Chinese community, his long report reflected upon not only the MCP, but also upon the loss of trust of the general population in the British administration. Entitled 'Unrest in Malaya', this document was submitted to the Colonial Office within a few months. In it, Pagden makes it clear that he had tried to provide information on the MCP since his return to the country. Prior to May 1946, when he was still working in Singapore (he then moved to Kuala Lumpur), he was informed that the MPAJA had formed and were keeping in reserve assassination squads 'for the removal of political opponents and others to whom they took a dislike'. He also states that he had included this information in his earlier reports, which also included a schematic diagram showing the interconnections between the various 'communist-controlled organisations'. He had given a copy of this diagram to the Secretary for Chinese Affairs.[115] Yet there is no indication that any of this information was passed to the Colonial Office until after the outbreak of the Emergency.

Within a few weeks, four former members of Force 136 (John Davis, Richard Broome and Jim Hannah, along with Robert Thompson who had served in Burma) approached the administration with their plan for what became known as 'Ferret Force', whose patrols would consist of an officer with jungle experience (either with Force 136 or the Chindits), about a dozen troops, and some trackers and liaison officers.[116] In terms of kills made and prisoners taken, Ferret Force was ultimately more successful against the guerrillas than was the regular army. Nevertheless, it was disbanded after only six months. The official line, as given in the press, was that the 'ferrets' had just been a stopgap and, their tactics having been taught to the regular army, there was no need to retain such an irregular force.[117]

Conclusion

The intelligence networks upon which the Malayan administration had relied before the Japanese conquest were decimated by the time the British returned to rule the country in 1945. There were two sides to this. Many Britons never came back, while those who did found the local Malayan population disillusioned. The colonial administration could not return the country quickly to pre-war conditions, and high prices, shortages of rice and violent crime all served to drive a wedge between the government and the people.

Even so, some men returned to work (some, it must not be forgotten, were Malayan Asians themselves) who could tap into the networks of Asian friends and associates that had existed before the war. Some of them had extraordinary levels of knowledge of, and access to, the MCP. Davis was in contact with Chin Peng in the second half of 1947; Hannah kept up with the Perak ex-MPAJA men; Pagden was on excellent terms with the two most important ex-MPAJA men in Selangor, Chau Yeung Pan and Liew Yao (Pagden was even invited to Liew Yao's wedding).[118] The MSS made one attempt to use Davis as a source during 1947, but there is no evidence that this was either successful, or followed through.[119] Pagden and Hannah, as we know, were both ignored, and there is also no indication that any of the Asians who had been in either the MPAJA or Force 136 were approached by the security services until after the Emergency had been declared.

The failure of the administrative hierarchy to listen to obviously worried men is more comprehensible when set within the broader context of political events. In the first three or four months of 1948, Malaya seemed to be on the path to peace: strike days and violent crime were falling, and it looked as if 'liberal imperialism', judiciously combined with a dose of old-fashioned repressive imperialism (regular banishments, for example), was working. Further, as Harper argues, 'the Labour government was reluctant to completely abandon the vestiges of its post-war plans for multi-racial colonial partnership in Malaya': this even, he adds, extended to an unwillingness to ban the MCP after the State of Emergency was declared.[120] In fairness to the government, it had responded to the upsurge in violence by beginning to prepare emergency legislation, though it remained reluctant to act in an obviously oppressive manner until after the Emergency was underway.[121]

What the administration did not have, despite its huge store of information regarding the MCP, was active, useable intelligence. As a consequence, the mandarins of the Colonial Office were stranded in what Yakov Ben-Haim, an economist whose ideas are applied to intelligence and security issues, has termed an 'info-gap', by which he means the disparity between what one knows and what one needs to know.[122] This info-gap was made wider by the lack of any threat assessment – by the failure of the Colonial Office, in Ben-Haim's terms, to get beyond concerns over uncertainty and develop methods of alleviating the 'adverse impact of surprise'. Despite some awareness among officials of the 'voluminous' nature of the *Journals* and their lack of clarity, the Colonial Office waited until April 1948 to ask the Malayan administration to produce political appreciations, none of which had been written before the Emergency was declared. It is conceivable that the Colonial Office was as overstretched as Dalley and his MSS. Much the same goes for the Malayan Police, who were forced to rebuild after the devastation of the Japanese occupation, while handling a country where smuggling, banditry and murder were rife. From the top to the bottom, the British administration in Malaya was less able to connect to the country it governed – and the country it governed was less willing to be connected to.

Karl Hack, as we have noted, argues that given such circumstances, and the information it had to hand, the administration did what it could. In February 1948, it set up a special committee to decide how best to counter the perceived 'communist threat'. When this committee reported back in May, it recommended more finely honed propaganda and improved conditions for labour. The authorities in Singapore accepted that direct suppression would be unpalatable to Whitehall, and counter-productive in so far as it would drive the communists underground.[123] There was still no move to bring the MSS into closer co-ordination with the police which, Dalley later averred, would have enabled a more organized swoop upon the MCP once the Emergency was declared.[124]

Yet this chapter now takes us a step beyond Hack's analysis, for it shows that, although the administration did what it could with what it knew, it had failed to tap valuable informants and thus make use of all the sources that might have been available to it. Moreover, there was a consistent failure – seen with the Force 136 reports and again with the *Journals* – to catalyse *information* into *intelligence*. Former members of Force 136, as can be seen from the contemporary letters and reports that they produced, understood that the MCP was continuing a project that it had begun during the Japanese occupation, and the planters were convinced that estate unrest was political at least as much as it was economic. But the colonial administration failed to utilize them as a source that could have offered a window into the MCP. Had the administration honed its vision, made full use of all sources of information, and analysed the information it gleaned, it would have been better informed. Whether this would have meant it would have been better prepared and thus able to respond more effectively is, given the evidence of overstretch that we have noted, another matter entirely.

CONCLUSION

This book, through the study of the Force 136 archive and related material such as letters and memoirs, has explored events in the interior of Malaya during the pivotal period of the Japanese occupation. It has sought to offer new insights into the events of the interregnum and to improve our understanding of the actions of the Malayan Communist Party (MCP) as the Emergency approached. The conclusions that can be drawn from this study fall into two broad categories, the first consisting of those that relate to the ambitions of the Malayan People's Anti-Japanese Army (MPAJA) and the wider Malayan communist movement. The second category relates to our understanding of British colonial intelligence gathering and British colonial policy, and the consequences – particularly the unintended consequences – that flowed from these.

Accounts from both Force 136 and the MPAJA show that the Blantan Agreement, struck at the end of 1943 was, for both sides, driven by necessity. Force 136 was keen to acquire useful local allies to assist in the expected reconquest of Malaya from the Japanese, and the MPAJA was hobbled as an anti-Japanese force by a lack of essential supplies. The guerrillas needed arms, food, medicines and money to enable them to provide active opposition to the Japanese, and also to allow them to prepare for the longer-term aim of their parent body, the MCP, of evicting the British and declaring a Malayan People's Republic. The impact of the Blantan Agreement was two-pronged. In material terms, it increased the capacities of the communists: troops were trained and taught tactics by Force 136 operatives, and arms – preferentially selected for jungle fighting and assassination – were spirited away from 'lost' Force 136 containers to be stashed in the jungle by MPAJA guerrillas. By the end of the war, the MPAJA was a stronger and more capable force than would otherwise have been the case. The MPAJA's alliance with the British also increased the post-war leverage that the MCP thought it should be able to apply against the colonial state. Though the evidence is that no explicit political promises were made to the communists, they nonetheless felt that they had earned political concessions: as in other places, cooperation during war was regarded as part of a bargain.

A side effect of the Blantan Agreement, unintended by the Special Operations Executive (SOE), was that the arms dropped to the MPAJA by Force 136 allowed the MCP to dominate the Chinese guerrilla movement to such an extent that the party was able to strengthen its claim for recognition by painting itself as the only guerrilla resistance. The MCP's attitude to other guerrilla organizations serves to emphasize that the party had long-term political ambitions that it nurtured even during the Japanese occupation. It did not see competing guerrilla groups as allies against the Japanese in either the short or the medium term, but as rivals to be suborned, exterminated or strangled in the cradle.

To this end, the MCP made concerted efforts to prevent Force 136 parties from establishing themselves in the Malay-majority districts where they were to operate, to the point where the Malay guerrilla unit planned by Operation *Multiple* was never even recruited. Despite this, the Force did manage to strengthen the Malay resistance – a policy adopted in the interests of ethnic balance. These units proved to be an unexpected proving ground for a small group of young elite Malays. From Force 136, Ibrahim Ismail of *Oatmeal* emerged as a senior figure within the army. From Wataniah, Yeop Mahidin went on to lead the Malaysian army reserves. Other Wataniah members – Tun Razak Hussein, Ghazalie bin Shafie – went on to have eminent political careers. These members of the Malay elite continued to play a role that they had performed before: they were prepared to help the British against those they considered a greater enemy. During World War II, it had been the Japanese, and during the Emergency, it was the communists.

During the Japanese occupation, the MCP also resisted the development of an alternative Chinese resistance. It lured groups allied to the Guomindang into the communist fold and, if evangelism failed, it turned to violence, using, if it had them, arms supplied by Force 136. So it was that the largest group that resisted the MCP's overtures, the Overseas Chinese Anti-Japanese Army (OCAJA), was driven by the MPAJA from the proto-state it had developed in northern Malaya and its key leaders killed. The Force 136 archive shows that the communists' attack on the 'Kuomintang State' was not the work of a group of breakaway cadres, for the involvement of the Perak Deputy State Secretary, Lau Mah, in this allegedly anti-bandit campaign indicates that the assault was given sanction by the highest levels of the MCP. We can now also see that the communists' killing of selected Guomindang leaders in mid-1948 was a return to an earlier policy of eliminating particular opponents. Moreover, these Force 136 sources reveal a story that has been lost to scholars who, when discussing the OCAJA, have utilized the discourse of 'banditry' employed by MCP leaders during and after the Japanese occupation, a discourse that has reduced a guerrilla army to gangs of thieves.

Information contained in the Force 136 reports that cover the period of the interregnum (mid-August to mid-September 1945) lends further weight to the argument that the MCP was fostering its long-term ambitions well before 1948. During this period, the MCP continued to remove its political opponents, killing people considered too close to the British, even though some of them had rendered good service to the communist resistance movement. As we saw in Chapter 6, MCP cadres eliminated Ho Thean Fook's acquaintance Kai Loh Weng because he had belonged to the Royal Army Service Corps, even though, during the formative days of the MPAJA, Kai had willingly led local cadres to the British arms truck full of weapons he had abandoned; communist cadres also disposed of Malays who assisted Force 136, such as the *Hebrides* agent Sarpin bin Shahabuddin, and a *ketua kampong* who had worked with *Fighter*. The Force 136 archive tells us that the MPAJA did not merely aim to influence the Chinese community, but to control the activity of those Malays who might provide an alternative political voice, or who indicated that they might have an allegiance to the British.

Furthermore, the MCP used the interregnum as a time to strengthen itself for future conflict. Although Lai Teck instructed the 'secret army' to disperse, and the 'open army' – the MPAJA – to disarm and disband, the MCP retained considerable stores of arms. Some of these the communists obtained during the interregnum from both the Malay police and the Japanese. Other weapons – carefully selected by the MPAJA for their usefulness for jungle fighting and assassination – had been, in effect, stolen from Force 136. Even after Lai Teck ordered the party to adopt a political stance, MCP cadres continued to work to obtain additional arms from the Japanese and the police. The Force 136 reports also make clear – supported by information from within the MPAJA – that the MCP was not, at the end of the war, a unified political grouping, but a disparate movement with a strongly radical wing. This radical wing was willing to turn to violence to attain its ends; in the interregnum it kept this alternative course of action open by stashing arms and preparing the population for revolution through political speeches. The revolutionary zeal of 1948 had been presaged by the MCP's activities during the period after the Japanese surrender.

The stashing of arms, the looting for monetary gain and the pursuit of rivals (actual or potential) by the MPAJA and, more widely, by the MCP indicates that Malaya's communist organizations contained cadres who saw their party as a revolutionary body. Lai Teck's fall and flight in 1947 ensured that the political posture that he had advocated lost credibility, allowing more radical members of the party to take charge and adopt equally radical policies. The consequence was insurrection. Within the colonial administration, different departments reacted by blaming each other for the failure to at least foresee, if not avert, the rise in violence. The army and the Colonial Office blamed the Malayan Security Service (MSS); Dalley of the MSS complained that it had been underfunded.

This analysis of the Force 136 sources also increases our understanding of a colonial administration plagued by intelligence failures that did not anticipate the upswing of killing and violence that became the Malayan Emergency. This lack of anticipation can – this book argues – be traced back to two main issues: a failure to utilize all sources of information and a lack of understanding of the constituents of good intelligence. These are two distinct issues but they go hand in hand and bring us to those conclusions that concern the colonial state rather than the MCP.

In the post-war period, the colonial administration did not have the access to local knowledge that it had enjoyed pre-war, largely as a result of the destruction wrought upon those networks by the war and the Japanese occupation. There were fewer Caucasians with pre-war experience in Malaya to tap into existing local networks, and many Asians had become disillusioned with the colonial state. The Empire that was supposed to protect them had crumpled before the Japanese and had, upon its return, proved both corrupt and inept. A ruling power that had already lost prestige in 1941–1942 was unable to regain it. Despite this, a considerable quantity of information still came in, from all communities and from all parts of the country, as is witnessed by the detailed nature of the MSS's *Political Intelligence Journal* and its ethnic and geographical scope.

Beyond this, there were additional sources of information available that were not tapped by the British administration: readily available contacts with people with long Malayan experience or former members of the MPAJA were not utilized. Some former Force 136 men had contacts at the very highest levels of the MCP. John Davis knew how to reach Chin Peng, Jim Hannah knew Col. Itu and met up with Lai Teck in the post-war period, and Hugh Pagden was on social terms with the two leading former MPAJA cadres in Selangor, taking them on insect-collecting trips and sharing his picnic with them. There is no indication that what these former Force 136 officers had to say was used by the MSS, and it also appears that they, and others with extensive local contacts, were also ignored by the rest of the administration. This was despite the fact that the Malayan colonial government was faced by a far harder task post-war than had faced it pre-war.

This failure to make use of willing and well-connected sources was compounded by the failure of the administration – from the men working in Malaya up to the bureaucrats in Colonial Office – to understand in time that a thick file of information is not the same thing – nor is it as useful – as a concise and well-analysed intelligence summary. This lack of analysis was not only a failing of the overstretched and understaffed post-war MSS, but something that had stalked Force 136 as well. The Force 136 reports presented a confused, conflicted and contradictory image of the MPAJA and MCP: here helpful, there apparently looting arms, somewhere else accused of abduction and murder. Close reading, however, reveals the major themes. The British Malayans who worked with the MPAJA tended to identify more with it than with other communist bodies, and thus saw the MCP's armed wing as distinct and separate, aloof from the 'trials' of collaborators and the looting of rubber stocks indulged in by the Malayan People's Anti-Japanese Union. The broad impression given by their reports is that the MPAJA was essentially a disciplined organization with which agreements could be made and kept: the MCP's armed wing, in this interpretation, was not particularly radical and therefore not particularly dangerous. The more cynical men – the ones who had been involved with other guerrilla bodies or who had dealt with MPAJA regiments that were out of easy contact with their own high command – struck a much more cautious note. Most suspicious of all were the handful of officers who had prior experience with communists in the Balkans: several of them uttered straightforward warnings about their concerns for the future, seeing the communists as an active threat to the colonial state.

Despite the existence of so many detailed reports, nobody drew out this complex picture, with all concerns highlighted, into a single intelligence report. It is possible that such a report might have been written, had it not been for the death of the head of Force 136's Malayan Country Section, Innes Tremlett, in October 1945 though, as a policeman, he would have been likely to have privileged the positive views of the policemen in Force 136 and on the ground in Malaya. As it was, however, the dominant Force 136 reports – those by John Davis and Richard Broome – and the unit history did not paint the MCP as a long-term threat. These reports did not make it clear that the MPAJA (and, by extension, the MCP) was a revolutionary organization prepared to annihilate the opposition, as vividly demonstrated by the fate of the OCAJA.

This failure by the colonial government to subject a complex picture to analytical scrutiny continued right through until the middle of 1948. The MSS's *Political Intelligence Journal* was difficult to understand, for the information was scattered through them and broad themes were not summarized or drawn together. It was perhaps for this reason that the Governor of Singapore, Sir Franklin Gimson, concluded that the MSS was unnecessarily obsessed by the MCP – a view, as we have seen, that influenced the mandarins of the Colonial Office. Despite its failure to use all sources, what the administration did not lack was evidence; what it lacked was analysis and, thus, active intelligence.

Moreover, the Malayan administration was deeply reluctant to listen to the warnings it received, including those from former members of Force 136. It did, however, understand that the situation was volatile and was preparing emergency legislation. Even so, with strike days and violent crime dropping in early 1948, it must have seemed, at least to the optimists within the administration, that 'liberal imperialism' was finally fulfilling the hopes that the Colonial Office had placed in it, and those who were delivering warnings of the immediate likelihood of armed disorder were disobligingly running against the grain. Former Force 136 men, with their contacts in the Asian community and their knowledge of the MCP, were aware that a call-up of former guerrillas seemed to be in progress. The police thought so too. But without evidence, the police were not allowed to act: the colonial government was anxious not to look any more oppressive than it had looked already. It did not seem to realize, however, that it had closed itself off from some key sources of local information, thus limiting what it knew about the MCP, and was also only just realizing that what it had to hand was information, rather than active intelligence.

Even so, it is entirely possible that, even with the best of intelligence, the Malayan Emergency could not have been prevented. It was not until the end of March that the MCP decided to move towards armed rebellion, and not until late May that it became clear to those observing the scene that a campaign of murder and arson was underway. There was limited time for information to be gathered and analysed into intelligence, tactics discussed and authorization given by Whitehall. As it was, colonial information gathering was poor, colonial intelligence analysis was almost entirely lacking, and the MCP's local cadres acted more quickly and more radically than the MCP's leadership had expected. Both sides were caught unprepared when five murders in one day compelled the administration to declare a State of Emergency.

Previous studies of clandestine activity have included much scholarly discussion of the unintended long-term political impacts of SOE's actions in the Balkans and Burma, and those of OSS (American Office of Strategic Services) in French Indo-China. This study has attempted to clear our view of the relationship between SOE and the resistance movements in Malaya, particularly with regard to its alliance with the MPAJA. While it is clear that SOE did not create the MPAJA, it succeeded in training and equipping an armed communist force in a country which, in 1945, became again a British colonial possession. We can now see that one of the consequences of SOE's short-term approach in Malaya was the development of the roots of the later insurrection.

Appendix A

THE BLANTAN AGREEMENT

The original was written on two sides of a sheet torn from a school exercise book by Richard Broome, then suffering from malaria.

From TNA HS 7/165

Record of Conference [illegible] 30, 31 DEC '43 between Messrs CHANG HONG [Lai Teck], CHEN CHING SHEN [Chin Peng]; Messrs Broome, Davis, TAN CHOON LIM [Lim Bo Seng], Major FS Chapman.

A. Terms of Cooperation

1 a. Mr. Chang Hong (C.H.) is the elected representative of the Malayan Communist Party, the Anti-Japanese Force and the Anti-Japanese Union, and can put into force any decisions agreed to in these meetings.
   b. Major J.L.H. Davis, Captain R.N. Broome and Mr. Tan Choon Lim are the Military Representatives (M.R.) of the Allied C-in-C, South ~~West~~ East Asia, and are fully empowered to cooperate with any anti-Japanese party in Malaya.
2 CH agrees that his party will fully cooperate with the Allied forces while retaking Malaya and for this purpose will follow all instructions of the Allied C-in-C in so far as military operations in Malaya are concerned.

B. Details of Proposals and Decisions

1 After giving a summary of the numbers and resources of the various anti-Japanese organizations in Malaya, CH asked in what way these organizations would be expected to cooperate.
   The MR summarised the military and Fifth Column activity hoped for and it was agreed that <u>at present</u>, beyond continuing to keep the people anti-Japanese, the only possible [? Semi-legible] <u>action</u> would be to foment

labour trouble and carry out sabotage against Japanese [? Semi-legible] naval dockyards etc. For the .... [next one a half lines, approx 11 words, are illegible] are combined action. CH also undertook to emphasize, in their present propaganda, the need for complete cooperation with Allied invading troops [? May read 'forces'].

2. Asked what kind of help his organ [?ization – half the word is missing] expected, CH replied (a) Arms and [?ammu – half the word is missing] nition. (b) Medical supplies including doctors. (c) Military training. (d) Financial assistance.

   The MR stated with regard to (a) and (b) that the Allied C-in-C will undertake to despatch to Malaya, by all possible means, the arms and supplies needed for effective cooperation. The introduction of Doctors from outside is difficult at present but the possibility will be investigated.

   (c) i The Chinese instructors who are ready in India will be introduced as soon as communications permit. ii Chinese students will be sent from Malaya for training as instructors and will be returned to Malaya. A party of 6 should be prepared to proceed to India shortly. iii the question of introducing European instructors at a later date will be investigated.
   (d) The MR have already asked for authority to finance. The reply is expected within a month. CH estimated 50–70,000 $ per month will meet present requirements.

3 After the MR had stressed the urgency of setting up the wireless installation, the details of part B2 (above) were discussed and an immediate detailed plan for the first shipment of arms and medical supplies was drawn up. Investigation of further specific supply routes was agreed upon.

The above is subject to the ratification of the combined [? half word struck out by hole punch] headquarters of the M.C.P., A-J.F., and A-J.U. and is subject to agreement on the following or similar clause to be added. "That cooperation shall continue during the period in which the army is responsible for the maintenance of Peace and Order in Malaya."

   [It is signed on one side by Chang Hong and on the other by JLH Davis, Major, R.N. Broome Capt and Tan Choon Lim.]

Appendix B

THE SECOND AGREEMENT

From TNA, HS 1/107

RECORD OF DECISIONS TAKEN AT CONFERENCE APRIL 17th, 1943 [sic].

<u>Present:</u>

Messrs.	Chang Hong [Lai Teck]
	Itu
	Chen [Chin Peng]
	Davis
	Chapman
	Broome
	Hannah

AJUF H.Q. will set up a C-in-C for the whole of their force in Malaya at the earliest possible moment. This C-in-C will be in constant personal touch with Col. Davis, representing S.E.A.C at any place convenient to AJUF.

AJUF will accept liaison Officers in all their groups and patrols. Each group will have one AJUF officer in command to whom a G.L.O. will be appointed. Each patrol will have one leader to whom a PLO will be appointed.

During build up period groups will be independent subject to general direction from AJUF H.Q. After 'D' Day, groups will be entirely independent on all military matters, receiving order direct from Task Force commander through G.L.O. Similarly, each Patrol will have authority in its own area subject to control by Group H.Q. After 'D' Day, patrols will be given greater independence subject to military necessity. All groups will be informed at once of the decision to accept liaison and details of liaison with patrols will be arranged by Group Commanders. Any difficulty or difference of opinion arising between Patrol of Group Commanders and their respective Liaison Officers must be immediately referred to AJUF H.Q. or Group H.Q. as the case may be.

AJUF Officers will be instructed by AJUF H.Q. how far their authority extends and will be expected to act on their own initiative within the terms of their instructions.

AJUF will use Fore 136 W/T links for transmission of orders to their units. These messages will not be interfered with. In AJUF messages the following code prefixes will be used.

KAPUT	- H.Q.	PERUP	- Group 5
SELUP	- Group 1	WESTUP	- Group 6
NORJUP	- Group 2[1]	EASTUP	- Group 7
SOUJUP	- Group 3	KEDUP	- Kedah
		LANUP	- Kelantan

Reference S.E.A.C, ISLD parties now in Malaya or coming in the future, AJUF will help them as far as possible. Their position with respect to MALT [*Gustavus*] will be cleared up as soon as possible.

FINANCE will be provided at 150 taels gold value per month in currencies and proportions agreed upon. Each group will get 21 taels value per month when liaison is set up. Subsidy for groups not yet in liaison will paid to AJUF H.Q. AJUF will use all this subsidy for immediate food purchases.

MEDICAL

One doctor will be sent in to each group and will visit patrols in turn to give medical attention and instruction.

When necessary, a SEAC officer will be detailed to receive drops in each group area. He will move from patrol to patrol as necessary.

AJUF will do their best to recruit interpreters for GLOs and PLOs.

GROUPS AND GLOs

GLO for Selangor and Negri will be dropped together in Selangor shortly. AJUF will instruct their units to receive them and take them to Selangor H.Q. The recognition signal between Selangor G.L.O. and Selangor H.Q. will be:-

GLO says "SINGAPORE"

H.Q. says "PENANG"

JOHORE – arrangements are already proceeding satisfactorily.

WEST PAHANG – This officer has already dropped in area. AJUF will instruct group to contact him and MALT will obtain further information to assist contact. Password will be: – GLO says "TAIPING". Pahang H.Q. says "ANSON".

EAST PAHANG – arrangements will be made later by West Pahang GLO.

PERAK – Major Hannah has already been appointed GLO to this group and will make arrangements direct with Perak group commander.

AJUF ask for liaison to be set up with a South Kelantan patrol now coming under No. 5 Group pending establishment of a Kelantan group. MALT will clear up position as regards Officers who have already contacted this patrol. [*Cairngorm*?]

AJUF is not yet strong enough in Kedah to warrant setting up liaison at present.

In next three months AJUF will be able to arm guerrillas as follows:

Selangor, Perak, North Johore, South Johore – 500 each
Perak, West Pahang, East Pahang – 300 each
Negri – 200
Kedah and Perlis – 100
Kelantan – 100

Later on these numbers can be increased.

DIFFICULTIES REGARDING FOOD SUPPLY.
To meet anticipated difficulties Force 136 will try to increase financial subsidy or
direct food supply as necessary.

From Chin Peng:

Chin Peng states in *My Side of History* that the meeting was 16th April, risky as
near a road and had Sgt. Humpleman (who was not involved in the negotiations)
added to the Allied side. Lai Teck, Chin Peng and Broome were all ill. He adds
on p. 114 that the British wanted to increase the number of guerrillas in Perak
from 500 to 800, and to have guerrilla patrols all down the north-south roads and
railways to attack the Japanese at the time of the Allied landings. He states that
John Davis outlined what would provided in the way of arms, gold, money and
food. In exchange the MPAJA was to accept liaison officer, with each officer being
accompanied by a platoon of Gurkhas. During a break, Lai Teck reassured the
guerrillas that, when and if the time came to turn on the British, they would not
need to worry about the Gurkhas, as a platoon of them would be no match for a
company of guerrillas.[2]

From Spencer Chapman

In *The Jungle Is Neutral*, Spencer Chapman describes the setting and lead up to
the April 1945 conference in some detail, but his description of its conclusions is
very brief:

> No written agreements were made or were necessary, as the conference was
> largely devoted to methods of carrying out the agreement previously made. The
> principle arrived at was the tactical decentralization of the guerrillas, increase of
> power for all their officers, and the encouragement of individual initiative.' He
> adds that reports of this conference were encoded that same night and relayed to
> Colombo; these must have formed the basis of the typed version above.[3]

Appendix C

TARGETED KILLINGS PRIOR TO THE DECLARATION OF THE EMERGENCY

From PIJ: *Political Intelligence Journal*; ST: *Straits Times*

	Date	Source	Employment	Cause	Location
1	17 May	PIJ 31/5 p. 396	Factory Manager	Ex-MPAJA	Nr. Ipoh
2	19 May	PIJ 31/5 p. 394	*Mandore*	Guomindang – both men were returning from a meeting	Machap, Malacca
3	19 May	PIJ 31/5 p. 394	*Mandore*	As above	As above
4	20 May	PIJ 31/5 p. 398	Merchant (Indian)	Witness, intimidation case	Penang
5	22 May	PIJ 31/5 p. 393 ST 17 June p. 1 confirms killed	Tapper	Refused to strike	Sua Betong Estate, Negri Sembilan
6	25 May	PIJ 31/5 p. 394	Contractor	Witness, intimidation case	Ladang Geddes Estate, Johore
7	25 May	PIJ 31/5 p. 394	Coolie	Collateral damage	Ladang Geddes, Johore
8	29 May[1]	ST 9 May, p. 1	Smallholder	None suggested	51st mile, Johore
9	2 June	PIJ 15/6 p. 427	*Kepala*	Guomindang	Mary Estate, Batang Berjuntai, Selangor
10	3 June	ST 8 June p. 6 and 17 June p. 1	Estate owner	Resisted MCP demands	Johore
11	3 June	PIJ 15/6 p. 427	Tin labourer	Blackleg; witnesses in intimidation case	Salak South, Selangor
12	3 June	PIJ 15/6 p. 427	Tin labourer	As above	As above
13	4 June	PIJ 15/6 p. 428	Mine manager (European)	Failed hold-up	Idris Hydraulic, Perak
14	5 June	PIJ 15/6 p. 428	Estate manager[2]	Anti-communist	Triang, Mentakab, Pahang
15	7 June	PIJ 15/6 p. 428	Contractor	In error for a non-union man	Tong Hing Estate, Johore
16	7 June	PIJ 15/6 p. 428	Settlement officer (Malay)	None suggested	Near Sungei Siput

	Date	Source	Employment	Cause	Location
17	7 June	PIJ 15/6 p. 428	Village headman (Malay)	None suggested	Near Sungei Siput
18	12 June	PIJ 15/6 p. 429	Contractor	Guomindang official	Rengam, Johore
19	12 June	PIJ 15/6 p. 429	Shopkeeper	Guomindang	Rengam, Johore
20	12 June	PIJ 15/6 p. 429	Shopkeeper	As above	As above
21	13 June	PIJ 15/6 p. 429	Not known	Probably mistaken for his brother	Sagil Estate, Johore
22	13 June	PIJ 15/6 p. 420 ST, 17/6 p. 1	Conductor	None suggested	Yong Kee Shian, Kesang, Malacca

Notes

1. As far as is known, with the exception of four, all of the victims were Chinese.

2. *Mandore*, conductor and *kepala* were terms used for foremen of varying levels of seniority.

Other killings

Eight labourers were killed in a police action on Chang Kang Swee Estate, Jementa, Johore on 1 June 1948.[3]

On 13 June, four Chinese were killed by Malays near Lenggong in northern Perak, thought to be in revenge for the killing of the two Malay officials a few days earlier elsewhere in the state.

NOTES

Introduction

1 See Alan Ogden, *Tigers Burning Bright: SOE Heroes in the Far East* (London: Bene Factum Publishing, 2013), pp. 249–50. The gross profit figure, of £77 million (£33bn at today's valuation), given by Ogden, can be sourced to M. R. D. Foot, *SOE: The Special Operations Executive 1940–1946* (London: Pimlico, 1999), p. 352.

2 For detail on the formation of SOE, see Foot, *SOE*, pp. 16–26.

3 Richard Aldrich, *Intelligence and the War against Japan: Britain, America and the Politics of Secret Service* (Cambridge: Cambridge University Press, 2000), pp. 93–4.

4 David Lampe, *The Last Ditch: Britain's Secret Resistance and the Nazi Invasion Plans* (Barnsley: Frontline Books, 2013; first published 1968), pp. 3–5. Lampe notes that 840 anti-tank guns had been left behind in France, leaving 167 for the defence of the United Kingdom.

5 The exposure of Britain's Asian possessions is analysed at length by Brian Farrell, *The Defence and Fall of Singapore, 1940–41* (Stroud: Tempus, 2005), pp. 57–73; the impact of the Tripartite Pact is discussed by Antony Best, *Britain, Japan and Pearl Harbor: Avoiding War in East Asia, 1936–41* (London: Routledge, 1995), p. 132.

6 Best, *Britain, Japan and Pearl Harbor*, p. 9; Ong Chit Chung, *Operation Matador: World War II: Britain's Attempt to Foil the Japanese Invasion of Malaya and Singapore* (Singapore: Marshall Cavendish, 2011; first published 1997), p. 143.

7 Best, *Britain, Japan and Pearl Harbor*, p. 135.

8 Field Marshall Lord Alanbrooke, *War Diaries, 1939–45*, ed. Alex Danchev and Daniel Todman (London: Weidenfeld and Nicolson, 2001), p. 205.

9 Best, *Britain, Japan and Pearl Harbor*, p. 120.

10 Richard Gough, *SOE Singapore 1941–42* (London: William Kimber, 1985), pp. 3–14; The National Archives, London (hereafter TNA), HS 1/207, 'History of SOE Oriental Mission, May 1941–March 1942', p. 1.

11 A recent issue of the journal *Intelligence and National Security* devoted to SOE virtually ignored Asia. See *Intelligence and National Security*, 20, 1 (March 2005). India is mentioned in the context of Italian POWs. In an article on currency transactions, Operation *Remorse* is discussed in passing, with the remark had it been extensively written up; the focus of the article then shifted to Europe.

12 Foot, *SOE*, pp. 130 and 350. Foot's focus is SOE in Europe.

13 Charles Cruickshank, *SOE in the Far East* (Oxford: Oxford University Press, 1983), pp. 193–203.

14 Lampe, in *The Last Ditch*, outlines the development of the idea of stay-behind parties in 1940 in the event of a German invasion of Britain; see especially pp. 2, 65–9 and 72–3. Col. Colin Gubbins of MI(R), who had been intimately involved in the formation of stay-behind parties ('Auxiliary Units') in England, was transferred to SOE before the end of 1940, and brought with him many of his instructors. Oriental Mission strongly promoted plans for stay-behind parties in Malaya from August 1941.

15 Dixee Bartholomew-Feis, *The OSS and Ho Chi Minh: Unexpected Allies in the War against Japan* (Lawrence, KS: University Press of Kansas, 2006); Maochun Yu, *OSS in China: Prelude to Cold War* (Annapolis: Naval Institute Press, 2011); Richard Duckett, *The Special Operations Executive in Burma: Jungle Warfare and Intelligence Gathering in World War II* (London: I.B. Tauris, 2017).
16 Maochun Yu, *OSS in China*, pp. 269–70.
17 Cruickshank, *SOE in the Far East*, pp. 81–2.
18 S. Woodburn Kirby, *The War against Japan, Vol. V* (London: HMSO, 1969), p. 250.
19 Aldrich, *Intelligence and the War against Japan*, p. 112; Farrell, *Defence and Fall*, pp. 239–40.
20 Gough, *SOE Singapore 1941–42*, pp. 230–3.
21 Farrell, *Defence and Fall*, p. 385.
22 Richard Duckett, 'The Special Operations Executive in Burma, 1941–45' (Unpublished doctoral thesis; The Open University, 2015), pp. 14–15 and 304.
23 Aldrich claims that in mid-1945 of 'the six main guerrilla groups', only three 'hosted SOE missions' (Aldrich, *Intelligence and the War against Japan*, p. 332). In fact, by the end of May, five Force 136 operations were active with regiments of MPAJA, with operations being prepared for the remaining three, and four others were either raising, or preparing to raise, Malay guerrillas.
24 Aldrich, *Intelligence and the War against Japan*, pp. 331–3.
25 Christopher Bayly and Tim Harper, *Forgotten Armies: Britain's Asian Empire and the War with Japan* (London: Penguin, 2005), p. 341. SOA, like Force 136, was a constituent unit of SOE. It was also referred to as Z Special Unit and the Services Reconnaissance Department.
26 Ogden, *Tigers Burning Bright*. For example, Ogden includes a table of the European stay-behind parties inserted into Malaya by Oriental Mission (pp. 151–4).
27 Ogden, *Tigers Burning Bright*, pp. 42, 46, 150, and 182. On p. 159, Major J.V. Hart is given as 'reinforcing' Operation *Carpenter*; Hart was in fact an ISLD agent infiltrated to *Carpenter*, but this is not made clear. Boris Hembry, *Malayan Spymaster: Memoirs of a Rubber Planter, Bandit Fighter and Spy* (Singapore: Monsoon, 2011), p. 267 (supported by TNA, HS 1/107, Operation *Carpenter* reports). Earlier in Ogden's book, it is not clear whether it was Oriental Mission or ISLD that trained and inserted parties of MCP cadres ahead of the Japanese advance.
28 Heather Williams, *Parachutes, Patriots and Partisans: The Special Operations Executive in Yugoslavia, 1941–1945* (London: C. Hurst Ltd., 2003); Roderick Bailey, *The Wildest Province: SOE in the Land of the Eagle* (London: Vintage, 2008). Some studies have examined the impact of OSS on Asian politics: see, for example, Scott L. Bills, *Empire and Cold War: The Roots of US-Third World Antagonism, 1945–47* (Basingstoke: Palgrave Macmillan, 1990), pp. 83–90.
29 It has been suggested that James Klugmann, an active communist working for SOE in Cairo, pulled strings and rigged reports to ensure that communist guerrillas were backed in the field over other groups. Roderick Bailey has concluded that, while Klugmann did seek to influence the course of events, his actions were immaterial, for SOE took a short-term view in the Balkans and supported the guerrillas who took the most effective action against the Axis. See Roderick Bailey, 'Communist in SOE: Explaining James Klugmann's Recruitment and Retention', *Intelligence and National Security*, 20, 1 (2005), pp. 72–97. For a wider discussion, see Williams, *Parachutes, Patriots and Partisans* and Bailey, *The Wildest Province*, as well as memoirs such as Fitzroy MacLean's *Eastern Approaches* (London: Penguin, 2009).

30 Mary P. Callahan, *Making Enemies: War and State Building in Burma* (Ithaca: Cornell University Press, 2003), for example, see pp. 70–81; Duckett, 'The Special Operations Executive in Burma, 1941–45'.

31 Callahan, *Making Enemies*, pp. 71, 78. Mountbatten's contact with Force 136 over policy for Burma is discussed on p. 318 of Philip Ziegler, *Mountbatten: The Official Biography* (London: Collins, 1985). Colin Mackenzie related how he saw Mountbatten at least twice a week, discussed matters with him and found him accessible (London, Imperial War Museum (hereafter IWM) Sound.9471, Interview with Colin Mackenzie, Reel 5).

32 Duckett, 'The Special Operations Executive in Burma, 1941–45', pp. 275, and 285–6.

33 Duckett, 'The Special Operations Executive in Burma, 1941–45', pp. 292–3.

34 See, for example, Woodburn Kirby, *The War against Japan,* V, p. 279 and Field Marshall Lord Carver, *Britain's Army in the 20th Century* (London: Pan Books, 1999), pp. 324 and 335.

35 Michael Burleigh, *Moral Combat: A History of World War II* (London: Harper Press, 2010), p. 559.

36 Thomas R. Mockaitis, *British Counterinsurgency: 1919–1960* (Basingstoke: Macmillan, 1990).

37 This is the underlying thesis that runs right through Ban Kah Choon and Yap Hong Kuan's *Rehearsal for War: The Underground War against the Japanese* (Singapore: Horizon Books, 2002).

38 Harry Miller, *Menace in Malaya* (London: Harrap, 1954).

39 Edgar O'Ballance, *Malaya: The Communist Insurgent War, 1948–60* (London: Faber and Faber, 1966); Cruickshank, *SOE in the Far East.*

40 Mockaitis, *British Counterinsurgency*, p. 112.

41 Chin Peng with Ian Ward and Norma Miraflor, *My Side of History* (Singapore: Media Masters Pte, 2003), pp. 11 and 109. Incidentally, in making this statement, he not only disregarded the efforts of the Guomindang and of the Malays, but also overlooked the civilian movement centred on the former policeman, Gurchan Singh, whose propaganda had been distributed from Penang to Singapore: see Gurchan Singh, *Singha: The Lion of Malaya Malaya, Being the Memoirs of Gurchan Singh*, ed. Hugh Barnes (London: Quality Press Ltd., 1949). Singa's agents – Indians, Chinese, Ceylonese, Malays and Eurasians – distributed his propaganda up and down the peninsula.

42 Chin Peng, *My Side of History*, pp. 26, and 133–4.

43 Bayly and Harper, *Forgotten Armies*, p. 416. For a view of the OCAJA as guerrillas, see TNA, HS 1/121, Major J.P.M. Clifford, *Hebrides Minerva* Operational Report.

44 Bills, *Empire and Cold War*, pp. 83–90. It appears that the members of at least some of the American operations in French Indo-China were unaware of the communist ideology of the Viet Minh.

45 For details on Lai Teck's life and times, see Leon Comber, 'Traitor of All Traitors – Secret Agent "Extraordinaire"', *Journal of the Malaysian Branch of the Royal Asiatic Society*, 83, 2 (2010), pp. 1–25.

46 T.N. Harper, *The End of Empire and the Making of Malaya* (Cambridge: Cambridge University Press, 1999), p. 49.

47 Wan Hashim, *Second World War in Malaya: Role of the Malay Guerillas: Force 136* (Kuala Lumpur: Institut Terjemahan Negara Malaysia Berhad, 2010), originally published in Bahasa Melayu as *Perang Dunia Kedua: Peranan Gerila Melayu Force 136* (Kuala Lumpur: Dewan Bahasa dan Pustaka, 1993). His intention is clear from his introduction.

48 Ban Kah Choon and Yap Hong Kuan, *Rehearsal for War*, pp. 55 and 146.

49 Paul Kratoska, *The Japanese Occupation of Malaya: A Social and Economic History 1941–1945* (London: C. Hurst and Co, 1998), pp. 295–6 and Cruickshank, *SOE in the Far East*, p. 295.

50 Bayly and Harper, *Forgotten Armies*, p. 451, and Christopher Bayly and Tim Harper, *Forgotten Wars: The End of Britain's Asian Empire* (London: Penguin, 2008), p. 341; Cheah Boon Kheng, *Red Star over Malaya: Resistance and Social Conflict during and after the Japanese Occupation 1941–1946* (Singapore: Singapore University Press, 2003), p. 74; F. S. V. Donnison, *British Military Administration in the Far East, 1943–46* (London: HMSO, 1956), pp. 386; Miller, *Menace in Malaya*, p. 46; Richard Clutterbuck, *The Long Long War: The Emergency in Malaya 1948–1960* (London: Cassell, 1967), p. 17.

51 For a discussion of this, see, Frank Costigliola, 'The Nuclear Family: Tropes of Gender and Pathology in the Western Alliance', *Diplomatic History*, 21, 2 (1997), pp. 163–83.

52 These include George Hesse (a Eurasian, and formerly a gunner in the FMSVF) and Lloyd Chin Fen, a Jamaican Chinese radio operator.

53 Stuart Duncan, '"Of Historical Interest Only": The Origins and Vicissitudes of the SOE Archive', *Intelligence and National Security*, 20, 1 (2005), pp. 14–26. The bonfires included papers held by individual Force 136 officers who were still serving in Malaya (Margaret Shennan in *Our Man in Malaya: John Davis CBE, DSO, SOE Force 136 and Post-war Counter-Insurgency* (Stroud: The History Press, 2007), p. 130).

54 Imperial War Museum (hereafter IWM), 4859, Papers of Lt. Col. F. Spencer Chapman, File 4, especially Encs. 42 and 48. This concealment of key information is discussed in detail in Chapter 2.

55 Neville Wylie, 'SOE: New Approaches and Perspectives', *Intelligence and National Security*, 20, 1 (2005), pp. 1–13.

56 Fraser was later instrumental in the expulsion of a number of Soviet diplomats. Obituary, *Daily Telegraph*, 19 July 2001, from <http://www.telegraph.co.uk/news/obituaries/1334494/Hugh-Fraser.html> [accessed 21 April 2012].

57 Among others, there are no personnel files for Lt. Col. P.E. Taylor (who remained in the army), Claude Fenner of the Malayan Police, or Dare Newell who had a long career in the SAS.

58 One, for example, wrote very critically and sarcastically about the views of 'misinformed senior officers'. TNA, HS 1/121, Major. J.P.M. Clifford, *Hebrides Minerva* Operational Report, pp. 4–5.

59 This is evident as regards the decisions of 'P' Division, discussed in Chapter 2.

60 The useful dispatches published in the *London Gazette* included those by General Arthur Percival and Air Chief Marshall Sir Keith Park.

61 See IWM, Sound.9471, Interview with Colin Mackenzie, Reel 5.

62 Gwyn Prins, 'Oral History' in *New Perspectives on Historical Writing*, ed. Peter Burke (Cambridge: Polity, 2001), pp. 120–52 (pp. 122 and 138).

63 Chin Peng, *My Side of History*.

64 For example, Chin Peng discusses the Lam Swee incident, where a senior MCP cadre defected, in both, *Dialogues with Chin Peng: New Light on the Malayan Communist Party*, ed. by C. C. Chin and Karl Hack (Singapore: Singapore University Press, 2004), p. 168, and *My Side of History* (p. 259). His upbringing and his conversion to communism are also among the many topics recounted in both books. It should be noted that although *My Side of History* was published before *Dialogues*, the discussions in *Dialogues* predate the writing of the memoir.

65 For example, Chin Peng, *My Side of History*, pp. 109–10, where he typifies the OCAJA guerrillas as bandits, though the Perak MPAJA fought them and cannot have failed to be aware of their anti-Japanese credentials. For a full discussion of other guerrillas, and the attitude of the MPAJA towards them, see Chapters 3 and 4. Interestingly, Chin Peng has virtually nothing to say about the health and feeding of the MPAJA, whereas Force 136 accounts, and the memoir of the MPAJA soldier Ho Thean Fook – *Tainted Glory* (Kuala Lumpur: University of Malaya Press, 2000) – make it clear that food was an Achilles' heel, as it would be again during the Emergency.

66 Karl Hack, 'The Origins of the Asian Cold War: Malaya 1948', *Journal of Southeast Asian Studies*, 40, 3 (2009), pp. 471–96.

67 MPAJA entering Slim River: Foss Papers; OCAJA on parade and Peter Dobrée at the end of operations: both TNA, HS 1/121; Peter Dobrée before operations: IWM, 10035, Papers of I.A. McDonald, group photograph.

Chapter 1

1 Cruickshank, *SOE in the Far East*, pp. 3 and 81–2; Aldrich, *Intelligence and the War against Japan*, p. 112.

2 Bayly and Harper, *Forgotten Armies*, pp. 133–5; Cheah Boon Kheng, *Red Star over Malaya*, p. 59; Kratoska, *The Japanese Occupation of Malaya*, pp. 291–3; Ban Kah Choon and Yap Hong Kuan, *Rehearsal for War*, pp. 31–3.

3 Bayly and Harper, *Forgotten Armies*, pp. 133–4; Kratoska, *The Japanese Occupation of Malaya*, pp. 290–1; Ban Kah Choon and Yap Hong Kuan, *Rehearsal for War*, pp. 33–4.

4 Aldrich, *Intelligence and the War against Japan*, pp. 105–6.

5 For example, Peter Dobrée, *Hot Rain Means Danger* (Ipoh: Yayasan Perak, Malaysia), 2007.

6 A.J. Stockwell, 'The Formation and First Years of the United Malays National Organization (U.M.N.O.) 1946–1948', *Modern Asian Studies*, 11, 4 (1977), pp. 481–513, esp. p. 484.

7 Kratoska, *The Japanese Occupation of Malaya*, p. 14; Bayly and Harper, *Forgotten Armies*, p. 41.

8 Karl Hack, *Defence and Decolonisation in Southeast Asia, Britain, Malaya and Singapore 1941–1968* (Richmond: Curzon, 2001), p. 46; Harper, *The End of Empire and the Making of Malaya*, p. 32. For a view of the lack of ethnic tension and the multi-ethnic tenor of daily life from an Asian who grew up during this period, see Yuen Yuet Leng, *Nation before Self and Values That Do Not Die* (Ampang, Malaysia: Self-published, 2011), pp. 3–9.

9 For example, IWM Sound.14876, L. H. N. Davis, Interview, for a pre-war view of the contacts developed by a district officer.

10 Bayly and Harper, *Forgotten Armies*, pp. 42–3. A 'Protector of the Aborigines' had recently been appointed, a young ethnologist named H.D. 'Pat' Noone (p. 267).

11 For the problems faced by the *Orang Asli,* see Dobrée, *Hot Rain Means Danger*, p. 33.

12 Kratoska, *The Japanese Occupation of Malaya*, p. 21.

13 See, for example, *Straits Times*, 13 May 1941, p. 11.

14 These were John Davis (*Gustavus*), Douglas Broadhurst (*Galvanic*), Claude Fenner (*Humour*) and (after the death in action of Major Paddy Martin) Ian Wylie (*Carpenter*).

15 This topic is discussed in detail on pp. 40–4.

16 Brian Farrell, *Defence and Fall*, pp. 98–9. Brigadier Ivan Simson, Percival's chief engineer, would later complain that he had not been allowed to build the defences that he felt the country required (Ivan Simson, *Singapore: Too Little, Too Late: Some Aspects of the Malayan Disaster* (London: Leo Cooper, 1970), esp. pp. 30–40). It may be argued that Simson had an axe to grind, but Farrell concludes that 'there is some corroboration for Simson' and notes Indian Division engineers mentioning his plans and drawings, adding, 'Whatever the truth of Simson's story, there is no doubt he tried to galvanise defence works': Farrell, *Defence and Fall*, p. 113. The lack of defences was evident to alert civilians (TNA, WO 106/2550B, 'The Malayan Campaign as seen by an Executive Government Officer', by G. Morgan, p. 2).

17 Aldrich, *Intelligence and the War against Japan*, p. 94.

18 Aldrich, *Intelligence and the War against Japan*, pp. 93–4.

19 Aldrich, *Intelligence and the War against Japan*, pp. 103–4; TNA, HS 1/207, 'History of SOE Oriental Mission', pp. 5–6. SOE's first scouting mission to Asia had been dispatched early in 1941.

20 Aldrich, *Intelligence and the War against Japan*, p. 101.

21 Antony Best, *British Intelligence and the Japanese Challenge in Asia, 1914–1941* (London: Palgrave Macmillan, 2002), p. 9.

22 Best, *British Intelligence and the Japanese Challenge*, pp. 9–10. Killery is one of those named by Best, as is the missionary Findlay Andrew, another member of Oriental Mission.

23 TNA, HS 1/112, 'OM Personnel' gives an idea of size of Oriental Mission and its geographic scope; TNA, HS 1/207, 'History of Oriental Mission' details its work – both the plans which came to fruition and those which did not.

24 TNA, HS 1/340, 'Far Eastern Mission', quoted in Duckett, 'The Special Operations Executive in Burma, 1941–45', p. 50.

25 TNA, HS 1/340, 'Far Eastern Mission', quoted in Duckett, 'The Special Operations Executive in Burma, 1941–45', p. 50.

26 Duckett, 'The Special Operations Executive in Burma, 1941–45', p. 51.

27 Gough, *SOE Singapore 1941–42*, pp. 25–9; F. Spencer Chapman, *The Jungle Is Neutral* (London: The Reprint Society, 1950), pp. 17–3; TNA, HS 1/112, 'OM Personnel'.

28 Aldrich, *Intelligence and the War against Japan*, p. 104; TNA, HS 1/207, 'History of Oriental Mission', p. 4.

29 The correspondence around this may be found on TNA, HS 1/115. This was in sharp contrast to the cooperation enjoyed by SOE's India Mission, which worked with the blessing of the Viceroy, Lord Linlithgow. India Mission would later absorb much of the staff of Oriental Mission. TNA, HS 1/340, 'To SO from CD, 24.12.41'. This document outlines the problems encountered in Malaya by Killery and his team.

30 TNA, HS 1/115, 'Copy of 1.100's Original Scheme', 27 August 1941, pp. 1–2.

31 Lampe, *The Last Ditch*, pp. 64, 66–8 and 113. The original stay-behind idea had its genesis in a pre-war visit, by General Thorne (later responsible for the defence of the British coastline during World War II) to East Prussia, where peasant farmers maintained dumps of food and arms that would only be used once an invading army had passed them by (p. 2).

32 David Lloyd Owen, *Providence Their Guide: The Long Range Desert Group, 1940–45* (London: Pen and Sword, 2000), pp. 11 and 13; Tim Moreman, *Long Range Desert Group Patrolman: The Western Desert, 1940–43* (Oxford: Osprey, 2010), p. 8.

33 Nagl, *Learning to Eat Soup with a Knife*, pp. xii–xiii. For an example of the processes by which this happened, see the contents of WO 193/911 ('Irregular Activities – Far East'), which includes correspondence between the War Office and commanders in the field and contains a long brief entitled 'Lessons of the Abyssinian Revolt'.

34 TNA, HS 1/340, 'Country Section', 16 December 1941, p. 5.

35 Cruickshank, *SOE in the Far East*, p. 61.

36 TNA, HS 1/340, 'Country Section', 16 December 1941, p. 5.

37 TNA, HS 1/115, 'Copy of 1.100's Original Scheme', 27 August 1941, pp. 1–2. The country was to be divided into six zones, each with two or three divisions. Each zone and each division would have been headed by a European, so at most twenty-four men would have been required.

38 Malay Regiment: Dol Ramli, *History of the Malay Regiment, 1933–42* (Singapore: University of Malaya, 1955), pp. 47 and 124; Eurasians in the Royal Artillery: *Straits Times*, 17 July 1940, p. 8; Johore Military Force and the Malayan Volunteers: John Brown, 'A Nominal Roll of the Volunteers' (including data on the JMF), unpublished, 2007. Brown's figures are based on records held at the National Archives, but he considered that these, for a number of reasons, underestimated the strength of the Volunteers so, if anything, there were more Asians in the Volunteers rather than fewer. The Volunteer forces included the Straits Settlements Volunteer Force (SSVF), the Federated Malay States Volunteer Force (FMSVF) and a number of smaller units, such as the Johore Volunteer Engineers. The SSVF was split on ethnic lines, whereas the FMSVF had been reorganized so that sections were mixed. That 'Asiatics' included Eurasians is clear from W.D. Reeve to Colin Mackenzie, 14 December 1942, TNA, HS 1/27, cited in Duckett, 'The Special Operations Executive in Burma, 1941–45', p. 69.

39 Malayan Police shotguns are mentioned in IWM, 10035, Papers of I.A. McDonald, p. 5.

40 TNA, HS 1/115, 'Copy of 1.100's Original Scheme', 27 August 1941, p. 1. The expectation of European leadership is discussed in Chapter 2.

41 Bayly and Harper, *Forgotten Armies*, p. 110; Mark Frost and Yu-Mei Balasingamchow, *Singapore: A Biography* (Singapore: Editions Didier Millet, 2009), p. 264.

42 TNA, WO 220/556, 'Major M [Colin Marshall] (Forests)', 'Report on Statements by Malayan Evacuees, Ex-Prisoners Etc.', p. E1. Marshall's unit was disbanded in late December 1941: Audrey Holmes McCormick, 'Volunteer Forces', at <http://www.malayanvolunteersgroup.org.uk/node/58> [accessed 16 April 2016]. 'Jungly' Marshall then moved to train 'forest guards' in East Pahang (near Sungei Lembing) but Japanese forces arrived too quickly for anything to come of this project (TNA, HS 1/120, F. Spencer Chapman, 'Report on report on AJUF'). Marshall then transferred to Dalforce, where he was second-in-command (Shennan, *Our Man in Malaya*, p. 17 and Jonathan Moffatt and Paul Riches, *In Oriente Primus* (Coventry: Self-published, 2010), p. 217.

43 This border patrol was raised by the chief game warden (E.O. Shebbeare) and the Noone brothers, Pat and Richard: Audrey Holmes McCormick, 'Volunteer Forces', at <http://www.malayanvolunteersgroup.org.uk/node/58> [accessed 16 April 2016]. Pat, whose job title was 'Protector of the Aborigines', took to the jungle, where he was later killed; Richard escaped and was taken on by SOA.

44 TNA, HS 1/207, 'History of Oriental Mission', p. 3.

45 TNA, HS 1/115, Percival to Mott, 22 November 1941.

46 TNA, HS 1/115, Memorandum from Percival to Killery, 11 November 1941.

47   TNA, HS 1/207 'History of SOE Oriental Mission', p. 3. This mission history is dated July 1941, and seems – from its scope and viewpoint – to have been written by Killery.

48   Aldrich, *Intelligence and the War against Japan*, p. 106; Bayly and Harper, *Forgotten Armies*, pp. 3, 5 and 23. Japan had invaded Manchuria in 1931.

49   Farrell, *Defence and Fall*, pp. 59–60.

50   Farrell, *Defence and Fall*, p. 397.

51   Aldrich, *Intelligence and the War against Japan*, p. 102 and Farrell, *Defence and Fall*, p. 136.

52   Ronald McCrum, *The Men Who Lost Singapore, 1938–1942* (Singapore: NUS Press, 2017), p. 234.

53   Richard J. Howarth, 'Geology behind Barbed Wire', *Proceedings of the Geologists' Association*, 126, 2 (April 2015), pp. 282–94.

54   Simson, *Singapore*, pp. 33 and 36–7.

55   Simson, *Singapore*, pp. 36–7. It might be argued that Simson was writing to protect his own reputation, but Farrell states that there is at least some corroboration for Simson's version of events (Farrell, *Defence and Fall*, p. 113).

56   Keith Simpson, 'Percival' in *Churchill's Generals*, ed. John Keegan (London: Weidenfeld and Nicolson, 1991), p. 271. McCrum, *The Men Who Lost Singapore*, p. 176, concurs with Simpson's verdict.

57   Norman Dixon, *The Psychology of Military Incompetence* (London: Jonathan Cape, 1976), p. 131. This quote occurs in a fascinating discussion of the failings of senior officers before and during the Malayan Campaign, pp. 130–44.

58   Percival continued to resist the construction of defensive works after the Japanese had invaded. Even in late December, according to Simson, Percival was still claiming that defensive works were bad for military and civilian morale (Simson, *Singapore*, pp. 68–9).

59   Oriental Mission's scorched earth activities included the 'blowing' of the tin smelter at Prai and the destruction of stores of aviation spirit: TNA, HS 1/207, 'History of SOE Oriental Mission', p. 15.

60   Shennan, *Our Man in Malaya*, pp. 6–7.

61   Shennan, *Our Man in Malaya*, pp. 7 and 16.

62   TNA, HS 1/109, F. Spencer Chapman, Report A, p. 2. This is at odds with the version given by Margaret Shennan, who claims that Lai Teck attended with another MCP man, and that the British side consisted of Spencer Chapman and John Davis. Since Spencer Chapman's report was written about two and half years after the events it describes, and he names all participants, it is probably accurate.

63   TNA, HS 1/109, F. Spencer Chapman, Report A, pp. 2–3.

64   During the course of the war, SOE was to find many guerrillas among the 'hill tribes' of Burma, but did not really consider the long-term political consequences: IWM, Sound.9471, Colin Mackenzie, Reel 2.

65   Chin Peng, *My Side of History*, p. 65; Bayly and Harper, *Forgotten Armies*, p. 134.

66   TNA, HS 1/115, 'OM Operations in Malaya', p. 14.

67   Spencer Chapman, *The Jungle Is Neutral*, pp. 27–8 and 46.

68   TNA, HS 1/115, 'OM Operations in Malaya', pp. 14–17.

69   Chin Peng, *My Side of History*, p. 68.

70   Chin Peng, *My Side of History*, p. 67; Ho Thean Fook, *Tainted Glory*, pp. 36 and 136.

71 The numbering of the first four MPAJA regiments follows the order in which groups were inserted into the jungle by 101STS: the 1st, 2nd, 3rd and 4th regiments were in, respectively, Selangor, Negri Sembilan, north Johore and south Johore. Only after this come the regiments in areas that the Japanese had, in fact, occupied earlier: Perak (5th), West Pahang (6th), East Pahang (7th) and Kedah (8th).

72 IWM, 10035, Private Papers of I.A. McDonald.

73 Diary of M.C. Hay (courtesy of the Hay family). It is difficult to generalize too widely about the state of mind of the Malayan Volunteers, for few contemporary accounts survive. Upon capitulation, those Asian troops still under arms were urged to return home and the Europeans, who were going into internment, were ordered to destroy all personal diaries and other related paperwork, so that there should be no written evidence available to incriminate Asian Volunteers who had headed back north. The official records of the FMSVF were also destroyed (Brown, 'A Nominal Roll of the Volunteers').

74 'Lessons from Hong Kong and Malaya' by Sir W. Battershill, G.E.J. Gent and W.L. Rolleston, from TNA, CO 877/25/7/27265/7, para. 22, cited in *British Documents on the End of Empire: Malaya Part 1 (Series B, Vol. 8)*, ed. A.J. Stockwell (London: HMSO, 2001), p. 33.

75 *London Gazette*, Second Supplement of 26 February 1948, Lt. Gen. Arthur Percival, 'Operations of Malaya Command', <http://www.britain-at-war.org.uk/WW2/London_Gazette/Malaya_Command/> [accessed 10 August 2015].

76 TNA, HS 1/115, 'OM Operations in Malaya', pp. 4–6.

77 There were eight official parties, plus another scratch party in Pahang, as well as at least one party, under Major James Barry, with the ISLD (MI5). See TNA, HS 1/115, 'OM Operations in Malaya', pp. 5–11; R.W. Holder, *The Fight for Malaya: The Jungle War of Maurice Cotterill* (Singapore: Editions Didier Millet, 2007), pp. 49–52; John Cross, *Red Jungle* (London: The Quality Book Club, 1957), pp. 24–9.

78 Spencer Chapman, *The Jungle Is Neutral*, p. 89. Even if the details Spencer Chapman obtained were doubled by exaggeration, this story still gives an indication of how effective well-founded and carefully dispersed stay-behind parties would have been.

79 Calculated from TNA, HS 1/112, 'OM Casualties' [undated], and data in Moffatt and Riches, *In Oriente Primus*.

80 Spencer Chapman, *The Jungle Is Neutral*, pp. 224–30; TNA, HS 1/109, Report.

81 *Singapore Free Press*, 15 August 1946, p. 1. Shinozaki was widely regarded in Malaya as having been a humane and decent man. Estimates for deaths in the *Sook Ching* vary widely, but the lowest figure is around 5,000.

82 TNA, HS 1/226 'OM Sumatra Operations', 11 May 1942, pp. 3–6 (sheets not numbered). For information of how events on the ground appeared in retrospect to those involved, see Gough, *SOE Singapore 1941–42*, pp. 169–87. Around 200 of those taken off from Padang were killed in the sinking of the *SS Rooseboom*.

83 'Excerpts from Lim Bo Seng's Diary' in *The Price of Peace: True Accounts of the Japanese Occupation*, ed. Foong Choon Hong, trans. by Clara Show (Singapore: Asiapac, 1997), pp. 148–59 (pp. 153–9). Lim Bo Seng does not mention the existence of the route, but it is obvious from the details of his journey and his fairly speedy arrival in Padang that he and his comrades were moved along it; for Tengku Mahmood, see TNA, HS 1/108, 'To C.D. from A.D.4, Major Tengku Mahmood Mahyideen', 16 February 1945. 'Tengku' is an alternative spelling of Tunku still used in Pahang, Kelantan and Selangor.

84   TNA, HS 1/226 'OM Sumatra Operations', 11 May 1942, p. 11 (sheets not numbered).
     The 800 included SOE's Alan Warren, who had masterminded the route but
     volunteered to remain behind in charge of stranded soldiers. Warren survived the war.
     (Ian Skidmore, *Marines Don't Hold Their Horses* (London: W.H. Allen, 1981), pp. 59
     and 67.

85   The story of Lim Bo Seng's escape is taken from 'Excerpts from Lim Bo Seng's Diary',
     pp. 148–59 (pp. 148–51). Another contemporary account that mentions the Padang
     route is IWM, 10035, Papers of I.A. McDonald.

86   The term 'British Malayan' is taken here to refer to Caucasian residents of Malaya who
     originated in Britain or one of the Dominions. The contentious issues surrounding
     this term are discussed at length by Tim Harper in 'The British "Malayans"' in *Settlers
     and Expatriates: Britons over the Seas,* ed. Robert Bickers (Oxford: Oxford University
     Press, 2010), pp. 233–68.

87   For a full and fascinating account of this, see IWM, Documents.10035, Papers of
     Major I.A. McDonald.

88   Dalforce: after a brief training, around a thousand men were stationed along the coast
     of Singapore Island. They were poorly armed, many with no more than the Greener
     shotguns formerly used by up-country Malayan Police and a parang, and some of the
     units took heavy casualties. The survivors were disbanded on 13 February, and told
     to burn their uniforms and bury their arms; an unknown number were rounded up
     and killed by the Japanese in the early days of their occupation of Singapore, in the
     'screening' of the Chinese population known as the Sook Ching. For a comprehensive
     discussion of Dalforce myth versus Dalforce reality, see Kevin Blackburn and Daniel
     Chew Ju Ern, 'Dalforce at the Fall of Singapore in 1942: An Overseas Chinese Heroic
     Legend', *Journal of Chinese Overseas,* 1, 2 (November 2005), pp. 233–59. See also
     IWM, Sound.4664, Frank Brewer Interview.

89   Those from the junk who returned with Force 136 were McDonald himself, Jock
     Hunter, Geoffrey Hasler, Fred Harrison and Jim Hislop. McDonald did not name all
     of the junk's passengers, so it is possible that there were others (see TNA, HS 1/108,
     Force 136 Operational Roll).

90   IWM, 3455, Papers of W.P.S. Brereton Martin; this information is drawn from two
     letters he wrote almost as soon as he reached Australia following his escape. Three
     others in the Martin party (Durward Sime, Douglas Browning and Alan Campbell-
     Miles) returned with Force 136, and another, H.M. Gray, with the ISLD (TNA, HS
     1/108, Operational Roll; Moffatt and Riches, *In Oriente Primus,* p. 145) gave Gray's
     nickname as 'Piper'; Hembry (*Malayan Spymaster,* p. 362) confirms 'Piper' Gray's
     infiltration with ISLD). Another escapee was Peter Dobrée, a gunner in the FMSVF,
     who will feature in later chapters. He recorded in his memoir that, 'We found we had
     stumbled upon the escape route organized [sic] by SOE' (IWM, 3328, Papers of P.G.J.
     Dobrée, p. 7).

91   Damien Lewis, *Judy: Dog in a Million* (London: Quercus, 2015), pp. 145 and 147.
     The story of the party is also recounted in Robert Weintraub, *No Better Friend: One
     Man, One Dog and Their Extraordinary Story of Courage and Survival in World War
     II* (London: Little Brown and Company, 2015). Judy, a pointer bitch, was their ship's
     mascot. She survived the war.

92   TNA, HS 1/207, 'History of Oriental Mission', p. 22. Oriental Mission's propaganda
     staff was taken on by the Far Eastern Combined Bureau (the Asian section of the
     Ministry of Information). Other staff were either paid off or transferred elsewhere
     within SOE.

93 Perhaps the most pronounced example of this was the return of Freddy Spencer Chapman to the East Pahang guerrillas after the end of the war. Having worked with them during the Japanese occupation, he was judged as being well placed to persuade this independent-minded group to come in, hand over their arms and disband. It was he who attended the meeting of senior MPAJA leaders that brought the situation under British control: TNA, HS 1/120, Major J.L. Chapman, *Siphon* Operational Report. (Confusingly, though Lt. Col. Freddy Spencer Chapman commanded the operation, Major Jack Chapman wrote the report.).

94 Chin Peng, *My Side of History*, p. 17, relates how Davis's history with the MCP cadres speeded the development of mutual trust: 'Davis was able to recount details of his association with several of our Perak comrades who had passed through the school. His SEAC letter of authorisation, together with the stories he related, quickly convinced me of his bona fides.'

95 Duckett has summarized Oriental Mission's work in Burma at <https://defenceindepth.co/2016/06/29/burma-1942-soes-role-in-defeat-into-victory/> [accessed 30 June 2016]. This describes how SOE was able to slow the Japanese advance through northern Burma, thus enabling the escape of more Allied troops, and preventing them from capturing Fort Hertz; had the Japanese gained the airstrip there, they would have been in a position to interdict the last remaining Allied supply route into China.

96 The strains on Japanese supply lines are discussed by Farrell, *Defence and Fall*, p. 294.

97 For reinforcements see Farrell, *Defence and Fall*, pp. 281 and 311 (I Australian Corps was pulled out of the Middle East to be sent to Malaya, but even before Johore had fallen to the Japanese, it was diverted to the Netherlands East Indies) and p. 295 (Hurricanes were dispatched to Malaya, but were diverted once it became clear to the RAF that air defence had become futile).

98 Farrell, *Defence and Fall*, p. 311.

Chapter 2

1 This account is drawn from TNA, HS 1/123, '"Siderhana Johannis" Escape Party' and Shennan, *Our Man in Malaya*, pp. 37–45. It is clear from photographs of the vessel, on the same file, that her sheets and sails were in no condition for the voyage. One of the escapees on board, who acted as navigator, was Ivan Lyon, who later led the SOA operation *Jaywick*, which destroyed Japanese shipping in Singapore harbour. He was killed during a second, similar, operation (*Rimau*), in October 1944. It should be noted that Richard Broome originally worked for the Malayan Civil Service, which shared the initials MCS with Force 136's Malayan Country Section.

2 As already noted, India Mission became known as Force 136 from March 1944.

3 Ban Kah Choon and Yap Hong Kuan, *Rehearsal for War*, p. 53.

4 See, for example, Cruickshank, *SOE in the Far East*, pp. 191–210 and 249–58; also Shennan, *Our Man in Malaya*. Shennan mentions other operations, but the only one examined in detail is *Gustavus*.

5 For example, Bayly and Harper, *Forgotten Armies* (particularly pp. 133–5 and 450–3) and Kratoska, *The Japanese Occupation of Malaya*.

6 This is covered in Chapter 6. The interregnum was the period between the surrender of Japan, when Japanese troops began to pull out of outlying areas and concentrate in

the main towns, and the reassertion of British authority, which took place across the country between the arrival of the first British troops in Penang at the end of August and the arrival of troops and administrators in outlying areas up to a month later.

7   The degree to which the 'Europe first' policy operated can be seen from the fact that only 10 per cent of SOE's resources went to the Far East. (Duckett, 'The Special Operations Executive in Burma, 1941–45', p. 129).

8   Raymond Callahan, *Burma 1942–45* (London: Davis-Poynter, 1978), p. 43 (cited in Duckett, *SOE in Burma*, p. 72) quotes the Joint Planning Staff as warning that India was at real risk of being lost.

9   Winston Churchill, *The Second World War, Vol IV: The Hinge of Fate* (London: Cassell, 1951), pp. 374–35, 529, 537, 687–9, 691–2; General Sir Archibald Wavell, 'Despatch on Operations in Iraq, East Syria and Iran', *The London Gazette*, 14 August 1946, p. 4093, <https://www.thegazette.co.uk/London/issue/37685/supplement/4093> [accessed 4 June 2015].

10 Duckett, 'The Special Operations Executive in Burma, 1941–45', pp. 143–4; TNA, HS 1/340, Cypher Telegram from Maymyo, 2 February 1941.

11 TNA, HS 1/226, 'OM and Escape from Malaya', p. 9, preliminary report dated 15 March 1942. Both Lo Ngai Soon (usually known as 'Chuan') and Jamal bin Daim were dropped into Malaya by Force 136.

12 TNA, HS 1/112, 'OM Personnel'. The majority of the Oriental Mission staff escaped alive, and many were redeployed within SOE, transferring to other departments, such as the Mediterranean Group or SOE China. The Force 136 designation was acquired in March 1944, though it did not come into regular use until towards the end of that year.

13 Aldrich, *Intelligence and the War against Japan*, pp. 157–8. Aldrich also observes that Mackenzie was a friend of Lord Linlithgow, the Viceroy, and that this connection eased India Mission's path, giving it a head start not enjoyed by Killery in Singapore. For more background on Mackenzie, see Duckett, 'The Special Operations Executive in Burma, 1941–45', pp. 111–12.

14 Report on Indian Mission, File 5, Private Papers of F. Spencer Chapman, IWM; Aldrich, *Intelligence and the War against Japan*, p. 158. Mackenzie's personality is also attested to by Alec Peterson, who was seconded from the India Mission staff to Mountbatten's HQ (IWM, Documents.13346, Private Papers of A.D.C. Peterson).

15 Chin Peng states that Innes Tremlett was Lai Teck's Special Branch handler (Chin Peng, *My Side of History*, p. 65), as does Leon Comber in *Malaya's Secret Police 1945–60: The Role of the Special Branch in the Malayan Emergency* (Singapore: Institute of Southeast Asian Studies, 2008), p. 95. However Shennan (*Our Man in Malaya*, p. 6) says that it was John Davis. She states in her footnotes that the information was provided by a former Malayan civil servant who claimed his information came directly from Davis (p. 255). Davis moved to Singapore in 1940, so it is feasible that he took over Lai Teck from Tremlett (IWM, 16953, Papers of J.H.L. Davis, Biographical Notes). Innes Tremlett's appointment as head of Malayan Country Section is noted in his 'SOE Record of Service' (TNA, HS 9/1482/8).

16 Duckett, 'The Special Operations Executive in Burma, 1941–45', p. 118, says that more than 6,000 Burmese troops reached India.

17 Gurkha platoons volunteered to work with SOE: Chris Bellamy, *The Gurkhas: Special Force* (London: John Murray, 2011), pp. 241–2; wills: see, for example, TNA, HS 9/1255/1 Form A.4 (A). The only recruits upon whom pressure seems to have been

placed to volunteer were those from the Mahara Examination Centre (see p. 69), who had the option of remaining interned, or joining one of the clandestine bodies.

18 Shennan, *Our Man in Malaya*, pp. 58–59. She sources her information to the draft of a letter Davis wrote to Basil Goodfellow, explaining why he should be allowed to remain in Malaya, whatever the risks. He also delineated another reason why a European should be with any exploratory party: as a way of proving its *bona fides*. The Japanese, he seems to be suggesting, could attempt to infiltrate the guerrillas using a party of Chinese; the presence of an Englishman – particularly of an Englishman likely to be known to some of the guerrillas – would persuade them that this really was a mission sent to them from outside the country. Ultimately, Goodfellow was persuaded.

19 David Cannadine, *Ornamentalism: How the British Saw Their Empire* (London: Penguin, 2002), pp. 6 and 8.

20 Cannadine, *Ornamentalism*, pp. 9–10.

21 Race: Catherine Hall, 'Remembering Edward Said', *History Workshop Journal*, No. 57 (2004), pp. 235–43, p. 242; excessive focus on elites: Ian Christopher Fletcher, 'Ornamentalism: How the British Saw Their Empire' (review), *Victorian Studies*, 45, 3 (2003), 532–4, particularly p. 533. Interestingly, Cannadine's argument ties in with work in evolutionary psychology, which indicates that 'race' as a classifier is very mutable and more easily 'overwritten by circumstance' than age and gender (See Robert Kurzban, John Tooby and Leda Cosmides, 'Can Race Be Erased? Coalitional computation and Social Categorization', *Proceedings of the National Academy of Sciences*, 98, 26 (2001), 15387–92. This study was broadly – though less emphatically – supported by Wouter Voorspoels, Annelies Bartlema and Wolf Vanpaemel, 'Can Race Really Be Erased? A Pre-registered Replication study', *Frontiers in Psychology*, <http://dx.doi.org/10.3389/fpsyg.2014.01035> [accessed 1 May 2016].

22 The Tengku was a major; Lim Bo Seng was not a member of the British Army, but was given the status of major (TNA, HS 9/1341, Personnel Record). Evidence for the backgrounds of the NCOs can be found in interviews with them carried out by the IWM. See, for example, Sound.12311, Alfred Edwin Holdham, who was the son of a coachbuilder, and a sergeant with Operation *Sergeant*; and Sound.13172, John William Ellis, also an NCO, who had worked in a shirt factory.

23 The carpet salesman was Bertie Wright of *Carpenter* (Bailey, *The Wildest Province*, p. 298), the Eurasian Geoffrey Frank of *Tideway*, whose English grandfather had been a private soldier (family information). This process was paralleled in Burma Country Section, where the head of the section dealing with propaganda and political subversion was an Anglo-Burman, Freddie Wemyss (IWM, Documents.13346, Private Papers of A.D.C. Peterson, p. 47).

24 TNA, HS 1/221, Mailes to Lincoln, 3 April 1944 and Watherson to Mott, 25 April 1944.

25 These organizations are referred to only vaguely in Shennan, *Our Man in Malaya*, pp. 51–52, but must be assumed to include ones like the British Association of Malaya (BAM). Escape lists were assembled to assist in the reunification of families. Shennan drew her information from records kept by John Davis who was, at the time, searching for Chinese agents but appears to have made a note of possible Europeans.

26 Hembry, *Malayan Spymaster*, p. 231.

27 John Davis's post-war address book is revealing in this regard: many of the names in it are of former colleagues in Oriental Mission and Force 136, including a number of Chinese (IWM, 16973, Papers of J.L.H. Davis).

28 At one point, Hembry was traced via the Railway Transport Office at Howrah Station who had handled his travel warrant. Hembry, *Malayan Spymaster*, p. 215.

29 TNA, HS 1/221, MPU to Mott, 21 October 1944. This letter names eight potential candidates, two refused outright, two could not be spared from other duties and of the remaining four only two – S.F. Owen and R.L. Melliar-Smith – were actually infiltrated. Men were free to pull out at any stage: one of the four candidates above who went on for training was 'sworn out' of the SOE later that year when he changed his mind (TNA, HS 1/221, SOE to Colonial Office, 5 December 1944).

30 TNA, HS 1/221, To Nigeria (Sir. A. Richards) from S. of S. Colonies, 12 April 1944 and To Gold Coast (Sir A. Burns) from S. of S. Colonies, 1 April 1944.

31 TNA, HS 1/221, From Nigeria (Sir. A. Richards) to S. of S. Colonies, 24 April 1944. This telegram requested that two men remain in post until July or August.

32 Cambridge University Library, Papers of Mubin Sheppard, 11084, Pt. III, File 9, Derek Headly to Mubin Sheppard, 1 April 1985. Headly here is talking not only of himself, but also of Doug Richardson.

33 The Malayan Planning Unit, set up by the Colonial Office, had two main functions: to organize and train staff for the British Military Administration which was to run Malaya following the defeat of Japan, and to revise the Malayan constitution, sweeping away the shambolic patchwork of governance of the pre-war period. In the event, the new constitution galvanized Malay political action like nothing else had ever done.

34 Stockwell, *British Documents on the End of Empire: Malaya Part 1*, p. liv.

35 For a full discussion of this, see A.J. Stockwell, 'Colonial Planning during World War Two: The Case of Malaya', *The Journal of Imperial and Commonwealth History*, 2, 3 (1974), pp. 333–51.

36 TNA, CAB 119/212, 'Chiefs of Staff Committee … Resistance Movements in Malaya', 3 June 1945, p. 2.

37 TNA, HS 1/221, Benham to Campbell, 24 May 1944 and MPU to Mott, 21 October 1944; TNA, HS 1/108, *Funnel* operational roll.

38 Shennan, *Our Man in Malaya*, pp. 51–2.

39 Maochun Yu, *The Dragon's War: Allied Operations and the Fate of China, 1947–1947* (Annapolis: Naval Institute Press, 2006), pp. 63–6. Tai Li was a notably ruthless individual whose secret police was described as 'a bunch of cutthroats' by an OSS operative (Aldrich, *Intelligence and the War against Japan*, p. 265).

40 TNA, HS 1/108, From C.D. to A.D.4, 16 February 1945.

41 TNA, CO 825/42/6, Tengku Mahmood Mahyideen, 'The Line our Propaganda to Malaya should take'.

42 Arkib Negara Malaysia (hereafter ANM), 2000/0006765, Derek Headly to Mubin Shepherd, 20 September 1979. Later in the war, Tun Mhd. Suffian went to London as head of the BBC's Malay section, before a distinguished career in Malaysian jurisprudence (*Daily Telegraph* Obituary, 20 September 2000 at <http://www.telegraph.co.uk/news/obituaries/1357064/Tun-Mohamed-Suffian.html> [3 July 2016].

43 Aldrich, *Intelligence and the War against Japan*, pp. 184–6. Aldrich draws entirely on US archival sources. Mention of Mahara in the records at the National Archives has proved entirely elusive, which may imply that additional Force 136 records remain to be released.

44 TNA, HS 7/165, 'History of Force 136 operations in Malaya', p. 19.

45 TNA, HS 1/115, 'Gurkha Support Groups', 18 July 1945; TNA, HS 1/107, Major S.F. Owen, *Funnel Green* Operational Report, p. 3. For the reputation of the Gurkhas, see Lionel Caplan, ' "Bravest of the Brave": Representations of 'The Gurkha' in British

Military Writings', *Modern Asian Studies*, 25, 3 (1991), 571–97. This source discusses the long-term essentializing of the Gurkhas, but does not mention their use in special forces in World War II, other than, fleetingly, in the Chindits. For the volunteer nature of the Gurkhas with SOE, see Bellamy, *The Gurkhas*, pp. 241–242. For how British troops viewed the Gurkhas, see George MacDonald Fraser, *Quartered Safe out Here* (London: HarperCollins Publishers, 2000; first published 1993), pp. 193–201.

46 TNA, HS 1/108 Operational Roll.

47 Capt. Geoffrey Frank: TNA, HS 1/108 Operational Roll; TNA, HS 9/539/2 and family information; Sgt. Robert Neubronner: TNA, HS 1/108 Operational Roll; TNA, HS 1/122, Operation *Multiple* Personnel Reports, and family information.

48 For example, although men recruited in Asia were sent on a parachute course in India, those recruited in Britain were trained at the SOE school at Ringway, outside Birmingham. (Bill Foss, Interview, Sevenoaks, May 2012).

49 See, for example, TNA, HS 9/539/2, Record of Service and HS 9/1000/7, Record of Service.

50 Duckett, 'The Special Operations Executive in Burma, 1941–45', pp. 128, 129 and 131.

51 For an example of wishing to contribute to the war effort: IWM, 653, Papers of H.R. Ross, Ross to his parents, 14 March 1942 ('I hate the idea of the Indian Army but if I return to England I feel that I am running away from my responsibility of becoming effective at the earliest opportunity'.) For another, in *Apa Khabar* (the journal of the Malayan Volunteers Group), January 2016, p. 13, George Templer to his mother; he discusses how he wants to join the Navy on his next leave as 'I can't bear the idea of enjoying myself for six months while there are other more important things to do.'

52 *Apa Khabar*, January 2016, '2nd Lt. Colin Symington – Escape from Singapore', pp. 6–8, 1942. Symington had been an officer in Dalforce and Col. Dalley, whose brainchild this was, had pushed hard for his Chinese-speaking European officers to be allowed to escape. In one of the complex coincidences typical of Malayan life, Symington had written a forestry manual that was about to be printed at the Caxton Press in Kuala Lumpur. The Japanese who was placed in charge of the Singapore Botanic Gardens was eager to get hold of this, and duly did so. The owner/manager of the Caxton Press was Victor Hessé, the father of George Hessé, who spent some of the occupation with the MPAJA, and then with Force 136. George will feature in later in this book. (Jeyamalar Kathirithamby-Wells, *Nature and Nation: Forests and Development in Peninsular Malaysia* (Singapore: Singapore University Press, 2005), p. 234; George Hessé, Interview, Perth, 2009).

53 IWM, 653, Papers of H.R. Ross, Ross to his parents, 14 March 1942. Bobby Ross was a member of the ill-fated Operation *Rimau* in late 1944, and was killed that October, fighting a rear-guard action to allow others to escape. Eventually, the survivors of the operation were picked up by the Japanese. They were executed in Singapore in July 1945.

54 An example of the sense of duty that pervades accounts by British Malayans may be found in IWM, 3455, Private Papers of W.P.S. Brereton Martin. Martin's account is contained in a letter he wrote just after he arrived in Australia, in March 1942. He carried out intelligence work behind Japanese lines during February 1942. On the night of 14 February he cycled back to his estate and woke up the *mandores* and conductors to find out how things were. He commented, 'It was a very long and tiring ride but I am glad I went, since … it was the last chance.'

55 IWM, 3328, Papers of P.G.J. Dobrée, 'Hot Rain Means Danger', p. 5.

56 TNA, HS 1/108, Operational Roll and HS 1/121, Lt. Col. P.G.J. Dobrée, *Hebrides* Operational Report.

57 Lim Bo Seng's birthplace is given as Amoy in his personnel file (TNA, HS 9/1341, Personal Record).

58 For example, Lim Bo Seng had encouraged Chinese labourers to go on strike at a Japanese owned iron mine at Dungun in northeast Malaya in the late 1930s: Xu Hai Liang, 'A Fighter's Thoughts on Anti-aggression' in *The Price of Peace,* ed. Foong Choon Hong, pp. 131–6 (p. 135) and S. Tsering Bhalla, 'My Father, the Hero' in *The Price of Peace,* ed. Foong Choon Hong, pp. 137–47 (p. 145). Lim Bo Seng was held in high regard by the British: in TNA, CO 537/3757, H.T. Pagden, 'Unrest in Malaya' (undated), para. 50, Hugh Pagden, a Force 136 staff officer, describes Lim Bo Seng as 'an outstanding man… one of the truly great men'.

59 'Excerpts from Lim Bo Seng's Diary', pp. 148–59. The entry for 11 February 1942 reads, 'To remain behind was entirely out of the question, considering my past activities'. That Lim Bo Seng was on a list of Chinese considered to be in danger may be deduced from TNA, CO 273/673/7, statement by a policeman named Boyle. This statement alleges that Lim Bo Seng was left behind by Innes Tremlett; Lim Bo Seng's own diary directly contradicts this.

60 Tan Chong Tee, *Force 136: The Story of a World War II Resistance Fighter* (Singapore: Asiapac, 1995), pp. 10 and 22.

61 Tan Chong Tee, *Force 136,* pp. 25–6.

62 Xu Hai Liang, 'A Fighter's Thoughts on Anti-aggression', in *The Price of Peace,* ed. Foong Choon Hong, pp. 131–6 (p. 133).

63 Huat Kin Koon, 'The Dilemma of Identity: Overseas Chinese in Malaya and the Quest for Nationhood, 1930–1949' (Unpublished doctoral thesis; London School of Economics and Political Science, 2006), pp. 25 and 64. The focus on China among Malayan Chinese during the 1930s is also clear from Chin Peng, *My Side of History,* pp. 41 and 43, where he refers to China as 'the Motherland', and describes the absorption of Malayan Chinese in events in China.

64 Roy MacLaren, *Canadians Behind Enemy Lines, 1939–1945* (Vancouver: University of British Columbia Press, 1981), p. 184.

65 MacLaren, *Canadians Behind Enemy Lines,* pp. 184–5 and 188; *Unwanted Soldiers,* 1999, dir. by Jari Osborne (National Film Board of Canada, 1999), <http://www.nfb.ca/film/unwanted_soldiers/> [6 May 2015]. This film was government funded and includes interviews with some of the men concerned.

66 TNA, HS 1/112, 'OM Personnel'; MacLaren, *Canadians Behind Enemy Lines,* pp. 184–5.

67 Information extracted from MacLaren, *Canadians Behind Enemy Lines,* pp. 200–32 and TNA, HS 1/108, Force 136 Operational Roll. Of the nine, eight were with Force 136 and one with 'E' Group.

68 Stockwell, *British Documents on the End of Empire: Malaya Part 1,* pp. lix and 168, fn. 16.

69 ANM, 2000/0006765, Wan Hashim bin Wan Teh, 'The Malay Resistance Movement against the Japanese during the Second World War', pp. 1 and 7 (Paper presented at Australian National University, 1985); ANM, 2000/0006765, Derek Headly, Background to Resistance in Malaya, p. 25.

70 ANM, 2000/0006765, Derek Headly, Draft of Chapter 2, p. 1.

71 TNA, CO 825/42/6, Tengku Mahmood Mahyideen, 'The Line our Propaganda to Malaya should take'.

72 ANM, 2000/0006765, Wan Hashim bin Wan Teh, 'The Malay Resistance Movement against the Japanese during the Second World War', p. 17. Wan Hashim sources the Tengku's views to an interview with the man with whom he shared a house in Delhi during the war.

73 W.K. Che Man, *Muslim Separatism: The Moros of Southern Philippines and the Malays of Southern Thailand* (Singapore: Oxford University Press, 1990), p. 65.

74 Aldrich, *Intelligence and the War against Japan*, p. 179.

75 Terence O'Brien, an RAF Special Duties pilot, in his memoir *The Moonlit War* blames most dissension between clandestines on ISLD (p. 218) and states that Force 136 and 'E' Group collaborated well, a claim supported by a letter of thanks written to the Force by 'E' Group's commander, Col. R.C. Jackman (TNA, HS 1/305, Jackman to Mackenzie, 27 September 1945). Force 136 was also prepared to let PWD use its air sorties for leaflet drops (e.g. TNA, HS 1/120, Airborne Operations Report (drop to Operation *Multiple*), Serial 879).

76 For 'E' group drops, see for example, TNA, HS 1/107, Major D. Sime, Operation *Carpenter* GLO Operational Report, p. 9. The *Oatmeal* party was successfully played back against the Japanese until the end of the war (see Chapter 3).

77 These two factors combined to cause stress and pressure in northern Malaya: TNA, HS 1/117, Major J.A. Hislop, *Sergeant* Operational Report, p. 3. Hislop found himself bumping up against Operation *Fighter* in an area with very few possible dropping zones.

78 Aldrich, *Intelligence and the War against Japan*, p. 93. For a particularly scathing take on ISLD, see O'Brien, *The Moonlit War*. O'Brien had experience both as a Chindit (and thus of conditions on the ground when working behind enemy lines) and as an RAF Special Duties pilot.

79 Hembry, *Malayan Spymaster*, p. 260; TNA, HS 1/304, 'Notes on I.S.L.D. Operation Evidence', 13 June 1945.

80 The joint operation is described in TNA, HS 1/121, Major G.A. Hasler, *Fighter* Operational Report, pp. 1–2. He and an ISLD officer, and their stores, had been dropped to *Hebrides*. This joint operation did not eventuate, as one man intended to work with Malays and the other with Chinese, so they went their separate ways without any apparent ill-feeling.

81 Aldrich, *Intelligence and the War against Japan*, pp. 96.

82 Aldrich, *Intelligence and the War against Japan*, pp. 103, 130 and 135.

83 Aldrich, *Intelligence and the War against Japan*, p. 133.

84 Aldrich, *Intelligence and the War against Japan*, pp. 140–1.

85 Aldrich, *Intelligence and the War against Japan*, p. 92.

86 TNA, HS 1/340, To AD/Z [Col. F.T. Davis, Director of SOE's Research, Development and Supply unit] from U.2. [Symbol unidentified, but U was the 'Americas' section], 17 March 1942.

87 Aldrich, *Intelligence and the War against Japan*, pp. 151 and 192.

88 TNA, HS 1/303, To D of I, HQ SACSEA, from HQ Force 136, 3 July 1945.

89 Duckett, 'The Special Operations Executive in Burma, 1941–45', pp. 135 and 139. Duckett sources the allegations against OSS to TNA, HS 1/227, a report from an inspection of India Mission, 8 January 1944–20 April 1944.

90 Aldrich, *Intelligence and the War against Japan*, p. 179.

91 TNA, HS 1/115, Cypher Telegram to Kandy, to B/B100 [Mackenzie], 5 January 45.

92 Aldrich, *Intelligence and the War against Japan*, pp. 191–2, outlines a project that relied upon overturning the long-running antipathy between the Malays of Kelantan

and the Thais just across the border, which he terms 'improbable'. That OSS's Malaya expert appears to have claimed connections with the 'burger' community casts some doubt upon quite how much he knew, since the people in question are known as the Burghers.

93 E. Bruce Reynolds, *Thailand's Secret War: OSS, SOE and the Free Thai Underground during World War II* (Cambridge: Cambridge University Press, 2004), p. 244; TNA, HS 1/308, To Group 'B' Force 136 (MCS) from HQ Force 136, 13 December 1944. (Group B was the Force 136 branch in Ceylon which included MCS).

94 Aldrich, *Intelligence and the War against Japan*, p. 193.

95 TNA, HS 1/123, *Oatmeal* Operational Report. *Jukebox* is also not mentioned in the memoir of *Oatmeal*'s leader, Ibrahim Ismail, *Have You Met Mariam?* (Johor Bharu: Westlight, 1984).

96 TNA, HS 1/308, To G. Ops, HQ Force 136 from OC, ADCS, 27 July 1945.

97 TNA, HS 1/308, To Kandy No. 707 from MCS, 12 June 1945. This telegram details the (non) liaison between OSS and Force 136 to date.

98 TNA, HS 1/308, To HQ Force 136 (OPS) from Group B Force 136 (MCS), 6 January 1945; TNA, HS 1/308, To Group 'B' Force 136 (MCS) from HQ Force 136, 13 December 1944.

99 TNA, HS 1/123, Major G.R. Leonard, *Pontoon* GLO's Operational Report, p. 10. The American Bithos, of whom Leonard speaks, was the leader of *Cairngorm*.

100 TNA, HS 1/308, To Group B Force 136 (MCS) from HQ Force 136 (Ops), 12 December 1944.

101 Aldrich, *Intelligence and the War against Japan*, p. 193; TNA, HS 1/308, Minutes of Meeting held on 15 May 1945. The agreement does not directly state that this was how the deal would pan out, but all OSS parties thereafter dropped to Force 136 reception parties and were expected to be under the tactical command of the local GLO.

102 TNA, HS 1/308, To HQ Force 136 (Ops) from Group B Force 136 (MCS), 13 July 1945. It is obvious from this letter that repeated requests were being made of OSS for this party to be infiltrated. See also TNA, HS 1/123, Lt. Col. Richardson's Operation *Beacon* Report.

103 TNA, HS 1/308, Tel: to Kandy No. 182 from Colombo, 31 July [1945]. The telegram ends, 'Please pass to OSS HQ for retransmission'.

104 Kirby, *The War against Japan, Vol. V*, pp. 65–70, outlines the tactics planned for *Zipper*. Force 136's role in relation to *Zipper* is discussed by Cruickshank, *SOE in the Far East*, p. 209.

105 O'Brien, *The Moonlit War*, p. 45. The B-24 Liberator was, by reducing payload, armour and gun turrets in exchange for extra fuel tanks, developed to close the 'air gap' in the mid-Atlantic during 1942 and (especially) 1943: Alan F. Wilt, *War from the Top: German and British Military Decision Making during World War II* (Bloomington: Indiana University Press, 1990), p. 212. The payload of these planes was compromised by the extra fuel tanks and they were almost defenceless, being reduced to one rear gun.

106 *Gustavus* was hamstrung for over a year: for detail on this period, see Shennan, *Our Man in Malaya*, pp. 75–95. *Carpenter*, another operation launched by submarine, ended up with extra mouths to feed, since the ferry party was unable to return to the submarine, and at the same time was unable to bring many of its stores ashore as the outboard engines on the rubber transport dinghies did not work (TNA, HS 1/107, Major D. Sime, *Carpenter* Operational Report, p. 3).

107 Duckett, "The Special Operations Executive in Burma, 1941–45', p. 108; TNA, HS 1/107, Lt. Col. J.L.H. Davis, *Gustavus* Operational Report.

108 TNA, HS 1/115, 'Copy of 1.100's Original Scheme'; TNA, HS 7/165, War Diary, p. 22.

109 TNA, HS 1/115, 'Plan for Malaya', 20 February 1945; Operation *Carpenter* had been launched in October 1944, with the aim of contacting the MPAJA.

110 TNA, HS 1/107, Major J.P. Hannah, *Funnel* GLO's Operational Report, p. 1.

111 It is difficult to be precise with these numbers, as some Malays were recruited locally, as were one Chinese and some European stay-behinds, and a handful of men died or were exfiltrated during the course of operations. The totals are drawn from the personnel roll on HS 1/108 (TNA) and the operational reports. The 'others' were two Eurasians (Capt. Geoffrey Frank and Sgt. Robert Neubronner) and a Baghdadi Jew, Capt. Mike Levy. In addition, one of the Gurkha jemadars seems, from his name, to have been Indian.

112 The likelihood is that the colour sequence was dictated by the order in which patrols were formed during training, and they would not necessarily infiltrate in this order. Each patrol worked to its own signal plan. In Malaya most of these were named after musical instruments (Operation *Galvanic*, for example, worked to the overall plan 'Guitar') and the patrol's 'colour' denoted its plan – so for, example, *Galvanic Blue* worked to the signal plan Guitar Blue. It is important not to confuse (as sometimes happens) the name of a signal plan with the name of an operation.

113 Although the Malay resistance group Wataniah reached a total armed strength of 173, only two European officers (one British and one American) were ever assigned to it. Many of its Malay officers appear to have had experience in the Malay Regiment, the Volunteers or the Local Defence Corps. (For details, see TNA, HS 1/123.) There were several hundred Guomindang guerrillas, but they were not divided into patrols in the same way as the MPAJA.

114 TNA, HS 1/107, Major T.A. Wilson, *Funnel Slate* Operational Report, p. 1.

115 TNA, HS 1/119, Major A.J. Hunter, *Galvanic Blue* Operational Report, p. 4.

116 See also, for example, TNA, HS 1/107, Major S.F. Owen, *Funnel Green* Operational Report, p. 4.

117 The rolling up of the *Gustavus* network is covered by Shennan (*Our Man in Malaya*, pp. 85–7) and Tan Chong Tee (*Force 136*, pp. 211–43) as well as TNA, HS 1/107, Major R.N. Broome, Report on *Gustavus*, pp. 3–4.

118 The story of the *Oatmeal* party is in TNA, HS 1/123. It is also covered in detail in its leader Ibrahim Ismail's book, *Have You Met Mariam?*

119 Cruickshank, *SOE in the Far East*, p. 209.

120 Jacques van Doorn, *The Soldier and Social Change: Comparative Studies in the History and Sociology of the Military* (London: Sage Publications Ltd., 1975), pp. 32 and 39.

121 Van Doorn, *The Soldier and Social Change*, pp. 21–2.

122 TNA, HS 1/119, Major A.T. Thomson-Walker, *Galvanic Orange* Operational Report, p. 4. Tin tailings were areas that had previously been mined, and consisted of spoil, scrub and pools of water.

123 TNA, HS 1/119, Major I.A. McDonald, *Galvanic Brown* Operational Report, p. 1.

124 Dobrée of Operation *Hebrides* fell victim to several of these: he was injured in an attack on his camp and forced with others to flee into the jungle (IWM, 3328, Papers of P.G.J. Dobrée, pp. 38–40).

125 Tan Chong Tee gives the whole story of arrest and death in *Force 136*, pp. 222–49; TNA, HS 1/107, 'Death of Major Martin'.

126 For example, TNA, HS 1/107, 'W/T Report by Sgt. Birrell of Operation Funnel'. Birrell commented, 'I have slaved (don't laugh) from 6.a.m. to 11p.m. many days to keep the battery charged', adding that he had 'made contact every sked [schedule] though sometimes atmospheric conditions were beyond a joke'; see also TNA, HS 1/107, 'Report on Carpenter Horn W/T by Sgt. Collinson'.

127 The 20 per cent figure is calculated across the Air Operations Reports for ninety flights, including one which ditched in the sea on the return leg, with few survivors, TNA, HS 1/120; 'skeleton' comment: TNA, HS 1/120, reverse of Air Operations Report, Serial 675. A photograph of Peter Dobrée of *Hebrides* taken during training, and another from the end of operations, show just how much weight he had lost (IWM, 10035, Papers of I.A. MacDonald, group photograph of British Malayan recruits in India and TNA, HS 1/121, photographs).

128 *Unwanted Soldiers*, 1999, dir. Jari Osborne (National Film Board of Canada), http://www.nfb.ca/film/unwanted_soldiers/.

129 For example, TNA, HS 1/122, Lt. Col. C.H. Fenner, Operation *Humour*, Report on Sgt. Hooker (he 'should never have been sent on an operation involving a small party'); TNA, HS 1/117, Major J.A. Hislop, Operation *Sergeant*, Report on Sgt. Holdham; TNA, HS 1/123, Major G.R. Leonard, Operation *Pontoon*, Report on Lt. Tonnison ('nervy and highly strung ... not a suitable type for operations of this nature.').

130 Although Operation *Carpenter* was in wireless contact from Johore in the south, the *Gustavus* group, which had infiltrated into Perak in August 1943, had been out of contact for almost a year, after the failure of a submarine rendezvous in early 1944, and though *Carpenter* had heard that they were alive, there were intense concerns for their safety and well-being (TNA, HS 1/107, Operation *Carpenter*, GLO Operational Report; Shennan, *Our Man in Malaya*, pp. 67 and 83). It is not clear if Hannah's refusal to work with *Evidence* came before or after the reception in Ceylon of a message from *Carpenter* informing HQ of the well-being and whereabouts of the *Gustavus* party (19 January: Shennan, *Our Man in Malaya*, p. 94). A listening watch was maintained on their signal frequency until *Gustavus* came up on the air, early in 1945 (Shennan, *Our Man in Malaya*, p. 97).

131 TNA, HS 1/304, 'Notes on I.S.L.D. Operation Evidence', 13 June 1945; TNA, HS 7/165 'Operations in Malaya', p. 33.

132 TNA, HS 9/912/8G.R. Leonard: Form TW/100; TNA, HS 1/119, Major A.J. Hunter: *Galvanic Blue* Personnel Reports.

133 TNA, HS 1/122, Lt. Col. C.H. Fenner, *Humour* GLO's Personnel Reports.

134 TNA, HS 1/119, Major A.J. Hunter, *Galvanic Blue* Personnel Reports; TNA, HS 1/107, Major S.F. Owen, *Funnel Slate* Personnel Reports. Hunter had played cricket on ethnically mixed teams pre-war and valued his friendships with Asians (family information, supported by *Malaya Tribune*, 10 April 1939, p. 12).

135 TNA, HS 1/122, Major D. Headly, Operation *Multiple* Personnel Reports. The supposed Eurasian inferiority complex was a very common trope at the time.

136 TNA, HS 1/121, Hasler, *Fighter* Operational Report, p. 7 ('But the one real failing... of the Malays that I found ... was their inability to keep their mouths shut and keep a secret for even a few days.'); TNA, HS 1/123, Lt. Col. J.D. Richardson, *Beacon* Operational Report, p. 6 ('The security of the Malays and of the Sakai had been remarkable and deserves special mention': this is supported by Reg Lawther, who was a major in the MPAJA in Pahang and had never heard of Wataniah: 'Notes of Interview with Reg Lawther', Elizabeth Moggie, Singapore, May 2016).

137 TNA, HS 1/122, Lt. Col. C.H. Fenner, *Humour* Operational Report, 'Confidential Reports on Officers: Major B.G. Phillips'.
138 TNA, HS 1/303, To HPD from HQ Force 136, 23 August 1945, Chinese Officer Personnel.
139 TNA, HS 1/303, To HPD from HQ Force 136, 23 August 1945, Chinese Officer Personnel.
140 For the trope of the arrogant European see, for example, Ho Thean Fook, *Tainted Glory*, p. 24 and Tan Chong Tee, *Force 136*, pp. 46, 48, 49 and 55.
141 Tan Chong Tee, *Force 136*, p. 29. Wu was, at the time, Secretary General of the Guomindang. He later rose to be Vice-Premier of the Republic of China.
142 Tan Chong Tee, *Force 136*, for example, pp. 47–8 and 196.
143 For the demise of the network, see Tan Chong Tee, *Force 136*, Chapter 22, and Shennan, *Our Man in Malaya*, pp. 85–6.
144 Shennan, *Our Man in Malaya*, p. 119, states that the Japanese diplomat, Mamoru Shinozaki, blamed Lai Teck for the betrayal of Lim Bo Seng to the Kempeitai when he was interrogated after the war. Shinozaki was well regarded by many Malayans, particularly by Eurasians who credited him with helping to protect their community.
145 TNA, HS 1/119, Lt. Col. D. Broadhurst, Operation *Galvanic* Personnel Report on Yui Ming Teh.
146 TNA, HS 1/119, Broadhurst, *Galvanic* Personnel Report on Tong Shu Shan.
147 TNA, HS 1/119, Broadhurst, *Galvanic* Personnel Report on Sgt. Lee Bing.
148 George Hesse, Interview, Perth, 2009.
149 Duckett, 'The Special Operations Executive in Burma, 1941–45', pp. 210–12.

Chapter 3

1 The quote is from Chin Peng, *My Side of History*, p. 11.
2 Chinese majority: for example, IWM, 14859, Papers of F. Spencer Chapman, 'The Chinese in Malaya', File 13, and Papers of C.E. Foss, nominal roll of the patrol *Funnel Green*; education: TNA, HS 1/109, F. Spencer Chapman, Report A, pp. 25–6.
3 Cheah Boon Kheng, *Red Star over Malaya*, p. 65; TNA, HS 1/121, John Creer, Report, p. 4.
4 TNA, HS 1/115, 'OM Operations in Malaya', p. 14. Davis's and Broome's work with Oriental Mission is covered in Chapter 1. Lim Bo Seng's role in the recruitment of the 'Dragons' is outlined in Chapter 2.
5 Shennan, *Our Man in Malaya*, p. 75, quoting John Davis. Davis might have been forewarned about Lai Teck, since intelligence from Malaya, which seems (given the date of the documents around it) to have come out of the country in late 1943, stated that 'Lai Tak' was the head of the MPAJU (IWM, 14859, Papers of F. Spencer Chapman Papers, File 4, paper headed 'Most Secret', p. 3). Spencer Chapman, who was also present, having been brought into the camp some time before by the MPAJA, had met Lai Teck at the Singapore meeting where SOE accepted the MCP's offer of assistance (*The Jungle Is Neutral*, p. 27) and might have recognized him too.
6 Chin Peng, *My Side of History*, p. 25; Shennan, *Our Man in Malaya*, p. 76.
7 Caroline Elkins, 'The Re-assertion of the British Empire in Southeast Asia', *Journal of Interdisciplinary History*, 39, 3 (2009), pp. 361–85.

8   Nicoletta F. Gullace, *The Blood of Our Sons: Men, Women and the Renegotiation of British Citizenship during the Great War* (New York: Palgrave Macmillan, 2002), pp. 3–4.

9   Pamela McElwee, '"There is Nothing that is Difficult": History and Hardship on and after the Ho Chi Minh Trail in North Vietnam', *The Asia Pacific Journal of Anthropology*, 6, 3 (December 2005), pp. 197–214.

10 Bayly and Harper, *Forgotten Wars*, p. 78.

11 Chin Peng, *My Side of History*, p. 26.

12 Bayly and Harper, *Forgotten Armies*, p. 451.

13 Bayly and Harper, *Forgotten Wars*, p. 32.

14 Elkins, 'The Re-assertion of the British Empire in Southeast Asia', pp. 361–85.

15 Cheah Boon Kheng, *Red Star over Malaya*, p. 74.

16 Ban Kah Choon and Yap Hong Kuan, *Rehearsal for War*, pp. 159 and 166.

17 Ban Kah Choon and Yap Hong Kuan, *Rehearsal for War*, p. vi. As noted previously, Ban Kah Choon and Yap Hong Kuan's book is problematic; nonetheless, they raise some interesting questions.

18 Ban Kah Choon and Yap Hong Kuan, *Rehearsal for War*. The main thesis runs right through the book, but the claim that the MPAJA was an effective fighting force before the arrival of Force 136 is made on p. 139.

19 Aldrich, *Intelligence and the War against Japan*, pp. 3 and 331.

20 Kratoska, *The Japanese Occupation of Malaya*, pp. 295–6.

21 Cruickshank, *SOE in the Far East*, p. 209. Duckett, 'The Special Operations Executive in Burma, 1941–45', p. 210. Duckett describes how the Karen levies raised by Force 136 prevented Japanese troops approaching from the northeast from reaching Toungoo before the XIV Army under General Slim, effectively damming them up at Mawchi. Slim's troops, however, were delayed by Japanese at Pegu, with the result that it was the seaborne troops of Operation *Dracula* who discovered in early May 1945 that the Japanese troops, whose commander felt that he did not have the troops he needed to defend the city, had abandoned Rangoon some days before.

22 TNA, CAB 119/212, Chiefs of Staff Committee, 3 June 1945, pp. 2–3. The three signatories to this document (Thompson, Dawson and Hubback) represented, respectively, the army, air force and navy.

23 TNA, CAB 119/212, Top Secret Cypher Telegram, SACSEA to AMSSO, 11 May 1945. AMSSO was the Air Ministry Special Signals Office, which handled cables for the Cabinet and other high-level bodies.

24 For a discussion of these conundrums, see Foot, *SOE*, pp. 341–6; Williams, *Parachutes, Patriots and Partisans*, Chapter 5; and Bailey, *The Wildest Province*, pp. 316–19.

25 A different political debate occurred over the acceptability of the Burma National Army (BNA) as guerrilla allies. The BNA had been formed by Aung San under the aegis of the Japanese, who made promises of independence to the army. Louis Mountbatten, from August 1943 Supreme Allied Commander South East Asia, regarded the BNA members as patriots who should be accepted as allies and found himself championing what was regarded as the progressive cause against the views of Reginald Dorman-Smith, the former governor, who was inclined to see them as traitors (Ziegler, *Mountbatten*, pp. 318–20).

26 Cruickshank, *SOE in the Far East*, pp. 83–4. Davis and his team first went into Malaya in May 1943; Davis exfiltrated in the June, and went back in during August. These movements are detailed in his report (TNA, HS 1/107).

27 Shennan, *Our Man in Malaya*, pp. 32–3.

28 Information on the composition of this sortie, *Gustavus I*, is surprisingly scant, but the totals of Chinese agents given by Shennan, *Our Man in Malaya*, pp. 62–63, and Tan Chong Tee, *Force 136*, p. 301, agree, though Shennan gives their code names and Tan Chong Tee their full names.

29 TNA, HS 1/107, John Davis, 'Operation Gustavus/Pirate'; TNA, HS 1/107, 'Record of Conference held at Camp, 30th–31st December 1943'. The immediate future was seen as 'a time of preparation for future combined action'; to this end, arms would be supplied.

30 IWM, 14859, Papers of F. Spencer Chapman, File 4, Memo, 13 October 1943, to A.D. and B.B. from O/X, Enc. 42. Sir George Moss, the adviser on Chinese affairs, an experienced diplomat, is not named on the document, but he was 'O/X'. A.D. was Col. G.F. Taylor, SOE's Director of Overseas Groups and Missions, and B.B. was the Far East section.

31 SOE had a mutually beneficial intelligence agreement with the Chinese Nationalist government, via a body called the Institute of International Relations, based in Chungking (Cruickshank, *SOE in the Far East*, pp. 151–3) and recruited in China through Lim Bo Seng (Shennan, *Our Man in Malaya*, p. 52).

32 IWM, 14859, Papers of F. Spencer Chapman, File 4, Cypher Telegram, 16 October, from B/B to New Delhi, Encs. 49 and 52.

33 IWM, 14859, Papers of F. Spencer Chapman, File 4, Intelligence, Enc. 82.

34 John Davis was able to prove his *bona fides* with Chin Peng because the work he had done with 101STS meant he knew some of the guerrilla leaders· Chin Peng, *My Side of History*, p. 17. 101STS is covered in Chapter 2.

35 Reg Lawther, unpublished memoir, pp. 11 and 28. Reg describes how he went into the jungle in fear of being conscripted by the Japanese, was selected for training as a cadre because of his linguistic abilities and how, once inducted into the party, was soon given the rank of major.

36 TNA, CAB 119/212, From SACSEA to AMSSO, 11 May 1945.

37 TNA, CAB 119/212, 'Chiefs of Staff Committee … Resistance Movements in Malaya', 3 June 1945, p. 2.

38 TNA, CAB 119/212, From SACSEA to AMSSO, 11 May 1945 and 'Memorandum from COS [Chiefs of Staff]', 3 June 1945, pp. 2–3.

39 TNA, CAB 119/212, Draft Telegram from AMSSO to SACSEA, May 1945.

40 TNA, CAB 119/212, 'Resistance Movements in Malaya: Second revised draft. Comments by SOE', pp. 1–2. SOE noted here that it wanted to arm the guerrillas, rather than use them as 'labour and guides' and supported this with the observation that the Karen levies in Burma 'have accounted for over 2,000 Japanese killed to date'.

41 TNA, CAB 119/212, 'Malaya Resistance Movement: Memorandum by Supreme Allied Commander South East Asia', 4 August 1945.

42 Tremlett: Comber, *Malaya's Secret Police*, p. 95; the four policemen were John Davis (*Gustavus*), Ian Wylie (*Carpenter*), Douglas Broadhurst (*Galvanic*) and Claude Fenner (*Humour*). All four eventually returned to the Malayan Police.

43 TNA, HS 1/109, F. Spencer Chapman, Report A, pp. 16 and 20.

44 The MPAJA was willing to recruit stay-behinds like Freddy Spencer Chapman and Robert Chrystal to train the troops. See, for example, Dennis Holman, *The Green Torture: The Ordeal of Robert Crystal* (London: Robert Hale, 1962), pp. 27–8, and 31.

45 Cheah Boon Kheng, *Red Star over Malaya*, pp. 64–5; Dorothy Thatcher and Robert Cross, *Pai Naa: The Story of an Englishwoman's Survival in the Malayan Jungle*

(London: White Lion Publishers, 1974), chapters 9 and 10. In Pahang, the fleeing guerrillas took their refugee sympathizers with them. However, as the occupation progressed, the MPAJA's attitudes towards squatters tended to harden, and uncooperative villagers, or those suspected of being pro-Japanese, were raided for food and money and sometimes killed (Cheah Boon Kheng, *Red Star over Malaya*, p. 65).

46 Cheah Boon Kheng, *Red Star over Malaya*, p. 83.

47 Ban Kah Choon and Yap Hong Kuan, *Rehearsal for War*, p. 131.

48 Chin Peng, *My Side of History*, pp. 79–80; TNA, HS 1/109, F. Spencer Chapman, Report A, p. 12. 101STS was the training school set up by Oriental Mission (SOE) in Singapore, at which around 160 communist cadres were trained in late 1941 and early 1942. This is discussed in Chapter 1.

49 Chin Peng, *My Side of History*, p. 80. For a detailed examination of the damage Lai Teck did to the party's leadership during the Japanese occupation, see Hara Fujio, 'Leaders of the Malayan Communist Party during the Anti-Japanese War' in *New Perspectives on the Japanese Occupation of Malaya and Singapore, 1941–1945*, ed. Akashi Yoji and Yoshimura Mako (Singapore: NUS Press, 2008), pp. 65–104.

50 Chin Peng, *My Side of History*, p. 80. Lai Teck's success looks less extraordinary, however, if one takes a long view of the MCP, and considers the legacies of Lai Teck's activity for the party he purported to lead. Aided and abetted by Special Branch, Lai Teck had been perfectly positioned pre-war to weed out his enemies or anyone capable of mounting a challenge (p. 84; quoting Satoru Onishi, the Kempei major who interviewed Lai Teck). Furthermore, at least some of the young cadres viewed their espousal of communism as being as powerful as a religious conversion (this was Chin Peng's take on his own acceptance of the party's doctrines). In this situation Lai Teck, as their leader, was almost guaranteed to be a figure to be venerated (p. 47).

51 Holman, *The Green Torture*, pp. 42–4. Others were people whose only mistake seems to have been that they stumbled into the wrong part of the jungle and thus compromised the security of a guerrilla camp (pp. 47–8).

52 In Perak at least there were dedicated 'traitor killing camps' (HS 1/109, F. Spencer Chapman, Report A, pp. 7–8). According to John Creer, who spent time with the MPAJA in the north of Malay during the occupation, he was told by another stay-behind, Robert Chrystal, that by the end of 1942 the Perak MPAJA had accounted for 152 traitors: traitor-killing began early in the occupation. (TNA, HS 1/121, John Creer, 'Report on Venus Party', p. 4). Holman, *The Green Torture*, pp. 39–44, and 47–51, discusses traitor-killing in some detail.

53 Ban Kah Choon and Yap Hong Kuan, *Rehearsal for War*, p. 96. They also argue that the purges springing from Lai Teck's duplicity strengthened the MPAJA relative to the civilian side of the party. After all, as they observe, it was from former MPAJA men (Chin Peng himself being one of them) that the challenge to Lai Teck's power eventually came (p. 94).

54 TNA, HS 1/109, F. Spencer Chapman, Report A, pp. 1 and 9.

55 TNA, HS 1/109, Slow communications: F. Spencer Chapman, Report A, p. 19. Referral up the chain of command: TNA, HS 1/115 'The A.J.F. in Southern Johore', 25 July 1945. This document appears to have been written by John Cross, who was inserted into Johore as part of an MI6 team just before the Fall of Singapore. He was exfiltrated in May 1945. AJF was one of the names used by Force 136 for the MPAJA.

56 Inflation is covered in detail in Kratoska, *The Japanese Occupation of Malaya*, pp. 196–205.

57 Kratoska, *The Japanese Occupation of Malaya*, pp. 248–58, discusses food rationing, but the ration system went beyond food: 'Even matches was on a ration' (Hyacinth Hess'e, Interview, Perth, 2009; Hyacinth lived in Malacca and Kuala Lumpur during the occupation).

58 Kratoska, *The Japanese Occupation of Malaya*, pp. 247, 276–7 and 319–20; Pamela Mayo, Interview, Brisbane, 2009 (Pam was a child in Singapore during the occupation; she herself saw the dying in the streets, and two of her cousins were employed on the 'dead body cart' which removed the corpses).

59 Even the *Orang Asli*, Malaya's aboriginal jungle-dwellers, grew crops to supplement their diet and even then could face serious shortages (IWM, 3328, Papers of P.G.J. Dobrée, p. 25).

60 TNA, HS 1/109, F. Spencer Chapman, Report A, pp. 28–9; Spencer Chapman, *The Jungle Is Neutral*, p. 148.

61 Spencer Chapman, *The Jungle Is Neutral*, p. 148.

62 The happy atmosphere of the camps is attested to by Freddy Spencer Chapman and Nona Baker. Spencer Chapman described the overall mood of the camps as 'extremely happy' and added, 'when they play games [they] make as much noise as a girls' school' (TNA, HS 1/109, F. Spencer Chapman, Report A, p. 26). Nona Baker found them 'happy-go-lucky' (Thatcher and Cross, *Pai Naa*, p. 94).

63 Spencer Chapman speaks of at least one massacre, where 160 people were killed. (TNA, HS 1/109, F. Spencer Chapman, Report A, App. B, p. 4). At other times, the Japanese contented themselves with burning out the village, or perhaps only the standing crops. For example, the village of Kambau in Johore was burned out in 1943 'by the Japs ... in their usual anti AJF [Anti-Japanese Force] patrolling' (TNA, HS 1/107, Major D. Sime, Operation *Carpenter* GLO Operational Report, p. 6.).

64 TNA, HS 1/109, F. Spencer Chapman, Report A, p. 31. The MPAJA leadership had been introduced to the *Orang Asli* – specifically, the Temiar of Upper Perak – by the anthropologist Pat Noone, who had gone to live with them when the Japanese invaded. (Holman, *The Green Torture*, pp. 57 and 59–60; TNA, HS 1/121, John Creer's Report, pp. 8; Dennis Holman, *Noone of the Ulu* (London: William Heinemann, 1958), p. 122).

65 Thatcher and Cross: *Pai Naa*, pp. 77–8; Lawther, unpublished memoir, p. 25.

66 TNA, HS 1/107, Major C.L.D. Newell, *Carpenter Brown* Operational Report, p. 2, who recorded that, unable to find a better dropping zone, they 'had to use the potato patch from which we drew our staple diet'.

67 Thatcher and Cross, *Pai Naa*, pp. 134–5.

68 Plenty: George Hess'e, who was with the 1st Regiment in Selangor, remembered eating rice, sweet potatoes, long beans, and dried fish, often flavoured with chilli, garlic or ginger and sometimes supplemented with game, such as wild boar, shot in the jungle. (George Hess'e, Interview 2, Perth, 2009). Short supply: Thatcher and Cross, *Pai Naa*, p. 148, record deaths from beriberi.

69 IWM, 14859, Papers of F. Spencer Chapman, File 4, Enc. 79, p. 4.

70 TNA, HS 1/107, Major D.R.W. Alexander, *Funnel Brown* Operational Report, p. 3. Spencer Chapman noted beriberi and a generalized vitamin deficiency (Spencer Chapman, *The Jungle Is Neutral*, p. 149; TNA, HS 1/109, F. Spencer Chapman, Report A, p. 27).

71 TNA, HS 1/107, Major D.R.W. Alexander, *Funnel Brown* Operational Report, p. 3.

72 Lawther, unpublished memoir, p. 24.

73 Ho Thean Fook, *Tainted Glory*, pp. 162 and 203.

74 TNA, HS 1/107, Major A. Rapoport, *Funnel* Medical Officer's Report, p. 3.

75 TNA, HS 1/107, Major A. Rapoport, *Funnel* Medical Officer's Report, p. 8. He classed multi-vitamins as his second most valuable drug, outranked only by the anti-malarial, mepacrine (TNA, HS 1/107, Major A. Rapoport, *Funnel* Medical Officer's Report, p. 2); see also TNA, HS 1/117, Major J.G. Dumoulin, Medical Officer's Report, Operation *Sergeant*, p. 2.

76 TNA, HS 1/107, Major A. Rapoport, *Funnel* Medical Officer's Report, pp. 3–4; Lawther, unpublished memoir, pp. 25 and 26.

77 Ho Thean Fook, *Tainted Glory*, p. 172.

78 Ho Thean Fook, *Tainted Glory*, pp. 147 and 159. Quinine seems to have been fairly readily available in the towns (Hyacinth Hess'e, Interview, Perth, 2009, recounts being given quinine in Kuala Lumpur to treat her own malaria). Other medicines, however, were in extremely short supply: 'there was no aspirin, nothing' (Pam Mayo, Interview, Brisbane, 2009).

79 Chin Peng, *My Side of History*, pp. 68 and 70.

80 Chin Peng, *My Side of History*, p. 71.

81 IWM, 14859, Papers of F. Spencer Chapman, File 4, Report on Malayan Chinese before the War, on Enc. 63.

82 Reg Lawther describes an unsuccessful arms raid on a police station, in which the patrol's Bren guns were lost and a number of guerrillas killed, and a successful one sometime later (unpublished memoir, pp. 29–31).

83 Chin Peng states that they had a reasonable stock of Lee Enfield .303s, the standard service rifle at the time, but found them too long, as well as a number of Brens which they lacked the training to use, and some Thomson submachine guns (tommy guns or TSMGs), which they liked (Chin Peng, *My Side of History*, p. 73. Hess'e, Interview, April 2009).

84 Ho Thean Fook, *Tainted Glory*, p. 136. In an established army, an officer or senior NCO will usually be issued with a side arm as an additional weapon.

85 Moggie, 'Notes of Interview with Reg Lawther' (2016).

86 A patrol of a hundred men would usually have around thirty assorted weapons (including pistols) and thirty to thirty-five grenades (many dud) (TNA, HS 1/109, F. Spencer Chapman, Report A, p. 21). The early parts of many operational reports indicate the size of the patrols once Force 136 officers began to arrive (see, for example, the early pages of most of the Patrol Liaison Officers' (PLOs) reports for Operation *Funnel*, TNA, HS 1/107: patrols varied in size from around 50 to about 150 and included new recruits brought into receive Force 136 training).

87 TNA, HS 1/107, Major D. Sime, Operation *Carpenter* Report, p. 2.

88 For a brief discussion on the impact of the climate on ammunition, see E.C. Foenander, *Big Game of Malaya* (London: The Batchworth Press, 1952), p. 53

89 IWM, 14859, Papers of F. Spencer Chapman, File 4, Encs. 71 and 79. Much of what is on this particular file appears to have been written by John Davis.

90 Cheah Boon Kheng, *Red Star over Malaya*, p. 64.

91 Cheah Boon Kheng, *Red Star over Malaya*, p. 64; Chin and Hack, *Dialogues*, p. 98. By comparison, the Japanese lost around 2,000 killed in the ten weeks of the Malayan Campaign of 1941–1942.

92 There is evidence that the MPAJA tended, possibly for purposes of propaganda and morale, to overstate its successes. For example, the first edition of the MPAJA's news-sheet 'Truth' announced that 'over 30' Japanese had been killed by the MPAJA during

an action at Gua Musang. John Creer, who was in the area at the time of this attack and witnessed its aftermath, stated that although nineteen Malay police had died, he doubted that any Japanese had been killed at all; further, this attack was not even carried out by the MPAJA. (TNA, HS 1/121, John Creer's Report, p. 5).

93   Ho Thean Fook, *Tainted Glory*, pp. 146 and 222. The aim of the other attack, at Lahat, was to seize arms and ammunition; this attack did not succeed.

94   Akashi Yoji, 'Japanese Research Activities in Occupied Malaya/Syonan, 1943–45' in *New Perspectives on the Japanese Occupation of Malaya and Singapore*, pp. 158–77 (pp. 160–1).

95   News, propaganda: IWM, 14859, Papers of F. Spencer Chapman, File 3, contains copies of two editions of the cyclostyled MPAJA news-sheet 'Truth'; see also Thatcher and Cross, *Pai Naa*, pp. 153–4 and 163. News, maps and money: see the story of the cut-off Australian sergeant, A.F. Shephard, in Joseph Kennedy, *When Singapore Fell: Evacuations and Escapes, 1941–2* (London: Macmillan, 1989), pp. 148–149. Shephard was just one of those they sheltered; his comrade Douglas Stewart of the Argylls was another (p. 149), as was Spencer Chapman.

96   Cheah Boon Kheng, *Red Star over Malaya*, p. 64. Ban Kah Choon and Yap Hong Kuan, *Rehearsal for War*, p. 139, state that the MPAJA was 'efficient' before the arrival of Force 136 supplies, but the comparatively low casualty figures, the poor health of the guerrillas and the shortage of arms cast doubt on this conclusion.

97   Chin Peng, *My Side of History*, pp. 111–13. According to George Hesse the secret army was 'the best known secret that everybody knew about' (email, 27 July 2011).

98   Chin Peng, *My Side of History*, p. 112

99   Chin and Hack, *Dialogues with Chin Peng*, p. 92.

100 TNA, HS 1/107, Major R.N. Broome, Report on *Gustavus*. p. 4.

101 Details on the formation and collapse of this network can be found in Tan Chong Tee, *Force 136*, pp. 176–251, and Shennan, *Our Man in Malaya*, pp. 75–89. Death of Lim Bo Seng: Tan Chong Tee, *Force 136*, pp. 242 and 249.

102 Ban Kah Choon and Yap Hong Kuan, *Rehearsal for War*, p. 159. Shennan, in *Our Man in Malaya*, p. 119, states that Lai Teck did tell the Japanese about Force 136, and that the Japanese diplomat, Mamoru Shinozaki, accused him of betraying Lim Bo Seng.

103 Shennan, *Our Man in Malaya*, p. 195. Shennan details the struggles of the *Gustavus* team and the MPAJA to bring the wireless to the camp and develop a working dynamo.

104 Paul Kennedy, *Engineers of Victory: The Problem Solvers Who Turned the Tide in World War II* (London: Penguin, 2013), p. xxv.

105 General Slim, quoted by Paul Kratoska, describes this in ringing terms: according to him, the Japanese, 'ran into ambush after ambush; bridges were blown ahead of them, their foraging parties massacred, their sentries stalked, their staff cars shot up. Air strikes, directed by British officers watching from the ground … inflicted great damage'. See Paul Kratoska, 'The Karen of Burma under Japanese Rule' in *Southeast Asian Minorities in the Wartime Japanese Empire,* ed. Paul Kratoska (London: RoutledgeCurzon, 2002), p. 31.

106 TNA, CAB 119/212, 'Resistance Movements in Malaya … Comments by SOE', pp. 1–2.

107 Duckett, 'The Special Operations Executive in Burma, 1941–45', p. 212.

108 TNA, HS 1/107, Major D. Sime, *Carpenter* Operational Report, pp. 1–3. This operation was led by the planter Paddy Martin, who had escaped from Pengarang.

109 TNA, HS 1/107, Major D. Sime, *Carpenter* Operational Report, pp. 4 and 8; and
      TNA, HS 1/107, 'Facts Relating to the Death of Major W.P. Martin'. Martin was
      killed when the Japanese raided an MPAJA camp following a successful airdrop in
      January 1945.
110 The first team of Operation *Funnel* dropped in on 27 February 1945 (TNA, HS 1/107,
      Lt. Col. J.P. Hannah, Operation *Funnel* GLO Operational Report, p. 1).
111 TNA, HS 1/107, 'Record of decisions taken at conference, April 17th, 1943 [sic: the
      date on the document is incorrect and should read 1945]'. Spencer Chapman also
      reports on this conference, though his comment is very brief, and he states that
      it 'was largely devoted to methods of carrying out the agreement already made'
      (Spencer Chapman, *The Jungle Is Neutral*, p. 338).
112 Chin Peng, *My Side of History*, p. 114. Although the MPAJA is generally described
      as consisting of a number of 'regiments', none of these contained more than
      1,000–1,200 men. A regiment usually contains upwards of 3,000 troops, under the
      command of a colonel or equivalent. The British, who placed a Lieutenant Colonel
      in tactical command of each of these guerrilla formations, clearly saw them as being
      more the size of the average battalion (around 600–1,000 men).
113 TNA, HS 1/115, Cypher Telegram from New Delhi, 15 July 1944; TNA, HS
      7/165, 'History of Force 136 operations in Malaya', p. 29; TNA, HS 1/107,
      bodyguards: Major I.D. Ross, *Funnel Blue* Operational Report, p. 2.
114 The personnel numbers can be calculated from TNA, HS 1/108. No accurate
      records of weapons drops seem to have been retained, but since only one submarine
      infiltration brought in significant quantities of arms (to *Carpenter* in mid-1945)
      and airdrops to the MPAJA did not begin until February 1945, it is reasonable to
      conclude that virtually all weapons issued to the MPAJA were brought in between
      those first airdrops and the war's end (after which no more weapons were provided).
      Incidentally, the first wireless contact from Malaya was from Operation *Carpenter* in
      Johore in October 1944.
115 C.E. 'Bill' Foss, Interview, 2012. Capt. Foss was with the patrol *Funnel Green*.
116 TNA, HS 1/107, Major D. Sime, Operation *Carpenter* GLO Operational Report, p. 6.
117 TNA, HS 1/107, Major S.F. Owen, *Funnel Green* Operational Report, p. 1, HS 1/107.
118 Major I.D. Ross, *Funnel Blue* Operational Report p. 1; Major S.F. Owen, *Funnel Green*
      Operational Report, p. 2, both HS 1/107.
119 TNA, HS 1/107, Major S.F. Owen, *Funnel Green* Operational Report, p. 3; see also
      Major I.D. Ross, *Funnel Blue* Operational Report, p. 1, and Personnel Report for
      Leong Ying; Major T.A. Wilson, *Funnel Slate*, Personnel Report for Capt. J. Davidson,
      both on TNA, HS 1/107.
120 TNA, HS 1/107, Major S.F. Owen, *Funnel Green* Operational Report, p. 2. Uniquely,
      the nominal roll for this patrol survived with the papers held by Bill Foss.
121 TNA, HS 1/107, Lt. Col. J.P. Hannah, Operation *Funnel* Report, p. 3; see also, for
      example, TNA, HS 1/119, Major A.J. Hunter, *Galvanic Blue* Operational Report.
122 TNA, HS 7/165, 'History of Force 136 operations in Malaya', p. 54.
123 The exact number of MPAJA troops under arms with Force 136 at the time of the
      surrender is unclear. The reasons for this will be explored in Chapter 6.
124 IWM, Sound.12785, Lloyd Chin Fen interview, Reel 4, and Capt. D.E. Trewaldwyn,
      Carpenter Blue Operational Report, p. 3 This rescue was effected by the 4th Regiment
      in south Johore, despite the fact that they were often on the run and regularly
      engaged by the Japanese. They were not the only aircrew helped by the MPAJA: see
      also the deposition by M.K.S. Panicker on FCO 141/7242. Panicker, an Indian estate

clerk in southern Negri Sembilan, prepared 'European food' for evaders who were passed through his estate by the MPAJA in March 1945.

125 TNA, HS 1/119, Lt. Col. D.K. Broadhurst, Operation *Galvanic* GLO Operational Report, p. 4. By the end of the war, Japanese aircraft were in a 'shocking condition' (IWM, 10994, Papers of L.M. Godfrey, 'Operation Arrest', App. B to Part III), and this would have limited, for example, the ability of the Japanese to carry out air reconnaissance of the camps.

126 See, for example, TNA, HS 1/107, Lt. Col. D.R.W. Alexander, *Funnel Brown* Operational Report, pp. 3, 4 and 6; and TNA, HS 1/117, Major T.A. Wight, *Sergeant Orange* Operational Report, p. 1. That they were correct in their suspicions concerning arms drops is borne out by the consolidated arms return, which will be discussed in detail in Chapter 6. In fairness to the MPAJA, it is plausible that some key items did go astray: after the war, a group of Malays fishing in a river in northern Malaya found $6,000 in British pre-war currency which was believed to have been dropped to the guerrillas (*Indian Daily Mail*, 3 September 1946, p. 4).

127 TNA, HS 1/115, 'Notes of a Meeting held at the Colonial Office', 9 November 1943. That the MPU was already considering the issue of a common citizenship and coming to some conclusions is clear from TNA, CO 865/18, 'Malaya: Creation of Malayan Union Citizenship', 1/9/43.

128 TNA, HS 1/115, 'B/B file copy', London, 11 November 1943; and CAB 101/66 B/4/7 cited in Huat Kin Koon, 'A Dilemma of Identity', p. 212, fn. 390.

129 TNA, HS 1/115, Edward Gent to Col. G.F. Taylor, 29 August 1944.

130 TNA, HS 1/117, Major T.A. Wight, *Sergeant Orange* Operational Report, p. 3.

131 TNA, HS 1/117, Major J.A. Hislop, *Sergeant* Personnel Report.

132 IWM, Sound.12785, Lloyd Chin Fen Interview, Reel 4.

133 For details of the new policy, see, for example, TNA, CAB 119/212, Top Secret Cypher Telegram from SACSEA, 11 May 1945.

134 TNA, CO 865/18, 'Malaya: Creation of Malayan Union Citizenship', 1/9/43. This renegotiation was the reason for the MacMichael Commission of October 1945. For detail, see Bayly and Harper, *Forgotten Wars*, pp. 130–134.

135 Philip Ziegler, *Mountbatten*, refers several times to Mountbatten's 'egalitarian instincts' and 'liberal' leanings – for example, pp. 299 and 314. It should be noted that Ziegler's view of Mountbatten, while generally favourable, is by no means sycophantic. His opinion on Mountbatten's liberalism is supported by the observations made by A.D.C. Peterson, who worked closely with him during the war (IWM, 13346, Private Papers of A.D.C. Peterson, p. 53).

136 IWM, 13346, Private Papers of A.D.C. Peterson, p. 53.

137 In his diary, Mountbatten pronounced himself to be 'completely on their side' (i.e. the BNA's) when arguing with those who wanted the BNA leadership arrested: *Personal Diary of Admiral the Lord Louis Mountbatten*, ed. Philip Ziegler (London: Collins, 1988), p. 206. The BNA had initially been set up by the Japanese, but had changed sides to fight for the British: Ziegler, *Mountbatten*, p. 318.

138 Ziegler, *Mountbatten*, p. 325. His liberal instincts are clear in his writings included in Stockwell, *British Documents on the End of Empire: Malaya Part 1*; for example, on p. 71 (writing in September 1944) he expresses the wish that the sultans should not be restored 'even as constitutional rulers', though he accepts (p. 72) that this might not be acceptable in the short term.

139 TNA, CAB 119/212, Top Secret Cypher Telegram from SACSEA, 11 May 1945.

140 TNA, CAB 119/212, Top Secret Cypher Telegram from AMSSO [Chiefs of Staff], 7 June 1945.

141 This order, dated 21 July 1945, is included as App. A to TNA, CAB 119/212, 'Malaya Resistance Movement: Memorandum by Supreme Allied Commander South East Asia', dated 4 August 1945. Mountbatten had issued this order to 'P' Division and for dissemination to officers in the field. It was in line with orders relayed by the Chiefs of Staff to Mountbatten on 7 June (TNA, CAB 119/212, Top Secret Cypher Telegram, from AMSSO [? semi-legible] to SACSEA, 7 June 1945).

142 TNA, CAB 119/212, 'Malaya Resistance Movement: Memorandum by Supreme Allied Commander South East Asia', 4 August 1945.

143 TNA, CAB 119/212, Top Secret memo, 5August 1945.

144 TNA, HS 1/109, Memorandum by Head of Malayan Country Section, para. 11.

145 TNA, CO 273/675/7, Minute by H.T. Bourdillon, 6 September 1945, in Stockwell, *British Documents on the End of Empire: Malaya Part 1*, p. 125.

146 Chin Peng, *My Side of History*, p. 119; TNA, HS 1/115, Cypher Telegram from Kandy, B/B.100 from B/B, 28 August 1945.

147 TNA, HS 1/115, Cypher Telegram from Kandy, desp 0850, 29 August 1945. This telegram is from 'B/B 100', which was Mackenzie's designation. (For a number of designations, including this one, see IWM, 14859, Papers of F. Spencer Chapman, File 5.) This telegram refers to Fenner's signal, which does not appear to have survived.

148 TNA, HS 1/115, Cypher Telegram to Kandy, B/B.100 from B/B, 29 August 1945.

149 Chin Peng, *My Side of History*, p. 135.

150 TNA, HS 7/165, 'History of Force 136 operations in Malaya', pp. 37–8.

151 *Straits Times*, 12 October 1945. There were numerous other articles over the next month or so, which went into detail about the proposals for federation and citizenship, and promises of eventual self-rule.

152 Harper, *The End of Empire and the Making of Malaya*, p. 78, sourced to TNA, CO 537/1533, Gent to Paskin, 20/9/46 and Paskin to Gent, 4/10/46.

153 Chin Peng, *My Side of History*, p. 26.

154 Chin Peng, *My Side of History*, pp. 133 and 26.

155 Chin Peng, *My Side of History*, p. 142.

156 Aldrich, *Intelligence and the War against Japan*, pp. 331–2.

157 For example, jungle carbines and PIATs were dropped to the MPAJA.

158 TNA, CAB 119/212, SACSEA to AMSSO, 11 May 1945; TNA, CAB 119/212, 'Chiefs of Staff Committee: Joint Planning Staff', 3 June 1945, p. 4.

159 Ban Kah Choon and Yap Hong Kuan, *Rehearsal for War*, pp. 144–5.

160 Citizenship: *Straits Times*, 14 November 1945, p. 2; The main planks of the Malayan Union were that all the states of Malaya – with the exception of Singapore, which was to remain a Crown Colony – were to be unified under one form of government for the first time and, alongside this, a Malayan citizenship would be offered to many members of the 'domiciled communities' who would qualify by either birth or prolonged residence. MCP operating openly: Cheah Boon Kheng, 'The Legal Period: 1945–8: The Malayan Communist Party and Its Relations with the Malays, British and "Bourgeois Nationalists"' in *Dialogues*, ed. Chin and Hack, pp. 255–9 (p. 255), where Cheah Boon Kheng explains that the MCP was able to operate semi-legally during 1945–1948, largely as a result of its wartime alliance with Force 136: it was exempt from having to register under the reintroduced Societies Ordinance.

161 Bayly and Harper, *Forgotten Wars*, pp. 362 and 501–3.

162 This feeling is clear in Chin Peng, *My Side of History*, pp. 133–44, where he complains, for example, that the MCP was under-represented in a post-war council, and bullied by the manner in which the courts were used.

163 Ho Thean Fook, *Tainted Glory*, p. 255; $200 of the $350 bonus was taken by the MCP.

Chapter 4

1 TNA, HS 1/123, letter 'From Singa [Yeop Mahidin] to Kiwi [Lt. Col. J.D. Richardson]', 24 June 1945, *Beacon* Operational Report, p. 12. The two men worked in tandem for some weeks before they met face to face. The quote seems to prefigure the working relationship that later developed between UMNO and the British administration.

2 TNA, HS 1/123, letter 'From Singa to Kiwi', received 14 July 1945, *Beacon* Operational Report, p. 17.

3 TNA, HS 1/123, letter 'From Kiwi to Singa', 31 July 1945, *Beacon* Operational Report, p. 28.

4 Foot, *SOE*, p. 350.

5 Foot, *SOE*, p. 350.

6 Abu Talib Ahmad, *The Malay Muslims, Islam and the Rising Sun, 1941–45* (Kuala Lumpur: Malaysian Branch of the Royal Asiatic Society, 2003), pp. 141–7.

7 Stockwell, 'The Formation and First Years of the United Malays National Organization (U.M.N.O.) 1946–1948', pp. 481–513, mentions Wataniah in the footnotes and includes a few scant details about the Askar Melayu Setia (AMS).

8 Chin Peng, *My Side of History*; by Chin and Hack, *Dialogues with Chin Peng*. The 'Additional References' in *My Side of History* include the SOE file HS 1/122, which contains the reports of not only the MPAJA operation, *Humour*, but also those of Operation *Multiple*, which was dispatched to contact Malays.

9 Harry Miller, *Menace in Malaya* (London: Harrap, 1954); Gene Z. Hanrahan, *The Communist Struggle in Malaya* (Kuala Lumpur: University of Malaya Press, 1971).

10 Hew Strachan, 'British Counter-insurgency from Malaya to Iraq', *RUSI*, 152, 6 (2007), pp. 8–11.

11 Mockaitis, *British Counterinsurgency*, p. 111.

12 Stockwell, The Formation and First Years of the United Malays National Organization (U.M.N.O.) 1946–1948'.

13 Bayly and Harper, *Forgotten Wars*, pp. 317 and 451–2; Cheah Boon Kheng, *Red Star over Malaya*, pp. 79–80, 285, and 170–3. Ban Kah Choon and Yap Hong Kuan, who argue in *Rehearsal for War* that the events of the Japanese occupation set the stage for later conflict, barely mention the Malay resistance (pp. 120–1).

14 Bayly and Harper, *Forgotten Wars*, p. 317; Cheah Boon Kheng, *Red Star over Malaya*, p. 20. The Malay agent Sarpin bin Shahabudin was recruited in Mecca in January 1943 (TNA, HS 1/121, 'Haji Sarpin bin Haji Shahabudin'); Operations *Carpenter* (to the MPAJA) and *Oatmeal* (to the Malays) were both launched in October 1944.

15 For a contemporary take on this, a search of Jstor is revealing: 'Wataniah Malaya' yields three hits, and 'MPAJA Malaya', fifty-seven.

16 Douglas Richardson, *Kiwi's Diary: A Journey of the Beacon's Party of Force 136 from Hulu Perak to Pahang during the Second World War* (Kuala Lumpur: Universiti Kebangsaan Malaysia, 1994).

17 Wan Hashim, *Second World War in Malaya: Role of the Malay Guerillas: Force 136* (Kuala Lumpur: Institut Terjemahan Negara Malaysia Berhad, 2010), originally published in Malaya as *Perang Dunia Kedua: Peranan Gerila Melayu Force 136* (Kuala Lumpur: Dewan Bahasa dan Pustaka, 1993).

18 For example, Kevin Blackburn and Karl Hack, *War Memory and the Making of Modern Malaysia and Singapore* (Singapore: NUS Press, 2012), p. 394.

19 Mervyn Cecil ffrank Sheppard came to Malaya as a member of the Malayan Civil Service in 1928. A POW during the Japanese occupation, he lived and worked in the country until his death in 1994. A convert to Islam, he took the name Mubin and was a pioneering figure in Malaysian history and heritage, president of the Malaysian Branch of the Royal Asiatic Society and a founder of the heritage organization Badan Warisan. See <https://badanwarisanmalaysia.org/tag/mubin-sheppard/> [accessed 2 July 2016].

20 There appears to be no other available evidence of communication between the British and any Malay resident in Malaya during the Japanese occupation. Though it is certain that the ISLD (MI6) ran Malay agents in the country (TNA, HS 1/121, *Fighter* Operational Report, pp. 3–4), their contact with the local Malay population is not known, as open records on this organization are extremely sparse.

21 The KMM, anti-feudal and anti-colonial, was formed in 1938. See Cheah Boon Kheng, *Red Star over Malaya*, p. 11. Both Cheah Boon Kheng and *Forgotten Armies* give considerable detail on the activities of the KMM and its relationship with the Fujiwara Kikan ('Fujiwara's Organization').

22 Mustapha Hussain notes towards the end of his memoir that he 'had been struggling for Independence since the age of twenty' (Mustapha Hussain, *Malay Nationalism Before UMNO: The Memoirs of Mustapha Hussain*, trans. by Insun Sony Mustapha and ed. by Jomo K.S. (Kuala Lumpur: Utusan Publications and Distributors, 2004), p. 390). It is difficult to establish how widespread support was for the KMM, as membership numbers do not seem to be available. Around 100–150 KMM members were arrested the British just before the outbreak of the Pacific War (pp. x and 140). Total membership appears to have numbered only in the hundreds: Mustapha recounts that his desire to make it a mass movement of 100,000 was 'shot down' by the president, Ibrahim Yaacob (p. 140). However, membership leapt up to 10,000 within two months of the Japanese victory, though the KMM was soon banned. (Cheah Boon Kheng, 'The Japanese Occupation of Malaya, 1941–45: Ibrahim Yaacob and the Struggle for Indonesia Raya', *Indonesia*, No. 28 (1979), pp. 84–120 (p. 103).

23 Brian Farrell, *Defence and Fall*, pp. 271–2; Kevin Blackburn, 'Colonial Forces as Post-Colonial Memories: The Commemoration of the Malay Regiment in Modern Malaysia and Singapore' in *Colonial Armies in Southeast Asia*, ed. by Tobias Rettig and Karl Hack (Abingdon: Routledge, 2005), p. 288; Karl A. Hack, 'Biar mati anak: Jangan mati adat [Better Your Children Die Than Your Traditions]: Locally Raised Forces as a Barometer for Imperialism and Decolonization in British South East Asia, 1874–2001', *South East Asia Research*, 10, 3 (2002), 245–75. For totals under arms, see Dol Ramli, *The Malay Regiment*, pp. 47 and 124.

24 Blackburn, 'Colonial Forces as Post-Colonial Memories', p. 291.

25 A total of almost a hundred fatalities can be calculated from nominal rolls of the dead in Justin Corfield and Robin Corfield, *The Fall of Singapore: 90 Days: November 1941– February 1942* (Melbourne: Talisman Publishing, 2012), pp. 140, 286, 356, 377, 384, 462, 465, 482, 488, 497, 517, 533, 573, 599, 637 and 707.

26 Brown, 'A Nominal Roll of the Volunteers'.

27 Nadzan Haron, 'The Malay Regiment 1933–1955: A Political and Social Study of a Colonial Military Establishment' (Unpublished doctoral thesis; University of Essex, 1988), pp. 311–17; Hack, 'Biar mati anak', 245–75. See also the memoir of the JMF soldier, Ibrahim Ismail, *Have You Met Mariam* (Johor Bahru: Westlight, 1985).

28 Bayly and Harper, *Forgotten Armies*, p. 68.

29 The Light Battery of the Federated Malay States Volunteer Force (FMSVF) was equipped with four 3.7" howitzers and included numerous non-Europeans in its ranks (Rebecca Kenneison, *Playing for Malaya: A Eurasian Family in the Pacific War* (Singapore: NUS Press, 2012), pp. 77–8); G Company of the Straits Settlements Volunteer Force consisted of heavy machine-gunners, who were all Eurasians.

30 Volunteers: total extracted from Brown, 'A Nominal Roll of the Volunteers'; Brown gives an exhaustive breakdown of his sources (mostly official) for the totals he gives, which are rather higher than the number of men he was able to name. The Local Defence Corps was the Malayan equivalent of the Home Guard in Britain.

31 For example, Bayly and Harper, *Forgotten Armies*, p. 124.

32 M.C.ff. Sheppard, *The Malay Regiment 1933–1947* (Singapore: Department of Public Relations, Malay Peninsula, 1947), p. 22.

33 Volunteers in general: TNA, CAB 106/156, Brigadier Robert Moir, D.S.O., M.C., 'Notes on the Federated Malay States Volunteer Force and Lines of Communication Operations in the Malaya Campaign 1941–42', p. 24; Jungle unit in particular: TNA, WO 220/556, 'Major M [Colin Marshall] (Forests)', Report on Statements by Malayan Evacuees, Ex-Prisoners Etc., p. E1. This unit has been briefly discussed in Chapter 1; Marshall had helped to raise the unit and was with it during the retreat.

34 Weapons: ANM, 2000/0006765, '[Illegible, possibly 'Some'] Comments on Lack of Malay Resistance Movement Earlier in Occupation'. (By inference, the author is Yeop Mahidin bin Mohamed Shariff. It is also clear from the context that this document was written after Malaya had become independent); proportion accepting demob Bayly and Harper, *Forgotten Armies*, p. 124; TNA, CAB 106/156, Moir, 'Lines of Communication'.

35 ANM, 2000/0006765, Wan Hashim, 'The Malay Resistance Movement against the Japanese during the Second World War'; Y. Mansoor Marican, 'Malay Nationalism and the Islamic Party of Malaysia', *Islamic Studies*, 16, 1 (1977), pp. 291–301.

36 Anthony Milner, *The Invention of Politics in Colonial Malaya* (Cambridge: Cambridge University Press, 2002), pp. 10, 15 and 244.

37 Cheah Boon Kheng, *Red Star over Malaya*, pp. 11 and 13.

38 See Y. Mansoor Marican, 'Malay Nationalism and the Islamic Party of Malaysia', *Islamic Studies*, 16, 1 (1977), pp. 291–301.

39 Frost and Balasingamchow, *Singapore*, 197.

40 Mustapha Hussain, *Malay Nationalism before UMNO*, p. 140.

41 Abu Talib Ahmad, *The Malay Muslims, Islam and the Rising Sun*, pp. 30–1 and 34.

42 The crisis of the Malayan economy under Japanese rule is discussed in Kratoska, *The Japanese Occupation of Malaya*, pp. 154–206.

43 TNA, HS 1/121, Major G. Hasler, *Fighter* Operational Report, p. 8.

44 Calculated from figures in Kratoska, *The Japanese Occupation of Malaya*, p. 274.

45 Wan Hashim, *Role of the Malay Guerillas* (Kuala Lumpur: Institut Terjemahan Negara Malaysia Berhad, 2010), p. 50. The Malay term for tapioca, *ubi kayu*, translates literally as 'wood tuber'.

46 Kratoska, *The Japanese Occupation of Malaya*, p. 277.

47 Kratoska, *The Japanese Occupation of Malaya*, p. 261. Kratoska also notes that the agricultural scheme at Endau, which was open to Chinese, was on Malay-owned land (p. 278).

48 See, for example, Peter Calvocoressi, Guy Wint and John Pritchard, *The Penguin History of the Second World War* (London: Penguin, 1999: first published as *Total War*, 1972), p. 646.

49 This argument is laid out in more detail in Yuki Tanaka, *Hidden Horrors: Japanese War Crimes in World War II* (Boulder, CO: Westview of HarperCollins, 1996), pp. 197–204; the point is made, by Tanaka and (in the introduction) by John Dower, that the brutality was not a consequence of Japanese exceptionalism, but of particular circumstances. The relay of violence (what John Dower terms the 'transfer of oppression') is illustrated in a cartoon by the former POW Sid Scales, where a Japanese warrant officer slaps a sergeant, who slaps a corporal, who slaps a senior private, who slaps a junior one, who slaps a POW, who kills a bedbug. See *Prisoners in Java: Accounts by Allied Prisoners of War in the Far East (1942–1945) Captured in Java*, ed. Java FEPOW 1942 Club (Southampton: Hamwic Publishers, 2007), p. 171.

50 Frost and Balasingamchow, *Singapore*, p. 285.

51 Abu Talib Ahmad, *Malay Muslims, Islam and the Rising Sun*, p. 50. The fear was well-founded: see, for example, IWM, 6626, Papers of L.D. Ashness, p. 69, where Ashness, a Catholic priest, records the rape of Chinese women.

52 Kratoska, *The Japanese Occupation of Malaya*, p. 111.

53 IWM, Sound.8476, Yeop Mahadin [sic] bin Mohamed Sharif, Interview; ANM, 2000/0006765, '[Illegible, possibly 'Some'] Comments on Lack of Malay Resistance Movement Earlier in Occupation'. It is clear from the context given in this paper that its author was Yeop Mahidin.

54 TNA, HS 1/123, Lt. Col. J.D. Richardson, *Beacon* Operational Report, pt. D. Ibrahim Yaacob, formerly leader of the KMM, claimed post-war that the Giyu Gun, a paramilitary organization of Malays raised by the Japanese but under Ibrahim's nominal command, had come to a formal agreement with the MPAJA that the Giyu Gun would not engage in offensive action against the MPAJA; however, MPAJA documents do not support this claim. For a detailed discussion of this, see Cheah Boon Kheng, *Red Star over Malaya*, pp. 71–72. *Beautais* is the spelling used by Richardson and Yeop Mahidin, but properly it seems to be *butai*, which means, approximately, a regiment or group.

55 Wan Hashim, *Role of the Malay Guerrillas*, pp. 46 and 50–1.

56 Che Man, *Muslim Separatism*, p. 62. Four of the five southernmost provinces of Thailand, Patani, Narathiwat, Yala and Satun, were originally part of *Patani Raya*: Greater Patani (Che Man, *Muslim Separatism*, p. 32). There were uprisings in Patani in 1922 and 1923 (pp. 63–4).

57 Che Man, *Muslim Separatism*, pp. 65 and 203. Che Man draws from a number of sources and discusses the shift by the Phibul government to confrontation with the Malays, the outlawing of Malay dress and language, and the banning of certain Islamic practices. For the flight of Malay-Muslims, particularly aristocrats, he cites a 1948 publication by GAMPAR, an association of ex-Patani Malays, founded in 1946 by, among others, Tengku Mahmood Mahyideen. GAMPAR's numbers seem to be broadly supported by a *Sunday Tribune* article of 14 March 1948, cited by Che Man, where hundreds of Patani Malays attend a protest meeting. The disquiet of the Patani Malays continued after the war (see, for example, *Straits Times*, 7 December 1946, 30 October 1947 and 7 March 1948).

58 Mustapha Hussain, *Malay Nationalism before UMNO*: disillusionment: pp. 249 and 254.
59 Kratoska, *The Japanese Occupation of Malaya*, pp. 86 and 89. For example, a surtax was imposed upon those aged 20 to 45 unable to read and write Thai by the end of 1943.
60 Robert Heussler, *Completing a Stewardship: The Malayan Civil Service, 1942–1957* (Westport, CT: Greenwood, 1983), p. 59.
61 Kratoska, *The Japanese Occupation of Malaya*. p. 64.
62 TNA, HS 1/123, Lt. Col. J.D. Richardson, *Beacon* Operational Report, p. 25.
63 ANM, 2000/0006765, Headly to Sheppard, 20 September 1977 and 'Contacts, Pahang' Wataniah, p. 2.
64 Tun Mohammed Hanif Omar, Interview, Kuala Lumpur, September 2016.
65 William Shaw, *Tun Razak: His Life and Times* (New York: Longman, 1976), p. 42. It might be tempting to suggest that as this quote is drawn from a later memoir, the Tun is guilty of the wisdom of hindsight. However, the sense of the disillusionment of the Malay community with the British comes through clearly in the diary of the civil servant, M.C. Hay. His entry for 31 January – the date the last of the British Army withdrew across the causeway into Singapore – states that 'The Malays in Johore were certainly lukewarm and this can hardly be wondered at when they saw us retreating without a fight'. (M.C. Hay, unpublished diary, by permission of the Hay family).
66 Shaw, *Tun Razak*, p. 48.
67 Bayly and Harper, *Forgotten Wars*, pp. 317 and 451–2 describe Wataniah as 'a cell of Malay fighters'; Cheah Boon Kheng, *Red Star over Malaya*, pp. 79–80, 170–3 and 285, briefly discusses Malay guerrilla activity, but does not expand beyond this.
68 Tengku Mahmood Mahyideen: Che Man, *Muslim Separatism*, p. 65; independence: Tun Razak quoted in William Shaw, *Tun Razak*, p. 42. The speed with which Wataniah would move to back UMNO after the war is also indicative of this (see below). UMNO's founder, Onn bin Jaafar, was clear that the reawakening of 'the spirit of Malay nationalism' was one of his aims (*Straits Times,* 26 May 1946).
69 Chin Peng, *My Side of History*, pp. 68–70.
70 ANM, 2000/0006765, Yeop Mahidin, 'Comments on Lack of Malay Resistance Movement earlier in Occupation'.
71 The Malays Fought as well as the Best Empire Troops', *Straits Times*, 6 May 1947, p. 8.
72 Sheppard, *The Malay Regiment*, pp. 25–6. Sheppard, although here obviously writing for the colonial government, was generally a reliable observer and author, so there is no reason to suspect him here of dishonesty or exaggeration.
73 ANM, 2000/0006765 'Comments on Lack of Malay Resistance Movement Earlier in Occupation'.
74 IWM, Sound.8476, Yeop Mahadin [sic], Interview. This is obviously post-hoc evidence; however, Yeop's intense suspicion of the MPAJA comes through clearly in his correspondence with Richardson within days of the Japanese surrender (TNA, HS 1/123, *Beacon* Operational Report, Singa to Kiwi, 20 August 1945 and 21 August 1945, pp. 34–35).
75 This tallies with information given by Tun Abdul Razak. A.J. Stockwell, *British Policy and Malay Politics during the Malayan Union Experiment* (Kuala Lumpur: Malaysian Branch of the Royal Asiatic Society, 1979), p. 71, sourced to interviews, 1971; Shaw, *Tun Razak* (Singapore: Longman, 1976), p. 48 (this information is not sourced, and may be taken from the same interviews).
76 Shaw, *Tun Razak*, p. 49. The Indian National Army was raised by the Japanese from among Indian POWs and locally resident Indians. Some Indian POWs joined willingly, while others did so under considerable duress, up to and including torture

and death. See, for example, David H. James, *The Rise and Fall of the Japanese Empire* (London: George Allen and Unwin, 1951), p. 253.

77 Shaw, *Tun Razak*, p. 49.

78 A brief description of the NAP is given in Foot, *SOE*, pp. 316–17.

79 ANM, 2000/0006765, 'Contacts Pahang Wataniah'; the intention was that, as the British came ashore, Japanese telecommunications in Pahang would be shut down. Wan Hashim, *Role of the Malay Guerrillas*, p. 103. The comparison with the NAP was first made by Derek Headly (GLO of *Multiple*) in his Draft Chapter 3, p. 12, in file 2000/0006765, ANM.

80 According to Kratoska, *The Japanese Occupation of Malaya*, p. 112, these associations were set up in Selangor in mid-1943 and in the other Malay states during 1944, essentially as bodies to provide relief for the destitute.

81 TNA, HS 1/123, Lt. Col. J.D. Richardson, *Beacon* Operational Report, p. 4.

82 Wan Hashim, *Role of the Malay Guerillas*, pp. 86–89. Roslan bin Johar had been a member of the 4th Pahang Battalion of the FMSVF and had escaped with his OC, Dennis Ambler, to Ceylon (ANM, 2000/0006765, Derek Headly, 'Background to Resistance in Malaya'; Roslan is given here as 'Roselan bin Salleh' but other sources, such as Wan Hashim, *Role of the Malay Guerrillas*, p. 86, have him as Roselan bin Johar).

83 TNA, HS 7/165, 'History of Force 136 Operations in Malaya', makes clear the value placed on this intelligence.

84 Davis's party (Operation *Gustavus*) did not come back up on the air until February 1945 (this is discussed in Chapter 2). *Carpenter* established a radio link with Force 136 HQ in late October or early November: the exact date is not clear from the operational reports on TNA, HS 1/107.

85 In brief, the wish to conciliate the Chinese government in Chungking had caused Force 136 heavily to downplay the level of communist involvement in the MPAJA from as early as October 1943 (IWM, 19859, Papers of F. Spencer Chapman Papers, File 3, Encs. 42, 48 and 82 refer). This 'line' endured: on 26 July 1945, a memo referred to the MPAJA as 'the so-called communists'. It was from B/B1: possibly Colin Mackenzie, the head of Force 136, whose designation was B/B100: there is no reference on file for 'B/B1'. (TNA, HS 1/115, 'Top Secret', 26 July 1945).

86 TNA, HS 1/115, 'Memorandum on Anti-Japanese Union and Forces', May 1945, from Colin Mackenzie. This issue was first brought to academic attention by Aldrich, *Intelligence and the War against Japan*, p. 330.

87 ANM, 2000/0006765, Wan Hashim, 'The Malay Resistance Movement against the Japanese during the Second World War', p. 17.

88 The late-colonial security forces were dominated by the Indians and, especially, the Malays; Comber, in *Malaya's Secret Police*, comments several times on the low number of Chinese in the police (pp. 34, 112 and 133).

89 Prior to this, he worked for the Public Relations Department in Pahang ('War Awards to Malayans', *Straits Times*, 8 December 1946). The Home Guard provided sentries for mines, plantations and New Villages during the Emergency.

90 TNA, HS 7/165, 'History of Force 136 Operations in Malaya', p. 8.

91 TNA, HS 7/165, 'History of Force 136 Operations in Malaya', App. B.

92 TNA, HS 7/165, 'History of Force 136 Operations in Malaya', p. 37; Richardson was clear that the 'objects' required of the Malay guerrilla force by Force 136 would be to 'Attack or deny targets as instructed' and to take their part in the reconquest of Pahang, including in the provision of guides and interpreters (HS 1/123, *Beacon*

Operational Report, Kiwi to HQ, 18 July 1945, p. 18). Force 136's priority was to prepare those guerrillas along the western coastal littoral where the first fighting was expected: their arms were all to be dropped before *Zipper* by the Special Duties Squadron, whereas the plan was to complete the arming of the Malay forces by Dakota from the beachheads. It is evident that this was due only to 'limited air lift from Ceylon' (TNA, HS 7/165, 'History of Force 136 Operations in Malaya', App. C,).

93　ANM, 2000/0006765, Derek Headly, 'Chapter 2', p. 1, notes that Ambler was a strong proponent of Malay forces; TNA, HS 1/115, 'Memorandum on Anti-Japanese Union and Forces', May 1945, from Colin Mackenzie.

94　ANM, 2000/0006765, Hashim, 'The Malay Resistance Movement against the Japanese during the Second World War', p. 17.

95　TNA, CO 825/42/6, Draft: Summary of Memorandum on Policy in Malaya by Tengku Mahmood Mahyideen (Enc. 48); the same information is contained at greater length in 'The Line Our Propaganda in Malaya Should Take', on the same file. This pleased members of the MPU: 'an enlightened Malay' had come to the same conclusions that they had (TNA, CO 825/42/6, McKerron to Monson, 3 December 1943). Ultimately, however, the Tengku's advice, in his own memorandum, to proceed with extreme tact and caution was ignored: in late 1945, the Malay sultans were presented with the new constitution of the proposed Malayan Union and the treaty changes it required, and more or less obliged to sign. Their degree of willingness varied, but they all turned against the idea in very short order.

96　Likewise failed due to technical problems; *Carpenter* infiltrated in mid-October 1944.

97　Ibrahim Ismail, *Have You Met Mariam?*, pp. 70–95. Force 136 HQ, quickly realizing that their agents were transmitting under duress, passed them immediately over to 'D' (Deception) Division, who proceeded to play the party back to the Japanese. The members of *Oatmeal*, acting with great coolness, kept the deception going until the end of the war. 'D' Division and *Oatmeal* have been credited by some sources with persuading the Japanese to believe that the British assault would come on the Kra Isthmus, not near Port Dickson, leading to the concentration of Japanese troops in the north. (See Ibrahim Ismail's obituary, *Daily Telegraph*, 26 January 2011, <http://www.telegraph.co.uk/news/obituaries/military-obituaries/special-forces-obituaries/8284728/Tun-Ibrahim-Ismail.html> [22 April 2012].

98　O'Brien, *The Moonlit War*, p. 45.

99　HS 1/121, Lt. Col. P.G.J. Dobrée, *Hebrides* Operational Report, p. 1. In due course it received two other operations, *Beacon* (January 1945) whose members had to walk to their operational area in Pahang, and *Fighter* (February 1945) which was to operate in Kedah. *Beacon*, in turn, received Operation *Multiple* (April 1945). (For *Multiple* and *Fighter*, see TNA, HS 1/108; for *Beacon*, see TNA, HS 1/121, Lt. Col. J.D. Richardson, Operational Report, p. 1). *Hebrides* also received at least one operation for the ISLD (MI6).

100　In Upper Perak, where Dobrée was based, word spread at speed and rumour stated that hundreds of men had been airdropped in: this lack of security only served to agitate the Japanese: Wan Hashim, *Role of the Malay Guerrillas*, p. 55. Hasler of *Fighter* had a similar problem (TNA, HS 1/121, Major G.A. Hasler, *Fighter* Operational Report, p. 7). By contrast, the security enjoyed by *Beacon* in Pahang was remarkable. The Malays and *Orang Asli* with whom Richardson dealt kept so quiet that, at the end of the war, neither the Japanese nor the local Chinese had the slightest idea that a guerrilla force was being armed and trained in the locality. (TNA,

HS 1/123, Lt. Col. J.D. Richardson, *Beacon* Operational Report, p. 6: 'The security of the Malays and of the Sakai had been remarkable and deserves special mention').

101 TNA, HS 1/121, Major G.A. Hasler, *Fighter* Operational Report, p. 3.

102 Ibrahim Ismail, *Have You Met Mariam?*, p. 70.

103 Young men from the kampongs: TNA, HS 1/121, Lt. Col. P.G.J. Dobrée, *Hebrides* Operational Report, p. 1; parachute cord: Wan Hashim, *Role of the Malay Guerrillas*, pp. 54–55.

104 ANM, 2000/0006765, Headly, Draft of *Hebrides* chapter, p. 19.

105 HS 1/121, Major G.A. Hasler, *Fighter* Operational Report, p. 8.

106 Richardson, *Kiwi's Diary*, p. 61; TNA, HS 1/123, Lt. Col. J.D. Richardson, *Beacon* Operational Report, Kiwi to Singa, 9 July 1945 (p. 16).

107 TNA, HS 1/123, Lt. Col. J.D. Richardson, *Beacon* Operational Report, Singa to Kiwi, 14 July, p. 17.

108 Wan Hashim, *Role of the Malay Guerrillas*, p. 62.

109 IWM, 3328, Papers of P.G.J. Dobrée, p. 33.

110 TNA, HS 1/121, Major G.A. Hasler, *Fighter* Operational Report, p. 3.

111 TNA, HS 1/121, Major G.A. Hasler, *Fighter* Operational Report, pp. 2 and 4. He commented that this was mainly because he lacked the right sort of contacts; once his presence was more widely known, after the Japanese surrender, 'I could have recruited at the rate of about 25 per day easily'. Given that Dobrée and Richardson easily managed to recruit men with military training, it seems that Hasler's explanation is credible, and not a consequence of reluctance on the part of local Malays.

112 See, for example, TNA, HS 1/123, Lt. Col. J.D. Richardson, *Beacon* Operational Report, p. 5. Wataniah had recruited six ex-Malay Regiment and fifty ex-FMSVF personnel.

113 ANM, 2000/0006765, Headly to Sheppard, 4 September 1979; TNA, FCO 141/7344, Record Sheet, Ng Boon Cheong (Decd); TNA, HS 1/121, Lt. Col. P.G.J. Dobrée, *Hebrides* Operational Report, p. 3; Cruikshank, *SOE in the Far East*, p. 207. Some of Dobrée's agents covered enormous distances, for it was over 400 miles from his camp to Singapore.

114 Wan Hashim, *Role of the Malay Guerrillas*, p. 62; *Straits Times*, 9 June 1946; TNA, HS 1/121, Lt. Col. J.D. Richardson, *Beacon* Operational Report, p. 15 (Singa to Kiwi: 'Most mukims [roughly equivalent to a parish] are practically dry as regards young men.')

115 IWM, Sound.8476, Interview with Yeop Mahadin [sic].

116 D.O. of Grik arrested and beaten up: IWM, 3328, Papers of P.G.J. Dobrée, p. 35; Salleh survived the Japanese, but died of liver cancer in November 1945 (TNA, FCO 141/7344, 'Casualties – Resistance Forces' and Record Sheet, Salleh, Dec'd,).

117 Wan Hashim, *Role of the Malay Guerrillas*, p. 92.

118 IWM, 14859, Papers of F. Spencer Chapman, File 2, 'Force 136 Operations in Malaya', Intelligence Appendix. Curiously, the same appendix speaks poorly of the intelligence returned by Operation *Beacon*, though Richardson assured Yeop Mahidin that what he sent was 'exactly what is wanted' (TNA, HS 1/123, Lt. Col. J.D. Richardson, *Beacon* Operational Report, Kiwi to Singa, 29 June 1945, p. 14).

119 TNA, HS 1/121, Lt. Col. P.G.J. Dobrée, *Hebrides* Operational Report, p. 2.

120 TNA, HS 1/123, Lt. Col. J.D. Richardson, *Beacon* Operational Report, Kiwi to Singa, 8 August 1945. This is supported by Richardson's confident assertion in his Operational Report (p. 5) that he would have reached a total of 950 recruits during

September. This must be compared to the total Malay population of Pahang, which
was around 128,500, of which at least 25 per cent would have been aged under
fifteen; of the remaining 96,000, half would have been women, and some would
have been elderly – and many of the young ones would have been unavailable due
to forced labour. In other words, at minimum, one adult Malay male out of every
forty-five of military age in Pahang was recruited into Wataniah. (Population figures
estimated from Pahang Malay total given in Kratoska, *The Japanese Occupation of
Malaya*, Table 1.2, p. 19.)

121 TNA, HS 1/123, Lt. Col. J.D. Richardson, *Beacon* Operational Report, p. 7; ANM,
1957/0341852, Derek Headly to Chief Secretary, BMA, 6 April 1946; TNA, HS 1/121,
Major G.A. Hasler, *Fighter* Operational Report, p. 8. The Giyu Tai was a paramilitary
force organized by the Japanese.
122 TNA, HS 1/122, Lt. Col. D. Headly, *Multiple* Operational Report, pp. 5–6.
123 TNA, HS 1/122, Lt. Col. D. Headly, *Multiple* Operational Report, p. 6.
124 Richardson, *Kiwi's Diary*, pp. 18–20. Richardson was a guest at a large celebration –
part trial of traitors, part propaganda meeting, where stress was laid on the actions
of 'Chinese bandits' who had exploited the local Malays. These 'bandits' will be
discussed in Chapter 4.
125 Richardson, *Kiwi's Diary*, p. 18; Chin Peng, in Chin and Hack, *Dialogues with Chin
Peng*, p. 149. Chin Peng adds that the MPAJA had several different Lau Mahs in its
ranks (it is a nickname, meaning 'Old Horse' in Cantonese), but it seems (from the
MPAJA Regiment involved) that the man Richardson met was the same man who
features also in the reports of Operation *Funnel* and attended the Victory Parade
in London in 1946. According to Anthony Short, *The Communist Insurrection in
Malaya 1948–1960* (London: Frederick Muller, 1975), p. 206, he was a member of the
Central Committee of the MCP after the war, and was killed in 1948.
126 TNA, HS 1/122, Lt. Col. J.D. Richardson, *Beacon* Operational Report, p. 3.
127 TNA, HS 1/122, Lt. Col. J.D. Richardson, *Beacon* Operational Report, p. 6; he
also asked Yeop Mahidin directly to 'let the A.J.U.F. [Anti-Japanese Union Forces]
know as little as possible about the M.R.M. [Malay Resistance Movement that is
Wataniah]' (p. 30). It appears that originally Richardson had hoped to agree with
the MPAJA discrete areas of operations for the communist guerrillas and Wataniah
(pp. 18–19: Kiwi to HQ, 24 July 1945).
128 TNA, HS 1/122, Lt. Col. D. Headly, *Multiple* Operational Report, pp. 5 and 6.
129 TNA, HS 1/121, Major G.A. Hasler, *Fighter* Operational Report, p. 8.
130 TNA, HS 1/121, Lt. Col. P.G.J. Dobrée, Personnel Reports. It is impossible to
establish from the available information when Sarpin was captured and killed, since
Dobrée does not specify. The MPAJA were nicknamed the *bintang tiga* or Three Stars
for their cap badge, said to represent each of Malaya's three main communities.
131 For example, TNA, HS 1/121, Major G.A. Hasler, *Fighter* Operational Report,
pp. 8–9.
132 The difficult relationship between rural Malays and Chinese merchants, and the
issues with the charging of interest, are outlined by Derek Headly (a man who spoke
very fluent Malay) in a draft chapter concerning the background to resistance in
Malaya (ANM, 2000/0006765, draft, pp. 5–6). His contentions are supported by the
long memorandum by Tengku Mahmood Mahyideen on TNA, CO 825/42.
133 TNA, HS 1/123, Lt. Col. J.D. Richardson, *Beacon* Operational Report, Singa to Kiwi,
22 August 1945, p. 9.

134 C.F. Yong, 'The Malayan Communist Struggle for Survival, 1930–1935', *Journal of the Malaysian Branch of the Royal Asiatic Society*, 69, 2 (271) (1996), pp. 1–22.

135 See, for example, TNA, HS 1/121, John Creer's Report, pp. 3 and 5.

136 Of the 60,000 Indian POWs taken in Malaya by the Japanese, around 20,000 defected to the INA, some willingly, others under considerable pressure (amounting in some cases to torture). See G.J. Douds, 'Indian POWs in the Pacific, 1941–45', in *Forgotten Captives in Japanese-Occupied Asia,* ed. Kevin Blackburn and Karl Hack (Abingdon: Routledge, 2007), pp. 73–74 and John Baptist Crasta, ed. Richard Crasta, *Eaten by the Japanese* (New York: Invisible Man Press, Inc., 2012), pp. 23–4. Towards the end of the occupation, either out of exasperation with the Japanese or from a desire to shift to the winning side, some INA troops offered their assistance to Force 136 (TNA, HS 1/107, Major I.D. Ross, *Funnel Blue* Operational Report, p. 2).

137 The differential treatment of Malaya's 'races' was noted by the former policeman, Gurchan Singh: he ran a propaganda network and carried out occasional acts of sabotage but generally, because he was an Indian, was not under suspicion. See Singh, *Singha: The Lion of Malaya*, p. 80. At least two of Gurchan's agents were Malays (pp. 64 and 93).

138 TNA, HS 1/109, F. Spencer Chapman, Report A, p. 30.

139 HS 1/122, Lt. Col. D. Headly, *Multiple* Operational Report, p. 2, and Thatcher and Cross: *Pai Naa*, pp. 165–166. In the closing weeks of the war, a group of Malays who had been impressed into the Giyu Tai (Volunteer Corps) deserted with their arms, intending to join Wataniah. Instead, they came across the MPAJA, which disarmed them and prevented them from joining Derek Headly, who was trying to track them down. Headly pursued their case for a demob bonus for several years. See correspondence on ANM, 1957/0341852.

140 Cheah Boon Kheng, *Red Star over Malaya*, p. 63.

141 Richardson and the Malays of Wataniah were concerned that the Malay population would believe Japanese propaganda that the Sultan of Pahang had been kidnapped by the MPAJA: TNA, HS 1/123, Ghazalie bin Shafie, 'Jap Device to Foster Enmity', p. 2 (this is discussed in more detail in Chapter 6). The nervousness of the Malay population comes through in Yeop Mahidin's communications with Richardson, for example, TNA, HS 1/123, Lt. Col. J.D. Richardson, *Beacon* Operational Reports, Singa to Kiwi, 21 August 1945, pp. 34–5.

142 Cheah Boon Kheng, *Red Star over Malaya*, pp. 210–23. Cheah Boon Kheng dates the start of the unrest to the earlier part of the year.

Chapter 5

1 The term 'Kuomintang State' was used by the OCAJA leader Yong Kong to describe the territory under the group's control. Holman, *The Green Torture*, p. 136.

2 Holman, *The Green Torture*, p. 169.

3 See T'ien-Wei Wu, 'The Chinese Communist Movement' in *China's Bitter Victory*, ed. James C. Hsiung and Steven I. Levine (London: Routledge, 1992), pp. 79–106 (pp. 98–9).

4 For example, TNA, HS 1/123, Major G.R. Leonard, *Pontoon* GLO's Operational Report, p. 6.

5   The earliest exposition of the idea that 'bandits' adopted the Guomindang flag to lend themselves legitimacy seems to have been in an article in the *Straits Times* of 25 July 48, p. 6.

6   Bayly and Harper, *Forgotten Armies*, p. 416; Cruickshank, *SOE in the Far East*, p. 208; Bayly and Harper, *Forgotten Wars*, p. 44; O'Ballance, *Malaya*, p. 47; Cheah Boon Kheng, *Red Star over Malaya*, p. 79.

7   C.F. Yong and R.B. McKenna, *The Kuomintang Movement in British Malaya, 1912– 1949* (Singapore: Singapore University Press, 1990), p. 199.

8   Cruickshank, *SOE in the Far East*, pp. 207 and 208.

9   Karl Hack and C.C. Chin, 'The Malayan Emergency' in *Dialogues with Chin Peng*, ed. Chin and Hack, pp. 3–37 (p. 5).

10 Short, *The Communist Insurrection*, p. 24, fn.7. Aside from Short, Richard Gough hints that they were perhaps slightly more than the 'robbers and murderers' described by the MPAJA (*The Jungle Was Red*, p. 72).

11 Ranajit Guha, 'The Prose of Counterinsurgency', in *Selected Subaltern Studies*, ed. Ranajit Guha and Gayatri Chakravorty Spivak (Oxford: Oxford University Press, 1988), pp. 46–84, esp. pp. 45–7.

12 For all of these reports, see TNA, HS 1/121.

13 For example: TNA HS 1/121, Creer's Report, p. 7, Creer laments the reluctance of Yong Kong and his detachment to accept any training from Robert Chrystal (a veteran of World War I); on p. 8 he states that at one stage 'CHRYSTAL swore he would have nothing more to do with the Chinese' (both Guomindang and communist); on p. 8 he describes one OCAJA leader as 'very vain' and accused him to his face 'of planning to murder me'. Also Holman, *The Green Torture*, p. 78, accused the Guomindang at Pulai of 'orgies and lawlessness' in the first nine months of the occupation.

14 TNA, HS 1/121, 'Copy of Signal No. 83', 18 August 1945, with the documents for Operation *Hebrides*; 'Mr. J.K. Creer's Notes on Dangerous Characters', September 1945 and John Creer's Report, pp. 2–3. The former document is signed off by Major Arthur Bromley-Davenport, but from the information it contains, the signal can only have been written by Creer. (It follows 'Mr. J.K. Creer's Notes on Dangerous Characters' which is also signed off by Bromley-Davenport.)

15 TNA, HS 1/121, Major J.P.M. Clifford, *Hebrides Minerva* Operational Report, pp. 2–5.

16 For examples of racial tropes and generalizations, see TNA, HS 1/121, John Creer's Report, pp. 10 ('Chinese intrigues') and 18 ('their behaviour still frequently baffles me').

17 Kratoska, *The Japanese Occupation of Malaya*, p. 86.

18 Holman, *The Green Torture*. Chrystal is often quoted, and the book was clearly based on extensive interviews.

19 John Creer's Report is at TNA, HS 1/121. Creer spent time with both the MPAJA and the OCAJA and his account is hard to understand, since he often fails to allocate named individuals to either group. Typing it into Microsoft Word to make it searchable enabled names to be tracked and allowed individuals to be ascribed to the appropriate guerrilla army. The slow job of transcription also made the shape of Creer's story more apparent.

20 Elizabeth Moggie, 'Notes on Visit to Kelantan', Personal Communication, 2017. I am extremely grateful to Mrs. Moggie for her investigations.

21 Holman, *The Green Torture*, p. 136.

22 Charles Tilly, 'War Making and State Making as Organized Crime' in *Bringing the State Back In,* ed. Peter Evans, Dietrich Rueschemeyer and Theda Skocpol (Cambridge: Cambridge University Press, 1985), pp. 170–2.
23 Tilly, 'War Making and State Making as Organized Crime', pp. 171–2.
24 Yong Kong's unit was based near Gua Musang where, according to Chin and Hack, the MPAJA claimed to have fended off bandits: Hack and Chin, 'The Malayan Emergency' in *Dialogues with Chin Peng,* ed. Chin and Hack, p. 5.
25 TNA, HS 1/121, Major J.P.M. Clifford's, *Hebrides Minerva* Operational Report, p. 4. Jelutong latex was used in the manufacture of chewing gum.
26 Cheah Boon Kheng, *Red Star over Malaya,* p. 78. The SOE was aware of an undercover Guomindang group (TNA, HS 1/164, 'OM China, 29th April 1942', p. 3); this may have been the means by which the Malayan Guomindang was instructed to raise guerrillas.
27 Kratoska, *The Japanese Occupation of Malaya,* p. 99. These account books may well have included the names of donors, who would have wanted to evade the Japanese.
28 Moggie, 'Notes on Visit to Kelantan' (2017), supported by 'Statement of Eyewitness Regarding the Death of Wong Yat Mun' and covering letter dated 15 December 1946 (in private hands, provided by Wee Pock Soon) and a translation of a memorial plaque originally at Bukit Cina Cemetery, Kok Lanas, Ketereh, Kelantan (provided by Wee Pock Soon), which commemorates ten members of the Kelantan Guomindang killed by the Japanese.
29 TNA, HS 1/115, 'OM Operations in Malaya', April 1942, p. 21. In keeping with the backgrounds of the Guomindang trainees, their course had a more urban slant than was the norm. Although a stores dump was established for these men near Johore Bharu on the Malayan mainland, Singapore was invested before they could be infiltrated and instead, 'They were turned over to "Dalforce" and used in the defence of the Island.'
30 Merchant, labour contractor, timber contractor and jelutong tappers: TNA, HS 1/121, John Creer's Report, pp. 2, 4 and 11; *kepala* (overseers) in rubber, timber and jelutong businesses: TNA, HS 1/121, Signal 83; gang robbers: Holman, *Green Torture*, p. 130.
31 TNA, HS 1/121, John Creer's Report, pp. 3 and 4.
32 TNA, HS 1/121, John Creer's Report, p. 3. Creer also states that between 1943 and 1944, this man was allied with the MPAJA before returning to the OCAJA (TNA, HS 1/121, J.K. Creer, 'Note on Dangerous Characters'). Clearly allegiances shifted.
33 Ho Thean Fook, *Tainted Glory*, pp. 230–1.
34 Phil Billingsley, *Bandits in Republican China* (Stanford: Stanford University Press, 1988), p. 273.
35 TNA, HS 1/121, John Creer's Report, p. 4.
36 TNA, HS 1/121, John Creer's Report, p. 5. It should be said that any references in this chapter to the Thai border will be to that pertaining before 1943 and again after 1945, not to that which applied during the cession of the four Malay states to Thailand between 1943 and 1945.
37 Daily life in MPAJA camps seems to have followed a strict timetable that varied very little from place to place. See, for example, TNA, HS 1/109, F. Spencer Chapman, Report A, pp. 24–5.
38 *Samsu*-drinking: Holman, *The Green Torture*, pp. 78, and 130 and TNA, HS 1/121, John Creer's Report, p. 12; hangovers: Holman, *The Green Torture*, p. 135. *Samsu* is rice wine, though during the occupation it was also made from tapioca.
39 Ho Thean Fook, *Tainted Glory*, p. 187.

40 IWM, 3328, Papers of P.G.J. Dobrée, p. 28, and TNA, HS 1/121, Robert Chrystal's Report, p. 3.
41 TNA, HS 1/121, John Creer's Report, p. 9.
42 TNA, HS 1/121, 'Copy of Signal No. 83', 18 August 1945. Cheong Shik Pho had been replaced by Wong Shin. Both men were still alive at the end of the war.
43 TNA, HS 1/121, John Creer's Report: sentries and bugles, p. 7 and parade grounds, p. 11.
44 TNA, HS 1/121, John Creer's Report, pp. 5, 7 and 11.
45 TNA, HS 1/121, John Creer's Report, pp. 4, 5, 9 and 11.
46 *Straits Times*, 25 July 48, p. 6. These men are described as 'bandits': already the 'bandit' trope was gaining traction in the public consciousness.
47 Ho Thean Fook, *Tainted Glory*, p. 38.
48 TNA, HS 1/121, John Creer's Report, pp. 5–6.
49 TNA, HS 1/121, Chrystal's Report, p. 3.
50 TNA, HS 1/121, John Creer's Report, p. 4 and p. 9.
51 TNA, HS 1/121, John Creer's Report, p. 14. Chrystal gives Wong Shin as Wong Shin Foon; for example, Holman, *The Green Torture*, p. 138.
52 Holman, *The Green Torture*, p. 78.
53 TNA, HS 1/121, John Creer's Report, pp. 4 and 5.
54 TNA, HS 1/121, John Creer's Report, pp. 9 and10.
55 TNA, HS 1/121, Captain J.P.M. Clifford, Operation *Hebrides* PLO's Report, p. 2.
56 TNA, HS 1/121, Captain C.L. Gabb, App. G to *Hebrides* Operational Report; TNA, HS 1/121, Capt. J.P.M. Clifford, App. G of *Hebrides Minerva* Operational Report; TNA, HS 1/121, Major A.R. Bromley-Davenport, App. G to *Hebrides Venus* Operational Report.
57 This can only be an educated guess. Western Kelantan, north Pahang and upper Perak were not thickly populated. These areas were also predominantly Malay, with perhaps 10 per cent Aborigines and – prior to the influx of new squatters – about 10 per cent Chinese. This information has been deduced from data in Saw Swee Hock, *The Population of Peninsular Malaysia* (Singapore: Singapore University Press, 1988), pp. 57, 62 and 66. Only 6 per cent of Kelantan's population was of immigrant origin.
58 TNA, HS 1/121, John Creer's Report, HS 1/121, pp. 5, 15 and 18; Holman, *The Green Torture*, p. 136.
59 TNA, HS 1/121, John Creer's Report, p. 4. This may be the same incident as described by Cheah Boon Kheng, *Red Star over Malaya*, p. 70, fn., which describes how, in 1943, Japanese troops searching for guerrillas and accompanied by Malays, raided a Chinese a settlement at Lenggong, burning the houses and taking the harvested rice. Several dozen Chinese were arrested, and some allegedly beaten to death.
60 Holman, *Green Torture*, p. 136.
61 TNA, HS 1/121, John Creer's Report, pp. 9–10.
62 TNA, HS 1/121, John Creer's Report, p. 12.
63 TNA, HS 1/121, John Creer's Report, p. 12.
64 TNA, HS 1/121, John Creer's Report, p. 12.
65 Holman, *Green Torture*, p. 137.
66 TNA, HS 1/121, John Creer's Report, p. 12.
67 Holman, *Green Torture*, p. 140.
68 Malays recruited: TNA, HS 1/121, John Creer's Report, p. 14; incidents where Malay police who went over to the MPAJA were disarmed: Thatcher and Cross, *Pai Naa*,

pp. 165–166; TNA, HS 1/123, Major J.D. Richardson, *Beacon* Operational Report, pp. 33–34. Both these instances were in Pahang.

69 TNA, HS 1/121, John Creer's Report, p. 11.

70 TNA, HS 1/121, John Creer's Report, p. 10.

71 TNA, HS 1/121, John Creer's Report, p. 16.

72 Holman, *Green Torture*, pp. 129 and 168.

73 TNA, HS 1/121, John Creer's Report, pp. 4 and 9.

74 TNA, HS 1/121, John Creer's Report, pp. 5 and 12.

75 Nakahara Michiko, 'Malayan Labour on the Thailand-Burma Railway' in *Asian Labour in the Wartime Japanese Empire: Unknown Histories,* ed. Paul Kratoska (New York: M.E. Sharpe, 2005), pp. 249–65 (pp. 254–6).

76 Kratoska, *The Japanese Occupation of Malaya*, p. 86.

77 Both Creer and Chrystal mention Yong Kong's contacts with Toh Misai; Creer relates how the Malays in Toh Misai's area had given ammunition to the Guomindang (TNA, HS 1/121, John Creer's Report, p. 10); Chrystal tells how Yong Kong heard there was a letter for them at Toh Misai's and took them there (Holman, *The Green Torture*, p. 142).

78 Holman, *The Green Torture*, p. 138.

79 Kratoska, *The Japanese Occupation of Malaya*, p. 81.

80 TNA, HS 1/121, John Creer's Report, pp. 9 and 11.

81 TNA, HS 1/121, John Creer's Report, p. 12. The all-Malay *Oatmeal* party, under Capt. Ibrahim's command, was captured within a few days of its coming ashore (see Chapter 4). That the news percolated deep into the *ulu* so quickly says much for the information network provided by the police.

82 TNA, HS 1/121, Chrystal's Report, pp. 4–5.

83 TNA, HS 1/121, John Creer's Report, Operation *Hebrides*, p. 16.

84 TNA, HS 1/121, John Creer's Report, p. 12; Holman, *The Green Torture*, p. 135.

85 Kathirithamby-Wells, *Nature and Nation*, p. 237.

86 IWM, 14859, Papers of F. Spencer Chapman, File 4, 'MOST SECRET Conditions in Perak (Malaya) in May-June 1943' (Enc. 16), p. 8; Kratoska, *The Japanese Occupation of Malaya*, p. 252.

87 Holman, *The Green Torture*, p. 137; the Thais took a levy a little further downstream at Kuala Krai, and the Japanese another at Kota Bharu.

88 Holman, *The Green Torture*, p. 137.

89 Holman, *The Green Torture*, p. 137. The price of gold increased substantially during the occupation (IWM, 14859, Papers of F. Spencer Chapman, File 4, Enc. 71).

90 For the questionable legal status of goldwashers and their conflicts with the colonial state, see TNA, HS 1/121, John Creer's Report, p. 4. The *Straits Times* of 12 March 1941 carried a letter from the game warden Theodore Hubback (with whom Creer originally lived in the jungle), complaining about the damage caused by illegal gold and tin mining, and the lack of action against it on the part of Pahang's administration.

91 Philip King, 'From Periphery to Centre: Shaping the History of the Central Peninsula' (Unpublished doctoral thesis; University of Wollongong, 2006), p. 205, referenced to Short, *The Communist Insurrection*, p. 180.

92 TNA, HS 1/121, John Creer's Report, p. 12. The reasons for the Japanese withdrawal will shortly be discussed.

93 TNA, HS 1/121, John Creer's Report, p. 14.

94 See, for example, TNA, HS 1/121, John Creer's Report, p. 12, where he recounts a ten-day journey from Dabong in Kelantan to the vicinity of Grik in Upper Perak; on the following page he describes travelling between small settlements in northern Kelantan; Chrystal also journeyed around (*The Green Torture*, pp. 60–77, just as the 'state' was being formed, and p. 176, towards the end of the war).

95 TNA, HS 1/121, John Creer's Report, p. 11.

96 Ota Koki, 'Railway Operations in Japanese Occupied Malaya' in *New Perspectives on the Japanese Occupation in Malaya and Singapore, 1941–1945*, p. 140.

97 Holman, *The Green Torture*, p. 136.

98 TNA, HS 1/121, John Creer's Report, p. 13.

99 The quote is from TNA, HS 1/121, John Creer's Report, p. 18.

100 Yong and McKenna, *The Kuomintang Movement in British Malaya*, pp. 85–9.

101 Huat Kin Koon, 'A Dilemma of Identity', p. 93.

102 Holman, *The Green Torture*, p. 78.

103 TNA, HS 1/121, John Creer's Report, p. 6.

104 See, for example, TNA, HS 1/121, John Creer's Report, p. 7.

105 TNA, HS 1/121, John Creer's Report, pp. 2–3 and 11; TNA, HS 1/121, Capt. C.L. Gabb, *Hebrides* Operational Report, pp. 1–2 and Moggie, 'Notes on Visit to Kelantan' (2017).

106 TNA, HS 1/121, John Creer's Report, p. 6

107 TNA, HS 1/121, John Creer's Report, pp. 6–10; supported by Holman, *The Green Torture*, pp. 78–83 and 130–132.The 'embezzlement' of funds meant for the OCAJA by the MPAJA is mentioned on TNA, FCO 141/7344, 'Record Sheet: Hong Kiong [Yong Kong]'.

108 TNA, HS 1/121, John Creer's Report, p. 10.

109 TNA HS 1/109, F. Spencer Chapman, Report A, p. 27. He added drily that 'I was told that this habit was discouraged by H.Q.'

110 Holman, *The Green Torture*, pp. 131–2; Hack and Chin, 'The Malayan Emergency' in *Dialogues with Chin Peng*, ed. Chin and Hack, pp. 3–37 (p. 5).

111 TNA, HS 1/121, John Creer's Report, pp. 11 and 12.

112 Chin Peng, *My Side of History*, p. 109

113 Robert Chrystal, quoted in the *Straits Times*, 31 July 1962, p. 9. In December 1945, fewer than 4,500 MPAJA fighters disbanded.

114 Holman, *The Green Torture*, pp. 168–9.

115 TNA, HS 1/121, John Creer's Report, p. 14.

116 Holman, *Green Torture*, p. 160.

117 TNA, HS 1/121, John Creer's Report, pp. 13–14.

118 TNA, HS 1/121, John Creer's Report, p. 15.

119 Cheah Boon Kheng, *Red Star over Malaya*, pp. 78–9.

120 TNA, HS 1/123, Lt. Col. G.R. Leonard, *Pontoon* GLO's Operational Report, p. 8. This incredible story, from initial contacts with the inhabitants of Merapoh to a fruitless Japanese air assault on the town, is detailed in a few pages of Leonard's report. This is the only instance I have come across, in all the Force 136 reports, of the MPAJA and an armed force of Malays working together.

121 TNA, HS 1/121, John Creer's Report, p. 11.

122 TNA, HS 1/114, Note on Interrogation of Ong Sin Bin, 3 July 1945, and copy letter from HQ Group B, Force 136 to HQ Force 136, 18 July 1945. Ong Sin Bin's junk had been sunk in January, so his information dated from the latter part of 1944 or early 1945.

123 Ho Thean Fook, *Tainted Glory*, pp. 186–8, 194–7, 202–3 and 230.

124 Chin Peng, *My Side of History*, p. 109. A group of swashbuckling guerrilla-bandits in Johore is described in Spencer Chapman, *The Jungle Is Neutral*, pp. 192–195, Holman, *The Green Torture* p. 132 and Holder, *The Fight for Malaya*, pp. 115 and 144.

125 Holder, *The Fight for Malaya*, p. 144.

126 Chin Peng, *My Side of History*, p. 109.

127 Foot, *SOE*, pp. 269–270.

128 Bailey, *The Wildest Province*, pp. 295–7.

129 Artemis Cooper, *Patrick Leigh Fermor: An Adventure* (London: John Murray, 2012), p. 157.

130 Holman, *The Green Torture*, p. 132

131 Comber, *Malaya's Secret Police*, p. 249; Cheah Boon Kheng, *Red Star over Malaya*, p. 78

132 TNA, HS 1/121, Major J.P.M. Clifford, *Hebrides Minerva* Operational Report, p. 2 and App. G; TNA, HS 1/121, Capt. C.L. Gabb, *Hebrides* Operational Report, App. G; TNA, HS 1/121, John Creer's Report, p. 16.

133 TNA, HS 1/121, John Creer's Report, Operation *Hebrides*, p. 15.

134 TNA, HS 1/121, annotated photograph.

135 IWM, 3328, Papers of P.G.J. Dobrée, p. 55.

136 IWM, 3328, Papers of P.G.J. Dobrée, p. 60; TNA, HS 1/121, John Creer's Report, p. 13.

137 Holman, *The Green Torture*, p. 142.

138 TNA, HS 1/121, Major J.P. Clifford, *Hebrides Minerva* Operational Report, p. 3.

139 Chrystal into Grik: Holman, *The Green Torture*, p. 178; Creer to Kota Bharu: TNA, HS 1/121, John Creer's Report, p. 18. Gough, *The Jungle Was Red*, p. 164, claims that '170 KMT guerrillas' had 'plundered the town'. This is not at all the account given by Creer who, with Major Bromley-Davenport, controlled the town with a mixed force of OCAJA and AMS. He states that the OCAJA made a few arrests and beat up 'one or two' people, 'but not badly' (p. 20), but that otherwise, there were no disturbances. Bromley-Davenport considered that the OCAJA had behaved with 'restraint' (TNA, HS 1/121, Major A.R. Bromley-Davenport, *Hebrides Venus* Operational Report, p. 4).

140 TNA, HS 1/121, John Creer's Report, p. 18.

141 TNA, HS 1/121, Copy letter, 'Kelantan, 18th October, 1945'.

142 Holman, *The Green Torture*, pp. 149 and 184.

143 IWM, 3328, Papers of P.G.J. Dobrée, p. 29.

144 TNA, HS 1/121, Capt. C.L. Gabb, *Hebrides* Operational Report, pp. 1–2. Tai Man had in fact been an estate contractor, known to Chrystal from before the war (Holman, *The Green Torture*, p. 176). He and Hong Chee eventually surrendered in April the following year: *Straits Times*, 18 June 1946, p. 3 and WO 203/2585, 'Emergency Ops', 25 and 27 April.

145 TNA, CO 537/1581, HQ Malaya Command Weekly Intelligence Summary No. 18, 2 March 1946, p. 4.

146 IWM, 3328, Papers of P.G.J. Dobrée, p. 64.

147 TNA, HS 1/107, Lt. Col. I. Wylie, GLO's Operational Report, *Funnel*, p. 2.

148 TNA, HS 1/121, Capt. J.P.M. Clifford's *Hebrides* Operational Report, App. F. Confusingly, this App. F, like most of those in the files, is headed 'MPAJA Personalities'. However, it names OCAJA leaders.

149 TNA, HS 1/121, 'Copy of Signal No. 83', 18 August 1945.

150 TNA, HS 1/107, Major R.N. Broome, Report on *Gustavus*, p. 13.

151   TNA, HS 1/123, Lt. Col. J.D. Richardson, *Beacon* GLO's Operational Report, p. 2.

152   Richardson, *Kiwi's Diary*, p. 19; Chin Peng, *My Side of History*, p. 110. Allegations of the abduction of women have also been made against the MPAJA: TNA, CO 537/1581, App. B to Weekly Intelligence Review, 31 May 1946, Ho Thean Fook, *Tainted Glory*, pp. 143 and 147 and Mahani Musa, 'Women in the Malayan Communist Party, 1942–1989, *Journal of South East Asian Studies*, 44, 2 (2013), pp. 226–49. Similar behaviour is also alleged during the Malayan Emergency: IWM, 20349, Papers of J.M. Miller, p. 5.

153   TNA, HS 1/123, Major G.R. Leonard, *Pontoon* GLO's Operational Report, p. 6. Leonard was somewhat sceptical about what Lau Mah had to tell him: 'Hearing only the PULAI [MPAJA] side of the story, I gathered that they [the 'bandits'] were terrible people, who cut out and ate raw the hearts and livers of any peace-seeking envoy sent to them by WANG LIT's guerrillas.' Lau Mah, as noted previously, was the Deputy State Secretary of the Perak MCP.

154   Chin Peng, *My Side of History*, p. 109.

155   TNA, HS 1/114, 'Brief for Head of P Division', 13 July 1945, p. 5.

156   *Straits Times*, 18 June 1946, p. 3 and *Singapore Free Press*, 25 June 1946, p. 3.

157   *Straits Times*, 15 April 1948, p. 4.

158   *Straits Times*, 12 April 1948, p. 4 and *Straits Times*, 22 April 1949, p. 5.

159   Yuen Yuet Leng, *Nation before Self*, p. 27. Dato Seri Yuen Yuet Leng served for many years in senior roles in the Malaysian police, including as Chief Police Officer of Perak and, at retirement, was the Sarawak Commissioner of Police.

160   Dato Seri Yuen Yuet Leng, Interview, Ampang, Malaysia, September 2015.

161   Chin Peng, *My Side of History*, p. 264. These Guomindang attacked and scattered a recently trained Malay unit of the Malayan National Liberation Army (MNLA) in 1949 or 1950, ending any hopes the MNLA had nurtured of attracting broad-based Malay support.

162   Chin Peng, *My Side of History*, pp. 109 and 11. It is also relevant to note that he fails to mention the two Malay resistance groups which operated towards the end of the war

163   Phillip Deery, 'The Terminology of Terrorism: Malaya, 1948–52', *Journal of Southeast Asian Studies*, 34, 2 (2003), pp. 231–47.

164   Chin Peng, *My Side of History*, p. 109.

165   *Straits Times*, 31 July 1962, p. 9.

166   The resistance of unarmed civilians – the propaganda network of the policeman Gurchan Singh (which reached from Penang to Singapore via a multi-ethnic network of agents), the Chinese and Eurasian families who concealed Gurkha and Anglo-Indian evaders – has been similarly ignored. For more on this, see Rebecca Kenneison, 'The Lion of Malaya': *Insights into Civilian Resistance* <http://www.warinasia.com/rebecca-kenneison/> [accessed 20 February 2019].

167   Chin Peng, *My Side of History*, p. 133.

168   TNA, HS 1/121, John Creer's Report, pp. 6, 8 and 13; TNA, HS 1/121, Chrystal's Report, p. 3.

Chapter 6

1   The quote is from Chin Peng, *My Side of History*, p. 123.

2   TNA, HS 1/123, Gazali [Ghazalie bin Shafie], 'Japanese Device to Foster Enmity between the Chinese and the Malays in Pahang Nipped in the Bud', p. 1.

3 TNA, HS 1/109, F. Spencer Chapman, Report A, p. 15. This is supported by Chin Peng, *My Side of History*, p. 14, and Reg Lawther, unpublished memoir, p. 18, who both record the use of Mandarin by the MPAJA.

4 Donnison, *British Military Administration in the Far East*, p. 155. The return of the British was slowed by a number of factors, including the pre-planned timing of Operation *Zipper*, and General McArthur's insistence that the main surrender be signed with Japan before landings were made elsewhere. According to Mountbatten's diary, British forces had been ready to reoccupy Penang on 22 August, but had been held back on MacArthur's orders (Ziegler, *Personal Diary of Louis Mountbatten*, p. 238). Lack of transport also slowed the arrival of troops to areas distant from the landing beaches.

5 Bayly and Harper, *Forgotten Wars*, pp. 42–4, 108–9 and 202–9; Ban Kah Choon and Yap Hong Kuan, *Rehearsal for War*, 169–70; Cheah Boon Kheng, *Red Star over Malaya*, pp. 195–240; Kratoska, *The Japanese Occupation of Malaya*, pp. 302–3; John Springhall, 'Mountbatten versus the Generals: British Military Rule of Singapore, 1945–46', *Journal of Contemporary History*, 36, 4 (2001), pp. 635–52.

6 Bayly and Harper, *Forgotten Wars*, pp. 213–14; Cheah Boon Kheng, *Red Star over Malaya*, p. 240; Kratoska, *The Japanese Occupation of Malaya*, pp. 303–4.

7 TNA, CO 537/3757, H.T. Pagden, 'Unrest in Malaya' (undated), para. 72.

8 TNA, HS 1/123, Major G.R. Leonard, Operation *Pontoon*, GLO Operational Report, pp. 14–15.

9 J.M. Gullick, 'Recollections of My Time in Malaya (1945–56), Pt. 1', *Journal of the Malaysian Branch of the Royal Asiatic Society*, 86, 2 (2013), pp. 59–76.

10 R.W. Holder, *Eleven Months in Malaya: September 1945 to August 1946* (Singapore: Editions Didier Millet, 2005), p. 71.

11 Bayly and Harper, *Forgotten Wars*, pp. 101–9; Kratoska, *The Japanese Occupation of Malaya*, pp. 339–46; TNA, CO 537/3757, H.T. Pagden, 'Unrest in Malaya' (undated), para. 73

12 Bayly and Harper, *Forgotten Wars*, pp. 197–209; Springhall, 'Mountbatten versus the Generals, pp. 635–52. Harper seems to confine the 'Malayan Spring' to late 1945 and early 1946, though, in Han Suyin's original coinage, the period extends to the outbreak of the Emergency.

13 Springhall, 'Mountbatten versus the Generals', pp. 637–8.

14 Bayly and Harper, *Forgotten Wars*, p. 204.

15 Cheah Boon Kheng, *Red Star over Malaya*, pp. 261, 263 and 299–300.

16 Ban Kah Choon and Yap Hong Kuan, *Rehearsal for War*, pp. 170–1.

17 Cheah Boon Kheng, *Red Star over Malaya*, p. 259.

18 The clandestine bodies were aware that arms containers had gone astray. Though perhaps writing with the wisdom of hindsight, Boris Hembry (of ISLD) relates in his memoir that he discussed with Force 136's Innes Tremlett and Claude Fenner their concerns over missing containers. (Hembry, *Malayan Spymaster*, p. 265.) This topic will be revisited later in this chapter.

19 Cheah Boon Kheng, *Red Star over Malaya*, p. 136.

20 Bayly and Harper, *Forgotten Wars*, p. 40.

21 Cheah Boon Kheng referred to the Force 136 files held at ANM and Harper cited a small number of the recently released papers at TNA.

22 TNA, HS 1/119, Major I.A. McDonald, *Galvanic Brown* Operational Report, pp. 4 and 6; IWM, 10035, Papers of I.A. McDonald (includes a contemporary report by the

clerk, Sinnadurai, and what appears to be an operational diary of September 1945);
George Hess'e, email, 4 October 2009.

23 TNA, HS 1/107, Major A.P. Grant, *Funnel Orange* Operational Report, p. 2 and Major
I.D. Ross, *Funnel Blue* Operational Report, p. 2.

24 Family information, courtesy of Ann and John Evans. Gorbex went on to act as an
interpreter and to work with the army's Field Security and War Crimes teams, as well
as assisting in the repatriation of Indian POWs (*Straits Times*, 5 February 1949, p. 11).
Gorbex and his immediate family had been involved in the propaganda network run
by the policeman Gurchan Singh: see Singh, *Singha*, pp. 64 and 170.

25 For example, Richardson, *Kiwi's Diary*, mentions them repeatedly – in almost every
entry for the first few months, and frequently thereafter. The Operation *Funnel* reports
also mention them regularly.

26 Lau Mah is mentioned by, among others, Douglas Richardson of Operation *Beacon*
(TNA, HS 1/123), John Creer (with the OCAJA in Kelantan: TNA, HS 1/121), David
Alexander of *Funnel Brown* and A.P. Grant of *Funnel Orange* (both TNA, HS 1/107).
For his position in the MCP, see Chin and Hack, *Dialogues*, p. 149.

27 Chin Peng, *My Side of History*, p. 121. Before Chin Peng stated that the move back
from rebellion had been Lai Teck's decision, there had been much scholarly discussion
of the reasons why the MPAJA might have pursued this course of action. According
to Lee Tong Foon, writing in 1977, Gene Z. Hanrahan's argument was that the MPAJA
was let down by feeble and vacillating leadership, which missed the chance to take
the opportunity that presented itself. Lee Tong Foon challenged this argument,
claiming instead that the MPAJA, after a wise assessment of its capacities, opted to
pull back from violence to mobilize its mass base and accomplish its ends by peaceful
means. (Lee Tong Foong, 'The MPAJA and the Revolutionary Struggle, 1939–45' in
Malaya: The Making of a Neo-Colony, ed. Mohamed Amin and Malcolm Caldwell
(Nottingham: Spokesman Books, 1977), pp. 109–11).

28 Esler Dening quoted in Bayly and Harper, *Forgotten Wars*, p. 37.

29 Chin Peng, *My Side of History*, p. 123.

30 TNA, HS 7/165, 'Record of Conference' [Blantan Agreement].

31 Standstill order: Cheah Boon Kheng, *Red Star over Malaya*, pp. 150 and 161. That
Force 136 received the standstill order is implied in many reports, and very clear in
TNA, HS 1/122, Major F.A. Olsen, *Humour Green* Operational Report, p. 1. Inevitably,
due to the fallibility of wireless communications, not all the Force 136 teams received
the order. Dobrée of *Hebrides* heard of the surrender but then his only radio operator
went sick, so he took a mixed party of AMS and OCAJA guerrillas into the nearby
town of Grik a few days later.

32 Cheah Boon Kheng, *Red Star over Malaya*, p. 151.

33 Chin Peng, *My Side of History*, p. 123.

34 Chin Peng, *My Side of History*, pp. 119 and 123.

35 Chin Peng, *My Side of History*, p. 124. Chin Peng relates that two of his colleagues
went to discuss terms with the Japanese in Johore, Negri Sembilan and Kedah, and at
their HQ in Taiping in Perak.

36 Chin Peng, *My Side of History*, p. 118.

37 Chin Peng, *My Side of History*, p. 118.

38 TNA, HS 1/107, Major Grant, *Funnel Orange* Operational Report, p. 2. Ringlet is
in Pahang, but on the border of Perak, and came under the 5th Regiment. Some
Danes and other 'neutrals' lived at liberty throughout the Japanese occupation;
others ended in the war at the 'agricultural settlement' of Bahau in Negri Sembilan,

which functioned more as an internment camp. See Fiona Hodgkins, *From Syonan to Fuji-Go: The Story of the Catholic Settlement of Bahau in WWII Malaya* (Singapore: Select Publishing, 2014), especially pp. 171–2. Rasmussen seems to have been one of a group of Danes who served in the Johore Volunteer Force and went to the Danish consulate at the surrender of Singapore. After about six months, they moved to Cameron Highlands and cleared a farm in the jungle, where they remained for the rest of the occupation (*West Australian* (Perth), 17 November 1945, p. 4, <https://trove.nla.gov.au> [accessed 13 March 2018], with thanks to Jonathan Moffatt).

39 On 21 August 1945, Yeop Mahidin claimed that the MPAJA had held up a lorry full of arms, and that on the same day MPAJA representatives had attended a meeting with the Japanese, asking for arms and ammunition; Richardson of *Beacon* was concerned enough to instruct the Japanese not to let any of their arms reach 'AJUF' (TNA, HS 1/123, *Beacon* Operational Report, letters dated 21 and 23 August, 1945, pp. 36, 39 and 42).

40 ANM, 1957/054990, Reports dated 17 September and 20 September.

41 Several reports stated that police arms had been taken in Trengganu (ANM, 1957/054990, Field Intelligence, 17 September 1945) and in east Pahang, from whence the leaders of the 7th Regiment were brought to Kuala Lumpur for consultations with Chin Peng (TNA, HS 1/120, F. Spencer Chapman, 'Report on AJUF' (Kuantan), p. 6). The Field Intelligence summaries also reported that 400 police arms had been taken in Upper Perak, though the exact location is not given and the thieves are not identified (ANM, 1957/054990, Summary of 15 September).

42 TNA, HS 1/121, John Creer's Report, p. 19.

43 Chin Peng, *My Side of History*, p. 118.

44 TNA, HS 7/165, 'Weapons issued to and recovered from the field in Malaya'; all the numbers for arms issued and surrendered, unless otherwise specified, have been drawn from this source. The percentage calculations are my own.

45 As close a check as possible was kept on weapons issued. The Foss Papers include a nominal roll; next to each name is a note of the type and serial number of the weapon the man was issued: '220240 Ah Lim STN [Sten] 28888' is a typical entry.

46 The totals were calculated from the copies of 'Appendix G', usually filed with the GLO's operational reports (a total of c. 3,100). However, there was no Appendix G for Operation *Gustavus*, which trained no guerrillas but did have a bodyguard and did arrive equipped with arms. In addition, some arms were noted as lost to the Japanese (sixty). The figures have been adjusted accordingly, with an educated guess being made for those instances where there is no Appendix G (*Gustavus*, c. 20). My figures give a deficiency of around 1,560 arms; the consolidated return gives a deficiency of 1,200. The only feasible explanation for this appears to be that the personal weapons of the Force 136 operatives were included in the infiltrated arms, but were not, reasonably enough, included on the disbandment returns. This would allow for a main weapon for every man infiltrated by SOE, plus side arms for most of the officers.

47 See, for example, TNA, HS 1/107, Major A.P. Grant, *Funnel Orange* Operational Report, p. 5; TNA, HS 1/117, Major T.A. Wight, *Sergeant Orange* Operational Report, p. 1; Gough, *The Jungle Was Red*, pp. 102–3. In addition, Major D.E. Trevaldwyn, *Carpenter Blue* Operational Report, p. 2 (TNA, HS 1/107), stated that MPAJA told him that the Japanese had raided an arms dump; the MPAJA source was regarded as being 'bad hat' (TNA, HS 1/107, Major D. Sime, *Carpenter* GLO Operational Report, p. 8) and thus his claim was regarded as suspect. Further, George Brownie of ISLD

stated in a later interview that, when counting the containers after a drop, 'there was always one missing and that one, you could be sure, had arms and ammunition' (IWM, Sound.11253, G.P. Brownie, Interview).

48 Chin Peng, *My Side of History*, p. 117.

49 Moggie, 'Notes of Interview with Reg Lawther' (2016).

50 Ho Thean Fook, *Tainted Glory*, p. 255. That the bonus total was $350 is confirmed by ANM, 1957/0341852, Derek Headly to Chief Secretary, BMA, 6 April 1946.

51 However, for many types of weapon, the sample sizes are small and thus prone to random fluctuation.

52 The silenced pistols were issued to the OCAJA, and all of them were recovered.

53 As an indication of the relative firepower of different weapons, under British law the licensing conditions for rifles are far more stringent than those for shotguns.

54 Reg Lawther, unpublished memoir, p. 22. Of the Lee Enfield .303, Chin Peng said, 'We had plenty of .303 rifles which, for men of our stature, were really too long and too heavy' (*My Side of History*, p. 73). Shotguns tend to be somewhat shorter than a Lee Enfield, but weigh around the same.

55 Moggie, 'Notes of Interview with Reg Lawther' (2016).

56 Leroy Thompson, *The Sten Gun* (Oxford: Osprey, 2010), p. 57. A loaded M1 Carbine weighed 6lb, and a loaded Sten Mk. II 8lb, compared to a Lee Enfield's 9lb and a Tommy gun's 11lb. At close range, the Sten had considerably more firepower than a Lee Enfield.

57 On the downside, it tended to jam and to fire when dropped. See Thompson, *The Sten Gun*, pp. 6, 12, 15, 49, 58 and 76. It was not a comely weapon, being described by one member of the Home Guard as looking as if its breeding was 'by Woolworth out of Scrap Heap' (Thompson, *The Sten Gun*, p. 31).

58 Chin Peng, *My Side of History*, p. 73.

59 See, for example, *Straits Times*, 5 June 1948, p. 1; 12 June 1948, p. 1; 15 June 1948, p. 1; 16 June 1948, p. 1; 17 June 1948, p. 1 and so on, on an almost daily basis.

60 Colin Smith, *Singapore Burning: Heroism and Surrender in World War II* (London: Viking, 2005), p. 301; Ian Skennerton, *British Small Arms of World War II: The Complete Reference Guide to Weapons, Maker's Codes and 1936–1946 Contracts* (Margate, Australia: Self-published, 1988), p. 34.

61 Chin Peng, *My Side of History*, p. 118.

62 *Straits Times*, 3 March 1947, p. 5 and 29 October 1947, p. 5. Pistols were excluded from this calculation, as their origins could not be judged. Another large dump was reported in the press on 13 August 1947, but it consisted entirely of ammunition and explosives, stored deep in a cave complex.

63 At least two former Force 136 liaison officers were killed: Fred Harrison (1949) and Tom Wight (1951). See Moffatt and Riches, *In Oriente Primus*, pp. 157 and 348.

64 Chin Peng, *My Side of History,* p. 184. He explains that half of this money went missing with Lai Teck, and the other was wasted on the unwise investments of local parties. The value is given in Malayan ('Straits') dollars.

65 TNA, HS 1/107, Major C.L.D. Newell, *Carpenter Brown* Operational Report, p. 3 (PWD stores at Batu Pahat, Johore), p. 7 (rubber, Rengam Estate, Johore; TNA, HS 1/123, Lt. Col. J.D. Richardson, *Beacon* Operational Report, Singa to Kiwi, 21 August 1945, p. 37 (lorries and petrol in Pahang; vehicles in Kuala Lumpur), and p. 47 (900 piculs – 53.5 tons – of rice at Jerantut); TNA, HS 1/118, Major G.C. Wilkinson, *Tideway Orange* Operational Report No. 1, p. 3 (rubber, office furniture, typewriters and lorries); TNA, HS 1/107, Major H.H. Wright, *Carpenter Slate* Operational

Report, pp. 7–8 (rice, Johore). TNA, HS 1/122, Major B.G. Phillips, *Humour Brown* Operational Report, p. 3 (rubber, Negri Sembilan; the MPAJA here also had access to lorries, though their source is not given nor even hinted at by the PLO); TNA, HS 1/107, Major A.P. Grant, *Funnel Orange* Operational Report, p. 4 (at tin mines, Perak: the PLO does not directly accuse the MPAJA of taking part, but he is critical of their dilatory attempts to stop the looting).

66 Food was scarce in Malaya during the Japanese occupation and into 1946. The BMA's rice allocation was cut several times, and there was an international rice shortage in 1946. Not until mid-1946, when it began opening cost-price restaurants, did the administration begin to devise new methods of tackling the food shortage. The restaurant scheme was hugely successful, and may have been a factor in helping Singapore and Malaya avoid outright famine. See Ho Chee Tim, 'Communal Feeding in Post-War Singapore', *Biblio-Asia*, 9, 3 (2013), pp. 2–9.

67 TNA, HS 1/107, Major C.L.D. Newell, *Carpenter Brown* Operational Report, p. 6.

68 Chin Peng, *My Side of History*, p. 130.

69 The close links between former members of the MPAJU (referred to by Ho Thean Fook as the Min Yuen) and the 'peace committee' running the small town of Papan are clear in Ho Thean Fook, *Tainted Glory*, pp. 241–2. The evidence that these committees wielded considerable power in Malaya's small towns can be found in, for example, TNA, HS 1/107, Major C.L.D. Newell, *Carpenter Brown* Operational Report, p. 4 and ANM, 1957/054990 Force 136 Field Intelligence, 21 September 1945.

70 Bayly and Harper, *Forgotten Wars*, p. 39.

71 TNA, HS 1/120, F. Spencer Chapman, 'Report on AJUF'.

72 Singapore: TNA, HS 1/107, Lt. Col. I.S. Wylie, Operation *Carpenter* GLO Operational Report, p. 2; Kuala Lumpur: TNA, HS 1/119, Major A.J. Hunter, *Galvanic Blue* Operational Report, pp. 5–6.

73 TNA, HS 1/107, Major A.P. Grant, *Funnel Orange* Operational Report, p. 2.

74 TNA, HS 1/107, Major A.P. Grant, *Funnel Orange* Operational Report, pp. 2 and 3.

75 Ho Thean Fook, *Tainted Glory*, p. 239; TNA, HS 1/107, Major D.R.W. Alexander, Operation *Sergeant*, App. F to GLO Operational Report.

76 Cheah Boon Kheng, *Red Star over Malaya*, p. 151.

77 TNA, HS 1/118, Major G.C. Wilkinson, *Tideway Orange* Operational Report, pp. 2–4; TNA, HS 1/118, Major A.P. Grant, *Funnel Orange* Operational Report, p. 3.

78 TNA, HS 1/107, Major A.P. Grant, *Funnel Orange* MPAJA Report, App. F.

79 TNA, HS 1/107, Major C.L.D. Newell, *Carpenter Brown* Operational Report, p. 5 and Major H.H. Wright, *Carpenter Slate* Operational Report, pp. 7–8.

80 TNA, HS 1/120, Spencer Chapman, 'Report on AJUF', p. 7.

81 TNA, HS 1/123, Lt. Col. J.D. Richardson, *Beacon* Operational Report, p. 38, Singa to Kiwi, 21 August 1945 (these policemen had all been disarmed by the Japanese and their deaths were seen as 'cold blooded murder'); TNA, HS 1/118, Capt. G.E.A. Whyte, *Tideway Orange* Operational Report, p. 1.

82 TNA, HS 1/121, Major G.A. Hasler, *Fighter* Operational Report, p. 9; FCO 141/7344, Record Sheet, Che Sah bin Hamid.

83 Shennan, *Our Man in Malaya*, p. 87; Tan Chong Tee, *Force 136*, p. 102. Davis's papers at the IWM also mention a Dang Sing Huat, who was also exfiltrated, trained, and brought back to Malaya. He seems to have vanished at the end of 1944. It is possible he is the same man as Cheng, and that one or other name was an alias, but equally he may have been a different person. (IWM, Documents.16593, Davis Papers, Box 4,

File 'Recommendations and Applications', letter Labour Office, Bentong, to Officer in Charge, CID, Ipoh, 11 December, year illegible).

84 TNA, HS 1/123, John Creer's Report, p. 8.

85 Ho Thean Fook, *Tainted Glory*, pp. 38–41 and 240.

86 FAC 'Jock' Oehlers, *That's How It Goes: Autobiography of a Singapore Eurasian* (Singapore: Select Publishing, 2008), pp. 107 and 159–60; Kenneison, *Playing for Malaya*, pp. 159–60.

87 ANM, 1957/054990, Field Intelligence Summary, 14 September.

88 A biography covering the experiences of a British soldier stranded in Johore, who spent a lot of time with the MPAJA, states that a Chinese who had helped him said of the MPAJA, as early as May 1945, 'Saya banyat takut dia' ('I fear them very much'): Robert Hammond, *A Fearful Freedom* (London: Leo Cooper, 1984), p. 159.

89 Cheah Boon Kheng, *Red Star over Malaya*, p. 295.

90 Exact numbers and proportions for the ethnic mix of the Malayan Police at the war's end are hard to come by, but Ian McDonald, PLO of *Galvanic Brown*, noted that when he and a small party of his patrol stopped a riot in Kajang, where the citizenry was attempting to storm the police station, he found that the policemen present consisted of '10 Sikhs, 2 Indians and 53 Malays'; there had been some Chinese police, but one had been taken by the crowd and 'a good many more had fled': TNA, HS 1/119, Major I.A. McDonald, *Galvanic Brown* Operational Report, p. 6.

91 Cheah Boon Kheng, *Red Star over Malaya*, p. 184, quoting Haji Buyong Adil, *Sejarah Johor* [History of Johor], Kuala Lumpur, 1971, p. 324. Modern memory: for example, Tun Mohammed Hanif Omar, Interview, Kuala Lumpur, September 2015. Tun Hanif, formerly the Inspector-General of Police, recounted how, as a young boy, he was warned not to reveal the whereabouts of some family members to the MPAJA, and how Telok Anson, where he lived, came under the control of 'the Chinese' who practised what the Tun described as 'the domination of the Malays'; Dato Syed Ahmad Idid, in 'My Father' (unpublished) relates how he saw his father dragged out of his office by MPAJA members soon after the end of the war and beaten in the street, before being rescued by his colleagues.

92 Cheah Boon Kheng, *Red Star over Malaya*, pp. 295 and 297.

93 Gullick, 'Recollections of My Time in Malaya (1945–56), Pt. 1', pp. 59–76.

94 Cheah Boon Kheng mentions that the Japanese may have a role here, but only when discussing the MPAJA's explanation for the outbreak of ethnic violence in Johore in mid-1945 (*Red Star over Malaya*, p. 217). The Malay version of events, which he also provides, does not mention the Japanese as an aggravating factor; according to the Japanese version of events, troops only intervened to defend the Malays (pp. 213–14).

95 Dato Sir Mahmud bin Mat, *Tinggal Kenangan: the Memoirs of Dato' Sir Mahmud bin Mat* (Ampang, Malaysia: Dewan Bahasa dan Pustaka, 1997), pp. 269–71 (the Dato was a member of the sultan's party); TNA, HS 1/123, Major G.R. Leonard, *Pontoon* GLO Operational Report, pp. 12–13; Gough, *The Jungle Was Red*, p. 163.

96 Mahmud bin Mat, *Tinggal Kenangan*, pp. 271–89. The OSS (American Office of Strategic Services) officer told the party that he had been advised that the Japanese were detaining important people (p. 271).

97 Wan Mansoor Abdullah, 'Ghazali the Civil Servant' in *King Ghaz: A Man of his Time,* ed. Rais Yatim and Prabhakaran S. Nair (Kuala Lumpur: National Archives of Malaysia, 2010), pp. 85–7.

98 TNA, HS 1/123, Gazali [Ghazalie bin Shafie], 'Japanese Device to Foster Enmity between the Chinese and the Malays in Pahang Nipped in the Bud', p. 2.

99 Dobrée, *Hot Rain Means Danger*, pp. 60–1 and 63.

100 Robert Chrystal, quoted in Holman, *Green Torture*, p. 182

101 TNA, HS 1/121, John Creer's Report, p. 18. The communists to whom Creer refers were those at Kuala Krai, who had obtained police arms from the Japanese. The OSS officer was probably a member of the missing American operation, *Cairngorm*.

102 Richardson, *Kiwi's Diary*, p. 82. The version of events in Gough, *The Jungle Was Red*, states that the MPAJA took over Raub before Wataniah moved in, but neither Richardson in his report nor Yeop (who was in Raub until 28 August and writing regularly to Richardson) provides any backing for this claim. Indeed, Richardson was more concerned that a Pahang state flag and a Union Jack be ready for when he and Yeop arrived in town by raft (TNA, HS 1/123, Lt. Col. J.D. Richardson, *Beacon Operational Report*, Kiwi to Singa, 26 August 1945, p. 45).

103 TNA, HS 1/119, Major J.A. Hunter, *Galvanic Blue* Operational Report, pp. 4–5.

104 TNA, HS 1/119, Major I.A. McDonald, *Galvanic Brown* Operational Report, pp. 8–10. The bandits were members of the Green Dragon Mountain Society, named later in the press as an ongoing problem (*Straits Times*, 20 July 1947, p. 6). On p. 10 of his operational report, McDonald records that the patrol guarded 440 tons of rubber worth $0.38/lb. The dollar denomination used is the pre-war Malayan or 'Straits' dollar.

105 All reports, TNA, HS 1/107: Major A.P. Grant, *Funnel Orange* Operational Report, p. 3; Major I.D. Ross, *Funnel Blue* Operational Report, p. 2; Major S.F. Owen (*Funnel Green*) had very few negative comments to make about the patrol to which he was attached.

106 TNA, HS 1/123, Major G.R. Leonard, *Pontoon* GLO's Operational Report, p. 10.

107 TNA, HS 1/117, Major J.A. Hislop, *Sergeant* GLO's Operational Report. Hislop's distrust is typified by comments such as 'CHEN LO [the leader] was reported sick but he was stated to be in Kroh by the messenger' and 'The D.O. [District Officer] was kidnapped – knowledge of this being denied by AH YANG and CHEN LO' – the implication being that, in Hislop's view, Ah Yang and Chen Lo cannot have failed to have known all about this incident.

108 TNA, HS 1/117, Lt. Col. D.R.W. Alexander, *Sergeant* Operational Report, p. 1. The Kedah MPAJA were sufficiently out of contact with MPAJA HQ as to use a different flag (TNA, HS 1/117, Major P. Chassé, *Sergeant Brown* Operational Report, p. 5).

109 Moggie, 'Notes of Interview with Reg Lawther' (2016) (Reg Lawther was an officer with this regiment.); TNA, HS 1/20, Major. J.L. Chapman, Operation *Siphon* GLO Operational Report, p. 1. Major J.L. Chapman is not to be confused with Lt. Col. F. Spencer Chapman, who was also with this operation.

110 TNA, HS 1/120, Major J.L. Chapman, *Siphon* GLO's Operational Report, p. 1.

111 TNA, HS 1/120, Lt. Col. F. Spencer Chapman, 'Report on AJUF', p. 6.

112 There were also two other groups: men with prior experience of SOE elsewhere, and men whose prior experience is not known (there were about seven of them, three or four having been recruited directly from a commando unit). Precision in numbers is surprisingly difficult: it might be expected that thirty-one patrols would result in thirty-one patrol operational reports written by thirty-one officers, but a few men were transferred from one patrol to another and therefore wrote two reports, one up to the date they left their original patrol and one from the date they arrived at their new one; they were often replacing men who were being transferred out of the field,

and were replaced by men who had previously been second-in-command of a patrol. Some men also fell into two categories: the British Malayan Douglas Broadhurst (the *Galvanic* GLO) had prior SOE experience in Asia (in Timor).

113 One of these was Hugh Munro of Operation *Sergeant* (see Operational Roll at TNA, HS 1/108) whose activities in Albania are detailed in Bailey, *The Wildest Province*, pp. 313–315. Munro aided in the escape of several people he felt were at risk from the communists and had one man smuggled aboard the boat which collected him in a specially made box; he then put out to sea, doused his lights and returned to a stretch of marshland to collect a married couple and their child.

114 TNA, HS 1/114, LFS/3266 [Col. L.F. Sheridan] to Edward Gent, 27 August 1945.

115 TNA, HS 1/119, Major I.A. McDonald, *Galvanic Brown* Operational Report, p. 5. The MPAJA cap badge consisted of three stars, symbolizing Malaya's three largest ethnic communities.

116 TNA, HS 1/122, Lt. Col. C.H. Fenner, *Humour* Operational Report, pp. 5–6.

117 TNA, HS 1/115, Progress Report No. 9, 31 July 1945.

118 TNA, HS 1/123, Major G.R. Leonard, Operation *Pontoon* GLO Operational Report, pp. 14–15 and 16. He added primly that this was 'language which myself and my party were not in the habit of using'.

119 TNA, HS 1/123, Major G.R. Leonard, Operation *Pontoon* GLO Operational Report, p. 17 and Report on Disbandment, p. 2.

120 TNA, HS 1/117, Lt. Col. D.R.W. Alexander, *Sergeant* GLO Operational Report, p. 1. Alexander was promoted from the rank of major upon transfer from Operation *Funnel*. Lim Hong Pei, a Chinese member of the *Sergeant* team, stated in a later interview that, during the Japanese occupation itself, the team had a good relationship with the local MPAJA: *Interview, Lim Hong Pei* (Penang, Malaysia, 1991), pp. 15–16.

121 TNA, HS 1/119, Lt. Col. D.K. Broadhurst, Operation *Galvanic* GLO Operational Report, p. 1.

122 For example, TNA, HS 1/107, Major D.R.W. Alexander, *Funnel Brown* MPAJA Report (App. F), recorded that 'Lo Mah' (Lau Mah) 'gave me nearly as much trouble as Itu'; TNA, HS 1/122, Lt. Col. C.H. Fenner, *Humour* MPAJA Report (App. F).

123 TNA, HS 1/107, Lt. Col. J.L.H. Davis, *Gustavus* Operational Report, p. 7.

124 TNA, HS 1/117, Major H.A.C. Munro, *Sergeant Brown* Operational Report, pp. 3–4.

125 TNA, HS 1/107, Major H.H. Wright, *Carpenter Slate* Operational Report, p. 9.

126 TNA, HS 1/117, Major H.A.C. Munro, *Sergeant Brown* Operational Report, pp. 2 and 3; TNA, HS 1/107, Major H.H. Wright, *Carpenter Slate* Operational Report, pp. 5 and 8.

127 TNA, HS 1/107, Major C.L.D. Newell, *Carpenter Brown* Operational Report, p. 4.

128 TNA, HS 1/107, Major D.E. Trevaldwyn, *Carpenter Blue* Operational Report, pp. 1–3.

129 TNA, HS 1/107, Major N.G. Reddish, *Carpenter Orange* Operational Report.

130 TNA, HS 1/107, Major D. Sime, *Carpenter* Personnel Reports. It is perhaps worth noting that this 'bias' was shared by at least one of the NCOs, Eric Child, who had previously served with the non-communist resistance in Greece, and had heard of the activity of the communist forces, whom he did not hesitate to accuse of 'slaughter' and killing 'all the bourgeoisie' (IWM, Sound.12665, Reel 1).

131 TNA, HS 1/119, Major P.T. Thomson-Walker, *Galvanic Orange* Operational Report and TNA, HS 1/107, Major T.A. Wilson, *Funnel Slate* Operational Report.

132 Nigel Clive, *A Greek Experience, 1943–48* (Salisbury: Michael Russell Publishing Ltd., 1985), pp. 84 and 86. In his book, Clive quotes a number of reports that he wrote at the time.

133 W. Stanley Moss, *Ill Met by Moonlight* (London: Cassell, 2014; first published 1950). For example, on p. 68 he states that the communist partisans threatened, if his party continued to pursue their own plans, to betray them to the Germans, and expose all their helpers and contacts.

134 Both men had spent time in communist camps, where they had at times been ill-treated and threatened.

135 TNA, HS 1/121, Capt. R Chrystal, 'Report on O.M. Left-behind Party No. 3 and Force 136 Operation Hebrides', 8th sheet.

136 TNA, HS 1/121, John Creer, 'Report on Venus Party', p. 6; and Capt. R Chrystal, 'Report on O.M. Left-behind Party No. 3 and Force 136 Operation Hebrides', p. 8.

137 TNA, HS 1/121, John Creer, 'Report on Venus Party', pp. 4 and 19.

138 TNA, HS 1/109, Major A.P. Grant, *Funnel Orange* Operational Report, p. 4.

139 TNA, HS 1/117, Capt. H.A.C. Munro, *Sergeant Orange* Operational Report No. 2, p. 3.

140 TNA, CO 537/3757, H.T. Pagden, 'Unrest in Malaya' (undated), para. 29.

141 TNA, CO 537/3751, Minute, 23 June 1948.

142 Han Suyin, Foreword to 'An Anthology of Modern Malaysian Chinese Stories' collected and translated by Ly Singko and Leon Comber (Singapore: Heinemann Educational Books, 1965), p. 11.

143 Bayly and Harper, *Forgotten Wars*, p. 121.

144 Ho Thean Fook, *Tainted Glory*, p. 240.

Chapter 7

1 The quote is from TNA, CO 537/3751, Minute, Rees-Williams to Seel, 11 May 1948.

2 Killings: *Straits Times*, 18 May 1948 and 24 May 1948 and *Malaya Tribune*, 24 May 1948; arson: *Singapore Free Press*, 11 May 1948 and *Straits Times*, 15 May 1948.

3 Cambridge University Library, Papers of Mubin Sheppard, 11084, Pt. II, File 3, 'Police Report, Kim Puay Sawmills at Subang' and 'Statement by Mr Tan Kim Puay in connection with the gun battle at the Kim Puay Sawmills at Subang'.

4 Chin Peng, *My Side of History*, pp. 205–9; Malcolm MacDonald, quoted in *Straits Times*, 8 June 1948, p. 6.

5 Chin Peng, *My Side of History*, p. 207; TNA, CO 537/3752, *Political Intelligence Journal*, 31 May 1948, pp. 384–385.

6 Philip Deery, 'Malaya 1948: Britain's Asian Cold War?', *Journal of Cold War Studies*, 9, 1 (2007), pp. 29–54.

7 For a detailed discussion of this, see Hugh de Santis, *The Diplomacy of Silence: The American Foreign Service, the Soviet Union and the Cold War, 1933–47* (Chicago: University of Chicago Press, 1979).

8 To colonial officials, especially those based in Whitehall, Malaya must have looked, by contrast, like an oasis of comparative calm. Contemporary headlines give a flavour of the times: '15 Die in Holy City Battles' and '1,300 Reported Killed in Attack on Indian Train' (*Straits Times*, 9 January 1948, p. 1, and 15 January 1948, p. 1).

9   Heussler, *Completing a Stewardship*, p. 159.
10 John Coates, *Suppressing Insurgency: An Analysis of the Malayan Emergency, 1948–1954* (Oxford: Westview Press, 1992), p. 35; Short in the introduction to Comber, *Malaya's Secret Police*, p. ix;
11 A.J. Stockwell, 'A Widespread and Long-Concocted Plot to Overthrow Government in Malaya'? The Origins of the Malayan Emergency', *The Journal of Imperial and Commonwealth History*, 21, 3 (September 1993), pp. 66–89.
12 Short in the introduction to Comber, *Malaya's Secret Police*, p. ix; Short, *The Communist Insurrection*, p. 40.
13 Harper, *The End of Empire and the Making of Malaya*, p. 95.
14 Bayly and Harper, *Forgotten Wars*, pp. 416 and 420–5.
15 Harper, *The End of Empire and the Making of Malaya*, p. 147.
16 Chin Peng, *My Side of History*, pp. 202–205; Bayly and Harper, *Forgotten Wars*, p. 416.
17 Hack, 'The Origins of the Asian Cold War', pp. 471–96.
18 This argument was put forward as early as 1954: see Miller, *Menace in Malaya*, p. 77.
19 Springhall, 'Mountbatten versus the Generals', pp. 635–52.
20 Hack, 'The Origins of the Asian Cold War', pp. 471–96, esp. p. 483.
21 See RHL, MSS.Ind.Ocn.s.254 (1) (Dalley Papers), 'Special Conference held under the chairmanship of H.E. the Governor-General, at 10a.m. on Thursday 26th June, 1947… Singapore'. At this event, MacDonald argued that 'British freedom-loving people' would resist the outlawing of the communists and that 'British democratic practice' should not criminalize the genuine idealist.
22 Stockwell, *British Documents on the End of Empire: Malaya Part 1*, p. lvi; Stephen Howe, *Anti-colonialism in British Politics: The Left and the End of Empire, 1918–1964* (Oxford: Clarendon Press, 1993), p. 141.
23 Christopher Andrew, *The Defence of the Realm: The Authorized History of MI5* (London: Penguin, 2010), fn. 45, p. 448. Bayly and Harper, *Forgotten Wars*, p. 247; Andrew, *The Defence of the Realm*, p. 448 (fn. 45); Calder Walton, *Empire of Secrets* (London: Harper Press, 2013), p. 165.
24 Oxford Dictionary of National Biography, <http://www.oxforddnb.com> [accessed 16 June 2016].
25 J.M. Gullick, 'Recollections of My Time in Malaya (1945–56), Pt. 2', *Journal of the Malaysian Branch of the Royal Asiatic Society*, 87, 1 (2014), pp. 53–81; Gullick notes another man, brought out from Britain to oversee measures to improve food supply, failed to comprehend that the issue was the shortage of rice, not other foodstuffs, and managed to antagonize the planters with an edict Gullick considered 'pointless' (p. 81). The shortage of rice was an ongoing problem, and a prompt to labour troubles, up until the Emergency, and the efforts of the administration's 'Grow More Food' campaign were pilloried in the *Straits Times* of 9 June 1947 (p. 4).
26 The brutal thinning of the ranks is discussed with respect to the Sungei Siput district of Perak by Boris Hembry, *Malayan Spymaster*, p. 307. His reliance on a pre-war Asian contact is discussed pre-Emergency on p. 308 (following on from p. 127) and during the Emergency on pp. 315–16. He also had sufficient local knowledge and contacts to establish his own private information network as the Emergency approached (p. 308). A randomly selected sample of fifty men who were commercially employed (planters, miners etc.) and whose wartime fate or post-war residence can be determined indicates that about 40 per cent did not return to Malaya: some were due for retirement and a small number opted not to return, but many died as internees or were killed in action.

27 Kathirithamby-Wells, *Nature and Nation*, p. 235. At least one senior European forester, Colin Symington (Chapter 1), died during the war.

28 See, for example, *Straits Times*, 19 October 1948 and 19 July 47, p. 8.

29 CUL, 11084, Sheppard Papers, D.O. Klang [probably Arthur Ramsay] to M.C.ff. Sheppard, 17 October 1947.

30 TNA, CO 537/3757, H.T. Pagden, 'Unrest in Malaya' (undated), paras. 73–82. Pagden was writing in retrospect, but in great detail, of Asian disaffection, charting the local mood over the course of several years. Contemporary comments about public displeasure with what was seen as the government's 'policy of leniency' towards collaborators may be found on TNA, CO 537/1581, Weekly Intelligence Summary, 9 March 1946, p. 7.

31 *Singapore Free Press*, 13 June 1946.

32 See Chin Peng, *My Side of History*, pp. 164–76. Chin Peng later searched for Lai Teck, only to find that he had been killed by communists in Thailand.

33 Short, *The Communist Insurrection*, p. 40.

34 Comber, *Malaya's Secret Police*, p. 96.

35 Roger Arditti and Philip H.J.Davies, 'Rethinking the Rise and Fall of the Malayan Security Service, 1946–48', *Journal of Imperial and Commonwealth History*, 43, 2 (2015), pp. 292–316, esp. p. 309.

36 TNA, CO 537/1581W.J. Morgan to Bourdillon, 28 March 1946.

37 See, for example, the intelligence summaries for 1946 on CO 537/1582.

38 Strikes were legal in all trades in Malaya post-war, as they had been in the pre-war years (though, from mid-1941, strikes were outlawed in essential war industries).

39 TNA, CO 537/1581, HQ Malaya Command Weekly Intelligence Summary, Week Ending 23 February 1946, p. 12 and App. D.

40 A good account of this is to be found in Richard McMillan, *The British Occupation of Indonesia, 1945–46: Britain, the Netherlands and the Indonesian Revolution* (Abingdon: Routledge, 2006). The Indonesian nationalists accused the British of paving the way for the return of the Dutch, and the Dutch accusing them of doing nothing to contain the nationalists.

41 Arditti and Davies, 'Rethinking the Rise and Fall of the Malayan Security Service, 1946–48', pp. 292–316.

42 Comber, *Malaya's Secret Police*, p. 40.

43 RHL, MSS.Ind.Ocn.s.254, Director MSS [Dalley] to Sir Ralph Hone, 13 July 1948.

44 These had been made by René Onraet, a pre-war Inspector-General of the Straits Settlements Police.

45 Andrew, *The Defence of the Realm*, p. 448.

46 Rory Cormac, *Confronting the Colonies: British Intelligence and Counterinsurgency* (London: C. Hurst and Co., 2013), p. 35 By this stage, of course, as Cormac notes, Dalley had organized Dalforce; in addition, escape attempts were by their nature risky. Moreover, Dalley's escape attempt was under orders, and he left on one of the last official evacuation vessels, the *Mary Rose* (IWM, 4664, Frank Brewer Interview, Reel 1; Richard Gough, *The Escape from Singapore* (London: William Kimber and Co Ltd, 1987), pp. 90 and 218–219). Dalley might have been a difficult (though by no means friendless) eccentric, but the charge of cowardice does not seem to stick.

47 Arditti and Davies, 'Rethinking the Rise and Fall of the Malayan Security Service, 1946–48', pp. 292–316.

48 C.A. Bayly, *Empire and Information: Intelligence Gathering and Social Communication in India, 1780-1870* (Cambridge: Cambridge University Press, 1996), pp. 3–4, fn. 9.

49 Marine Corps Doctrinal Publications 2, *Intelligence*, Washington, 1997, at <http://www.globalsecurity.org/military/library/policy/usmc/mcdp/2/mcdp2_chp1.pdf> [accessed 5 February 2015].

50 For example, Short's statement that with the loss of Lai Teck 'the light at the top of the stairs went out' perhaps unintentionally implies that the MSS was left blundering about in the dark (Short, *The Communist Insurrection*, p. 40).

51 TNA, HS 9/1482/8, untitled obituary, commencing 'His many friends...'.

52 That reassignment was underway before the New Year is evident from the personnel file of Geoffrey Frank of *Tideway* (TNA, HS 9/539/2).

53 Stuart Duncan, "Of Historical Interest Only': The Origins and Vicissitudes of the SOE Archive *Intelligence and National Security*, 20, 1 (March 2005), pp. 14–26.

54 TNA, HS 1/119, Lt. Col. D.K. Broadhurst, Operation *Galvanic* GLO Operational Report, App. F.

55 TNA, HS 1/107, Lt. Col. J.H.L. Davis, *Gustavus* Operational Report, p. 8 (undated; after disbandment in December 1945).

56 Chrystal quoted in Holman, *The Green Torture*, p. 185.

57 These included the 'Who's Who' series on politically prominent Malayans, which focused almost entirely on leading Chinese of all political persuasions.

58 In military intelligence, the letter indicates the reliability of the source and the number indicates the degree to which the information has been confirmed. Thus A1 means that the source is entirely trusted and the information has been confirmed; B3 that the source is fairly reliable and the information is logical, but is not confirmed. F6, the lowest, is from an untested or unreliable source, and unlikely to be true.

59 For a very brief discussion of this, see Bayly and Harper, *Forgotten Wars*, p. 351.

60 For example, comment was made in the *Journal* of 15 February 1948 that an employee of the AMCJA was applying to become an agent of a communist press agency, Telepress (p. 82). One would have needed to have read the *Journal* of 15 January 1948, pp. 21–22 to appreciate that a virtual contract for news and publicity was being considered between Telepress and the London AMCJA representative. See TNA, CO 537/3751.

61 TNA, CO 537/3757, H.T. Pagden, 'Unrest in Malaya' (undated), para. 98; Victor Purcell, *Malaya: Communist or Free?* (London: Victor Gollancz, 1954), p. 54.

62 Chin Peng, *My Side of History*, p. 199.

63 TNA, CO 537/3751, *Political Intelligence Journal* of 15 January 1948, p. 20. One of the men named, Sidney Herbert Cox, was the subject of a 'communist: record file' that is, according to National Archives website, still retained – MEPO 38/65. <http://discovery.nationalarchives.gov.uk/details/r/C10881752> [accessed 21 August 2016].

64 TNA, CO 537/3751, O.H. Morris to Williams, 7 May 1948; Rees-Williams to Seel, 11 May 1948.

65 Chin Peng, *My Side of History*, p. 201.

66 TNA, CO 537/3751, *Political Intelligence Journal*, 29 February 1948, pp. 120–127.

67 TNA, CO 537/3751, Extract, Sir Franklin Gimson to Bourdillon, 7 February 48, Enc. 5.

68 TNA, CO 825/74/3, H.T. Bourdillon to Acheson, 2 April 1948.

69 TNA, CO 537/3751, O.H. Morris to Seel, 25 February 1948.

70 TNA, CO 825/74/3, O.H. Morris to Rees-Williams, 18 June 48. Bourdillon himself had felt that if the authorities in Malaya were to write them, they might only give a narrow view of events (TNA, CO 825/74/3, H.T. Bourdillon to Acheson, 2 April 1948).

71   TNA, CO 825/74/3, Rees-Williams to Seel, 6 July 1948.

72   Brian Stewart, *Smashing Terrorism in the Malayan Emergency: The Vital Contribution of the Police* (Subang Jaya, Malaysia: Pelanduk Publishers, 2004), p. 317.

73   Harper, *Making of Malaya*, p. 146.

74   TNA, CO 825/74/3, Rees-Williams to Seel, 6 July 1948. It appears that the CO was not on the regular circulation list for the SIFE reports.

75   TNA, CO 825/74/3, one of series of extracts from other documents, collated on 9 July 1948. The date of the original from which it is taken is unclear, but the comment within this extract that 'Sir F. Gimson... doubts Col Dalley's judgment' – when Dalley had been proven correct in his anxieties regarding the MCP – might imply that it was written before the Emergency. Gimson, it will be remembered, considered that Dalley focused too closely on the activities of the Malayan communists.

76   TNA, WO 208/3931, Col T.N. Grazebrook to Lt. Col. C.H. Tarver, 7 July 1948. This happened once the MSS 'got into its stride', so was probably during 1947.

77   TNA, WO 208/3931, Col T.N. Grazebrook to Lt. Col. C.H. Tarver, 7 July 1948.

78   Hack, 'The Origins of the Asian Cold War', pp. 471–96.

79   Chin Peng, *My Side of History*, p. 208, states that the MCP leadership planned to meet in August 1948 to hone their plans. This claim is broadly supported by information provided to the senior policeman Yuen Yuet Leng by some former senior MCP cadres, who stated that the insurgency was 'triggered off prematurely' by cadres who, knowing that a rebellion was planned, had become unwilling to tolerate the government's repressive measures and jumped the gun (quoted in Stewart, *Smashing Terrorism in the Malayan Emergency*, p. xxx).

80   TNA, CO 539/2140, Intelligence Summary, 12 March 1947, p. 10; *Straits Times*, 8 May 1941 and 23 March 1947, <http://www.viweb.freehosting.net/talalla-bros.htm> [accessed 13 August 2010], and family information from Richard Talalla. Henry, the eldest son, was shot down and killed over France in July 1944. To 'the King's Chinese' might be added 'the King's Ceylonese': many members of the Sinhalese, Burgher, Chetty and Jaffna Tamil communities regarded themselves, in pre-war Malaya, as loyal subjects of the Empire.

81   *Straits Times*, 24 December 1947, p. 7.

82   *Straits Times*, 6 February 1948, p. 4. Fletcher's had been the scheming mind behind Operation *Remorse*, the smuggling and currency exchange venture which earned SOE £77 million: M.R.D. Foot, *SOE*, pp. 351–2.

83   Of course, there were some men who fell into both categories: a number of Force 136 officers returned to planting after the war.

84   J.P. Hannah, Memoir, p. 179.

85   TNA, CO 537/3757, H.T. Pagden, 'Unrest in Malaya' (undated), App. 7.

86   Shennan, *Our Man in Malaya*, p. 135.

87   Hannah, Memoir, p. 179, punctuated as in original.

88   TNA, CO 537/3757, H.T. Pagden, 'Unrest in Malaya' (undated), App. 4. Pagden gives no information on the background of the officer who told Sime to get out, but his tone suggests that the officer had no prior Malayan experience.

89   Shennan, *Our Man in Malaya*, p. 148.

90   Shennan, *Our Man in Malaya*, pp. 149–50.

91   Moggie, 'Notes of Interview with Reg Lawther' (2016). Reg states that he was never approached.

92   Noel Barber, *War of the Running Dogs* (London: Cassell Military Paperbacks, 2004: first published 1971), pp. 29–30.

93   Hack, 'The Origins of the Asian Cold War', pp. 471–96.

94   Hack, 'The Origins of the Asian Cold War', pp. 471–96.

95   CUL, 11084, Sheppard Papers, D.O. Klang to M.C.ff. Sheppard, 17 October 1947.

96   *Straits Times*, 22 April 1948, p. 6. Two initially sceptical British union men, Stanley Awberry MP, and F.W. Dalley, had visited Malaya and confirmed that this was the case. Chin Peng admits that the MCP had substantial control of many Malayan unions (*My Side of History*, pp. 193 and 244). See also, for example, TNA, CO 537/3752, *Political Intelligence Journal*, 15 June 1948, p. 436. On two estates in Perak, the communists ordered the labourers to leave under threat of 'violence and the destruction of their homes'.

97   Coates, *Suppressing Insurgency*, p. 35.

98   Hannah, in a letter to Davis quoted in Shennan, *Our Man in Malaya*, p. 151.

99   Shennan, *Our Man in Malaya*, p. 152.

100 TNA, CO 537/3757, extract from letter dated 5 June 1948, provided by Pagden.

101 TNA, CO 717/172, 'Delegation to the Secretary of State for the Colonies, Tuesday 22nd June 1948', pp. 3–4. The representative complaining about Gent was H.H. Facer, the vice-president of the United Planting Association of Malaya. None of the other representatives made any move to contradict him, nor even to qualify his comments.

102 See Appendix C for details.

103 Bayly and Harper, *Forgotten Wars*, p. 426; Comber, *Malaya's Secret Police*, p. 36.

104 TNA, CO 637/3752, *Political Intelligence Journal*, 31 May 1948, p. 394 and 15 June 1948, pp. 427 and 429. This is contrary to Yong and McKenna, *The Kuomintang Movement in British Malaya*, p. 217, who imply that the MCP did not begin assassinating Guomindang members until the Emergency had already begun, stating that 'Overt KMT support for the Malayan government during the Malayan Emergency brought MCP retaliation'. This is evidently not the case: MCP action pre-dated this.

105 For detail, see Appendix C.

106 TNA, CO 537/3752, *Political Intelligence Journal*, 31 May 1948, pp. 393, 394, and 396 and 15 June 1948, pp. 427 and 428; *Straits Times*, 8 June 1948, p. 6.

107 In addition, a mine manager was shot dead by an impatient cadre during a failed wages heist, and two Malay officials were killed, perhaps seen as agents of the state though no cause was suggested (TNA, CO 537/3752, *Political Intelligence Journal*, 15 June 1948, p. 428). There were also two other killings for which no cause was given, and another three men were killed by mistake – one probably in error for his Guomindang-member brother, the others collateral damage (TNA, CO 537/3752, *Political Intelligence Journal*, 31 May 1948, p. 394 and 15 June 1948, pp. 420, 428 and 429; *Straits Times*, 9 May 1948, p. 1).

108 Hannah, Memoir, p. 180.

109 TNA, CO 537/3752, *Political Intelligence Journal*, 31 May 1948, pp. 384–5.

110 This is the grading system known as the Admiralty Code.

111 Dato Seri Yuen Yuet Leng, Interview, Ampang, Malaysia, September 2015. He was Chief of Police in Perak in the 1970s, taking over from the former MPAJA guerrilla, Khoo Chong Kong, who had been assassinated.

112 *Straits Times*, 14 June and 15 July 1948.

113 Men who had worked in Malaya with the Inter-Services Liaison Department were also approached, including Colin Park, the son of Air Chief Marshall Sir Keith Park. He was killed in action while serving with Ferret Force (Hembry, *Malayan Spymaster*, p. 335).

114 Shennan, *Our Man in Malaya*, p. 152.
115 TNA, CO 537/3757, H.T. Pagden, 'Unrest in Malaya' (undated), para. 33.
116 *Sunday Tribune*, 29 September 1948, with IWM, 15555, Papers of Major F. Crawford.
     Even before Ferret Force had been suggested, George Leonard (who had led *Pontoon*
     and returned to life as a game warden) and Francis Olsen (of Oriental Mission
     and then a patrol leader with *Humour* who was, by this time, the owner of a small
     sawmill) had been sworn into the police and were going on reconnaissance near
     Bahau (Short, *The Communist Insurrection*, p. 133, fn. 29).
117 *Singapore Free Press*, 6 January 1949, p. 6.
118 Shennan, *Our Man in Malaya*, pp. 135, 149–50; TNA, CO 537/3757, H.T. Pagden,
     'Unrest in Malaya' (undated), App. 7. Liew Yao was killed early in the Emergency,
     and was mourned by Chin Peng as 'undoubtedly one of my best military
     commanders' (*My Side of History*, p. 228).
119 Shennan, *Our Man in Malaya*, p. 148.
120 Harper, *End of Empire and the Making of Malaya*, p. 142.
121 Hack, 'The Origins of the Malayan Cold War: 1948', pp. 471–96 (p. 494).
122 Yakov Ben-Haim, 'Policy Neutrality and Uncertainty: An Info-Gap Perspective',
     Intelligence and National Security, published online 18 December 2015 and available
     at <http://tx.technion.ac.il/~yakov/IGT/pol-neut005.pd> and DOI:10.1080/0268452
     7.2015.1121683.
123 Hack, 'The Origins of the Asian Cold War', pp. 471–96.
124 RHL, MSS.Ind.Ocn.s.254 (1), Dalley Papers, Director MSS [Dalley] to Sir Ralph
     Hone, 13 July 1948.

Appendix B

  1 There appears to have been a typographical error made here. It looks as if the code
     for the Negri Sembilan guerrillas has been omitted, without a corresponding Group
     number being dropped, until Group 4 – which should relate to the 4th Regiment
     in south Johore (SOUJUP, who are given as Group 3). Sometimes in the reports
     ones encounters a guerrilla leader referred to using these codes: COGSELUP, for
     example, was Chau Yeung Pan, the leader ('Chief of Guerrillas' – COG) of the
     Selangor MPAJA.
  2 Chin Peng, *My Side of History*, p. 113.
  3 Spencer Chapman, *The Jungle Is Neutral*, p. 338.

Appendix C

  1 The *Journal* does not note this murder, but the news article claims that the police
     connected the gang who killed the smallholder with a gang who raided a nearby
     estate in an attempt to kill the manager (which the *Journal* did note).
  2 The same page of the *Journal* also records the death of the Chinese manager of the
     Triang Estate on 7 June. It is possible that this was a different man.
  3 TNA, CO 537/3752, *Political Intelligence Journal*, 15 June 1948, p. 427.

SOURCES AND BIBLIOGRAPHY

London: The National Archives (TNA), Kew

CAB 106 – War Cabinet and Cabinet Office: Historical Section: Archivist and Librarian Files

CAB 119 – War Cabinet and Cabinet Office: Joint Planning Staff: Correspondence and Papers

CO 273 – Colonial Office: Straits Settlements Original Correspondence

CO 537 – Colonial Office and Predecessors: Confidential General and Confidential Original Correspondence

CO 539 – Colonial Office and Predecessors: Accounts Branch: Miscellanea

CO 717 – Colonial Office: Federated Malay States: Original Correspondence

CO 825 – Colonial Office: Eastern Original Correspondence

CO 865 – Colonial Office: Far Eastern Reconstruction Original Correspondence

FCO 141 – Foreign and Commonwealth Office and Predecessors: Records of Former Colonial Administrations: Migrated Archives

HS 1 – Special Operations Executive: Far East Registered Files

HS 5 – Special Operations Executive: Balkans: Registered Files

HS 7 – Special Operations Executive: Histories and War Diaries: Registered Files

HS 9 – Special Operations Executive: Personnel Files (PF Series)

WO 32 – War Office and Successors: Registered Files (General Series)

WO 106 – War Office: Directorate of Military Operations and Military Intelligence, and Predecessors: Correspondence and Papers

WO 193 – War Office: Directorate of Military Operations and Plans: Later Directorate of Military Operations: Files Concerning Military Planning, Intelligence and Statistics

WO 203 – War Office: South East Asia Command: Military Headquarters Papers, Second World War

WO 208 – War Office: Directorate of Military Operations and Intelligence

WO 220 – War Office: Directorate of Civil Affairs: Files, Reports and Handbooks

London: Imperial War Museum (IWM)

Private Papers

6626, Reverend L.D. Ashness
14859, Lieutenant Colonel F. Spencer Chapman
15555, Major F. Crawford
16593, Colonel J.L.H. Davis
3328, Major P.G.J. Dobrée
10994, L.M. Godfrey
7896, Major P.S. Leatheart
10035, Major I.A. McDonald
3455, Major W.P.S. Brereton Martin
20349, J.M. Miller
13346, A.D.C. Peterson
653, Lieutenant H.R. Ross
1049, R.F. Scott

Interviews

11752, Bailey, Frederick Arthur
4664, Brewer, Frank
11253, Brownie, George Primrose
12665, Child, Eric
12785, Chinfen, Lloyd Beresford
8726, Davis, John Lewis Haycraft
13172, Ellis, John William
12311, Holdham, Alfred Edwin
8641, Landes, Roger
9471, Mackenzie, Colin Hercules
10192, Thompson, Robert Grainger Ker
8476, Yeop Mahadin [sic]

Cambridge: Cambridge University Library (CUL)

11084, Sheppard Papers

Oxford: Rhodes House (RHL)

MSS.Ind.Ocn.s.215, W.C.S. Corry
MSS.Ind.Ocn.s.254, J. Dalley
MSS.Ind.Ocn.s.23, E.C. Foenander

Cambridge: Library of St. John's College

Records, F. Spencer Chapman

Kuala Lumpur: Arkib Negara Malaysia (ANM)

1957/0341852: Compensation
1957/054990: Force 136 Field Intelligence Reports
1957/0625480: Officers ex-Force 136
1957/574113: Force 136 Transport
2000/0006765: Papers of Mubin Sheppard

Singapore: National Archive of Singapore:

Documents

Hedwig Anuar's Diary

Oral History Department, transcripts

Abdul Wahab Ghows
Broadhurst, Douglas
Lim Ho Hup
Nair, Devan
Seah Tin Toon

Singapore: Institute of South-East Asian Studies

Portion of J.P. Hannah, unpublished memoir.

Papers in Private Hands

Papers of C.E. 'Bill' Foss.
Diary of M.C. Hay.

Unpublished Memoirs

J.P. Hannah, Untitled Memoir (in the hands of Tim Hannah).
Syed Ahmad Idid, *My Father*.
R.E. Lawther, Untitled Memoir.

Interviews

C.E. 'Bill' Foss, Sevenoaks, Kent, 2012.
George Hess'e, Perth, Australia, 2009.
Hyacinth Hess'e, Perth, Australia, 2009.
Pamela Mayo, Brisbane, Australia, 2009.
Tun Mohammed Hanif Omar, Kuala Lumpur, 2015.
Barry Neubronner, Arlesford, Essex, 2012
Tan Sri Yeun Yuet Leng, Ampang, Malaysia, 2015.

Other Unpublished Sources

John Brown, 'A Nominal Roll of the Volunteers', 2007.
Roy Follows, information via email
George Hess'e, information via email
Don Levy, 'Major Michael George Levy', undated.
Elizabeth Moggie, 'Notes of Interview with Reg Lawther', Singapore, May 2016.
Elizabeth Moggie, 'Notes of Interview with Reg Lawther', Singapore, August 2016.

Newspapers and Magazines

Apa Khabar (Journal of the Malayan Volunteers Group)
Singapore Free Press
Straits Times

Printed Primary Sources

Published Diaries

Danchev, Alex and Daniel Todman, eds., *War Diaries, 1939–45: Field Marshall Lord Alanbrooke* (London: Weidenfeld and Nicolson, 2001).
'Excerpts from Lim Bo Seng's Diary' in *The Price of Peace,* ed. Foong Choon Hong, trans. by Clara Show (Singapore: Asiapac, 1997), pp. 148–59.
Ziegler, Philip, ed., *Personal Diary of Admiral the Lord Louis Mountbatten, 1943–1946* (London: Collins, 1988).

Published Memoirs

Chin Peng with Ian Ward and Norma Miraflor, *My Side of History* (Singapore: Media Masters Pte, 2003).

Churchill, Sir Winston, *The Second World War, Vol. V: The Hinge of Fate* (London: Cassell, 1951).

Clive, Nigel, *A Greek Experience, 1943–48* (Salisbury: Michael Russell Publishing Ltd, 1985).

Crasta, John Baptist, *Eaten by the Japanese: The Memoir of an Unknown Indian Prisoner of War,* ed. Richard Crasta (New York: Invisible Man Press, Inc., 2012).

Cross, John, *Red Jungle* (London: The Quality Book Club, 1957).

Dobrée, Peter, *Hot Rain Means Danger* (Ipoh: Yayasan Perak, 2007).

Francis, Jerry, *The Turbulent Years in Perak: A Memoir* (Petaling Jaya, Malaysia: Alpha Sigma, 2008).

Fraser, George MacDonald, *Quartered Safe Out Here* (London: HarperCollins, 2000).

Gilmour, O. W., *With Freedom to Singapore* (London: Benn, 1950).

Gordon-Creed, Geoffrey, *Rogue Male: Death and Seduction in World War II with Mister Master Geoff,* ed. Roger Field (London: Coronet, 2011).

Hembry, Boris, *Malayan Spymaster: Memoirs of a Rubber Planter, Bandit Fighter and Spy* (Singapore: Monsoon, 2011).

Holder, R.W., *Eleven Months in Malaya: September 1945 to August 1946* (Singapore: Editions Didier Millet, 2005).

Ho Thean Fook, *Tainted Glory* (Kuala Lumpur: University of Malaya Press, 2000).

Ibrahim Ismail, *Have You Met Mariam?* (Johor Bahru: Westlight, 1984).

Mustapha, Hussain, *Eastern Approaches* (London: Penguin, 2009).

Moss, W. Stanley, *Ill Met by Moonlight* (London: Cassell, 2014; first published 1950).

Mustapha Hussain, *Malay Nationalism before UMNO: The Memoirs of Mustapha Hussain,* trans. by Insun Sony Mustapha, ed. K.S. Jomo (Kuala Lumpur: Utusan Publications and Distributors, 2004).

O'Brien, Terence, *The Moonlit War: The Story of Clandestine Operations in South-East Asia, 1944–5* (London: Collins, 1987).

Oehlers, F.A.C. 'Jock', *That's How It Goes: Autobiography of a Singapore Eurasian* (Singapore: Select Publishing, 2008).

Percival, Lt. Gen. Arthur, *The War in Malaya* (London: Eyre and Spottiswoode, 1949).

Richardson, Douglas, *Kiwi's Diary: A Journey of the Beacon's Party of Force 136 from Hulu Perak to Pahang during the Second World War* (Kuala Lumpur: Universiti Kebangsaan, 1994).

Simson, Ivan, *Singapore: Too Little, Too Late: Some Aspects of the Malayan Disaster* (London: Leo Cooper, 1970).

Singh, Gurchan, *Singha: The Lion of Malaya, Being the Memoirs of Gurchan Singh,* ed. Hugh Barnes (London: Quality Press Ltd., 1949).

Smiley, David, *Albanian Assignment* (London: Sphere Books Ltd., 1985).

Spencer Chapman, F., *The Jungle Is Neutral* (London: The Reprint Society with permission from Chatto and Windus, 1950).

Tan Chong Tee, *Force 136: The Story of a World War II Resistance Fighter* (Singapore: Asiapac, 1995).

Yuen Yuet Leng, *Nation before Self and Values That Do Not Die* (Ampang, Malaysia: Self-published, 2011).

Other Published Primary Sources

Interview, Tunku Abdul Rahman (Penang: University Sains Malaysia, 1989).
Interview, Lim Hong Pei (Penang, University Sains Malaysia, 1991).
Interview, Tsang Jan Nam (Penang, University Sains Malaysia, 1991).
Prisoners in Java: Accounts by Allied Prisoners of War in the Far East (1942–1945) Captured in Java, ed. Margaret Martin (Southampton: Hamwic Publishers, 2007).
Smashing Terrorism in the Malayan Emergency: The Vital Contribution of the Police, ed. Brian Stewart (Subang Jaya, Malaysia: Pelanduk Publications, 2004).

Printed Official Records and Sources

Cruickshank, Charles, *SOE in the Far East* (Oxford: Oxford University Press, 1986).
Donnison, F.S.V., *British Military Administration in the Far East, 1943–46* (London: HMSO, 1956).
London Gazette, 14 August 1946, p. 4093, General Sir Archibald Wavell, 'Despatch on Operations in Iraq, East Syria and Iran'. https://www.thegazette.co.uk/London/issue/37685/supplement/4093
London Gazette, Supplement of 22 January 1948, Air Chief Marshall Sir Robert Brooke-Popham, 'Operations in the Far East from 17th October to 27th December 1941'. http://www.ibiblio.org/hyperwar/UN/UK/LondonGazette/38183.pdf
London Gazette, Second Supplement of 26 February 1948, Lt. Gen. Arthur Percival, 'Operations of Malaya Command'. http://www.britain-at-war.org.uk/WW2/London_Gazette/Malaya_Command/
London Gazette, Supplement of 19 April 1951, Air Chief Marshall Sir Keith Park, 'Air Operations in South East Asia' http://www.ibiblio.org/hyperwar/UN/UK/LondonGazette/39202.pdf
Sheppard, M.C.ff., *The Malay Regiment 1933–1947* (Singapore: Department of Public Relations, Malay Peninsula, 1947).
Stockwell, A.J., ed., *British Documents on the End of Empire: Malaya Part 1 (Series B, Vol. 8), The Malayan Union Experiment* (London: HMSO, 2001).
Woodburn Kirby, Major-General S., *The War Against Japan, Vol. 5, The Surrender of Japan* (London: HMSO, 1969).

Film

Unwanted Soldiers, 1999, dir. Jari Osborne (National Film Board of Canada), http://www.nfb.ca/film/unwanted_soldiers/

Unpublished Doctoral Theses

Duckett, Richard, 'The Special Operations Executive in Burma, 1941–45'. Open University, 2015.
Huat Kin Koon, 'The Dilemma of Identity: Overseas Chinese in Malaya and the Quest for Nationhood, 1930–1949'. London School of Economics and Political Science, 2006.

King, Philip, 'From Periphery to Centre: Shaping the History of the Central Peninsula'. University of Wollongong, 2006.

Nadzan Haron, 'The Malay Regiment 1933–1955: A Political and Social Study of a Colonial Military Establishment'. University of Essex, 1988.

Books, Chapters and Articles

Abrams, Philip, 'Notes on the Difficulty of Studying the State (1977)', *The Journal of Historical Sociology*, 1, 1, pp. 58–89.

Abu Talib Ahmad, 'The Impact of the Japanese Occupation on Colonial and Anti-Colonial Armies in Southeast Asia' in *Colonial Armies in Southeast Asia,* ed. Tobias Rettig and Karl Hack (Abingdon: Routledge, 2005), pp. 213–38.

Abu Talib Ahmad, *The Malay Muslims, Islam and the Rising Sun, 1941–45* (Kuala Lumpur: Malaysian Branch of the Royal Asiatic Society, 2003).

Aldrich, Richard, 'Britain's Secret Intelligence Service in Asia during the Second World War', *Modern Asian Studies*, 32, 1 (1998), pp. 179–217.

Aldrich, Richard, *Intelligence and the War against Japan: Britain, America and the Politics of Secret Service* (Cambridge: Cambridge University Press, 2000).

Aldrich, Richard, 'Putting Culture into the Cold War: The Cultural Relations Department (CRD) and British Covert Information Warfare', *Intelligence and National Security*, 18, 2 (2003), pp. 109–33.

Andrew, Christopher, *The Defence of the Realm: The Authorized History of MI5* (London: Penguin, 2010).

Arditti, Roger and Philip H. J. Davies, 'Rethinking the Rise and Fall of the Malayan Security Service, 1946–48', *The Journal of Imperial and Commonwealth History*, 43, 2 (2015), pp. 292–316.

Ban Kah Choon, *Absent History: The Untold History of Special Branch Operations in Singapore, 1915–1942* (Singapore: Raffles, 2001).

Ban Kah Choon and Yap Hong Kuan, *Rehearsal for War: The Underground War against the Japanese* (Singapore: Horizon Books, 2002).

Bailey, Roderick, 'Communist in SOE: Explaining James Klugmann's Recruitment and Retention', *Intelligence and National Security*, 20, 1 (2005), pp. 72–97.

Bailey, Roderick, *The Wildest Province: SOE in the Land of the Eagle* (London: Vintage, 2008).

Barber, Andrew, *Kuala Lumpur at War 1939–1945* (Kuala Lumpur: Karamoja Press, 2012).

Barber, Noel, *War of the Running Dogs* (London: Cassell Military Paperbacks, 2004; first published 1971)

Bartholomew-Feis, Dixee, *The OSS and Ho Chi Minh: Unexpected Allies in the War against Japan* (Lawrence, KS: University Press of Kansas, 2006).

Bayly, C.A., *Empire and Information: Intelligence Gathering and Social Communication in India, 1780–1870* (Cambridge: Cambridge University Press, 1996).

Bayly, Christopher and Tim Harper, *Forgotten Armies: Britain's Asian Empire and the War with Japan* (London: Penguin, 2005).

Bayly, Christopher and Tim Harper, *Forgotten Wars: The End of Britain's Asian Empire* (London: Penguin, 2008).

Bellamy, Chris, *The Gurkhas: Special Force* (London: John Murray, 2011).

Ben-Haim, Yakov, 'Policy Neutrality and Uncertainty: An Info-Gap Perspective', *Intelligence and National Security*, published online 18 December 2015, DOI:10.1080/0 2684527.2015.1121683

Best, Antony, *Britain, Japan and Pearl Harbor: Avoiding War in East Asia, 1936–41* (London: Routledge, 1995).

Best, Antony, *British Intelligence and the Japanese Challenge in Asia, 1914–1941* (London: Palgrave Macmillan, 2002).

Bhalla, S. Tsering, 'My Father, the Hero' in *The Price of Peace,* ed. Foong Choon Hong, trans. by Clara Show (Singapore: Asiapac, 1997), pp. 137–147.

Billingsley, Phil, *Bandits in Republican China* (Stanford: Stanford University Press, 1988).

Bills, Scott L., *Empire and Cold War: The Roots of US-Third World Antagonism, 1945–47* (Basingstoke: Palgrave Macmillan, 1990).

Blackburn, Kevin, 'Colonial Forces as Post-Colonial Memories: The Commemoration of the Malay Regiment in Modern Malaysia and Singapore' in *Colonial Armies in Southeast Asia,* ed. Tobias Rettig and Karl Hack (Abingdon: Routledge, 2005), pp. 302–326

Blackburn, Kevin and Daniel Chew Ju Ern, 'Dalforce at the Fall of Singapore in 1942: An Overseas Chinese Heroic Legend', *Journal of Chinese Overseas*, 1, 2 (2005), pp. 233–59.

Burleigh, Michael, *Moral Combat: A History of World War II* (London: Harper Press, 2010).

Butcher, John G., *The British in Malaya, 1880–1941: The Social History of a European Community in Colonial South-East Asia* (Kuala Lumpur: Oxford University Press, 1979).

Callahan, Mary P., *Making Enemies: War and State Building in Burma* (Ithaca: Cornell University Press, 2003).

Calvocoressi, Peter, Guy Wint and John Pritchard, *The Penguin History of the Second World War* (London: Penguin, 1999; first published as *Total War*, 1972).

Cannadine, David, *Ornamentalism: How the British Saw Their Empire* (London: Penguin, 2001).

Caplan, Lionel, ' "Bravest of the Brave": Representations of 'The Gurkha' in British Military Writings', *Modern Asian Studies*, 25, 3 (1991), pp. 571–97.

Carver, Field Marshall Lord, *Britain's Army in the 20th Century* (London: Pan Books, 1999).

Che Man, W.K., *Muslim Separatism: The Moros of Southern Philippines and the Malays of Southern Thailand* (Singapore: Oxford University Press, 1990).

Cheah Boon Kheng, 'The Japanese Occupation of Malaya, 1941–45: Ibrahim Yaacob and the Struggle for Indonesia Raya', *Indonesia*, No. 28 (October 1979), pp. 84–120.

Cheah Boon Kheng, *Red Star over Malaya: Resistance and Social Conflict during and after the Japanese Occupation, 1941–1946* (Singapore: Singapore University Press, 2003, 3rd edition).

Cheah Boon Kheng, 'The Legal Period: 1945–8. The Malayan Communist Party and Its Relations with the Malays, British and "Bourgeois Nationalists" ' in *Dialogues with Chin Peng: New Light on the Malayan Emergency,* ed. C. C. Chin and Karl Hack (Singapore: Singapore University Press, 2004), pp. 255–9.

Chin, C. C. and Karl Hack, eds., *Dialogues with Chin Peng: New Light on the Malayan Emergency* (Singapore: Singapore University Press, 2004).

Chua Ai Lin, 'Nation, Race, and Language: Discussing Transnational Identities in Colonial Singapore, Circa 1930', *Modern Asian Studies*, available on CJO 2012, DOI:10.1017/S0026749X11000801.

Clutterbuck, Richard, *The Long Long War: The Emergency in Malaya 1948–1960* (London: Cassell, 1967).

Coates, John, *Suppressing Insurgency: An Analysis of the Malayan Emergency, 1948–1954* (Oxford: Westview Press, 1992).

Comber, Leon, *Malaya's Secret Police 1945–60: The Role of the Special Branch in the Malayan Emergency* (Singapore: Institute of Southeast Asian Studies, 2008).

Comber, Leon, 'Traitor of All Traitors – Secret Agent "Extraordinaire"', *Journal of the Malaysian Branch of the Royal Asiatic Society*, 83, 2 (2010), pp. 1–25.

Cooper, Artemis, *Patrick Leigh Fermor: An Adventure* (London: John Murray, 2012).

Corfield, Justin and Robin Corfield, *The Fall of Singapore: 90 Days: November 1941 – February 1942* (Melbourne: Talisman Publishing, 2012).

Cormac, Rory, *Confronting the Colonies: British Intelligence and Counterinsurgency* (London: C. Hurst and Co., 2013).

Costigliola, Frank, 'The Nuclear Family: Tropes of Gender and Pathology in the Western Alliance', *Diplomatic History*, 21, 2 (1997), pp. 163–83.

Deery, Philip, 'Malaya 1948: Britain's Asian Cold War?', *Journal of Cold War Studies*, 9, 1 (2007), pp. 29–54.

Deery, Phillip, 'The Terminology of Terrorism: Malaya, 1948–52', *Journal of Southeast Asian Studies*, 34, 2 (2003), pp. 231–47.

Dennis, Peter, *Troubled Days of Peace: Mountbatten and South East Asia Command, 1945–46* (Manchester: Manchester University Press, 1989).

Dixon, Norman, *On the Psychology of Military Incompetence* (London: Jonathan Cape, 1976).

Dol Ramli, *History of the Malay Regiment, 1933–42* (Singapore: University of Malaya, 1955).

van Doorn, Jacques, *The Soldier and Social Change: Comparative Studies in the History and Sociology of the Military* (London: Sage Publications Ltd., 1975).

Douds, G.J., 'Indian POWs in the Pacific, 1941–45' in *Forgotten Captives in Japanese-Occupied Asia,* ed. Kevin Blackburn and Karl Hack (Abingdon: Routledge, 2007), pp. 73–93.

Duckett, Richard, *The Special Operations Executive in Burma: Jungle Warfare and Intelligence Gathering in World War II* (London: I.B. Tauris, 2018).

Duncan, Stuart, "'Of Historical Interest Only": The Origins and Vicissitudes of the SOE Archive', *Intelligence and National Security*, 20, 1 (March 2005), pp. 14–26.

Elkins, Caroline, 'The Re-assertion of the British Empire in Southeast Asia', *Journal of Interdisciplinary History*, 39, 3 (2009), pp. 361–385.

Farrell, Brian P., *The Defence and Fall of Singapore, 1940–1942* (Stroud: Tempus, 2005).

Fletcher, Ian Christopher, 'Ornamentalism: How the British Saw Their Empire' (review), *Victorian Studies*, 45, 3 (2003), pp. 532–42.

Foenander, E.C., *Big Game of Malaya* (London: The Batchworth Press, 1952).

Foot, M.R.D., *SOE: The Special Operations Executive 1940–1946* (London: Pimlico, 1999).

Frost, Mark and Yu-Mei Balasingamchow, *Singapore: A Biography* (Singapore: Editions Didier Millet, 2009).

Gough, Richard, *SOE Singapore 1941–42* (London: William Kimber, 1985).

Gough, Richard, *The Jungle Was Red: SOE's Force 136 Sumatra and Malaya* (Singapore: SNP Panpac, 2003).

Guha, Ranajit, 'The Prose of Counterinsurgency' in *Selected Subaltern Studies,* ed. Ranajit Guha and Gayatri Chakravorty Spivak (Oxford: Oxford University Press, 1988), pp. 46–84.

Gullace, Nicoletta F., *The Blood of Our Sons: Men, Women and the Renegotiation of British Citizenship during the Great War* (New York: Palgrave Macmillan, 2002).

Gullick J.M., 'Mubin Sheppard' [Obituary], *Journal of the Malaysian Branch of the Royal Asiatic Society,* 68, 2 (1995), pp. 2–6.

Gullick, J.M., 'On the Nature of Military Government: The Case of the BMA in Negri Sembilan', *Journal of the Malaysian Branch of the Royal Asiatic Society,* 79, 2 (2006), pp. 85–101.

Gullick, J.M., 'Recollections of My Time in Malaya (1945–1956), Pt. 1', *Journal of the Malaysian Branch of the Royal Asiatic Society,* 86, 2 (2013), pp. 59–76.

Gullick, J.M., 'Recollections of My Time in Malaya (1945–56), Pt. 2', *Journal of the Malaysian Branch of the Royal Asiatic Society,* 87, 1 (2014), pp. 53–81.

Hack, Karl, 'Biar mati anak: Jangan mati adat [Better Your Children Die Than Your Traditions]: Locally Raised Forces as a Barometer for Imperialism and Decolonization in British South East Asia, 1874–2001', *South East Asia Research,* 10, 3 (2002), pp. 245–275.

Hack, Karl, *Defence and Decolonisation in Southeast Asia, Britain, Malaya and Singapore 1941–1968* (Richmond: Curzon, 2001).

Hack, Karl, 'The Origins of the Asian Cold War: Malaya 1948', *Journal of Southeast Asian Studies,* 40, 3 (2009), pp. 471–96.

Hack, Karl and C.C. Chin, 'The Malayan Emergency' in *Dialogues with Chin Peng: New Light on the Malayan Emergency,* ed. C. C. Chin and Karl Hack (Singapore: Singapore University Press, 2004), pp. 3–37.

Hall, Catherine, 'Remembering Edward Said', *History Workshop Journal,* No. 57 (2004), pp. 235–243.

Hammond, Robert, *A Fearful Freedom* (London: Leo Cooper, 1984).

Hanrahan, Gene Z., *The Communist Struggle in Malaya* (Kuala Lumpur: University of Malaya Press, 1971).

Han Suyin, 'Foreword' in *Modern Malaysian Chinese Stories,* trans. and ed. Ly Singko and Leon Comber (Singapore: Heinemann Educational Books (Asia), 1965), pp. 2–35.

Harper, Tim, 'The British 'Malayans' in *Settlers and Expatriates: Britons over the Seas,* ed. Robert Bickers (Oxford: Oxford University Press, 2010), pp. 233–68.

Harper, T.N., *The End of Empire and the Making of Malaya* (Cambridge: Cambridge University Press, 1999).

Harper, T.N., 'Globalism and the Pursuit of Authenticity: The Making of a Diasporic Public Sphere in Singapore', *Sojourn,* 12, 2 (1997), pp. 261–92.

Harper, T.N., 'The Politics of Disease and Disorder in Post-War Malaya', *Journal of Southeast Asian Studies,* 21, 1 (1990), pp. 88–113.

Heussler, Robert, *Completing a Stewardship: The Malayan Civil Service, 1942–1957* (Westport, CT: Greenwood, 1983).

Hirschman, Charles, 'The Making of Race in Colonial Malaya: Political Economy and Racial Ideology', *Sociological Forum,* 1, 2 (1986), pp. 330–61.

Ho Chee Tim, 'Communal Feeding in Post-War Singapore', *Biblio-Asia,* 9, 3 (2013), pp. 2–9.

Hodgkins, Fiona, *From Syonan to Fuiji-Go: The Story of the Catholic Settlement of Bahau in WWII Malaya* (Singapore: Select Publishing, 2014).

Holder, R.W., *The Fight for Malaya: The Jungle War of Maurice Cotterill* (Singapore: Editions Didier Millet, 2007).

Holman, Dennis, *The Green Torture: The Ordeal of Robert Chrystal* (London: Robert Hale, 1962).

Holman, Dennis, *Noone of the Ulu* (London: William Heinemann, 1958).

Howarth, Richard J., 'Geology behind Barbed Wire', *Proceedings of the Geologists' Association*, 126, 2 (2015), pp. 282–94.

Howe, Stephen, *Anti-colonialism in British Politics: The Left and the End of Empire, 1918–1964* (Oxford: Clarendon Press, 1993).

James, David H., *The Rise and Fall of the Japanese Empire* (London: George Allen and Unwin, 1952).

Kathirithamby-Wells, Jeyamalar, *Nature and Nation: Forests and Development in Peninsular Malaysia* (Singapore: Singapore University Press, 2005).

Kennedy, Joseph, *When Singapore Fell: Evacuations and Escapes, 1941–2* (London: Macmillan, 1989).

Kennedy, Paul, *Engineers of Victory: The Problem Solvers Who Turned the Tide in World War II* (London: Penguin, 2013).

Kenneison, Rebecca, *Playing for Malaya: A Eurasian Family in the Pacific War* (Singapore: NUS Press, 2012).

Kerkvliet, Benedict J., *The Huk Rebellion: A Study of Peasant Revolt in the Philippines* (Lanham, MD: Rowman and Littlefield Publishers, 2002).

Kratoska, Paul, *The Japanese Occupation of Malaya: A Social and Economic History 1941–1945* (London: C. Hurst and Co., 1998).

Kratoska, Paul, 'The Karen of Burma under Japanese Rule' in *Southeast Asian Minorities in the Wartime Japanese Empire*, ed. Paul Kratoska (London: RoutledgeCurzon, 2002), pp. 21–38.

Krikler, Jeremy, *Revolution from Above, Rebellion from Below: The Agrarian Transvaal at the Turn of the Century* (Oxford: Clarendon Press, 1993).

Kurzban, Robert, John Tooby and Leda Cosmides, 'Can Race Be Erased? Coalitional Computation and Social Categorization', *Proceedings of the National Academy of Sciences*, 98, 26 (2001), pp. 15387–92.

Lampe, David, *The Last Ditch: Britain's Secret Resistance and the Nazi Invasion Plans* (Barnsley: Frontline Books, 2013; first published 1968).

Lau, Albert, *The Malayan Union Controversy, 1942–1948* (Singapore: Oxford University Press, 1991).

Lee Tong Foong, 'The MPAJA and the Revolutionary Struggle, 1939–45' in *Malaya: The Making of a Neo-Colony,* ed. Mohamed Amin and Malcolm Caldwell (Nottingham: Spokesman Books, 1977), pp. 95–119.

Levi, Giovanni, 'On Microhistory' in *New Perspectives on Historical Writing*, ed. Peter Burke (Cambridge: Polity, 2001), pp. 97–119.

Lewis, Damien, *Judy: Dog in a Million* (London: Quercus, 2015).

Lewis, Jon E., *SAS: The Autobiography* (London: Robinson, 2011).

Lloyd Owen, David, *Providence Their Guide: The Long Range Desert Group, 1940–45* (London: Pen and Sword, 2000; first published 1980).

MacLaren, Roy, *Canadians Behind Enemy Lines, 1939–1945* (Vancouver: University of British Columbia Press, 1981).

Marican, Y. Mansoor, 'Malay Nationalism and the Islamic Party of Malaysia', *Islamic Studies*, 16, 1 (1977), pp. 291–301.

McCrum, Ronald, *The Men Who Lost Singapore, 1938–1942* (Singapore: NUS Press, 2017).

McElwee, Pamela, '"There is Nothing that is Difficult": History and Hardship on and after the Ho Chi Minh Trail in North Vietnam', *The Asia Pacific Journal of Anthropology*, 6, 3 (2005), pp. 197–214.

McMillan, Richard, *The British Occupation of Indonesia, 1945–46: Britain, the Netherlands and the Indonesian Revolution* (Abingdon: Routledge, 2006).

Miller, Harry, *Menace in Malaya* (London: Harrap, 1954).

Mills, L.A., *British Malaya 1824–1967* (London: Oxford University Press, 1966).

Milner, Anthony, *The Invention of Politics in Colonial Malaya* (Cambridge: Cambridge University Press, 2002).

Mitchell, Tim, 'The Limits of the State: Beyond Statist Approaches and Their Critics', *The American Political Science Review*, 85, 1 (1991), pp. 77–96.

Mockaitis, Thomas R., *British Counterinsurgency, 1919–1960* (Basingstoke: Macmillan, 1990).

Moffatt, Jonathan and Paul Riches, *In Oriente Primus* (Coventry: Self-published, 2010).

Mohd. Rizal bin Mohd. Yaakop, 'The British Legacy on the Development of Politics in Malaya', *Tawarikh: International Journal for Historical Studies*, 2, 1 (2010), pp. 41–60.

Moreman, Tim, *Long Range Desert Group Patrolman: The Western Desert, 1940–43.* (Oxford: Osprey, 2010).

Nagl, John, *Learning to East Soup with a Knife: Counterinsurgency Lessons from Malaya and Vietnam* (Chicago: University of Chicago Press, 2002).

Nakahara Michiko in *Asian Labour in the Wartime Japanese Empire: Unknown Histories*, ed. Paul Kratoska (New York: M.E. Sharpe, 2005), pp. 249–64.

O'Ballance, Edgar, *Malaya: The Communist Insurgent War, 1948–60* (London: Faber and Faber, 1966).

Ogden, Alan, *Tigers Burning Bright: SOE Heroes in the Far East* (London: Bene Factum Publishing, 2013).

Ong Chit Chung, *Operation Matador: World War II: Britain's Attempt to Foil the Japanese Invasion of Malaya and Singapore* (Singapore: Marshall Cavendish, 2011).

Ota Koki, 'Railway Operations in Japanese-occupied Malaya' in *New Perspectives on the Japanese Occupation in Malaya and Singapore, 1941–1945,* ed. Akashi Yoji and Yoshimura Mako (Singapore: NUS Press, 2008), pp. 139–57.

Prins, Gwyn, 'Oral History' in *New Perspectives on Historical Writing*, ed. Peter Burke (Cambridge: Polity, 2001), pp. 120–52.

Purcell, Victor, *Malaya: Communist or Free?* (London: Victor Gollancz, 1954).

Pye, Lucian W., *Guerrilla Communism in Malaya: Its Social and Political Meaning* (Princeton: Princeton University Press, 1956).

Reiter, Dan, 'Exploring the Bargaining Model of War', *Perspectives on Politics*, 1, 1 (2003), pp. 17–43.

de Santis, Hugh, *The Diplomacy of Silence: The American Foreign Service, the Soviet Union and the Cold War, 1933–47* (Chicago: University of Chicago Press, 1979).

Saw Swee Hock, *The Population of Peninsular Malaysia* (Singapore: Singapore University Press, 1988).

Shaw, William, *Tun Razak: His Life and Times* (New York: Longman, 1976).

Shennan, Margaret, *Our Man in Malaya: John Davis CBE, DSO, SOE Force 136 and Postwar Counter-Insurgency* (Stroud: The History Press, 2007).

Short, Anthony, *The Communist Insurrection in Malaya 1948–1960* (London: Frederick Muller, 1975).

Siebold, Guy L., 'Core Issues and Theory in Military Sociology', *Journal of Political and Military Sociology*, 29, 1 (2001), pp. 140–59.

Simpson, Keith, 'Percival' in *Churchill's Generals,* ed. John Keegan (London: Weidenfeld and Nicolson, 1991), pp. 256–76.

Skennerton, Ian, *British Small Arms of World War II: The Complete Reference Guide to Weapons, Maker's Codes and 1936–1946 Contracts* (Margate, Australia: Self-published, 1988).

Skidmore, Ian, *Marines Don't Hold Their Horses* (London: W.H. Allen, 1981).

Smith, Colin, *Singapore Burning: Heroism and Surrender in World War II* (London: Viking, 2005).

Springhall, John, 'Mountbatten versus the Generals: British Military Rule of Singapore, 1945–46', *Journal of Contemporary History*, 36, 4 (2001), pp. 635–52.

Stenson, Michael R., *Repression and Revolt: The Origin of the 1948 Communist Insurrection in Malaya and Singapore* (Athens, OH: Ohio University Center for International Studies, 1969).

Stockwell, A.J., *British Policy and Malay Politics: British Policy and Malay Politics during the Malay Union Experiment, 1945–48* (Kuala Lumpur: Malaysian Branch of the Royal Asiatic Society, 1979).

Stockwell, A.J., 'Colonial Planning during World War Two: The Case of Malaya', *Journal of Imperial and Commonwealth History*, 2, 3 (1974), pp. 333–51.

Stockwell, A.J., 'The Formation and First Years of the United Malays National Organization (U.M.N.O.) 1946–1948', *Modern Asian Studies*, 11, 4 (1977), pp. 481–513.

Stockwell, A.J., 'Policing during the Malayan Emergency, 1948–60: Communism, Communalism and Decolonisation' in *Policing and Decolonisation: Politics, Nationalism and the Police, 1917–65*, ed. David M. Anderson and David Killingray (Manchester: Manchester University Press, 1992), pp. 105–122.

Stockwell, A.J., '"A Widespread and Long-Concocted Plot to Overthrow Government in Malaya"? The Origins of the Malayan Emergency', *Journal of Imperial and Commonwealth History*, 21, 3 (1993), pp. 66–89.

Stoler, Ann Laura, '"In Cold Blood": Hierarchies of Credibility and the Politics of Colonial Narratives', *Representations*, No. 37 (1992), pp. 151–89.

Strachan, Hew, 'British Counter-insurgency from Malaya to Iraq', *RUSI*, 152, 6 (December 2007), pp. 8–11.

Tanaka, Yuki, *Hidden Horrors: Japanese War Crimes in World War II* (Boulder, CO: Westview of HarperCollins, 1996).

Thatcher, Dorothy and Robert Cross, *Pai Naa: The Story of an Englishwoman's Survival in the Malayan Jungle* (London: White Lion Publishers, 1974).

Thomas, Martin, *Empires of Intelligence: Security Services and Colonial Disorder after 1914* (Berkley: University of California Press, 2008).

Thompson, Leroy, *The Sten Gun* (Oxford: Osprey, 2010).

Tilly, Charles, 'War Making and State Making as Organized Crime' in Peter Evans, *Bringing the State Back In,* ed. Dietrich Rueschemeyer and Theda Skocpol (Cambridge: Cambridge University Press, 1985), pp. 169–91.

Turnbull, Mary, *A History of Modern Singapore* (Singapore: NUS Press, 2009).

Walker, Barrington, ed., *The History of Immigration and Racism in Canada: Essential Readings* (Toronto: Canadian Scholar's Press, 2008).

Wan Hashim, *Second World War in Malaya: Role of the Malay Guerillas: Force 136* (Kuala Lumpur: Institut Terjemahan Negara Malaysia Berhad, 2010), originally published in Bahasa Melayu as *Perang Dunia Kedua: Peranan Gerila Melayu Force 136* (Kuala Lumpur: Dewan Bahasa dan Pustaka, 1993).

Wan Mansoor Abdullah, 'Ghazali the Civil Servant' in *King Ghaz: A Man of His Time,* ed. Rais Yatim and Prabhakaran S. Nair (Kuala Lumpur: National Archives of Malaysia, 2010), pp. 85–7.

Weintraub, Robert, *No Better Friend: One Man, One Dog and Their Extraordinary Story of Courage and Survival in World War II* (London: Little Brown and Company, 2015).

Wesseling, Hans, 'Overseas History' in *New Perspectives on Historical Writing*, ed. Peter Burke (Cambridge: Polity, 2001), pp. 71–96.

White, Jim, 'History from Below' in *New Perspectives on Historical Writing*, ed. Peter Burke (Cambridge: Polity, 2001), pp. 27–40.

Williams, Heather, *Parachutes, Patriots and Partisans: The Special Operations Executive in Yugoslavia, 1941–1945* (London: C. Hurst and Co., 2003).

Wilt, Alan F., *War from the Top: German and British Military Decision Making during World War II* (Bloomington: Indiana University Press, 1990).

Wouter Voorspoels, Annelies Bartlema and Wolf Vanpaemel, 'Can Race Really Be Erased? A Pre-registered Replication Study', *Frontiers in Psychology* (2014), <http://dx.doi.org/10.3389/fpsyg.2014.01035>.

Wu, T'ien-Wei, 'The Chinese Communist Movement' in *China's Bitter Victory*, ed. James C. Hsiung and Steven I. Levine (London: Routledge, 1992), pp. 79–106.

Wylie, Neville, 'SOE: New Approaches and Perspectives', *Intelligence and National Security*, 20, 1 (2005), pp. 1–13.

Xu Hai Liang, 'A Fighter's Thoughts on Anti-aggression' in *The Price of Peace,* ed. Foong Choon Hong, trans. by Clara Show (Singapore: Asiapac, 1997), pp. 131–6.

Yong, C.F., 'The Malayan Communist Struggle for Survival, 1930–1935', *Journal of the Malaysian Branch of the Royal Asiatic Society*, 69, 2 (1996), 1–22.

Yong, C.F., 'The Origins and Development of the Malayan Communist Movement, 1919–1930', *Modern Asian Studies*, 25, 4 (1991), pp. 625–48.

Yong, C.F. and R.B. McKenna, *The Kuomintang Movement in British Malaya, 1912–1949* (Singapore: Singapore University Press, 1990).

Yu, Maochun, *The Dragon's War: Allied Operations and the Fate of China, 1947–1947* (Annapolis: Naval Institute Press, 2006).

Yu, Maochun, *OSS in China: Prelude to Cold War* (Annapolis: Naval Institute Press, 2011).

Ziegler, Philip, *Mountbatten: The Official Biography* (London: Collins, 1985).

Miscellaneous Online Sources

Badan Warisan: https://badanwarisanmalaysia.org/tag/mubin-sheppard/

China Heritage Quarterly: http://www.chinaheritagequarterly.org/features.php?searchterm=019_vale_morrison.inc&issue=019

Daily Telegraph Obituaries: http://www.telegraph.co.uk/news/obituaries/military-obituaries/special-forces-obituaries/8284728/Tun-Ibrahim-Ismail.html http://www.telegraph.co.uk/news/obituaries/1357064/Tun-Mohamed-Suffian.html

Defence in Depth, Summary of SOE in Burma: https://defenceindepth.co/2016/06/29/burma-1942-soes-role-in-defeat-into-victory/

Malayan Volunteers Group: http://www.malayanvolunteersgroup.org.uk

http://www.malayanvolunteersgroup.org.uk/node/58, Audrey Holmes-McCormick, 'Volunteer Forces'.

Oxford Dictionary of National Biography: http://www.oxforddnb.com

Scottish Herald Obituary: http://www.heraldscotland.com/sport/spl/aberdeen/
david-alexander-1.389832
Sejarah SMKTP: http://wwwsejarahsmktp.blogspot.co.uk/2009/07/pasukan-wataniah.
html
US Marine Corps publications: 2, *Intelligence*, Washington, 1997, at http://www.
globalsecurity.org/military/library/policy/usmc/mcdp/2/mcdp2_chp1.pdf
Victoria Institution, Kuala Lumpur: http://www.viweb.freehosting.net/talalla-bros.htm

INDEX